STUDIES IN EUROPEAN POLITICS.

STUDIES

IN

EUROPEAN POLITICS

BY

MOUNTSTUART E. GRANT DUFF

KENNIKAT PRESS
Port Washington, N. Y./London

STUDIES IN EUROPEAN POLITICS

First published in 1866
Reissued in 1970 by Kennikat Press
Library of Congress Catalog Card No: 72-110901
SBN 8046-0884-9

Manufactured by Taylor Publishing Company   Dallas, Texas

ADVERTISEMENT.

THE seven Chapters which form this volume were, in their original shape, contributed as articles, during the last three years and a half, to the *North British Review*, the *National Review*, and *Fraser's Magazine*. They are now reprinted, by the kind permission of the conductors and proprietors of those periodicals.

The third, which is from the *North British*, and the seventh, from *Fraser*, having appeared quite recently, are hardly at all altered. To the first and second, also from the *North British*, considerable additions have been made; while the two German papers, which were published in the *National* in 1863 and 1864, are very greatly altered and enlarged; less, however, than the sixth, the nucleus of which was a paper in *Fraser* of March 1863.

All the seven articles were based upon some personal acquaintance with the countries to which they refer, as well as on a good deal of reading; and warm thanks are due to many foreign friends for information and criticism.

Undertaken primarily for the writer's own instruction, and as part of a scheme of study, these articles were "studies" in the most literal sense of the term, and they are now. republished in the hope that they may abridge the labour of other persons engaged in similar pursuits.

CONTENTS.

CHAPTER I.

SPAIN.

PAGE

Increased facility of Spanish travel . . . 1

Different classes of travellers in Spain 1

Political travellers . . 1

Books recommended to them 2

The constitution of 1812 . 4

The reign of Ferdinand . 5

Accession of Queen Isabella 5

Commencement of the civil war 5

The Estatuto Real . . 6

Mendizabal . . . 7

Isturiz and Galiano . . 7

Mutiny of La Granja . . 7

Constitution of 1837 . . 8

Convention of Vergara . 9

Conduct of the Queen-mother 10

Revolt of Barcelona . . 10

Regency of Espartero . 11

Unsuccessful rising at Pamplona 12

Coalition against Espartero, and his fall . . . 13

Transition ministry of Lopez 13

Olozaga and the queen . 14

Gonsalez Bravo . . . 14

Narvaez and the constitution of 1845 . . . 15

The Spanish marriages . 16

Cabinet of Narvaez and Sartorius 16

1848 at Madrid . . 16

Ministry of Bravo-Murillo . 17

Ministry of Sartorius . 17

Pronunciamento and Revolution of 1854 . 18

The Constituent Cortes . 19

Ministerial crisis . . 20

O'Donnell in power . . 20

PAGE

Reactionary government of Narvaez . . . 21

Ministerial changes . . 21

O'Donnell and the "Union-Liberal" . . . 21

The war with Morocco . 22

The fall of O'Donnell . 24

Short-lived ministries . 24

The Narvaez cabinet of 1864 25

The troubles of 1865 . 26

The present administration 27

Views of Mr. Buckle on Spain 28

The Spanish monarchy . 29

The existing constitution . 29

The Ministry of Grace and Justice . . . 30

The Ministry of the Interior 32

The Ministry of Public Welfare 34

Material revival of Spain . 35

Railways, roads, foreign trade, etc. 35

The Ministry of Finance, Spanish credit . . . 39

Sale of church property . 41

The Ministry of War . 42

The Spanish soldier . . 42

The Ministry of Marine . 44

The Ministry of the Colonies 45

The Ministry of Foreign Affairs 46

Parties in Spain . . 47

The newspaper press . . 47

Contemporary literature . 49

Education . . . 51

State of religion . . 54

Protestantism . . . 56

The dynasty . . . 60

The present and future of Spain 61

CHAPTER II.

RUSSIA.

PAGE

Western European opinion on
Russia 65
Its elements . . . 65
Clarke—Custine—Presumptu-
ous foreign policy . . 65-6
Alexander I. . . . 66
What the Holy Alliance really was 67
Congress politics . . 68
Last days of Alexander I. . 69
Early dangers of the reign of
Nicholas . . . 69
The Crimean war . . 70
Death of Nicholas, and break-
up of his system . . 71
Alexander II. . . . 71
Period of fermentation . 71
The Russian peasants . 72
  a. The *Odnodvortzi* . 72
  b. The Cossacks . . 72
  c. The free labourers . 73
  d. The foreign colonists . 74
  e. The crown peasants . 74
  f. The peasants of the apan-
    ages . . . 74
  g. The peasants of the *Arendes* 74
  h. The peasants of the crown
    establishments . 75
  i. The Yamschiki . . 75
  j. The serfs proper . 75
M. Nicholas Tourguéneff . 75
The Russian commune . 77
The personal serfs . . 81
History of the emancipation
project . . . 81
The proclamation of enfranchisement 83
M. Milutine . . . 83-4
Possible effects of the emancipation . . . 85-6
Gathering in London in the
spring of 1861 . . 87
News arrives of the first collision at Warsaw . . 87

PAGE

The Polish question . . 87
Poland under Alexander I. . 88
Poland under Nicholas . 88-9
Wielopolski, André Zamoyski 89
The Agricultural Society . 90
The year 1863 . . 91
The conscription . . 91
Difficulties of the Polish ques-
tion 92
The religious element in the
insurrection . . . 95
The venerable feud of the
" Filioque" . . . 95
The Greek Church . . 95
Its wide extent and great
power 96
Its influence on the peasantry 96
Its art and its music . . 97
Its want of learning . . 97
Reforms which it requires . 97
The Dissidents . . 99
Schédo - Ferroti's book — *La
Tolerance, etc. en Russie* . 99
The Greek and Anglican
Churches . . . 101
England and Russia—Have
they anything to fear from
each other ? . . . 102
Russia in Central Asia . 102
Our policy in Asia should be
one of strict alliance . 103
Constantinople and the Eastern
question . . 103-4
Russia in Germany . . 105
Pansclavism . . . 105
Extract from Chamiakoff . 106
Russia strong for defence but
weak for aggression . 107
Circassia . . . 109
Russian finance . . 109
Russian parties . . 109
Constitutionalism in Russia 110
Herzen and the *Kolokol* . 112

	PAGE
Democratic basis of Russian society	113
The Russian nobility	113
The Tchinovniks	114
Russian law	115
Russian literature	116
Russian journalism	117
The universities	118
Education	119

	PAGE
Uncertainties of the future	120
Events of the last twenty months	121
L'Écho de la Presse Russe	125
Milutine in Poland	127
M. N. Tourguéneff on the Polish land question	127-31
Results of the present reign	131-2

CHAPTER III.

AUSTRIA.

Provisional character of all political arrangements in Austria	133
Critical state of that empire	133
Books on Austria	134-6
The modern history of Austria begins with Joseph II.	136-7
Leopold II.	137-9
The SYSTEM	140
The Emperor Francis	141-2
Prince Metternich	142-4
The Greek insurrection	145
End of the diplomatic period	145
Hungary in 1825	146
The Bohemians	147
The Greek revolution	148
The Polish struggle of 1831	148
The SYSTEM to the death of the Emperor Francis	149
Decline of Metternich's influence	150
The Emperor Ferdinand	150
The Triumvirate	151
The Tyrol	152
Hungarian grievances	152
First appearance of Kossuth	153
Stephen Széchenyi	153
Transylvanian agitations — Wesselenyi	154
Croatia	155
Hungarian parties and politics	156-7

The 1st of March 1848	158
General disaffection	159
The Galician massacres	160
Occupation of Cracow	161
The 13th of March at Vienna	163
The laws of 1848 in Hungary	163
The Hungarian war and its results	164-5
Schwartzenberg and Bach	166-7
The Bach system and the reaction	167-73
Fall of M. Bach	173
The strengthened council of the Empire, May 1860	173
The October diploma	174
Count Goluchowski	175
Baron Nicholas Vay	176
M. Schmerling	177
The patent of February 1861	177
The Hungarian Diet meets	178
The Hungarian Diet is dissolved	179
The Schmerling administration	180-1
The three letters from Pesth	182-3
Deak	184
Retirement of M. Schmerling	185
The September manifesto	186
Vienna in September 1865	187
The autumn of 1865 in Austria (note)	188

	PAGE		PAGE
Difficulties of Austria.	180-90	Austria and the Eastern question	
The commercial treaty	. 191	tion	. 197
The nationalities	. 193	Austria and Poland .	. 198
Venetia . . .	194-5	The future . . .	. 199
Germany and Austria .	195-6	The threatened war .	. 200

CHAPTER IV.

PRUSSIA.

Unattractiveness of Prussian politics	201	Its manifesto . . . 229
Recent history of Prussia .	201	Constitution of the new parliament 229
Four well-marked periods .	202	Leading liberal politicians . 230-1
Death of Frederick William III.	202	The military question . 231
Frederick William IV. .	203	Resignation of ministers and dissolution . . . 231
1840-47	204	The Von der Heydt cabinet 231
The "Historical" school .	205	The new parliament . . 232
The "Vereinigte Landtag"	205-6	Vincke and Sybel . . 232
1848 in Berlin .	206-10	M. von Bismarck-Schönhausen 233
Gains of the revolutionary period	210	His history and character . 234-5
Commencement of the reaction	210	Quarrel between the House and the ministers—prorogation 236
Manteuffel . . .	211	Press ordinances . . 236
Retirement of the democratic party	211	The speech of the Crown Prince at Dantsic . . 237
The constitution . .	212	Dissolution and new parliament ˉ 238
The crisis of 1850 and Olmütz	212	Death of Frederick VII. of Denmark . . . 238
The reaction continues .	213	The Schleswig-Holstein question becomes dangerous . 239
Stahl, Gerlach, and the king	215-16	M. Bismark and the Lower House 239
Vincke	217	The Danish war . . 240
The Prussian war and the Crown Prince . .	218	The autumn of 1865 . . 241
Violence of the reaction .	220	The short session of 1866 . 241
Popular education in Prussia	221	Difficulties of Prussian Liberals 242
Illness of the king . .	222	The army 243
Regency with full powers .	222	The Feudal party . . 244
The new government .	222-6	Mecklenburg . . . 245
Character of the regent .	226	The situation in the spring of 1866 . . 246-9
The coronation at Königsberg	226	The future . . 250-1
The military question .	227	
Re-appearance of the democratic party as the German party of progress . . .	228	

CHAPTER V.

THE GERMANIC DIET.

PAGE

Distinction between a federative state and a confederation of states . . . 252

Germany is the latter — a Staaten-Bund not a Bundes-Staat 252

The Holy Roman Empire . 253

The Confederation of the Rhine 254

The negotiations of 1814 255-7

The Federal Act . 257-8

The Final Act . . . 259

The Ministerial Conferences of 1820 and 1834 . . 260

Plans of Federal reform . 260

The Vor-Parlament . . 261

The Frankfort Parliament . 261

The League of the Three Kings and the "Union" . . 262

The Gotha party . . 263

The *Interim* at Frankfort . 263

Saxony and Hanover secede from the "Union" . . 264

The Erfurt Parliament . 264

The threatened war of 1850 265

Ascendancy of Nicholas . 265

Fall of Radowitz and the "Union" . . . 266

The Dresden Conferences . 266

PAGE

Elation of Prince Schwartzenberg 266

France, England, and Russia interfere . . . 266

The Confederation as it is . 267

The Diet . . . 268-76

The Federal army . . 270

Austria and Prussia . . 270

The minor German States (*note*) . . . 272-6

Plans of Federal reform . 276

The *National-Verein* . . 277

The Duke of Saxe-Coburg . 278

Official steps for Federal reform . . . 279-80

Count Bismark's recent proposal 281

The three Ideas . . 281

The "Great-German" Idea . 282

The "Trias" Idea . . 283

The "Small-German" Idea . 284

The threatened war . . 284

German unity . . 285-6

Estrangement between England and Germany . . 287

Its cause — the Schleswig-Holstein imbroglio . . 287

Better hopes for the future . 288

CHAPTER VI.

HOLLAND.

Physical character of the Netherlands . . 289

Contrast of their ancient and modern condition . . 290

Wonderful achievements of the Dutch . . . 290

The comic side of Holland . 290

Books on Holland . 291-2

The modern history of Holland begins with the French Revolution . . . 292

Creation of the kingdom of the United Netherlands . 293

PAGE

Four periods—
  1. 1815 to 1830.
  2. 1830 to 1840.
  3. 1840 to 1848.
  4. 1848 to the present time 293
The Dutch royal family . 294
Achievements of the fourth
  period .   .   . 294
Life and character of Thorbecke .   .   294-5
The " April movement" . 296
Steady progress.   .   . 297
Holland is in advance of every
  country in Europe in two
  departments of national
  life. These are—
  a. Her ecclesiastical system
  b. Her elementary educa-
    tion .   .   297
History of theology in Hol-
  land from the Reformation
  downwards .   .   298
The Synod of Dort . . 298
Influence of the Cartesian
  philosophy .   .   299
The eighteenth century in
  Holland . . 299-300
Van der Palm .   .   301
The reaction in Holland . 301
Bilderdyk.   .   .   301
Da Costa .   .   . 301
M. Groen van Prinsterer . 302
The high Tory and Confes-
  sional party .   303-6

PAGE

The Vinet school in Hol-
  land .   .   . 306
The theologians of Gronin-
  gen   .   . 307-9
The theologians of Leyden 309-11
The " modern" theologians 311
The Walloon churches . 312
M. Albert Réville . . 313
M. Opzoomer . . 315
The theologians of Utrecht. 315
Spinoza .   .   . 316
The Jansenist Church of Hol-
  land   .   . 316
Other dissenting sects . 317
Ecclesiastical organisation . 318
Prospects of the Dutch Church 318
Noble reply of the General
  Synod .   . 320
Education in the Netherlands 321
Cuvier's report . . 321
M. Victor Cousin's report . 321
Mr. William Chambers's book 321
Mr. Matthew Arnold's report 322
The " Society for the Public
  Good" .   . 322
The school law of 1806 . 322
The debates of 1857 . 323
M. Émile de Laveleye's book 323
Working of the law of 1857 323-5
Dutch secondary education, till
  lately, very imperfect .326-7
The Dutch Universities .327-9
Colonial reforms now under dis-
  cussion .   .   .330-1

CHAPTER VII.

BELGIUM.

Death of King Leopold . 332
His reign deserves to be
  studied.   .   . 332
Creation of the kingdom of
  the United Netherlands . 322
Causes of its failure .   . 333

" The Union" .   .   . 334
The four glorious days . 334
The Provisional Govern-
  ment .   .   . 334
The Congress .   . 335
Leopold becomes king . 335

	PAGE
Services of Lord Palmerston to Belgium	336
Political life of the new nation	336
Liberals and Clericals	336
Useful measures	337
M. Devaux and his article in the *Revue Nationale*	338
The De Theux cabinet	338
The Rogier cabinet	338
The Nothomb cabinet	338
The Van de Weyer cabinet	339
M. de Theux again First Minister	339
Reform meeting at the Hotel de Ville in Brussels	340
M. Rogier and M. Frère-Orban	340
Their programme	341
Fall of the July monarchy	341
The year 1848 in Belgium	342-3
Party conflicts	344
Ministry of conciliation	344
M. de Brouckere	345
The Vilain xiiii. and De Decker cabinet	346
The *Jamais* of M. Vilain xiiii.	348
The Episcopal aggression	348
The " Loi des Couvents"	349
Riots	350
The king's letter	351
Fall of the ministry	352
M. Rogier once more in power	352

	PAGE
Session of 1858	353
New questions	353
Abolition of the Octroi	354
Commercial treaty with France	355
Question of Antwerp	356
Commercial treaty with England	356
Abolition of the Scheldt dues	357
Enlightened views on fiscal reform	357
M. Dechamps	358
His programme	359
The dead-lock of parties	359
The Encyclical of December 1864	360
The session of 1865	361
The death of King Leopold	361
In what condition did he leave his country	362
Moral and material progress	362-3
Recent works on Belgium	363
The Walloons and the Flemings	364
Belgian literature	365-6
The periodical press	366-7
Population, pauperism, taxation	367-8
M. Dechamps—his article in the *Revue Générale*	368
M. de Laveleye's article in the *Revue des Deux Mondes*	369
Clericals and Liberals	369-73
Richard Cobden, *Roi des Belges*	373
France and Belgium	373-7

PREFATORY NOTE.

WHILE these sheets have been passing through the press, the diplomatists of three great countries have been engaged, with more or less of zeal, in attempting to preserve the peace of Europe. There seems now little reason to doubt that their efforts have been unsuccessful, and that more than one of the questions, which we have discussed, may be brought to a speedier settlement than any one expected a few months ago. Still, whatever may be the result of the encounters of armies, and however long they may continue, it will be necessary, when the storm has passed away, to remember accurately the position of affairs before its first mutterings began to be heard; and it is hoped that the present work may not be wholly useless to those who desire to do so. Ere yet, then, the whole face of the Continent is covered with the smoke of battle, let us take one last glance at the seven countries to which this volume is devoted.

Spain, fortunate in her isolated position, would have indeed gone out of her way to seek misfortune if she had contrived to become involved in the present

European complication. At this moment her government appears to be making a somewhat more earnest
effort than usual to put herself right with her creditors, and to obtain, so to speak, a *locus standi* in the
great money-market of the world.

Meanwhile English newspapers are full of reflec-
tions upon her doings in the Pacific; and it is most
assuredly not our business to justify them, anxious as
we are to see the rights of commerce, in time of war,
ever more and more protected. Nevertheless, we
should wish that more prominence were given to
the Spanish side of the question. All Europe is
interested in restraining the petulance of the South
American States, whose one bond is an intense jealousy
and dislike of the old Continent. Those who imagine
that their ill humour is the fruit of past injuries, and
is directed only against Spain, might turn with advantage to the extremely interesting essay prefixed by M.
Calvo, the Chargé d'Affaires of Paraguay, to his
valuable collection of the Treaties of Latin America.
They will there find that England comes in for considerably more than her fair share of detestation, and
is accused of "intolerable oppression." It is difficult,
as any one who pursues the tangled thread of our
relations with these promising, but still imperfectly-
civilised communities, will readily discover, always to
hit the exact mean between over-severity and weakness. Of one thing, however, there can be no doubt,—

that any interference on the part of Spain in South America, which goes beyond what is absolutely necessary for the protection of Spanish subjects and Spanish commerce on that Continent, is simple madness. If she must play the Quixote, she had much better find vent for her superfluous enthusiasm in another quarrel with the Moors.

What secrets may be known to those wonderful persons who telegraph to Mr. Reuter the contents of autograph letters from the Czar to the Kaiser, we cannot pretend to say; and it is quite possible that the policy of Russia in the present crisis may be as evil as we are often told that it invariably is. So far, however, as any information which looks authentic has reached us, the conduct of the Autocrat and his advisers has been very fair and loyal. Every one, at least, will admit that we seem to be separated, not by seventeen years, but by whole ages, from the famous proclamation which marks the culminating point of the insanity of Nicholas:—" Nobiscum Deus, audite populi et vincemini, quia nobiscum Deus !"

The Prussian press, as we gather from its faithful exponent in Brussels, is decidedly favourable to peace, and, although watching with great care all that passes on the Danube, is chiefly occupied with internal affairs, more especially with the new judicial institutions, which came into operation at Petersburg and Moscow in the month of April. These institutions will, we trust, be one step more on the road to legal as distinguished from arbitrary government; but large deductions will doubtless have to be made from the enthusiastic observations of the Minister of Justice, who lately declared that the new code of procedure was "almost the *dernier mot* of juridical wisdom."

In the far East we see, by the latest news, that Russia has good cause, not for alarm, but for anxiety. The defeat which her arms lately sustained, at the hands of the Emir of Bokhara, must have been more serious than was at first supposed—so serious indeed as to require that something considerable should be done, in order to recover her lost *prestige*. We are far from saying, that if Russia ends by annexing the whole of that part of Tartary which is still independent, it will not be right for us to consider, most seriously, whether there are not some points which we ought to secure as outworks of our Indian Empire. Because we once played, what a brilliant writer has called, "the great game of Central Asia" extremely badly, that is no reason why we should conclude that it will never have to be played at all. Far from neglecting the advance of Russia towards the South, we think we should watch it with the greatest possible attention; but this should be done in a friendly, not in a hostile spirit, the ultimate object being, as we have elsewhere said, to arrive at a mutual understanding in Asia,—an understanding which may, before our frontiers, still separated by enormous distances, shall touch each other, be so close as to lead us to feel that each other's neighbourhood is a guarantee against the insurrectionary tendencies of the Mussulman populations in our respective dominions. The worst forms of fanaticism, which we have to dread in India, cannot well be more formidable than the peculiarly-odious type which the religion of the prophet has assumed in Turkistan.

In treating of this subject there are two things equally to be deprecated—an excessive indifference to Russian advance, and a foolish fear of it. We are glad to observe that Mr. Long has taken up the cudgels for Russia in Calcutta. If his views are a little too favourable to that power, as we have hinted, they are, we repeat, far nearer the truth than those which have often prevailed in India, and the discussion which he cannot fail to bring about in the press of Bengal, will tend to enlighten public opinion.

In suspending for a time the publication of the *Moscow Gazette*, the Russian government has only carried out the existing press law of the empire, and we cannot attribute any political significance to the course which it has adopted. Its latest appointments, on the contrary, were highly approved of by that journal. Of these the most important was the substitution of Count Tolstoi, as Minister of Public Instruction, for the more liberal Golownine. Count Tolstoi has taken a very prominent part in the direction of ecclesiastical affairs, and his appointment indicates a desire to fall back upon the church for aid against Herzenism, Nihilism, Polonism, and all the other spectres with which the Russian reactionists think they have a mission to fight. A curious standard of comparison between the relative enlightenment of the retrograde party, immediately east and west of the Vistula, is afforded by a recent article in the *Kreuz Zeitung*, which, while highly approving Count Tolstoi's appointment, and praying for the revivification of the Greek Church, points out that the best way to attain that object would be to grant religious toleration, and this at the very moment when, at least in the western provinces of Russsia, that church is assuming an exclusive and intolerant attitude, by no means in accordance with her traditions. The rescript of the Czar, lately addressed to Prince Gagarine, is another symptom of a desire to invoke the aid of superstition as a protection against " antisocial machinations."

Austria continues her slow progress down the easy slope of Avernus. The war into which she seems as anxious as either of her adversaries to plunge, can bring to her, at least, the satisfactory solution of no one of the questions which have so long tormented her. She may well drive back Victor Emmanuel from the Quadrilateral, she may well overbalance by sheer force of numbers the advantage derived by her German foe from that formidable needle-gun, which we are told makes one soldier do the work of three ; but who, that knows the forces now at work in Europe, can doubt that Italy and Prussia must conquer in the end ?

It appears to be generally expected that Hungary will forget her grievances and support the Kaiser in his attempt to establish, once for all, his preponderance in Germany. We shall believe this when we see it. The chivalrous Magyars showed, even in that famous Diet when they rallied round the Empress-Queen, that they had a tolerably sharp eye to their own interests. If the ingenious author of *Pearls and Mock Pearls of History* ever republishes, in an enlarged form, that interesting article, we should recommend him to examine what basis of historical truth there really is in that famous story of the " Moriamur pro rege nostro," the one *fact* (?) in Hungarian history familiar to Englishmen, before the war of 1848-49, and which has been *set* by Lord Macaulay in a brilliant passage—the same, by the way, in which he has exalted the tiny mound called the Königsberg into the " Mount of Defiance." As is that hillock to the castle-hill of Presburg which rises over it, so we trust will be the real to the anticipated enthusiasm of Hungary in this evil war.

And Prussia—can she escape censure ? Certainly not ; for unless we separate the people from the government, she is far more in the wrong than her opponent in' the quarrel which is the *proximate* cause of war.   Nor can we altogether separate the people from the government, for if the annexationist schemes of Count Bismark in the Duchies had not been seconded last year by the enthusiasm of many who ought to have known better, he might not have advanced so far.   The best we can say is that the attitude of the nation in view of the approaching danger has been worthy of an intelligent and civilised community.   It seems impossible to believe that the war could be long continued without the complete break-down of the present system of government; and if that break-down is sudden and final, if the vast change which would be involved in the substitution of the policy of, say, M. Roggenbach, for that of M. Bismark, were soon to follow the commencement of hostilities, it would undoubtedly be a not inadequate return for a good deal of suffering.

That Prussia, even in the best event, has, if she once goes to war, a good deal of suffering to pass through, we cannot for a moment doubt.   It may be, as some military authorities tell us, that the superiority of her weapons will give her a great advantage; but her whole social system will be far more disorganised by war than that of her antagonist, and she will have to use up on the battle-field material far more valuable than any which her adversary will use, or even possesses. We may smile at those excited gentlemen who believe that the scenes in Schiller's " Camp of Wallen-stein" are going to be reproduced all over North Germany, and we do not for a moment believe that the Seressaner or Likaner of 1866 is more of a barbarian than many of the private soldiers in other armies ; but the fact of his not being on a par with the soldiers of Alva, or the Pandours who followed Trenck, will not make him exactly a pleasant visitor.

The smaller states of Germany, divided now by their sympathies, will ere long be divided only by geographical lines, for it can hardly be that, if war is once commenced, their neutrality will be respected by their mighty neighbours. He would be a bold man who would prophesy how many of them will stand erect when the threatened troubles are at an end.

Holland, with characteristic prudence, desires to keep as far from the combatants as possible, and very reasonably proposes to make arrangements for withdrawing Limburg from the Germanic Confedera-tion, with which it has never, *de facto,* been as closely connected as Luxemburg.

The colonial debates which were proceeding when the paper on Holland was printed, resulted in the carrying of an amendment which ministers considered fatal to their measure of reform, and they have ac-cordingly resigned, and have been succeeded by a cabinet of Conservative, though not Tory, colour. It is hardly probable that M. van Zuylen van Nyevelt and his colleagues can, in the present state of parties in Holland, long retain power; and perhaps the only effect of their return to office may be once more to unite all Liberal factions, and to lead to the passing of a measure of colonial reform more comprehensive than that which was recently under discussion.

Belgium, though on the whole in sufficiently good heart, is naturally beset by the anxieties which afflict the mind of a householder who sees his neighbour's house on fire, and learns that there is some difficulty in getting up the fire-engines. Accordingly we were not much surprised to find an article in a recent number of the newspaper which is most closely connected with M. Frère, in which England is well rated for not taking more active steps to prevent the outbreak of hostilities, the writer being no other than M. Hymans, whose excellent work on the reign of Leopold was our chief guide in the earlier part of the paper which treats of that country, but who does not represent precisely that shade of Belgian liberalism with which, in its views on the questions now under discussion, we have the greatest sympathy.

In Brussels, as in London, the question of electoral reform is becoming daily more important, nor can there be any doubt that the passing of the measures which Her Majesty's government has brought forward this session, would greatly assist the best Belgian Liberals.

Happy the country which, at so solemn a moment, is able to watch with interest the encounters of champions whose respective war-cries are a *seven* and an *eight* pound franchise! Over half the fairest cities of Europe the thunder-clouds seem closing as we write, and for some time to come we must be content to find our best comfort in the old German distich—

> Herrscht der Teufel heut' auf Erden,
> Morgen wird Gott, Meister werden.

London, *June* 9, 1866.

CHAPTER I.

SPAIN.

THE opening, in August 1864, of the line from Beasain to Olazagutia, through a country as rugged, although fortunately more beautiful than, those strange Basque names, completed the railway communication· between Madrid and Paris. Amongst many good results which will flow from this, not the least will be the invasion of the Peninsula by many travellers, who have hitherto taken, all too literally, the witty saying, that "Africa begins with the Pyrenees." Such travellers will belong, for the most part, to one of two categories : those who go abroad in search of novelty, and those who are attracted to the Peninsula by the love of art. To these two classes we do not address ourselves, for they have, in numerous well-known books, every literary help that they can possibly need.

May we not hope, however, that in addition to those who go to Spain as the nearest preserve of picturesque barbarians, or as one of the great museums of the world, there will be some who will go with other views—some who will cross the Bidassoa in the hope of seeing for themselves whether the vague rumours of revival, which reach our shores, are true or false ; whether there is any hope that that nation, once so famous, is going to take part in the forward movement of Europe ; or whether it is indeed true, as Mr. Buckle tells us, that " she lies at the further extremity of the Continent, a huge and torpid mass, the sole representative now remaining of the feelings and knowledge of the Middle Ages ?"

Travellers, who have this purpose in view, will find that they have embarked upon an enterprise, which is made unnecessarily difficult by the erroneous notions about Spain which prevail even amongst well-informed persons in England, as well as by the scantiness of the information with regard to her condition, which is readily accessible. It is mainly for the purpose of clearing away from the path of such investigators some preliminary difficulties, that we have drawn up this paper—not without hope that some one, who may be benefited by its hints, may repay the obligation with interest ; may give us, in a not too bulky volume, a full and accurate estimate of the state and prospects of Spain.

This is perhaps the place to say a word or two as to some books which such an investigator may take with him, or may buy in Madrid. They are not very numerous, and none of them is by itself of surpassing importance ; but they are the best that exist, written by persons of very different views and characters, and one who is anxious to ascertain the truth, may, by a sensible use of them, arrive at pretty correct conclusions.

First, we have Minutoli, whose work may be taken as a very exact inventory of Spanish affairs in 1851. Minutoli writes from the *Standpunkt* of a Prussian bureaucrat who thinks that Berlin is illuminated by *Intelligenz* in a quite supernatural manner, and who believes that the *via prima salutis* is to have an efficient and upright *Beamtenthum*. He is anxious for the development of all manner of wealth, for the furtherance of the happiness of the greatest possible number ; but he distrusts the power of the people to work out its own wellbeing, and is consequently a good friend to the

Moderado *régime* which extended from 1843 to 1854. His book is, it will be observed, somewhat out of date, but it still is serviceable, though we must warn those who would read it, that it stands in the same relation to the typical blue-book in which that stands to a sensation novel.

Then we have Mr. Wallis, who wrote in 1853, and who looks at Spain through the spectacles—and very colourless ones they are—of an accomplished, highly-cultivated American gentleman, a warm friend to free institutions, but possessed of a more than aristocratic hatred of popular clap-trap. His book is only too easy to read ; but his means of information were ample, his head is clear, and his conclusions, after making allowance for a little unsoundness on questions of trade, will commend themselves to most Englishmen.

Next comes Rico y Amat, a prejudiced Tory writer, but very useful for giving the sequence of events down to 1854, discussing all parliamentary matters in great detail, and quoting many important documents at full length. In strong contrast to him is the go-ahead Orense, Marquis of Albaida, who, dissatisfied with the conduct of his brother Progressistas, has cast in his lot with the Democrats. The views of the politicians who were hurled from power in 1854 may be gathered, by one who has eyes to look for them, from a very slight but clever little book called the *Attaché at Madrid*, which, professing to be translated from the diary of a young German diplomatist, who spent part of 1853 and 1854 in the Spanish capital, and published in America, really owes its origin to one who had the best information, and excellent reasons for wishing well to the cause of Sartorius. When the reader has laid it down, he may take up Garrido's work, which we have used in its German form. Garrido belongs to the extreme left, as may be guessed when we mention that his book was translated by Arnold Ruge, and that he was introduced to the ex-editor of the *Hallischen Jahrbücher* by Dr. Bernard. It would be as imprudent unconditionally to accept his view of matters, as to find nothing to object to in those of Rico y Amat, or of the author of the *Attaché at Madrid,* but his pages are full of statistics and information of all kinds, deserving to be read and weighed most carefully.

The articles in the *Annuaire des Deux Mondes,* which extend in unbroken succession from 1850 to 1865, are some-what Moderado in tone, but extremely valuable and interesting. The Spanish papers in the *Revue* itself are not, perhaps, so happy as those on several other countries ; but some of them—such as C. de Mazade's on Larra, and on Donoso Cortes—will repay perusal even now. The life of Olozaga, lately published —surely the hugest political pamphlet which ever appeared —should also be consulted.

No one, of course, will omit to read the *Handbook* and the *Gatherings,* both full of that wisdom of Spain which is trea-sured up in her proverbs, and quite indispensable, in spite of their constant offences against good taste. Captain Widdring-ton's works are still valuable, while most of the modern English books of travel in the Peninsula are absolutely worthless.

Spain has slipped, of late years, so thoroughly out of the notice of Englishmen, that it would be mere affectation to pre-tend to imagine that one in a thousand knows even the A B C of her recent history and politics. We must, therefore, briefly relate the events of the present reign, for some know-ledge of these is quite necessary to those who would compre-hend her actual position.

The Cortes of Cadiz, in 1812, devised a Constitution,

which, in spite of many blemishes and shortcomings, was on the whole most creditable to its framers. It sinned, indeed, against several of the first principles of Liberalism, but it cordially accepted many others ; and, considering the circumstances of the country, it unquestionably went too far in a democratic direction. In 1814, Ferdinand VII. overthrew this Constitution, restored the Inquisition, and ruled for six years despotically. In 1820, the revolt of Riego, and the movements which followed it, again inaugurated a brief period of liberty, which continued until the Spanish patriots were put down by the French, under the Duc d'Angoulême, and the *re dissoluto* was once more able to ride rough-shod over all that was honest and virtuous from the Bidassoa to the lines of Gibraltar. This terrible time lasted until the day when Ferdinand VII. was trundled off to his last home in the Escurial, in the way which Ford has described with so much grim humour. The last act of importance in the wretched man's life had been the confirmation of the right of succession of his daughter Isabella II., as against his brother Don Carlos. The pretensions of that personage had been already loudly proclaimed, and he hardly waited for the challenge of the Royalists to erect his standard. That challenge soon came, for on the 24th October 1833, the voice of the herald, according to ancient custom, was heard in Madrid, proclaiming " Silencio, silencio, silencio, oyid, oyid, oyid, Castilla, Castilla, Castilla, por la Senhora reina Doña Isabel II. que Dios guarde." Bilbao was the first place to pronounce for the Pretender, and ere long the whole of the north was in arms, and the civil war had begun. How that war raged, and how many souls, heroic and other, it sent to Hades, it is unnecessary to say. How it ended we shall presently have occasion to relate, but we must confine our narrative, for the present, to that portion of Spain which acknowledged the rightful sovereign, merely reminding the reader that Don Carlos represented two totally distinct interests,—first, that of bigotry and corruption generally, in all parts of the Peninsula; and, secondly, the infinitely more respectable aspirations of the Basques, who, attached to liberty, but possessed of little enlightenment, desired to remain a semi-republican island in the midst of an Absolute Spain, rather than to lose the local franchises which they knew, in the general freedom of a Constitutional Spain, which had not yet come into existence, although its advent was near at hand.

The queen-mother, obliged by the force of circumstances to rely on the support of the Liberal party, but anxious to be as little liberal as possible, accepted the resignation of Zea Bermudez, who represented the party of enlightened despotism, and called to her councils Martinez de la Rosa, who had suffered much for his attachment to Constitutional principles during the late reign, but who from 1833 till his death in 1862, was one of the most eminent of the Moderado or Conservative statesman of Spain. By his advice she promulgated the *Estatuto real*, a Constitution incomparably less liberal than that of Cadiz, but still a Constitution, and one professing to be founded upon the ancient and long-disused liberties of the land. This document, we may observe in passing, may, like that of 1812 and all its successors, be read at length in Rico y Amat's History. By the *Estatuto* were created an upper house of "Proceres," and a lower house of "Procuradores." These soon met, and the discussions which took place in them, combined with the agitation out of doors, and some diplomatic misadventures, soon obliged Martinez de la Rosa to retire. He was followed by Toreno; but he, too, was unable to hold his own. A far more energetic and enlightened minister was required, and that minister soon appeared in the great reformer Mendizabal.

He it was who concentrated the forces of the revolutionary agitation, which had already broken out in the provinces, and gave them a definite direction. This he did chiefly by three great measures, which will cause his name ever to be held in honour by all Spanish patriots. These three measures were the closing of the monasteries, the sale of all the lands belonging to the regular clergy, and the organisation, on a thoroughly popular basis, of the National Guard. All this he effected in a very short space of time, for his cabinet, attacked at once by the most impatient Liberals, by the retrograde party, and by French intrigue, had a hard battle to fight, and soon gave way to an administration, of which the leading spirits were Isturiz and Galiano.* These politicians, however, utterly failed to carry the country with them, and their days of power were few and evil. Readers of the *Bible in Spain* will recollect the strongly-contrasted descriptions of Mr. Borrow's visit to Mendizabal at the zenith of his power, and to Isturiz, when that minister had already begun to hear the mutterings of the storm which was soon to burst upon his head. That storm was the mutiny which broke out amongst the troops stationed at the royal residence of La Granja, which is situated in the

---

* Alcalá Galiano was born at Cadiz in 1789, entered the diplomatic service in 1812, took an active part in the revolution of 1820, and was banished for his share in it. During the eight years that he passed in England, he was a frequent contributor to the *Westminster and Foreign Quarterly*. On his return to Spain he again entered political life ; became a bitter opponent of the first two Constitutional ministries, and a supporter of Mendizabal. Like the Duke of Rivas, however, and many others, he soon changed his politics, and the second half of his life was passed as a Moderado. He enjoyed a great reputation as an orator, and his lectures at the Madrid Ateneo were in their day extremely celebrated. He died as Minister of Public Welfare in 1865.

mountainous country to the north of Madrid. The leader of
this mutiny was a certain Sergeant Garcia, and the chief objects
of the discontented soldiery were to force the Queen Regent
to dismiss her ministers and to proclaim the Constitution of
1812. In these objects they were completely successful.
Christina yielded to the threats of the mutineers, and power
passed once more into the hands of the movement party.

After the assassinations, disorders, and escapes across the
frontier, which are usual in Spanish political crises, the new
government, which was of course composed of men of Liberal
politics, convoked the famous Constituent Cortes of 1837.
Out of its labours arose the new Constitution, which was
based on that of Cadiz, but differed from it in many particulars.
Argüelles, who had been one of the principal authors of the
former, was also concerned in the latter, and was indeed a
member of the committee which drew up the resolutions on
which it was based. Its tone is much less democratic than
that of its predecessor; and the fact that Olozaga and other
distinguished Liberals supported it created much dissatisfaction in the ranks of their followers. We are far, however,
from thinking that, in the circumstances of Spain, the changes
which they introduced were otherwise than necessary. With
regard to the one point in which the Constitution of 1837
made more concession to Liberal opinions than that of 1812,
there can be no question among honest and intelligent men.
The Cortes of Cadiz proclaimed the Roman Catholic religion
to be the only true one. The legislators of 1837 contented
themselves with asserting as a fact that the Spanish nation
professed the Roman Catholic religion, and bound itself to
maintain that form of faith.

This great work had not been long completed, when the

ministry which had been called into existence by the mutiny of Granja succumbed in its turn to another military revolt, excited by the partisans of those whom it had so summarily displaced, and Espartero, whose military reputation was already great, became for a brief period the President of the Council; for a brief period, we say, for, defeated in the elections, he was succeeded by the reactionary Ofalia; he again by others of little note, till the Convention of Vergara came to alter the whole position of affairs.

The reader will recollect that during all these ministerial changes, revolutions, and makings of constitutions, the Philistine was still in the land. The advanced posts of Don Carlos had been seen from the walls of Madrid; Gomez had made a sort of military progress from one end of the country to the other; La Mancha was in the hands of one rebel, Valencia was overrun by another; and the whole of the mountainous north was a camp of the "factious." Fortunately for the cause of Queen Isabella, there were dissensions in the enemy's ranks not less bitter than those which distracted the capital. The military party and the clerical party hated each other with a deadly hatred; and at last their animosity became so embittered that Maroto, the most important of the lieutenants of Don Carlos, took the law into his own hands, and put some of the most conspicuous of his opponents to death. This was the beginning of the end; and after infinite intrigues, the little Basque town of Vergara saw the signature of the document which assured the throne of the young queen, put a period to the war of Navarre, and made the pacification of Arragon merely a question of time. Espartero's attitude had now been for some time of the greatest possible interest to all who watched the politics of Spain. He was evidently inclining more and more towards the Progressista party, while his relations with the Moderado government became ever colder. A letter addressed by his secretary to one of the Madrid papers had openly condemned the conduct of the ministry in dissolving the Cortes, with a view to get rid of the Progressista majority; and the party which was now about to resort to revolutionary measures in Madrid reckoned on his assistance.

The struggle in the Cortes of 1840 was fierce but short. The galleries, as was usual in those stormy times, took an active part in the political combat; and on one occasion the scenes of 1793 seemed about to be repeated. In spite of the gallant resistance of the Progressista party, the government carried several reactionary laws,—the most important of which was one for the modification of the municipal system, which would have had the effect of very much diminishing the influence of the Liberals throughout the country, and of strengthening unduly the powers of the Crown. Just at this crisis, when Madrid was in a most uneasy state, and nearly all the large towns hardly more tranquil, the young queen was advised to take warm sea-baths at Barcelona, and to that place she repaired, accompanied by her mother. Christina had not been long in the Catalan capital, when she announced to Espartero that she had given her assent to the law relating to the municipalities. To this ungracious declaration he replied by resigning his position as commander-in-chief. His resignation was not accepted; and he then informed the Regent that he was about to retire from the city, as he could be of no further use to her. Hardly had he done so than Barcelona rose in rebellion, and the ministers who had accompanied the queen fled hither and thither. The movement begun amongst the turbulent Catalans rapidly spread all over Spain. Madrid

pronounced on the 1st of September, whereupon the Regent
gave way, and Espartero was ordered to form a new government. Her new advisers insisted that she should issue a
manifesto, in which she should throw upon the late cabinet
the whole responsibility of the recent attempts at reaction,
that she should solemnly promise that the law relating to the
municipalities should not be carried into execution, and that
the Cortes should instantly be dissolved. These terms she
refused, resigned the regency, and took refuge in France, addressing from Marseilles to the Spanish people a proclamation in which the sentiments of her heart were expressed or
disguised, in the ornate language of Donoso Cortes. The
abdication of Christina left the first place in the state without
an occupant, and it was necessary to fill it as speedily as possible. The question which now became urgent was, How
should this be done? Two opinions divided the suffrages of
the victors in the recent struggle. The advanced Progressistas
were in favour of a regency of three. The immediate *entourage*
of Espartero desired the elevation of their chief to undivided
authority. It was this last view which prevailed ; for the
Moderados, seeing that the question was an apple of discord
to their enemies, threw all their influence into the scale of
Espartero, feeling sure that they should succeed in embroiling
him with the majority of those whose alliance had placed the
successful soldier in a position to play the great game of
politics. So it came about that, on the 8th of May 1841,
Espartero was chosen by the Cortes to be sole Regent ; and
no sooner was he fairly installed in his office, than the edifice
of his power began to crumble under his feet. His descent
was more rapid than even his rise, for the circumstances in
which he found himself required infinite skill in intrigue,—a

quality of which the honest and well-meaning Duke of Victory had a very small share. His great mistake was his surrounding himself from the very first with ministers and private advisers who had not the confidence of his party, and who soon became known to the public by several injurious epithets. Some called them *Ayacuchos,* from the name of one of the battles in South America which had been most disastrous to the Spanish arms,—the insinuation being that they were a mere clique of military *old fogies;* while others spoke of them as *Santones,* intending thereby to ridicule their want of revolutionary energy.

The Moderado party soon took advantage of the weakness of the government; and in October 1841 a military revolt broke out at Pamplona, at Madrid, and elsewhere, in the interest of Christina. The Regent showed a good deal of decision. A file of soldiers at Vittoria sent to his account Montes de Oca, who had been Minister of Marine in the former government. General Leon met a similar fate at Madrid ; while O'Donnell got safe to France, living " to fight another day."

Espartero, however, had other adversaries more formidable than even the Moderados. More than once he was obliged to put down with a strong hand the Democratic agitations of Barcelona ; and each successive act of vigour directed against those who, after all, formed the extreme left of his own party, cost him a large portion of his popularity. Then the French government did all it could by underhand methods to assist Christina, and to discredit Espartero, and at last a hostile vote in the Lower House destroyed his ministry. By this time the Progressista party was so disorganised that his second cabinet was not more generally satisfactory than his first. His third, at the head of which was Lopez, who had distinguished himself very much as a popular orator, came too late, and was too short-lived. Its fall, which was the result of Espartero's firm support of his friend Linaje against it, was another blow to his influence ; nor did the friendship of England at all tend to his greater popularity amongst a proud and ignorant people. Of the many accusations brought against him, not the least potent in exciting hatred was his alleged subservience to our commercial policy. And now the end came fast. A coalition, which comprised large numbers both of the Progressista and Moderado party, was formed throughout the country. *Pronunciamentos* followed. Narvaez, O'Donnell, and many of the exiled or fugitive generals, entered Spain. Treachery helped the work that disunion had begun ; and in the beginning of August 1843, the idol of September 1840 was on his way to England, whither he was presently pursued by a decree which stripped him of all his titles, honours, and decorations.

Lopez was the next First Minister. His intentions were, we believe, not otherwise than honest, but his position was an untenable one. Himself an advanced Progressista, he found himself obliged to place all the military powers of the country in the hands of the Moderado generals, who had borne the brunt of the contest with the Duke of Victory. He soon saw that the game was lost, and passed through the Cortes a measure for proclaiming the queen of full age eleven months before the time which the Constitution prescribed. This done he placed his resignation in the hands of Her Majesty, and retired from power a sadder and a wiser man. He had much occasion for sadness, for the knell of his party was very soon to sound ; nevertheless it was a Progressista ministry which succeeded his, and there was still one act of the play to be played out.

The new President of the Council was Olozaga, who was then, and is still, a foremost figure amongst the Progressistas.

Hardly was he fairly in the possession of power, when there occurred an incident of so strange a kind, that it only requires to be seen through the mist of ages to have the romantic interest of the Gowrie conspiracy. The President of the Council could reckon upon the ardent support of a minority in the Cortes, but of a considerable majority in the electoral body. It was therefore his obvious interest to appeal, as soon as possible, to the country, and a decree dissolving the legislature shortly appeared. Hardly, however, had it been promulgated, when strange rumours arose in Madrid, to the effect that the decree for the dissolution of the Cortes to which the young queen owed the declaration of her majority, had been obtained, not only by undue moral pressure, but by personal violence ; and these rumours acquired additional confirmation, after a decree had appeared revoking the former one and dismissing the minister. Expectation was raised to its height, when, on the day appointed for the discussion, a personage new to such functions took his seat in the Congress, with the ministerial portfolio under his arm. This worthy defender of the throne was no other man than the editor of the Spanish *Satirist* of that day—Gonsalez Bravo ; and the paper which he proceeded to read was a full account, signed by Her Majesty, of the violence which had been employed by the late Premier. The discussion was long and stormy. Its principal feature was of course the speech of Olozaga, which even his adversaries admit to have been a very great effort, and in which he contrived to exculpate himself without bringing home to his sovereign the charge of falsehood. The real history was probably that the minister was somewhat more peremptory in his manner than is usual, as a man of Olozaga's character and commanding appearance might well either be, or appear to be, when urging a matter of pressing national importance upon a puzzle-headed young woman, and that the worthless persons who surrounded the queen, and who were entirely in the hands of the opposite party, magnified the importance of the incident in her eyes, until they actually brought her to sign a paper in which she perhaps hardly knew how to distinguish the false from the true.

Olozaga, after his defence, fled to Lisbon to avoid the by-no-means-chimerical danger of assassination ; and the meaning of the intrigue gradually unfolded itself, as it was seen that Gonsalez Bravo was merely an instrument in the hands of Narvaez—-the bridge, as some one said at the time, by which that ambitious warrior meant to arrive at power with his pure Moderado following. When the bridge was passed, the ministry of Gonsalez Bravo disappeared, and the Duke of Valencia, whom he had served so well, ruled in his stead, and advanced with firm steps upon the road of reaction. The leading measure of his government—its flower and crown in the eyes of the Moderado party—was the revision of the Constitution, and the promulgation of the new Constitution of 1845. We have already seen that the Constitution of 1837 was less liberal than that of 1812. That of 1845 was in its turn far less liberal than its predecessor. The liberty of the press was curtailed ; the Senate became a nominated, not an elective body ; the Cortes lost its right of assembling by its own authority, in case the sovereign neglected to summon it at the proper time, and the principle of the national sovereignty disappeared from the preamble. The most significant change, however, in the circumstances of the hour was

that which precluded the necessity of the approbation of the
Cortes as a preliminary to the royal marriage. This was the
event which was the pivot of intrigue for several years.

Those who would understand the complications of Spanish
politics during the period that immediately preceded and immediately followed the marriage of the young queen to her
cousin Don Francisco de Assis, must find the clues of half-
a-dozen plots, in which the interests of courtiers, ministers, and
confessors were strangely interwoven with the hopes of Carlist,
French, Neapolitan, and Portuguese competitors for the doubtful blessing of the royal hand. Most readers will, we presume,
be satisfied to remember that no less than six ministries rose
and fell in an incredibly short space of time, and that all of
them were more or less of a Moderado complexion. At length
a cabinet was formed, in which the chief places were filled
by Narvaez, and Sartorius Count of San Luis, a very young
man, who had acquired fame first as a journalist, and then as
a politician. It was this government which was in power
when the events of February 1848 threw Europe into confusion. It contrived to pilot Spain through that stormy time
with tolerable success. More than once the Democratic party
took up arms. There was fighting in the streets of Madrid,
and many persons were transported, but the amount of blood-
shed was not very great. This ministry fell, like so many of
its fellows, before a palace intrigue, the wire-pullers in which
were ecclesiastical persons. Its successors, however, only
remained in place twenty-four hours, long enough to win a
place in Spanish history as the " *ministerio del relampago* "—
the lightning ministry—so rapidly did they flash out of and
into obscurity. Narvaez and Sartorius returned to power with
a somewhat modified list of colleagues, and tried to fortify

their power by new elections, in which the authority of the government was exercised in so barefaced a manner, that it scandalised even Madrid, and the assembly which resulted from this pressure was called the *"Congreso de familia."* All this zeal was, however, in vain. The intrigues of Christina, who had quarrelled with Narvaez, were too much for him, and down once more went the Sartorius ministry. It was now the turn of Bravo Murillo, who claimed the confidence of the country as a financial genius and economical reformer. So determined was he to have this confidence entire, that he actually succeeded in excluding from the new Cortes the very man who had peopled the last one with his creatures, and Sartorius found himself for a time in private life. The rock upon which Bravo Murillo ran was an attempt to imitate the *coup d'état,* and to remodel the Spanish Constitution by getting the Cortes to sanction *en bloc* nine new laws, which would have undone nearly all that had been done since the death of Ferdinand. His attempt, eagerly backed by the court *camarilla,* utterly failed. In vain he sent Narvaez across the frontier. The country would have none of his reforms, and he too passed into nothingness, leaving behind him as his legacy the Concordat of 1852, by which the pope, to a certain extent, accepted the measure of Mendizabal in 1836, and other accomplished facts, obtaining in return many concessions. Several short-lived cabinets succeeded, and on the 18th September 1853 Sartorius was again the President of the Council, with the Marquis of Molins, Calderon de la Barca, General Blaser, and others, to assist him.

The last months of 1853 and the first of 1854 passed uneasily. Every day the scandals of the court and of the ministry became more flagrant, and the measures of repression more severe. General after general was sent out of Madrid, and the persecutions of the government fell, be it observed, not on the Progressistas, who were keeping quite aloof from public affairs, but upon all the sections of the Moderado party, except the immediate followers of Sartorius. Accusations of the grossest pecuniary corruption against many persons in high places were bruited about, and almost universally believed. The crisis came in June 1854. "Will you not come with us?" cried General Dulce to the Minister of War, as he rode in the grey of the morning out of Madrid, to try, as was supposed, a new cavalry saddle. "I should like nothing better," answered General Blaser, "but I am too busy." In a few hours it was known that Dulce had been joined by O'Donnell, and that the long-expected revolt had taken place. An indecisive action took place between the queen's troops and the revolted generals at Vicalvaro, whence the name Vicalvarist—which is now very generally given to the followers of O'Donnell ; and that commander issued a proclamation at Manzanares, explaining that the *pronunciamento* was made in favour of constitutional government and of morality. Up to this point the rising, it cannot be too distinctly understood, was a Moderado rising, and Narvaez himself, as afterwards appeared, was deeply implicated in the conspiracy. But on the 17th of July the whole aspect of affairs changed. An *émeute* took place in Madrid, and the revolt of O'Donnell was swallowed up in a revolution. After a very agitated period, things began to settle down. The Moderado *régime* of eleven years was fairly at an end, and the queen, with the Counts of Lucena and Luchana, O'Donnell and Espartero, was awaiting the meeting of a Constituent Cortes, which was to decide, amongst other things, whether the Bourbon dynasty was to continue to rule in Spain. It met on the 9th November 1854, and soon decided that question—194 as against 19 were quite willing to keep Queen Isabella on the throne if she would conduct herself with tolerable propriety. The discussions on the other bases of the new Constitution took more time. There was a very long one early in 1855, upon the question of religious toleration, and other matters were hardly less warmly debated. The greatest work, however, of the Constituent Cortes was their carrying out to its legitimate issue the leading measure of Mendizabal's administration, and freeing the soil of Spain, with inconsiderable exceptions, from the tyranny of the dead hand, and from the colossal entails under which it had so long suffered. The queen resisted, in the interest of the church, but yielded after a private interview with O'Donnell and Espartero at Aranjuez. Next to this great measure, which, although one of its immediate results was a Carlist rising in Arragon, gave very general satisfaction, the best acts of this assembly were those which it passed in furtherance of the material interests of the country. Its other purely political performances were not so successful. It settled the Constitution, but never promulgated it, and several of the most important laws which were necessary to supplement that Constitution were never finished. It should be the first care of all such bodies to do quickly whatever their hand finds to do, for if their deliberations continue long, they invariably become unpopular, since they are always accused of wishing unduly to prolong their own power, while agitators are quite sure to take advantage of a provisional state of things to pursue their own objects. So it happened in Spain in the spring of 1856. Disturbances, and above all incendiary fires, became the order of

the day.   By the middle of 1856 people began to weary.   The
conflicts in the Cortes between the moderate Progressistas on
the one hand, and the advanced Progressistas, backed by the
Democrats, on the other, were frequent and severe.   Not less
marked was the division in the cabinet between O'Donnell
and Espartero.   At length a quarrel, occasioned by an attack
which was made by Escosura, the Minister of the Interior,
upon the Moderado views of O'Donnell, brought about an open
rupture, and at four o'clock in the morning, on the 14th July,
a ministerial crisis took place.   (In Madrid, ministerial crises
always seem to take place in the small hours, thanks to the
owl-like habits of society it that capital.)   When the Madri-
lenian housewives came back from market, they were able to
tell their lords that a revolution had taken place since they
went to bed.   Their lords committed the imprudence of flying
to arms, and thereby gave O'Donnell and the queen the excuse
they wanted for a little *coup d'état*.   O'Donnell and his
colleagues, the most important of whom was Rios y Rosas,
straightway dissolved the Cortes, and as the Constitution, which
it had elaborated, had never been promulgated, fell back upon
the Moderado Constitution of 1845, supplemented by an additional act of their own, good as far as it went, although of
extra-legal origin.

Henceforth they worked steadily, and with no unnecessary
severity, to bring back matters to the position in which they
would have been if the military revolt begun by O'Donnell
and his friends in 1854 had not been followed by a revolution.
This, considering their views, which were those of Liberal
Conservatives (Union-Liberal), was natural enough ; but it
was also quite natural that when the court and its corrupt
adherents saw that it was possible to go so far in a reactionary

course, they should wish to go a little further ; and so, after
three months of power, O'Donnell was tripped up, and Narvaez
came in with a cabinet in which he was by no means the
most anti-liberal element. He pushed the reaction a good
deal further, and, above all, made an arrangement with Rome
by which the sales of church lands already effected were recognised, but all further sales were stopped, and other concessions were made to the clergy. The Constitution of 1845
was likewise altered in so far as the composition of the
Senate was concerned. Narvaez fell in the autumn of 1857,
overthrown partly by the results of his interference in one
of those bedchamber questions which are so constantly
arising in the palace of Madrid, and partly by the odium
excited by the rabid reactionary tendencies of his colleague
Nocedal. He was succeeded by General Armero, who took
for his motto : " The Constitution of 1845—neither more nor
less."

As, however, the Narvaez Government had turned out too
reactionary for its own party, the Armero Government turned
out to be too much the other way. In other words, the Moderados hardly knew their own mind. One combination more
was tried. M. Isturiz, the *vir pietate gravis* of his side of politics, was sent for, and formed an administration, which had no
particular fault, except that it commanded the sympathies of
nobody ; and when it followed its predecessors, as it very soon
did, the queen once more called O'Donnell to her councils.
O'Donnell came back, determined to represent the Union-
Liberal more thoroughly than ever, and to construct, if possible,
some machine by which, amidst the decomposition of parties,
he might contrive to guide the politics of Spain. So conciliatory was he, that in one province it is said he had a Progress-

ista civil governor, a Moderado secretary, and a military commandant who belonged to the Union-Liberal. The new Congress was composed of equally diverse elements, and gave him infinite trouble, when very luckily the Italian war of 1859 came to call off the attention of the people from internal affairs; and so kind were the influences of the Palmerstonian star under which he was born, that no sooner was that contest over, than the Moors began to make themselves so intolerably unpleasant, that he had an excellent excuse for proposing to his countrymen to go to war on their own account.

The speech of the President of the Council, announcing the commencement of hostilities with Morocco, caused the greatest rejoicings in all parts of the country ; and through the five months during which the war lasted, the Government had little to complain of, even from the Opposition press. The Spanish arms were, of course, victorious, and peace was soon restored. It was fortunate that this was so, since, if the struggle had lasted longer, the attempt of Ortega—who, in the beginning of April 1861, landed at the mouth of the Ebro with the garrison of the Balearic Isles, of which he was captain-general, with a view to renew the Carlist wars—might have been more inconvenient. As it was, the danger did not last above twenty-four hours ; Ortega was taken and shot, the Conde de Montemolin and his second brother were arrested, and liberated after signing a re-nunciation of their supposed rights,—a renunciation which, as they had pledged their honour in it, and were their father's sons, they naturally made haste to disavow, so soon as they were in a place of security. Their sudden and most strange deaths at Trieste, a few months after, deprived these transactions of any importance, and left their brother Don Juan at the head of the family. With the return of tranquillity the struggle

of parties recommenced, and was envenomed as well by the
severities which were exercised, or alleged to have been exercised, in putting down a sort of Socialist rising or Jacquerie
which broke out during the summer at Loja, not very far from
Malaga, as by the constantly-increasing influence of the clerical
camarilla. O'Donnell, who had now been in power for a
longer time than any minister since Spain became a constitutional country, had become fond of office, and, in order to keep
it, allowed his measures to be far too much moulded by the
court, which was under the control of the Nuncio, acting
chiefly through the Nun Patrocinio, one of those personages—
half-deceiver, half-enthusiast—who are so common in Catholic
countries. In the end of 1861, the attacks in both branches
of the legislature became very frequent and fierce. Olozaga
particularly distinguished himself by his plain speaking ; and
when O'Donnell, with a strange want of tact, appealed from
him to the other great Progressista leader, Don Pascual Madoz,
it was only to draw from that statesman a warning to the
administration to change its ways, " lest some one might say,
at the head of 2000 horse, that he would no longer serve a
government which was dishonoured by a *camarilla*,"—the
quotation being taken from O'Donnell's own rebel manifesto.
A more dangerous adversary perhaps than two men so well
known for their advanced Liberal opinions, was Rios y Rosas,
who, as we have seen, was the leading spirit of O'Donnell's
cabinet in 1856, the very incarnation of the Union-Liberal.
When a politician of his colour reminds the sovereign that
princes, who are too long obstinate, generally finish their lives
in exile, the state of affairs has become alarming. O'Donnell,
knowing that his internal policy would not bear inspection,
and satisfied with the success of his Moorish diversion, still

continued to try to distract popular attention by bold diplomatic strokes. If the additional Concordat, published in 1860, made too great concessions to the clerical interest, had he not soon the re-incorporation of St. Domingo, and the impetuous action of the Spanish commander on the Mexican coast, to flatter the national vanity? The Liberal party from the first pointed out to what these measures must lead; but ministers live from hand to mouth in Spain, and that is the best course which keeps things quiet for the moment.

The O'Donnell cabinet continued all through 1862, reaped what little glory was to be gained from the successes obtained, in concert with France, in Cochin-China, and incurred much additional unpopularity from the results of the Mexican expedition. It fell at length early in 1863, and the Marquis of Miraflores succeeded the Duke of Tetuan. The new chief allowed one of his colleagues to issue a most imprudent circular, restraining, after the model of imperial France, the right of electoral meetings. The result of this mistake was, that the whole Progressista and Democratic parties refused to take part in the elections. Miraflores succeeded in getting a Congress, composed of various fractions of the several Conservative parties, but fell before an adverse vote of the senate, on the question of reforming the composition of that body, as arranged in 1857.

The Mon. Cabinet settled for a time the difficult question about the composition of the senate by restoring in its integrity the Constitution of 1845; but, agitated by rumours of revolutionary projects in various quarters, they acted in an extremely arbitrary manner—exiling Prim, for example, to Oviedo, and trying obnoxious journalists by councils of war. In the meantime, the conflict with Peru and St. Domingo, and the state of the finances, got more and more desperate. In September 1864 Narvaez was sent for, and came into power with a cabinet which contained, besides himself, no less than four ex-Presidents of the Council.

The Narvaez Government * seemed at first inclined to a moderate and conciliatory policy. In spite of the known character of their chief, who is always ready to cut himself out of a difficulty, sword in hand, sanguine people imagined that ministers might contrive to keep their places without shedding blood. They began by condoning press offences, by repaying fines which had been imposed on newspapers, by proposing to withdraw from the San Domingo *imbroglio* and the Peruvian folly, made as if they would do something to restore Spanish credit, and allowed full liberty of discussion during the elections. No sooner, however, were these over, than M. Gonsalez Bravo, who had already, in the month of October, attempted to restrain the free-speaking of professors, issued, on November the 25th, a circular curtailing this same liberty of discussion. That document excited much amusement in England, and elsewhere, from the absurdity of forbidding the press to do what had just been proved to be perfectly harmless. The truth was, however, that a struggle

---

* Narvaez was born in the year 1800. In 1822 he took the side of the Liberal party, and after the French invasion was obliged to live very quietly at Loja, his native place, until the death of Ferdinand. In 1834 he returned to the army, and distinguished himself upon several occasions, more especially in 1836, when he overtook and defeated the famous Carlist leader Gomez. From this time forward he became sufficiently important to be considered as a sort of rival to Espartero. His first attempts were, however, unsuccessful; and after a fruitless endeavour to put himself at the head of a party, he fled to France, whence, in 1843, he returned, as we have seen, to take a decisive part in the overthrow of the best and most patriotic of Spanish politicians. His history from that date has been sufficiently commented on in the preceding pages.

which had been going on in the cabinet had been decided in favour of the less liberal fraction of it. This was first betrayed to the outer world by the retirement of M. Llorente. Presently a cabinet crisis occurred, ostensibly about the withdrawal from San Domingo, really from a court intrigue ; and the Narvaez ministry seemed on the point of being replaced by a new combination. Replaced it was not, however, and the session of the Cortes of 1865 opened under its auspices. By this time, however, it had drawn closer to the violent Catholic party, and had gone further away from any Liberal *velléités* which it may at first have had.

Just at this crisis the queen made over to the nation the whole of the remaining patrimony of the Crown in return for a sum much below its presumed value, for which the Treasury became liable. Two views could be taken of this. It might be regarded as a grand and patriotic act, or as a good bargain. Foreigners generally took the former view— so did some Spaniards ; but others were not so amiable. Amongst these last was M. Emilio Castelar, professor at the University of Madrid, and editor of the newspaper called the *Democrazia.* He published a very strong article against the royal benefaction. The government immediately prosecuted him, as it had a right to do; but it did more. It insisted on the Rector of the University, M. Montalvan, proceeding academically against the opposition journalist. This he declined to do, and he was immediately dismissed. The students then applied for permission to give him a serenade. This was first granted—then refused. Crowds collected in the streets. On the night fixed for the serenade, the 7th of April, there were more crowds, but no disturbance. On the 10th, however, some stones were thrown ; the troops were ordered to fire; about a dozen people were killed, and more than 100 wounded.

These violent proceedings called forth the most bitter attacks in the Cortes, and ministers came out of the debate terribly damaged in spite of the eloquence and daring of M. Gonsalez Bravo, who bore the brunt of the onset. The disquiet of the public mind reacted on the finances, and M. Barzanallana retired in desperation after having added one more wild expedient to the wretched make-shifts of Spanish Chancellors of the Exchequer. At length, in June 1865, the whole cabinet, utterly discredited, bankrupt in reputation, and at its wit's end, vanished into space; while O'Donnell once more reigned in its stead.*

We wish we could say that he had decidedly mended matters, but he has done something. Italy has been recognised—a fact far more important in its bearing upon internal than external affairs. Hopes have been held out to the negro in Cuba, the press is more gently handled, a sort of Parliamentary Reform Act has been passed—no *panacea*, alas! for the evils—at least of Spain; the rash attempt of Prim was suppressed with singular gentleness and good temper, but the "complaint in the chest" is still alarming, and the wretched Chilian squabble will not improve it.

If we consider the advanced age of Espartero and Olozaga, the blunders of their party, the repeated failures of Narvaez, the scanty following and slender political experience of the democratic leaders, we cannot help coming to the conclusion that the government of O'Donnell is perhaps the best which

---

* For a clear and very detailed account of the last Narvaez administration, the reader is referred to an article by M. Charles de Mazade in the *Revue des Deux Mondes* for September 1865.

Spain is at present likely to get ; * but let the name of the government be Union-Liberal, or Progressista, or Democratic, it must keep the court within bounds, and govern *tolerably*, or another 1854 may at any time occur.

The reader who has followed us thus far will be able to judge for himself, whether the country which has passed through so many political vicissitudes in thirty years, can be fairly described, in the words of Mr. Buckle, as "a torpid mass." We shall now briefly sketch its existing government, endeavouring to answer, as shortly as possible, the more important questions which an intelligent inquirer into the state of an European community is likely to ask. It will be seen, we hope, that the Spain of to-day, with all her faults, is hardly a representation of "the feelings and knowledge of the Middle Ages." †

Doña Isabel Segunda, Queen of the Spains, rules over the conterminous, but most hetrogeneous, provinces of Spain proper (la Peninsula) ; over the "adyacentes," including the Canaries, the Balearic Isles, the small places (Presidios) on the north coast of Africa, with Fernando Po and Annabon in the Gulf of Guinea ; and over certain colonies in America and Asia (Ultramar). España Presidial is, in some respects, under the same, in others under different regulations, from

* The author of a sensible article on Spain in *Fraser* for December 1865, says : " We are far from assenting generally to the shallow doctrine—

> For forms of government let fools contest ;
> Whatever's best administered is best.

But we do think that the existing form of government in Spain is good enough for all useful purposes, if it were only well administered ; by which we mean, if the politicians engaged in the practical working of the machinery, whether in office or opposition, would simply act like the politicians similarly engaged in England—no very exalted or unattainable standard of public virtue."

† A great deal of miscellaneous information upon Spain is collected in Mr. O'Shea's *Guide*, published in 1865. The bulk, the frantic prejudices, the bad

the rest of the monarchy. The colonies, of which we shall speak hereafter, are subject to an exceptional *régime*.

By the Constitution now in force—which is, as we have seen, that of 1845—the sovereign can do no wrong, and ministerial responsibility is fully recognised. The legislative power resides in the Crown and in the Cortes, but far too large a space is left for the arbitrary action of authority, and royal decrees often do the work which ought to be done by the legislature. The Cortes consist of two bodies—a Senate and a *Congreso* of Deputies; but behind both, and stronger than both, are the private influences of the palace. Ministers can generally make both Houses pretty " safe," but clouds gather in a clear sky, and they fall even with the Cortes at their feet. It does not fare much better with the guarantees of public and individual liberty common to most constitutions. They are pompously paraded in the Moderado great charter, but convenient little clauses are introduced, which leave the rulers free to do pretty much what they please. In short, the existing Spanish Constitution deserves what has been said of it by many persons, and by none more pointedly than by Gonsalez Bravo, the late repressive Home Minister. It is neither one

taste, the inaccuracy of Ford's work, together with the changes that have taken place since he wrote, make it perfectly natural that some one should attempt to become his rival. At the same time his merits are so great that his name ought to remain attached to the English tourist's *Handbook for Spain* for at least a generation longer; and we think that Mr. O'Shea would have conferred a greater benefit upon his countrymen, to say nothing of having done a more graceful act, if he had confined himself to publishing a work avowedly as a supplement to that of his predecessor. Such a book would have been bought by every one who went to Spain under the guidance of the elder traveller. Mr. O'Shea's *Guide*, in spite of its very considerable merit, will be unable to compete with a judiciously-corrected edition of the *Handbook*, and only those who have a very strong interest in Spain will, we should think, buy both.

thing nor another; the product neither of frank despotism nor of frank constitutionalism.

The government of Spain is carried on by nine ministers. The Premier, who is, unhappily, but too often a soldier, is called the President of the Council, and is supposed to direct the general policy of the country. His colleagues are—

The Minister of Grace and Justice.

The Minister of the Interior (*de la Gobernacion*).

The Minister of Public Welfare (*de Fomento*).

The Minister of Finance (*de Hacienda*).

The Minister of War.

The Minister of Marine.

The Minister of the Colonies.

The Minister of Foreign Affairs (*de Estado*).

To the province of the Minister of Grace and Justice belongs everything that is connected with the administration of the law, both in the civil and ecclesiastical courts; and he superintends the proceedings of all legal functionaries, from the judges of the supreme tribunal at Madrid, down to the *Alcaldes*, or mayors of the towns, and to the *juges de paix* in the country districts. The state of the department committed to his charge is not one of the things upon which Spain can be congratulated, for the confusion, delay, and uncertainty of Spanish law is a frequent subject of complaint in the country. According to Mr. Wallis, the last collection of laws which had any pretension to completeness was published in 1806. This *Novissima recopilacion* was founded on the *Nueva recopilacion* of Philip II. Neither of these two documents, however, quite excludes the authority of some more ancient codes, which are understood to be in force, in cases not otherwise provided for.

We need hardly say that the laws promulgated in 1806 have been altered in a thousand ways since.

The criminal law, as revised in 1853, is decidedly humane. The punishment of death is only inflicted in cases of wilful murder. The gallows, to which the Iberian mind has a peculiar objection, has been superseded by the garrotte, to which it attaches, for some reason or other, more agreeable associations. Corporal punishments and the pillory have been abolished. Trials take place in public, but there are no juries, and have never been any, except in cases connected with the press. A curious description of his own trial, at Lerida, for publishing a pamphlet which was charged with a seditious tendency, is given by Garrido. The jury was, however, once more abolished in press cases after the counter-revolution of 1856. Prisoners are often detained a most unreasonable time before they are tried ; while caprice, bribes, and the protection of the powerful, have still far too much influence upon the lot of the criminal. Mr. Wallis, himself a lawyer, and with a keen interest in all that relates to his profession, bears testimony to the high character of the leading advocates at Madrid, and was evidently much struck with the advantage which they have over American lawyers, and, to a certain extent, over English barristers, in finding all the lower and mechanical part of litigation taken off their hands by the attorney and the notary, or *escribano*. This last-named personage is a kind of middleman between the attorney and the court. " Every picture," says Mr. Wallis, " that is painted of the law's delay, and of the costly injustice, for which men curse it, has for its chief figure the *escribano*.

" ' Con semblante infernal y pluma en mano.' "

All evidence "goes before the judge in the shape of declarations

made before the *escribano*, and reduced by him to writing.   Indeed there is nothing which concerns the case, in law or in fact,
of which the *escribano* is not the conductor, from the judge to the
parties, and from the parties to the judge, and to each other."

This is an evil inherent in the system. We fear, however,
that whatever evils there are inherent in the system of Spanish
justice, they are far surpassed by the evils which have been
engrafted on it.   The worst of these is the venality and partiality of the judges.   As long as these prevail there is a canker
at the root of all prosperity.

In the office of the Minister of the Interior, all the threads
of a most elaborately-centralised system meet in one point.
France, as France was under Louis Philippe, supplied the
model upon which the victorious Moderados of 1845 re-organ-
ised their own country ; and the changes, which have been
introduced since, have not been favourable to local liberties.

The whole mainland of Spain is divided, for administrative
purposes, into forty-seven provinces.   Over each of these is
an officer who bears, in the province of Madrid, the title of
Political Chief, and in the other forty-six that of Civil Governor.   Each of these personages is assisted by counsellors,
appointed, like himself, by the Crown, and by a consultative
body whose members are elected by the province.   The local
administration is carried on by *Alcaldes*, who are also nominees
of the government, and are helped in the discharge of their
functions by elected councils, larger or smaller, according to
the population of the district ; those same *Ayuntamientos*, of
which we have already spoken, and whose power, before the
reaction abridged it, was the mainstay of the Liberal party.
In the very smallest places there is a still humbler administrator, who is called the *Alcalde pedaneo*.

All these Alcaldes, great and small, must do as the minister of the hour commands, and they are the principal instruments by which the elections are worked so as to produce the results which are desired by the party in power.

The management of the police forms another part of the multifarious duties of the Minister of *Gobernacion*. Minutoli speaks well of it ; and all men speak well of the allied service called the *Guardia Civil*, which looks after the safety of the roads, and is due to General Narvaez. The danger to which the traveller is exposed from robbers in Spain has, of course, been materially diminished by the increase of railways ; but even the common roads are much safer than they were.

There is really hardly anything that does not fall within the province of the minister of whom we are writing; and Minutoli, in describing his functions, speaks *de omni scibili*. Of the charitable institutions of Spain he expresses warm approbation, and on this head the reader will do well to consult the *Attaché at Madrid*, always remembering that he is reading the work of a Roman Catholic neophyte.

Of the lunatic asylums, the state of which Ford describes as very bad, Minutoli also gives a painful account. On the other hand, he says that the prison at Valencia was, under the management of Col. Montesinos, the very best which he ever saw in Europe, except that of Munich under Obermayer, and he certainly adduces some most remarkable facts in support of his opinion. The aptitude of Col. Montesinos for his work must have been quite exceptional, and his prison very unlike some others in Spain ; for about the very time that he was doing wonders at Valencia, the Carcel del Corte at Madrid was, as we know from Borrow, in a frightful condition.

The management of the post in Spain does scant credit to

ministerial wisdom. Nothing more ridiculous can be imagined, and its irregularities are complained of by all travellers. Tourists cannot be too earnestly cautioned not to have letters of importance addressed to them at the post-office in Spain. They should always be sent to the house of some banker, or other well-known person.

The persecution of the press is another most important part of this minister's functions ; and whatever else he may neglect, he generally fulfils this part of his duty with great zeal. Still, even under Narvaez, there was more freedom for public writers in Spain than in France.

The Ministry of Public Welfare has the care of the mines, of agriculture, of the scanty but priceless forests, of all public works, of the studs, of the telegraphs—in short, of commerce and material improvement of every kind.

The rapid development of the wealth of Spain during the last twenty years has excited more attention beyond her own boundaries than any other phenomenon connected with her recent history ; but the very reasonable and proper attitude of the London Stock Exchange, towards a defaulting state, has had the indirect effect of closing the channels by which we in England should in the natural course of things have heard of her prosperity. It is chiefly from France that those supplies of capital have come which have swelled the not inconsiderable hoards of the natives, which appear to have been kept out of harm's way during the troubles, and to have come to light in recent and more peaceful times. Travel where you will in Spain, you will see more evidence of poverty than of abundance ; but even in the poorest districts, let there be a piece of clerical or other land to be sold by the authorities upon advantageous terms, and it is curious to see how many people are able to offer for it. Not less interesting is it to notice that the ill-will of the church has had so little effect in preventing the acquisition of estates once devoted to pious uses.

On the subject of the material revival of Spain—a revival to which nothing save peace has contributed so much as the sale of lands which belonged to the clergy—a long array of most carefully-marshalled and significant figures appeared in an article of the too short-lived *Home and Foreign Review*. The writer, who had peculiar means of information, shows that the population is steadily increasing, having risen more than five millions between 1797 and 1860 ; that there is every reason to suppose that agricultural production has increased during the same period more rapidly to the south than to the north of the Pyrenees ; that the use of meat is becoming more common, and the number of cattle and other domestic animals rapidly multiplying. Not less cheering is it to learn that the consumption of coal has more than quadrupled in the last few years, and that the possessors of iron mines are not less prosperous, while exports and imports had increased by 350 per cent between 1843 and 1860.

There is no more agreeable feature in the last ten years of Spanish history than the rapid development of railway communication. We have seen that the line from Bayonne to Madrid is quite finished. A gap occurs in the railway communication between the capital and Cordova; but when that city is once passed there is no interruption till the traveller arrives at Cadiz. Fifteen hours of very comfortable railway travelling connect the seat of government with the port of Alicante, and with the capital of the wealthy and important province of Valencia; while ere long we may hope to see the locomotive traversing the whole length of the coast-line from the city of the Cid to Perpignan. Already, in 1864, passengers were set down at the Saguntum station, and were, indeed, carried considerably past it to the northward.

From Barcelona the line is only completed along the Catalonian shore as far as Gerona, but one can go straight across the country from sea to sea, without any diligence travelling. Montserrat; Manresa, so famous in the life of Loyola; Lerida, the Ilerda of Horace ; Calahorra, the ancient Calagurris; and Tudela, are all stations upon this line, the latter half of which is singularly picturesque, ascending as it does the upper valley of the rapid and beautiful Ebro, and descending the course of the Nervion, affording through almost every mile the most beautiful views, and doing infinite credit to the engineering skill of its daring constructors. The journey from Miranda to Bilbao is the very poetry of railway travelling. The railway already connects Pamplona with Saragossa, and Saragossa with the metropolis ; while the lounger of the Puerta del Sol can hurry to the fresh breezes of Santandar, without any of " les belles horreurs," which Mr. Borrow has so feelingly described. Even Zamorra, whose desolation had become as much of a jest in Spanish literature as that of Cumæ in the days of Juvenal, can now be reached by railway ; and if only the lines from Santa Cruz to Cordova, and from Madrid to Badajoz, were completed, the tourist would really have very little reason to complain. Several ther important lines are in progress, and not a few minor ı nes are already completed; but we need not give further details, as Spain has already an *Indicador* of its own, on the plan of the well-known French publication.

The roads that are to feed these railways advance more

slowly, but still they advance. We can well believe that the Marquis of Albaida tells an " ower true tale," when he says that the promise of a road or a bridge is one of the commonest bribes held out by the Alcaldes to induce their fellow-townsmen to vote for the government candidates,—the " Diputados di Amen," as they are wittily called. Not less true, we fear, is it that these roads and bridges are oftener promised than made.

The coasting vessels and those for foreign trade advance in numbers, and in the frequency of their voyages, while something is being done for the harbours, which, especially along the eastern coast, are far from being what they must be, if Spain is to become, as she surely one day will, a great maritime power.

Judging by the number of houses which bear upon them the device of some insurance company, we should have thought that fire insurance was more generally practised than the figures before us would lead us to believe. Banking is very far behindhand, and credit walks still with lame and staggering feet.

Turn where we will, we see what marvellous changes an increase of science would work in this splendid country. There are rivers of wine, but it is rarely fit to drink. There are lakes of oil, but it is equally abominable. There are acres of peaches, but the fruit is a sort of turnip. There is no want of industry. The Spaniard works hard with his hands, as those of our engineers who have superintended railways in Spain are ready to testify. Sobriety is a common virtue. Intelligence is not wanting, and elementary education is not so very backward. It is intelligent direction which is wanted, central direction, if nothing better can be got, independent local direction where that is possible. How many Spaniards, however, are there who have imitated Espartero, who devotes the greater portion of his time to making his property near Logroño a model for his neighbours?

It is melancholy when we reflect that vast spaces of fertile land in Spain have been utterly waste since the days of Philip III., to know that every year large numbers of industrious persons emigrate to Oran and elsewhere, and that the attempts at colonisation in Andalusia have not been crowned with any great success. The religious difficulty here, as elsewhere in the old world, has done much to keep far from the borders of Spain the most hardy and useful colonists.

Garrido has accumulated, in his fifteenth and sixteenth chapters, statistical tables illustrative of the commerce and manufactures of Spain. We should be more tempted to quote their principal figures, if they were more complete, and if some of the more important industries,—as, for instance, the cotton-spinning of Catalonia,—were not exotics fostered by unwise laws. Of all Spanish exports the most important is wine, and of all Spanish wines the most important is sherry. We observe that the amount sent out of the country doubled between 1841 and 1861, though the price advanced by about 80 per cent. It should not be forgotten that, as Ford points out, sherry, although grown in Spain, is chiefly made by and for foreigners. There is less wine drunk at a Spanish *table d'hôte* in a month than at a German one in a day.

One of the most important matters to which the department of Fomento could devote itself, would be the increase and better distribution of the water supply of Spain. Drought is, next to misgovernment, the great curse of the country. The formation of reservoirs to catch the winter rains must one day be set about in good earnest, if Spain is ever to support a population at all equal to that which we see in many other countries. The replanting of those forests which human shortsightedness and folly have destroyed, is another urgent necessity; but its difficulty is, alas! proportionate to its importance.

The multiplication of canals for purposes of irrigation would be another great boon, but unfortunately this too is, from the character of the Spanish rivers, far from easy. Long and loud has been the clamour in favour of making the upper Tagus and upper Douro navigable, but neither they nor the Ebro are as yet of much use for purposes of transit. One is tempted to believe that the Moors, as they quitted the soil of Europe, laid a curse on the waters of Spain,—so unsuccessful have their conquerors been in imitating their dealings with that wayward element.

It was the brilliant and unfortunate Larra who proposed to inscribe over the gate of the Madrid Exchange, "Aqui yace el crédito Español," and who observed, that when that was done, everybody would compare the building to the Pyramids of Egypt, marvelling that a work so vast should be raised for the sepulture of a thing so little. The English translation of the suggested inscription has the advantage, as Ford perceived, of the double meaning of the verb. Things are somewhat better than they were in those days of repudiation and bankruptcy, but still the Spanish Finance Minister has a bad time of it.

The best source of information to which we can refer those who wish to know the most important facts about the public debt and the actual state of the money matters of Spain, is two sections of the article "Espagne," in Block's *Dictionnaire*

General de la Politique. They are both written by Barzanallana,
who was, as we have seen, Finance Minister in the last Narvaez
Government. He gives as the total amount of the debt on the
1st January 1862,—14,603,231,950 reals, but it has of course increased since. He also states the amount of the budget voted
on the 4th March 1862 at 2,003,853,536 reals, for the ordinary
expenses of the state, as against 2,009,938,000 reals, the esti-
mated ordinary revenue ; while more than 560,000,000 reals
were assigned to extraordinary expenses, which it was expected
would be met by receipts not forming part of the ordinary
revenue. We may remind our readers that a sum in reals may
be converted into one in pounds sterling, with sufficient
accuracy for ordinary purposes, if it is divided by 100.

Many of the methods of raising the revenue are much complained of by intelligent Spaniards. The tariff is still ruin-
ously protective. The tobacco and other monopolies are
opposed to the most elementary principles. The barbarous
octroi minimises the internal commerce of the country, loses
many hours of every day to thousands of industrious people,
and fosters the vicious propensities of a whole army of officials,
whose illegitimate gains, as every traveller knows, are far
greater than their honest ones. An elaborate and vexatious
system of stamps interferes with almost every transaction of
life. With one hand the Minister of Finance beckons into
existence a host of *contrabandistas,* and with another an
army of *carabineros* to keep them in check. The lottery still
sows demoralisation broadcast over the whole Peninsula. In
short, there are few economical heresies which are not embraced as great truths by Queen Isabella's government, in
spite of the efforts of many enlightened persons who translate
Bastiat, and otherwise attempt to dispel the darkness of the land.

Of the wrongs of the bondholders we will say nothing. There are few Spanish topics which are so familiar to the newspaper reader. Those, however, who would learn what can be advanced on the Spanish side of the case, might look with advantage at the pamphlet called *Spain and Morocco*, by Mr. Owen Ross.

So obvious are the benefits which would accrue to Spain from an honest arrangement with her creditors, and so perfectly able is she to make one which would be accepted as satisfactory, that we cannot doubt that such will be made. Made it would have been ere this, if the present state of things had not been useful to speculators, whose influence at Madrid is more powerful than any consideration of national prosperity, to say nothing of national honour.

We have seen that in the year 1858 the Neo-Catholic party, which had attempted to stop the sale of the national church lands, was obliged to give way to the politicians of the " Union-Liberal." They recommenced the good work, and an enormous amount of real property has now passed from the dead to the living hand. The money received by the state has been and is being applied to many good objects— *inter alia*, to the construction of harbours and lighthouses, to canals, roads, and bridges. Unfortunately, vast sums have been squandered on preparations for and munitions of war ; while, according to Garrido, not one penny has been spent in promoting the increase of knowledge—*the* great want of Spain.

Assuredly finance is not the bright side of Iberian affairs. And yet let any one compare the figures of recent budgets with those of the days of Spain's prosperity and pre-eminence, asking himself, after he has done so, what people mean when they say that she has declined. Her relative position has changed, and she has not advanced as she ought to have done ; but how much of that halo of greatness which surrounds her past is mere delusion ? It should not be forgotten that the figures we have cited are only those connected with the central government. Very large sums are raised for public purposes by the provincial councils and by the municipalities. It should also be borne in mind that the debt has been much increased by the state's having given to the former owners of lands held in mortmain, obligations upon the National Treasury instead of the estates which they lost.

The events of the Peninsular War left on the English mind a somewhat too unfavourable impression of the Spanish soldier. Faults, which were really attributable only to his officers or to the War Department, were unhesitatingly ascribed to him ; and his demerits are even now popularly accepted as part of the low estimate of Spain which is usual amongst us. And yet the great Captain who freed the Peninsula by no means shared these views. He did not hesitate to express the highest opinion of the warlike virtues of the Spanish private ; and a person is still living who can testify to his having said, " The British soldier—if you treat him well—if you feed him—if you clothe him—will go anywhere and fight anybody ; but the Spanish soldier—if you *don't* treat him well—if you *don't* feed him—if you *don't* clothe him—will do the same."

The necessities of the civil wars directed very great attention to the better organisation of the royal troops in Spain ; and when peace returned, the wants of the service were not lost sight of. Minutoli, who had himself served for twenty-four years in the Prussian army, gives a most detailed account of the whole military system, satisfying in his scrupulous

pages alike the curiosity of the drill-sergeant and of the army
tailor. His summing-up is highly favourable to the efficiency
and high character of the troops of Queen Isabella, who, when
he wrote, had been for some time reposing on their laurels.
When, a few years afterwards, they were called to make proof
of their valour and endurance in the war with Morocco, they
earned, it will be remembered, much praise at the hands of the
Times correspondent, whose letters have since been republished,
and should be referred to by those who are anxious to form an
opinion as to the real importance of Spain.

Official returns of the year 1863, quoted in the *Statesman's
Year-book*, give 151,668 men as the total strength of the
Spanish military forces; but more than 22,000 of these belong
to the Carabineros and to the Guardia Civil; while more than
44,000 are militiamen. There are also troops in the Canaries
and in the colonies, which are not included in the above. The
army is recruited by conscription; but great privileges are
given to volunteers, who receive a large bounty, and substi-
tutes are freely permitted. Minutoli calls particular attention
to the artillery, which is destined to act in mountainous districts,—an arm of the first importance in the land of Sierras.
The exercises of the army in general, and of the cavalry in
particular, are arranged on the French model. We have no
very certain information as to how far Spain is keeping pace
with the latest improvements in military science; but a government which is almost always presided over by generals should
hardly be behindhand in such matters. The Spanish navy,
which had sunk very low, rose rapidly into importance under
Charles III., and at the commencement of the present century
was still in a very flourishing condition. The great disaster
of Trafalgar inaugurated another period of decline, from which

it is only now recovering. Perhaps it is to the filibustering expeditions against Cuba, more than to any other cause, that we must attribute the very marked improvement that is now visible in the Marine Department. Some credit is also due to the Marquis of Molins, now minister in London—better known by his name of Roca di Togores—whose poetical and rhetorical merits raised him to the office of First Lord of the Admiralty about the time that the Cuban question became alarming. As early, however, as 1845, things had begun to mend ; and Minutoli speaks of as many as 78 vessels being in process of construction, or undergoing large repairs, in the spring of 1851. Ever since there has been a gradual advance, and now, like other and greater powers, Spain is turning her attention to the construction of ironclads, of which she has several afloat.

The officers of the Spanish navy are very highly spoken of by Mr. Wallis and others. Both the war and commercial marine suffer much from the obstinate adherence of the authorities to a system based upon the French maritime inscription. The sailor too has, it would appear, other griev-ances, of which the chief are a low rate of pay and severe punishments. It is probable that the Spanish Government will follow in the wake of their great neighbour in undoing the mistakes of Colbert ; but Garrido says that it as yet is only the Democratic party which urges this change.

The minister who now presides over the colonies of Spain has not a very laborious office. Her gigantic colonial empire has now sunk to Cuba, Porto-Rico, a corner of the Virgin Islands, part of the Philippines,* the Marian Archipelago, with

* The reader who is curious about these unfamiliar regions should consult a recent article in the *Revue des Deux Mondes*, and *Der Stille Ocean und die*

the far-scattered Carolinian group.   The whole population of these possessions may be 8,000,000, so that Holland has now many more colonial subjects than her once terrible antagonist.

The want of good faith the Spanish Government has displayed in all that relates to the slave-trade, has been a frequent subject of complaint in this country.   Since the treaty of 1817, the slaves in Cuba have enormously increased, and almost every captain-general has made large sums by conniving at the importation of slaves from Africa.   The most conspicuous exception to this rule was General Valdez, who administered the island during the regency of Espartero, and whose name is a synonym for honour.   The Democratic party is of course thoroughly opposed to the existing system, and its writers do not cease to point out that soon or later the sins of the past and present will be washed out in blood.   The absolute stoppage of the slave-trade, with gradual emancipation immediately begun and steadily persevered in, are the only possible methods of conjuring the frightful calamity which impends over the Queen of the Antilles.   The downfall of the Confederacy has been a warning to her to set her house in order.*

The really liberal party in Spain, as we have seen, is altogether opposed to attempts at " re-vindications" of colonial empire.   Garrido even goes so far as to assert, that Spain, if she lost the colonies which she has, would be all the stronger, and there is much to be said on that side of the question. He admits, however, that public opinion is not ripe for such a change as this, and Spain will have done all that England can expect, if she tries to imitate what we have done during

Spanischen Besitzungen im Ostindischen Archipel, published at Vienna in 1860 by the gifted Austrian savant and diplomatist, M. Ch. de Hügel.

* It is said that very strict orders to enforce the laws against the slave trade have been sent by O'Donnell to the present captain-general.

the last thirty years, without attempting to place herself abreast of our most "advanced" colonial politicians. Her dependencies are still governed by an arbitrary system, for the laws promised in the Constitution of 1837 have never been introduced. The captain-general of Cuba, if we believe the Democratic press, is as despotic as a pasha.

The Secretary for Foreign Affairs is generally placed in the list of Spanish ministers immediately after the President of the Council. We have put him last, wishing thereby to indicate that there is none of his colleagues who does not occupy a more really important position. The advice of every man of common sense, who desires the welfare of Spain, to the Spanish Foreign Minister, will, if he understands the circumstances of that country, be, for thirty years to come, a very simple one. " Try to forget that Spain has ever exercised any influence beyond her own borders. Instruct all your ambassadors to confine themselves to protecting the lives and rights of their countrymen in foreign lands, and to keeping you well informed, taking especial care to hear as much and to say as little as possible." If this policy were persevered in, and the other ministers were as active as their colleague was tranquil, Spain would not, at the end of the period we have named, have to ask humbly to be admitted into the councils of Europe. She would be one of the " Great Powers," in virtue of being a *great power.*

Parties in Spain at the present time may be thus divided :—

I. The Royalists, "pures et simples," who are again split into three fractions : the Carlists, the Neo-Catholics, and the Royalists of Isabella II.

II. The Constitutionalists, who are either—

Moderados of several shades ;

Men of the Union-Liberal ;

Moderate Progressistas ;

Advanced Progressistas.

III. The Democratic party, which has two subdivisions, according as its members are

Democratic Progressistas or Socialist Republicans.

Neither the Constitutional Progressistas nor the Democrats have taken any part, as we have seen, in the recent elections, but they, like all the other sections, have their representatives in the press.*

* In the autumn of 1864, the Carlists had for their principal organ the *Esperanza*, a large paper, of very little merit, but which had, we believe, a great circulation. Practically, this party, of course, can only strengthen the hands of the clerical faction, the Neo-Catholics, whose chief paper was *El Pensamiento Español*. It must be remembered that Neo-Catholicism in Spain means something very different from the comparatively moderate views to which it is applied in France. In the latter country we connect it with the name of Montalembert, and with certain *velléités* towards Liberalism, while in Spain it is the creed of the " real old bats of bigotry." The only paper in Spain which supports the principles of the *Correspondant* was, in 1864, so far as we are aware, the *Diario di Barcelona*, an old-established journal, which was then under the direction of M. Mañe y Flaquer, a man of intelligence and ability. The Royalists, who have rallied round the present dynasty, had the *Regeneracion* for their organ.

The Moderados had the *Reino*, the *Contemporaneo*, and several other journals.

The Union-Liberal had the *Epoca*, the *Politica*, etc.

The Progressistas had, amongst others, the *Novedades* and the *Iberia*, the latter of which was perhaps the best Spanish paper which then appeared. It is strange that it is hardly ever quoted by the English press, while the names of very inferior journals appear frequently.

The *Democrazia*, which is edited, as already mentioned, by Castelar, who has attracted much attention by a series of lectures at the Ateneo, upon the civilisation of the first five centuries, represents the opinions of the Democratic Progressistas ; while the *Discusion* is the organ of the Socialist Republicans. Till 1864, that journal was under the guidance of a Catalan, M. Pi y Margall, and it still has great influence in Barcelona and its neighbourhood. In literary merit it seemed to us very inferior to the *Democrazia*, with which it lived on the worst possible terms.

Garrido gives 279 as the number of the journals of Spain.
Of these, 62 were daily and political, 52 belonged to the
bishops, 58 to the government, and the other 93 were devoted
to particular branches of knowledge, to commerce, and so forth.
These figures have probably not been very much altered in the
last two years ; and although the state of things which they
disclose is not one to make us over-sanguine, yet compare it
with the accounts which we have of Spain from 1823 to 1833,
and we seem to have entered a new world.

Students of Spanish literature who have been led down to
the reign of Charles IV. by the learned and only too-pains-
taking Ticknor, may well be excused if they decline to pursue
its history to our own times with such imperfect helps as they

The writer in *Fraser*, already quoted, observes :—

" The Moderado *El Español*, of the 31st October last, employed the following language, which may be taken as a specimen of the licence of Spanish
journalism :—' Vicalvarism (O'Donnellism), that political plague, that nega-
tion of all idea, that deleterious miasma that decomposes and envenoms the
political atmosphere of parties, and for which the word *country* is synonymous
with *prize;* that group of apostates and political pillagers, that sect without
faith, without creeds, without history except what defines a period of illegality,
of violence, of pilfer, and of blood ; that vermin's nest which has bred and
grown with the pest ;—Vicalvarism, that denies the history of all parties—
that presumes, insensate ! to deny the merit and the glory naturally and legiti-
mately corresponding to historical combinations,—that is not a party with
which we ought to measure our strength, is not a legitimate and noble adversary whom we ought to combat.'

*   *   *   *

" Sir James Mackintosh, happening to be at Paris at a time of more than
ordinary looseness of morals, notes down in his journal : ' I hear that Madame
—— is excluded from society. I really should like to know what her offence
can be.' Just so, when, after reading such specimens of permitted journalism
as have fallen under our observation, we hear that a newspaper writer has
been prosecuted, we are driven to wonder what his offence can be. In the
midst of their violence, the opposition papers take good care not to attack the
government for the gravest errors of commission or omission, when in accordance with the national feeling—such as the war with Chili, or the culpable
delay in restoring credit."

can find. They must not, however, conclude, as too many do, that nineteenth-century Spain has no literature worthy of the name. The only substitute for Ticknor which we can suggest to them, of course a very imperfect one, is the two-volume collection of extracts from Spanish contemporary writers, edited by Ochoa for Baudry in 1840. A biographical notice of each author is prefixed to the passages taken from him. Amongst many now dead they will find the names of Hartzenbusch, Pacheco, the Duke of Rivas, Ventura de la Vega, and not a few others who are still alive. There are also several writers who have appeared since Ochoa's collection was given to the world. Such is Campoamor, whose short pieces, called *Doloras*, are of really very great merit, and may be most strongly recommended to those lovers of fugitive poetry who have come to the end of all that the better known literatures have to offer in this kind.

If quantity were of great importance in literature, great would be the place which would be filled in the eyes of his contemporaries by Don Modesto Lafuente, the twenty-second volume of whose history of Spain only brings us down to 1814; but those best entitled to speak with authority upon such a subject accuse him of much too great haste, and of pandering to some of the worst prejudices of his countrymen. The history of the reign of Charles III., by Ferrer del Rio, relates in minute detail the annals of a period which is very imperfectly known, and has been favourably received by foreign critics. Like these, the great statistical work of Don Pascual Madoz has found its way into good English libraries. Amador de los Rios is retracing in fuller detail the ground already so well traversed by Ticknor. Beginning, however, with the beginning, he thinks it necessary to go back not only to Lucan and

Martial, but even to Portius Latro, the worthy rhetorician who was the teacher of Seneca.

The Marquis of Pidal, long prominent in politics, is a historian of a higher order, and unlike Lafuente, who is said to have spent only five days at Simancas, has brought many new facts to light.

The lady who writes under the assumed name of Fernan Caballero is perhaps better known out of her own country than any living Spanish writer, and at least one of her novels has been translated into English. It is unfortunate that her influence, such as it is, is thrown into the scale of the anti-liberal party. This is the case, too, with the popular poet and romance writer, Don Antonio de Trueba. Those who care to know more about living Spanish writers may turn to the work of Latour, *Etudes Littéraires sur L'Espagne.* We should warn them, however, that this author is but the one-eyed in the kingdom of the blind, and we only recommend him because, superficial and prejudiced as he is, we know no better guide. When will some one do for Spain what Marc Monnier, in *L'Italie est elle la Terre des Morts?* has done for the sister Peninsula?

Although the state of education in Spain is very far from being satisfactory, even when compared with other Catholic countries, it would be a sad mistake to suppose, as too many do, that it is no better than Mr. Borrow found it. In the year 1832 there were in the whole country only 700 educational establishments, and in 1839 these had, thanks to the civil wars, increased only to 900. In the end of 1851, Minutoli calculated that were—

17,009 Boys' Schools, attended by	626,882	scholars.
5,021 Girls' Schools, attended by	201,200	„
287 Asylums for Children, educating	11,100	„
Total	839,182	„

On the 1st of January 1861, according to official returns quoted by the writer in the *Home and Foreign Review* already alluded to, the number of children receiving instruction had risen to 1,046,558, and the proportion between the sexes had materially altered ; for whereas in 1851 there were three times as many boys as girls in the schools, the ratio in 1861 was as nine to four—a change which can hardly fail to be fruitful of good to the next generation.   Minutoli, speaking from personal observation in many parts of Spain, says that in spite of their low salaries the schoolmasters are in general very tolerable, and that he came from time to time upon schools which were quite excellent.

All this progress has been made in little more than a quarter of a century, for the first school-law that seems to have had any effect was framed in 1838.   In 1797 there were not 400,000 children attending the primary schools.

Very little good, we fear, can be said of the class of schools corresponding to the French Lycées.   They are few in number, and ill attended.   Hence the Universities have to do much of the work that ought to be got over in the years of boyhood— an evil of which we know something nearer home.   In Spain, Greek, which in the sixteenth century had a very heretical flavour, has never been much studied, and we were recently assured by an eminent professor of the University of Madrid, that the instruction in Latin usually given in Spanish schools was extremely imperfect.

The Universities are ten in number, but of these Madrid is the only one which is organised on the scale of a great national establishment.   It represents the famous University of Alcalá—whose name we connect with Cardinal Ximenes and the Complutensian Polyglott.   It alone bears the title of

"Central," while its humbler sisters are only "District Universities." These are situated at Barcelona, Granada, Oviedo, Salamanca, Seville, Santiago, Valencia, Valladolid, and Saragossa.

The darkness of the Middle Ages still lies deep upon Valladolid and Salamanca, but in Seville the ideas of our time have at least one worthy exponent. In the capital of Catalonia the Scotch philosophy contrives to reconcile itself with the fervent Catholicism of Balmez, a foeman more worthy the steel of Protestant controversalists than any whom Spain has produced since the commencement of her decline ; and the general tone of that University appears for the moment to be singularly alien to the Democratic tendencies which have of late been so prominent in the most active and turbulent of Spanish provinces. The University of Saragossa shares in the general decay of the old capital of Arragon; a decay whose persistence is all the more remarkable, when it is remembered how favourably it is situated with respect to railway communication. The library of this institution is really one of the most touching spectacles which the lover of letters is likely to see in any part of Europe. Room after room may be traversed without finding almost a single book likely to interest any one, except the *bibliomane.* Yet even here, where so little provision is made for giving solid instruction to the students, we could mention the name of one professor who is honourably distinguished among his reactionary colleagues by liberality and intelligence.

A detailed account of the Madrid University, with all the apparatus of higher, secondary, and primary instruction which it sets in motion, is to be found in a convenient little volume, the *Memoria-Anuario de la Universidad Central.* On paper, at least, everything seems well ordered, and in a course of steady improvement. Whether Dr. Pattison and Mr. Arnold would give as pleasant a picture of the actual working of the machine is quite another question. It is, however, undoubtedly doing good service to sound learning; and the tone of the very important philosophical faculty is extremely liberal. Not the least remarkable of its professors is M. Sanz del Rio, whose *Ideal de la Humanidad para la vida* now lies before us. Tell it not in Gath, but it is the philosophy of Krause which is now taught to the rising generation in the metropolis of the *autodafè*—of Krause, who found in freemasonry the germ of that higher order in which he believed that all states and churches would one day merge. Vera is preaching Hegel at Naples, and Krause is indoctrinating the "only court." It is enough to bring Philip II. out of his grave again.

Garrido observes, that although the law of 1856, which now governs public instruction in Spain, was framed by a very reactionary cabinet, the ideas of the time have been too strong for its contrivers, and it is to a great extent working in a liberal direction. He tells an amusing anecdote of the troubles of an unfortunate boy at a school in Andalusia, who, when examined by the priest with regard to the creation of the world, made the same answer which he had been taught to make in the natural history class of the same establishment. Everywhere throughout Spain, the old and the new, superstition and enlightenment, are in presence of each other, but nowhere do they meet in sharper conflict than in the educational institutions. All attempts to make the scientific works used even tolerably conformable to the teaching of the church seem to have been given up. Education is certainly cheap, even when we consider that Spain is a poor country ; and indeed it is difficult to understand how tolerably competent professors can be secured for the very small remuneration which is offered.

It is unfortunate that we cannot refer those who desire to know something of the religious state of Spain, to any recent work which can bear comparison with Doblado's *Letters*, which are now more than forty years old, for there is no subject on which it is more difficult for a foreigner to speak. A few facts, however, we may note as certain :—*First*, The existing Spanish Constitution, although it still contains no clause proclaiming religious toleration, is in this one respect very much more liberal than that of Cadiz, which distinctly committed the nation to intolerance. At present the legislation of Spain recognises the liberty of religious opinions, but does not recognise the liberty of religious worship. The distinction is a pitiful one for these our days, but still it is very real, and represents the abolition of an enormous amount of tyranny and annoyance. *Secondly*, The territorial power of the priesthood, once so great, has ceased to exist ; monasteries are a thing of the past, and in their place we find only a few scattered mission-houses, while the whole number of ecclesiastics has been diminished by many thousands. *Thirdly*, Although it might be imagined that the sacrifice of so large a portion of its worldly advantages might have been repaid to the Spanish clergy by an increase of spiritual influence, this has certainly not been the case, and every traveller knows that neither they nor their office are respected by large sections of the community.

Some curious evidence with regard to this point is supplied by a book published in 1851, and entitled, *The Practical Working of the Church in Spain*. Its authors (for more than one hand contributed to its pages) belong or belonged to that section of English Churchmen who talk of Dr. Pusey as " one whose words are priceless." It may then readily be inferred that they went to the Peninsula expecting to see and hear much with which they could sympathise. They thought that they were entering a land of " happy peasants, all holy monks, all holy priests, holy everybody ;" and great, accordingly, was their consternation when they found ceremonies profaned, confession laughed at, and the clergy despised. In Malaga and Cadiz, in Seville and Cordova, through all south-eastern Spain, they beheld the old religion sinking into contempt. The priests candidly confessed that they had lost their hold over the middle class; or, to use their own peculiar diction, they said, " If it was not for the poor, there would be no worship of God in the land." Sometimes, when a sermon of an exceptionally startling kind woke up the slumbering consciences of the masses, the ancient fanaticism flared up again in a ghastly way ; but it was a mere momentary revival, and things soon returned to their accustomed course. We strongly recommend those who are interested in Spain to read this little work, because the testimony which it gives is evidently wrung from its authors with great reluctance. They had no sympathy with some of the more flagrant delusions of the Roman system,—with its Mariolatry, for example ; but with much that to a real Protestant is quite as objectionable, they were thoroughly at one.

If we turn to the debates which took place in the Constituent Cortes with regard to religious toleration, and which have been published in a separate volume, we shall see that not only were several of the amendments brought forward by the Liberal party very respectably supported, but that the reasons given by some of the most influential persons in support of the less liberal proposal of the committee, which was ultimately adopted, were by no means such as could be acceptable to conscientious bigots, while the counter-proposal which was brought forward by the Neo-Catholic party met with very little favour. The motion of Montesinos, deputy for Caceres in Estremadura, to establish complete religious toleration, was only lost, on the 15th of January 1855, by 103 votes to 99. There is little doubt that if it had not been for the difficulties occasioned by the bigotry of Queen Isabella, and the fear of introducing another element of disturbance into an already-agitated country, the amendment we have just alluded to would have been carried.

There can be no doubt that the barbarous suppression of the Reformed tenets was one of the chief causes of the decline of Spanish glory, but we do not feel by any means sure that the introduction of a considerable leaven of Protestantism into sixteenth-century Spain might not have exercised so powerful a dissolving force as to have undone the work of Ferdinand and Isabella, by breaking the country once more into two or more separate kingdoms. No one has a right dogmatically to assert that this would not have been so, until he has well weighed and considered the centrifugal forces which have long worked, nay which are even now working, in Spanish politics. It is not impossible that the historians of the twentieth century may think that they understand why it was that the good cause was allowed so utterly to fail; and as they narrate the discomfiture which assuredly awaits the " Great Church" in the Peninsula, may see how fatal to the interests of superstition has been that national unity of which its advocates have said so much. The shades of Ægidius and San Roman are, if we mistake not, likely to be far more thoroughly avenged upon their

enemy than they would have been by the kind of partial
success which followed efforts similar to theirs in France or
Southern Germany; and those who read their story by the
light of what is now passing in Spain may comfort themselves with the saying—

> "Though the mills of God grind slowly,
> Yet they grind exceeding small."

It would, however, be a mistake to suppose that there is
any tendency towards the Confessions of the sixteenth century on the part of any appreciable number of Spaniards.
The expedition of Mr. Borrow, except in so far as it produced
a book which has been well called "Gil Blas in Water-
Colours," was a perfect failure, as is well explained in Captain
Widdrington's second work. The more recent movement, to
which the name of Matamoros is attached, has not even the
proverbial importance of straws that show which way the
wind blows. If any exhortations of ours were likely to reach
the class of persons who find a vent for their superfluous
energy in missions to the Mediterranean, we would advise
them for the present to devote all their attention to Italy.
There they will find, under the protection of an enlightened
government, a fair field and certainly no disfavour. There,
by a plentiful expenditure of money and zeal, they will be
able thoroughly to test how far their views are suitable to
Latin populations in the nineteenth century. The cause of
progress can only gain by their having full scope for their
operations, whether judicious or otherwise. In Spain the case
is very different : they have to deal with a half-enlightened
government, and with a people which, so long as we hold
Gibraltar, will be apt to look with intense dislike on everything which has a peculiarly English colour. Whatever they

do, let them at least not make Gibraltar the pivot of their operations. The only result of doing so will be to stultify their own efforts, and to alienate the sympathy of Spaniards from any of their converts who may get into trouble. Our own impression is, that the form of Romanism which prevails in Spain is lower, and retains less of the real spirit of Christianity, than that which exists in any other Catholic country with which we are acquainted. Over the lower classes it still has very considerable hold ; but rather as a superstition than as a religion. On the other hand, the creed of the bulk of the men among the educated classes is pure indifferentism, and probably in their hearts the majority of those who are opposed to religious toleration oppose it in order that they may not have the trouble of settling what attitude they are to take up towards the religion of the state. At present they are Catholics, as a matter of course, just as they are Spaniards. If they could be anything else, they would be ashamed to profess belief in a system which they utterly despise. This state of things need surprise nobody : it is the natural result of the forcible suppression of free thought, and is seen in a less degree even in those countries— pagan and other—where public opinion, and not penal legislation, is the supporter of the existing creeds. We cannot expect this miserable hypocrisy, injurious alike to morality, to literature, and to statesmanship, soon to pass away ; but a beginning is made. Any one who knows Spain could mention the names of Spaniards who are as enlightened in these great matters, and as earnest, as the best amongst ourselves ; and just as surely as the opinions of Luther and Melancthon would, through the Enzinas family and many others, have taken root in Spain and converted a large minority of the nation, if the persecutions of Philip II. and his successors had not made it absolutely impossible, so one or other of the forms of pure Christianity which, under various names and with differences more or less marked, but not of vital importance, are becoming the creed of most thinking men in the countries of Europe generally recognised as progressive, will most certainly, before the end of this century, have great influence in rapidly reviving Spain. Only let all concerned remember that any attempt on the part of foreigners to hasten this good work will only retard it. There is an excellent Castilian proverb which impatient reformers would do well to remember : "*No por mucho madrugar, amanece mas temprano :*" " However early you get up in the morning, the dawn comes never the sooner."

All this is not very like the Middle Ages ; and we cannot help thinking that if Mr. Buckle had lived, he would have found it necessary to reconsider the latter part of his elaborate and valuable treatise on Spain. We think that the key to modern Spain is to recollect that she is essentially not mediæval, but that, in the room of the old faith, loyalty, and *pundonor*, she has not as yet got any great national belief, philosophy, or idea, in the light of which to live. The old principles were bad enough, yet let no man condemn them too utterly, till he has seen the Cathedral of Toledo, and read what is best in Calderon. Nearly all the moral and social phenomena which we now observe amongst the educated classes of Spain, may be explained by the influence of a superficial French culture acting upon a people in whom long tyranny had dried up the springs of national life.

The question which underlies all other questions in the Peninsula is the question of the dynasty. Will this wretched

Bourbon race ever be able honestly to reconcile itself with constitutional government, or must it be trampled down at Madrid as elsewhere. Our readers will have gathered that, altogether apart from the play of the political forces, there is an evil influence which is perpetually interfering with the action of government. As long as there is the *camarilla* in the palace, there will be a constant danger of revolution in the streets. It is more than probable that Queen Isabella would ere this have been set aside, if it were possible to put anybody in her place; but against every candidate whose claims have ever been canvassed, there are great objections, and he must be an ardent republican, indeed, who would seriously propose to try his favourite form of government in such a country. As long as the queen persists in giving her confidence to priests, swindlers, and favourites, it is impossible to say what may happen from hour to hour; but if the royal difficulty could be got over, and the intelligence of the country could be once for all reconciled with its dynasty, which we should be heartily glad to see, the next great political step should be, if not to restore the Constitution of 1837, at least very much to alter that of 1845, and, above all, to sweep away those dishonest saving clauses which leave it open to a minister to exercise despotic authority under constitutional forms. It may be doubted, however, whether even good political change is so important for Spain as quiet and decently-honest government. Anyhow, the improvement that would be effected, if all parties would consent to abstain from the exercise of that undue influence which has been employed against all in turn, would be so enormous, that all questions sink by comparison into insignificance. Corruption by private persons has never made much progress in Spain, although

there, as in France, it is upon the increase. If these reforms
could be effected, Englishmen could look with great equanimity upon a nominated Senate, and the continued abeyance
of the National Guard, although we are far from venturing to
assert that real reforms will be carried out without recurrence
to the use of that powerful but dangerous instrument. Another crying evil, which it would be most important to
sweep away, is the intolerable number of functionaries and
pensioners, who eat up the revenues of the state, and eke out
their wretched pay by bribery and oppression. This, however, is an evil with which the constitutional government of
Spain finds it as difficult to deal as does the Autocrat himself. It is easier to say that Spain ought to have half the
number of employés which she now has, and to double their
salaries, than to propose any feasible means of effecting such
a reform. It is no less clear that her policy ought to be
to have a small, thoroughly well-appointed army, which,
in the improbable case of a really necessary war, might
act as a nucleus round which her population—than which
none in Europe more easily adopt the habits of the soldier—
might rapidly rally. Nor would it be less desirable that
Spanish generals should confine themselves to their own
art, standing aloof from politics, and imitating, in this respect,
their naval brethren. We have alluded already to the ruinous
results which have followed the unfair dealing of Spanish
Finance Ministers, to the abominations of the tariff, and the
whole fiscal system, as well as to the extreme impolicy of the
excessive centralisation which prevails in every department of
the state. We cannot, however, too strongly impress upon
our readers that the punctual execution of the laws which
even now exist in Spain, bad as these laws in many parti-

culars are, would very much improve the position of the country. Everywhere there is slackness, gross dishonesty, want of business habits, and falsehood. With regard to all this side of Spanish affairs, the observations of Ford cannot be too frequently read, or too carefully treasured. Against such evils as these the best government can do but little, and any man who, like Espartero and some of his friends, stood erect amidst the general abasement, deserves, although their conduct amounts to little more than a protest, to be placed upon the same level as far more successful reformers in more fortunate lands. The railways and the abolition of passports have done, and will do, much to diminish that intense provincial jealousy which is one of the greatest difficulties of Spanish rulers. Intercourse with foreign nations, which has now become so easy, will gradually force the Spaniards of the upper and middle classes, both men and women, to become more educated. The bull-fight, at once an index and a stimulant of national brutality, is now more flourishing than ever; but this may be accounted for by increased wealth, and everywhere there is an intelligent minority which protests against it. We should, however, only be too happy to think, that the hundredth anniversary of the day on which Jovellanos attacked it would see it beginning to vanish.

If Spain had only, at the commencement of the present reign, adopted a reasonable policy towards her colonies, she might ere this have stood towards them in a position at once honourable and profitable, and have acted in Europe as the head of the Spanish race in all parts of the globe. As it is, it is more probable that she will lose the last of them, than that she will be wise in time, and introduce a good government. Her colonial, like her foreign policy, has remained that of

Ferdinand VII. There is surely no power in Europe to which non-intervention is more recommended by nature, for the Pyrenees, as has been truly said, "damp the sound of her voice." She has but two real foreign interests, and both these are peninsular: the union with Portugal, and the possession of Gibraltar. The former of these will, we think, certainly come about when both nations arrive at a higher point of development, for such a union will increase the power of both in geometrical ratio. We should not, however, be deceived, for as yet nothing is prepared for it, and the *Pedrist* intrigues of 1854 were quite premature. There are hardly two capitals in Europe which have so little intercourse with each other as Lisbon and Madrid. When the frontier is cut by half-a-dozen railways it will be very different, and ere that time may we not hope to see a really free and good government in both countries? At present, Portugal is politically much in advance.* With regard to Gibraltar, we do not care to discuss the question either from an English or a Spanish point of view. Those who imagine that it will not have one day to be very seriously discussed, must have odd ideas about the future of the Mediterranean. There seems, however, at present to be little likelihood of its becoming a subject of immediate interest in this generation.

Spain would have made a very great step towards pros-

---

* There is an interesting paper on Portugal in the *Revue des Deux Mondes* for 1864. In the opinion of its intelligent author, the tendency of public feeling in Portugal is altogether against any *rapprochement* to Spain. Since the idea of annexation was taken up by a portion of the Spanish press in 1861, he says that it has become the fashion in Portugal to affect ignorance even of the language of their nearest neighbours. " The two nations are brothers, but brothers who desire to live apart." A similar dislike on the part of Scotland, did not, however, prevent the Union, and the logic of interest and events will one day perhaps be too strong for national prejudice.

perity, if she could only understand, that all intelligent Englishmen wish that she should rise to a point of national wealth and real power, such as she has never as yet attained. They are quite aware that, in the present condition of the world, Spain cannot be prosperous without being enlightened, peaceful, and industrious ; and they well know that the transformation of the Iberian Peninsula into an enlightened, peaceful, and industrious state, would not only be a great blessing to mankind, but would add enormously to the wellbeing of their own country, which is becoming every day more and more the workshop and the *entrepôt* of the world. Nor will the complete regeneration of Spain be less important to us in an intellectual than in a material point of view. Consider what she did when she was enslaved to a faith only less bloody than that which she overthrew in Mexico,—a faith at which all intelligent Romanists now shudder ; then judge what she may do when the fine intellects of her people are freed from the bondage of ignorance, and she has her fair share of the knowledge of those facts of the universe, which are now acquired for humanity. So surely as a new product of any value is discovered, it soon finds it way to England. So surely as a new idea is born into the world, it soon finds its way hither also ; and no nation can now become rich or wise without largely contributing to the increase of our riches and wisdom.

CHAPTER II.

RUSSIA, said a French historian to an English friend, is a siren, with whom it is dangerous to parley. "Just look at Haxthausen's book; he starts as a very good German, but he becomes more Muscovite than Muscovy, before he gets to the end." If the remarkable man who used these words had ever thought of Russia, except as a subject for dithyrambic rhetoric, he would probably have reflected that to say of a country that, the more you examine it, the better your opinion of it is likely to be, is to pass upon it a very equivocal kind of censure. We place his remark, however, at the very commencement of this article, in order that the reader may not be unwarned, but may suspect us, if he finds anything more favourable to Russia than he anticipates, to have listened too long to the voice of the siren.

What are the elements which make up the ordinary ideas about Russia, now floating in English society? First, there is a general feeling of dislike, not unmingled with disgust, which may be traced up perhaps to the publication of Dr. Clarke's travels. That writer, who influences many who never read a line of his works, visited Russia during the reign of the Emperor Paul, and suffered, like most who did so, from the caprices of that maniac. His descriptions have been criticised, but were probably in the main correct, and the state of

society, which he found in Russia, was eminently detestable.
The impression which his book left upon the mind of Western
Europe was heightened by the bitter diatribes of Custine ; and
even those who would have been willing to look, with a
friendly eye, upon the Russian people and their advancing
civilisation, have been revolted by the impudent pretensions
of their government to give law to Europe, and by that long
succession of presumptuous follies which, commencing with
1814, only came to an end when the heart-strings of the Emperor Nicholas cracked in the agony of defeat and humiliation.
The bloody repression of two Polish insurrections, the long
grim tyranny of Nicholas, and the fact that the events of even
the present reign come to us coloured, as has been well said,
either by the views of Germans who fear, or of Poles who
hate Russia, have combined to make the task of any one
who asks the Liberal party in England to look upon the
empire of the Czars as it really is, very far indeed from an
easy one.

Alexander I., during the earlier years of his reign,
seemed inclined to give his attention to the internal affairs of
his empire.　Too soon, however, he was dragged into the
whirlpool of the revolutionary wars, and ere long the utter
failure of Napoleon's mad attempt put him in a position to
dictate to the Continent.　He caught too, beyond his own
frontiers, that strange malady of religious enthusiasm which
broke out all over Europe, when the subject nations began
first to hope for an opportunity of shaking off the domination
of France.　Opposition to the Revolution estranged the pupil
of Laharpe from the doctrines of his master.　The influence
of Madame de Krüdener made the eldest son of the Holy
Eastern Church a mystic according to the Western manner.

After the peace he still cherished hopes of making Warsaw a centre, whence a modified Liberalism might be conducted, at the good pleasure of the Czar, from one city of Russia to another ; but the difficulties he met with from a people, which then as now cared much more for national freedom than for forms of government, of however liberal a character, gradually altered the views of Alexander about Poland, while he became engaged ever more and more deeply in the Congress politics, of which Metternich was the moving spirit. Before he died he was little more than the Minister of Foreign Affairs for Russia, while the legitimate functions of the Autocrat were discharged, and discharged detestably, by his all-powerful favourite Araktchéïeff. We have said that Alexander was gradually led into this unfortunate policy ; indeed, nothing would be more mistaken than to suppose that even the signature of the Holy Alliance was coincident with his reaching any very advanced point on the political " descensus Averni." So much nonsense has been talked of late about the Holy Alliance, in connection with the Carlsbad and Kissingen interviews of 1864, that we shall not do wrong to remind our readers what that agreement really was.

The document called the Holy Alliance was originally sketched at Paris, in the French language, by Alexander's own hand, after a long and animated conversation with Madame de Krüdener and Bergasse. It was suggested, perhaps, by words spoken by the king of Prussia after the battle of Bautzen, but was chiefly the result of the influence upon a mind always inclined to religious ideas, of the conversation of Madame de Krüdener and of the philosopher Bader, the admirer of Tauler, Jacob Boehm, and St. Martin, the deadly foe of Kant and his successors in Germany—a man

who may be called, in a certain sense, the father of the
Tractarian movement, and who used to speak of the Reformation as a *deformation,* just as Richard Froude did at Oxford
some twenty years afterwards.

The Czar dreamt of founding a Communion of states,
bound together by the first principles of Christianity. He
hoped to see the Turk driven out of Europe, and he had not
much more affection for the Pope than for the Turk. The
king of Prussia signed the paper from motives of friendship
for the Czar, without attaching much importance to what he
did, to the vexation of Madame de Krüdener, to whom, of
course, his carelessness appeared a sort of profanation. The
emperor of Austria, the least sentimental of mankind, at first
declined to sign, "because," he said, "if the secret is a political
one, I must tell it to Metternich ; if it is a religious one, I
must tell it to my confessor." Metternich accordingly was
told, and observed scornfully, " *C'est du verbiage.*" Indeed no
one of the princes who adhered to the Holy Alliance, with
the single exception of Alexander himself, ever took it
seriously. It was doomed from its birth. As M. de Bernhardi observes : " It sank without leaving a trace in the
stream of events, never became a reality, and never had the
slightest real importance." What *had* real importance was
the continuance of the good understanding between the
powers who had put down Napoleon, and their common
fear of France.

This good understanding and that common fear led to
the treaty of the 20th November 1815, by which it was
stipulated that the Powers should, from time to time, hold
Congresses with a view to regulating the welfare of nations
and the peace of Europe. It was these Congresses, and not

the Holy Alliance, which kept up close relations between
the rulers of Russia, Prussia, and Austria, and enabled them,
when the liberal movement on the Continent, which followed
the conclusion of the war, began to be alarming, to take
measures for a combined system of repression.

Alexander I., when he lay on his deathbed at Tag-
anrog, had wandered far away from his mystic benevo-
lence of ten years before. The danger of revolution had
come much nearer, and although he did not know all before
he closed his eyes, he knew enough to understand that the
whole of his system, and even the lives of the imperial
family, were in imminent danger. It is well, perhaps, for
his reputation as a humane and well-meaning sovereign, that
he did not return to encounter the rival conspiracies of the
south and of the north—the republicanism of Pestel, or the
constitutionalism of Ryléïeff.

His brother Nicholas, who succeeded him after a short
but most dangerous interval, was a man of narrow views,
and brave rather from the force of will than from impulse.
At the critical moment when the attempted revolution had to
be encountered and put down, he behaved with great spirit,
but his nerves were unquestionably shaken by what occurred.
Long afterwards he said to an English diplomatist, who remarked to him that only two thrones in Europe were secure,
that of England and of Russsia : " Speak of England, if you
please, but I, you know, sit upon a volcano." When he came
to examine into the state of the empire, he found nothing to
reassure him. All was in disorder. He set to work, and
from that time till his death, although his principles were
false, and the objects which he set before him were impossible,
it cannot be denied that he tried hard to improve the country

over which he ruled.   He had, however, inherited from Alexander the unfortunate legacy of the foreign policy, which had
been inaugurated during the years which followed the Peace ;
and his own imperious temper, no less than his extreme fear
lest the revolutionary spirit should cross his frontiers, led him
to plunge deeper into the complications of Western Europe.
He strove so successfully to show his hatred to liberalism, if
not to counteract its efforts, that the name of Russia became
detested by every intelligent man in Europe, and only the
few who were led by accident fully to examine the character
of the man, and the nature of the circumstances in which he
was placed, could ever think of Nicholas except as a demon
reigning over one of the circles of the *Inferno*.   Those who
knew the truth could make more allowances, and could perfectly understand how it was that the type of all absolutism
should have quizzed Lord Heytesbury about the fears with
which the English Tories regarded the Reform Bill, and have
assured that minister, that if he had been the sovereign of
England, he would have found no difficulty in assenting to it.

The mistaken foreign policy of two reigns brought its own
punishment.   The conduct of Russia in the commencement of
the Crimean dispute is intelligible enough, and it would not
be impossible to justify some of the claims of the Czar.
Certainly the war would never have occurred, if it had not
been for the utter abhorrence with which Russia was regarded
by all the liberal and progressive elements of Western society.
The English Cabinet went to war for Turkey, but enlightened
public opinion supported it, because it saw an opportunity of
striking a heavy blow at the stolid power which lent itself to
prop up every decaying throne and every worn-out authority
from the Vistula to the Ocean.

The great struggle began, and although short, was decisive. It ended too soon, perhaps, for the glory of the English arms, but not before the object which the nation, as distinguished from the government, had at heart, was thoroughly attained, for peace was followed by the utter break-down of the whole system of Nicholas at home and abroad.

With the death of the great oppressor, and the accession of a sovereign who was justly supposed to resemble rather his uncle than his father, a change came over the tone of society in St. Petersburg and Moscow. All tongues seemed to be loosed. The government was as freely criticised in many drawing-rooms as if it were not still omnipotent, and even to the press an altogether unwonted latitude was allowed. Numerous projects of reform—social, political, and industrial—were put forward and discussed. Out of all this fermentation there has hardly come, up to this time, a proportionate amount of solid advantage, although it would be most unjust to deny that Russia is much better prepared for reforms of many kinds than she was ten years ago. One extremely important measure has indeed become law ; we allude, of course, to the emancipation of the serfs. There is, we trust, every reason to believe that as this was a change without which no real improvement in any direction was possible, so it will be only the first of a series of measures which may reflect glory upon the reign of Alexander II., laying broad and deep the foundations of the true greatness and prosperity of Russia ; and we hope indeed to show, ere we conclude, that many salutary innovations are tolerably far advanced.

Before we give some account of the emancipation of the serfs, it will be necessary to take care that our readers should have a clear notion of the condition of the Russian peasant before 1861. It is quite a mistake to suppose that all Russian peasants were serfs up to that year. Several large exceptional classes must be deducted from the mass of the peasantry, before we come to those who were actually serfs.

First, There were the small proprietors, or *odnodvortzi*—a word which signifies possessors of a single house or court. M. N. Tourguéneff, who wrote in 1847, calculates their numbers at 1,400,000. They were not to be distinguished from the other peasants, either by their dress or manner of life ; but they retained the recollection of the days when they had been in the position of the *schliachta*, or *"petite noblesse"* of Poland, about which we have lately heard so much ; and these recollections combined with their personal freedom before the law, to keep up their self-respect, although they were too often treated by their wealthier neighbours, and by the agents of government, as if they were actually serfs.

Secondly, The Cossacks, a numerous body, or rather aggregation of bodies, scattered through different parts of the empire enjoying peculiar privileges, and forming the nucleus round which cluster many of the most incredible stories which are told about Russia.

When Napoleon said that in fifty years Europe would be either Cossack or republican, he made a false prophecy in the most unlucky language possible. "Free as a Cossack" is a common proverb in Russia. The truth of the matter is that the first Cossack communities were composed of bands of heterogeneous adventurers, who, at first little better than brigands, were at length allowed to establish themselves on the frontier of the empire, with a view to protect it against the Tartars and other barbarous tribes. In return for a nominal allegiance, and for their warlike service, they were permitted to rule themselves after their own fashion. The most celebrated of the Cossack associations is that of the Don. Dr. Clarke visited it before the changes which were introduced into its organisation by Alexander I., and he gives a very curious and far from unpleasing picture of Cossack manners and mode of life, contrasting them very favourably with those of the inhabitants of Great Russia. They are now chiefly known as largely contributing to the light troops of the empire, and making themselves extremely useful in keeping up communication, cutting off stragglers, and so forth. For actual fighting they are not well adapted. Small, rough-looking men, on small, rough-look-ing horses, they swarmed in Poland during the recent insur-rection, and no doubt had their fair share in the atrocities that were so freely committed on both sides. At the same time, we believe that M. Tourguéneff is supported by the testimony of all entitled to judge, in saying that the Cossack is not naturally cruel ; probably it may be very truly said of him, as was said by one who was laughing over the alarming stories about the Croats, which were circulated in Germany during the Hungarian war, and into which reminiscences of the days of Tilly and Pappenheim very largely entered : "Ah ! the modern Croat is much improved, he prefers plunder to murder."

Thirdly, The free labourers, a class which was called into existence during the reign of Alexander I. They were cal-culated by M. Tourguéneff at only about 70,000, because the endless formalities with which the transformation of serfs into peasants of this class was attended, had prevented the benevolent design of the emperor being carried out as fully as he had expected.

Fourthly, The foreign colonists, numbering about 84,000, and dispersed over very distant regions. Full and interesting accounts are given of some of these by Haxthausen, more especially of the Mennonite settlers in the south of European Russia.

Fifthly, The enormous class of the Crown peasants, who, although very much harassed by the employés, were really free " comme on l'est en Russie," as M. Tourguéneff observes, who, inhabiting the domains of the Crown, were, in addition to the capitation-tax, only bound to pay a small sum, of the nature of rent, in return for their share of the communal lands. It has been often said that these peasants were worse off than the serfs themselves, because they were oppressed by the inferior agents of government, and were without the protection of any seigneur. This is, however, a complete mistake, as is proved by the fact that the happiest serfs were always ready to make great sacrifices to pass into the hands of the Crown, and so to become Crown peasants.

Sixthly, The peasants of the apanages—serfs in all but the name—consisting of the inhabitants of a large number of properties which were separated under Paul I. from the domains of the Crown, to be a special provision for the members of the imperial family.

Seventhly, The peasants of the *arendes,* a class which was created by Alexander I., who put an end to the bad old custom of giving away to private persons domains belonging to the Crown, with the peasants inhabiting them ; thus reducing these peasants to the position of serfs ; but instead of it introduced the nearly equally bad custom of giving to persons whom he desired to favour, leases of portions of the Crown lands called *arendes*. The lot of the peasants who were in this way let to private persons, was extremely wretched. The custom existed only in the Baltic provinces, and in those governments which formed part of ancient Poland.

Eighthly, Peasants attached to the establishments of the Crown, employed in the government mines, factories, and works, and sometimes even in those of private persons. They formed a large and often very ill-used class, calculated by M. Tourguéneff at about 200,000.

Ninthly, The peasants attached to the administration of the post, or *yamschiki,* also very hardly used, but not falling within the class of serfs.

The government, by recent legislation, has facilitated the acquisition of a portion of land by each family of Crown and apanage peasants, so that in less than fifty years the whole of this immense mass of men will be turned into peasant proprietors, holding in fee-simple, except in so far as the rights of the commune may continue to exist.

At length we arrive at that large and interesting class which has recently passed from serfdom to liberty amidst the applause and thanksgiving of the whole civilised world. And before we go further, we should advise all those who take an interest in the question of serf-emancipation to make themselves acquainted with that portion of M. Nicholas Tourguéneff's book, *La Russie et les Russes,* which deals with this subject. That excellent and very distinguished man was, in early life, attached as Russian Commissary to Stein during the advance of the armies of the Czar upon Paris. After the peace he returned to his own country, and was the first, or almost the first, to press the importance of the serf question upon the Russian reformers of that period. He and his brother, along with some other much larger proprietors, presented a project of emancipation to Alexander I. Fortunately for M. Tourguéneff, he was travelling abroad when the attempted revolution of December 1825 broke out. Summoned to return by the government of Nicholas, he wisely refused, and Mr. Canning treated with silent contempt a proposal for his extradition from England. There can be no doubt that in the then temper of the Czar he would have been sent to Siberia or put to death, although there was not a tittle of evidence to connect him with any of the treasonable designs which were undoubtedly cherished by some of the persons with whom he was more or less connected. For many years he has lived in Paris, and was there at the time when he composed the book to which we are calling attention, and which, although nineteen years have elapsed since its publication, is still one of the best which we possess upon Russia. No living man has laboured so long and so steadily for the emancipation of the serfs, not only because he sympathised most deeply with a body of men whose excellent qualities he well knew, but because, half-a-century ago, he saw, what few then perceived, that this great reform was a *sine quâ non* for all real progress in Russia.

The novels of his namesake, M. Ivan Tourguéneff, are also most valuable, as giving a faithful picture of the working of serfdom ; and some portions of Haxthausen compared with, and to some extent corrected by, the appendix to M. Hertzen's *Du Développement des Idées Revolutionnaires en Russie*, ought to be read by any one who desires to have a fair notion of the state of the Russian serf up to 1861.

Every person in Russia who does not belong to the nobility, or the *bourgeoisie,* must necessarily belong to some *commune.* The *commune* of Russia is simply a slightly modified form of the village community which was one of the earliest institutions of the Indo-Germanic race, and is still the basis of society in Hindostan.

Modern jurisprudence, following the mature Roman law, looks, in the words of Mr. Maine, " upon co-ownership as an exceptional and momentary condition of the rights of property ;" but in India, and we may add in Russia, this order of ideas is reversed. It is separate proprietorship that is exceptional, while co-ownership is normal. The word *mir,* by which the Russian describes his *commune,* is the same word which he uses when he wishes to speak of the Kosmos. Haxthausen says, and we think he is right, that it is untranslatable by any word in the Romance or Teutonic languages, and he gives a most curious list of proverbs which illustrate the idea of sanctity attached to it.

The *commune* or microcosm is, or rather should be, in theory as regards the state, a single individual. The state has no right to go beyond it. It is responsible for all its members, and its deliberations ought to be regarded by all external to it, as we in the West should regard the workings of a man's own mind. Each *commune* possesses a certain amount of land, and has the absolute power of parcelling out this land in equal portions to the individuals who compose it, the individual obtaining only the usufruct, while the property remains in the *commune.* The *commune* decides without appeal what portion of the taxes imposed by government upon itself, is to be borne by each of its members, or rather, by the land whose usufruct belongs to each member. Every

male dwelling in the *commune* has a right, as soon as he
arrives at majority, to demand a portion of land, and then
becomes entitled to a voice in the communal affairs, and is
subject to pay his share of taxes. The elective head of the *commune,* or *Starost,* has great authority over every individual, but
no authority over the commune itself. M. Hertzen points out
that M. Haxthausen makes a great mistake in saying that
the authority of the Czar is reflected in the Starost. The
truth is, that the Starost can only act despotically when he
is supported by the public opinion of the commune. This
local administration was, before the emancipation, and still is,
in fresh observance. The power of the seigneur stopped with
the commune. In the words of M. Hertzen : " Le seigneur
peut réduire la terre concedée aux paysans ; il peut choisir
pour lui le meilleur sol ; il peut agrandir ses bien-fonds, et,
par là, le travail du paysan ; il peut augmenter les impôts,
mais il ne peut pas refuser aux paysans une portion de terre
suffisante, et la terre, une fois appartenant à la commune,
demeure complètement sour l'administration communale la
même en principe que celle que régit les terres libres ; le
seigneur ne se mêle jamais dans ses affaires."

An Englishman finds it very difficult to understand how
such a degree of self-government was consistent with serfdom,
but his surprise is diminished when he reflects that these
communes were very much isolated, and had often but little
communication even with the communes which formed part
of their own group. The serf since the days of Peter the Great
bowed low his head, in the words of M. Hertzen, and allowed
misfortune to pass over him. It is his absolute retirement,
within the circle of the commune, from everything like political life, that accounts for his having kept many good qualities,

which, if the whole weight of tyranny had pressed upon him, would have crushed all good out of his character.

How was it, however, that not only an absolute government, but the thousand petty local tyrants, respected the organisation of the commune? The answer to this is, that there are some things which every government must respect, and on the few occasions on which the Russian government was imprudent enough not to respect the communes—as, for instance, in the affair of the military colonies under Alexander I.—it was met by a resistance which, coming from one of the gentlest of races, seemed so preternaturally savage that it has for a long time taken good care to let well alone.

The justice of the village tribunal is, it would appear, of a very rough-and-ready kind, and by no means dispenses with the argument from the stick, which is so frightfully common in Russia. Those who have witnessed a meeting of villagers to discuss their common affairs, give a curious account of the gradual process by which a conventional unanimity is arrived at; and it has been well pointed out how completely this Sclavonic idea of a conventional unanimity broke down, when, transferred from the narrow circle of the commune, it was adapted, in the Polish Diet, to great affairs.

Most persons will see in the communal institutions of Russia merely an interesting sample of arrested social development, and will look with interest for the slow and gradual breaking-up of the communes, and their replacement by individual ownership. M. Hertzen is, or was in 1853, of a different opinion. He thinks, or thought, that Russia with her commune stands before an epoch in which the anti-communal civilisation of feudalism and the Roman law has come to a deadlock, and he dreams or dreamt that " the barbarians of the

north, and our home barbarians, may find out that they have
a common enemy—the old feudal monarchical edifice, and a
common hope—the social revolution." His friend, M. Ogareff,
wrote his *Lettres a un Anglais*, published in 1862, chiefly to
bring out and defend the Socialist side of Russian institutions.
They are well worth studying.*

The communal institutions of Russia are far older than its
serfdom. They saw that evil institution begin, as they have
seen it end. Serfdom, properly so called, only began in Russia
with the reign of the usurper Boris Godunoff, and with St.
George's day of the year 1593. It was on that day that the
peasants, whose right of moving from one master to another
had been for some time confined to that festival, became
through enormous districts *adscripti glebæ*. Afterwards, however, and more especially in the reign of Peter the Great,
things became much worse, but it was Catherine II. who
completed the iniquity by introducing serfdom into the wide
region called Little Russia, which did not form part of the
empire of Boris Godunoff.

The agricultural serfs were divided into two great classes :—
Those who were obliged to work for a certain length of time,
generally three days in the week, for their masters, and those
who were bound to pay an *obrok* or rent. This rent was almost
always moderate, and the peasants who paid it were generally
the happiest. This was particularly the case in the great central governments of Jaroslav, Kostroma, and Vladimir, whose
inhabitants wander all over Russia, exercising their various

---

* Only very recently a Russian paper announced that the mission of that
country was to proclaim the universal equality of all citizens before the state,
and the duty of the state to give lands in fee-simple to all its citizens.—(See
the *Revue des Deux Mondes*, for March 15, 1866.)

trades, and paying to their seigneur a small acknowledgment.
A few *grand seigneurs* possessed serfs who were enormously
wealthy. This was the case more especially with the great
family of Cheremetieff. Of course, according to law, all the
property of these wealthy serfs belonged to their masters, but
a custom stronger than law prevented this right being often
enforced, although there were exceptions, and sometimes very
melancholy exceptions, to this rule, for an account of some of
which we may refer to *La Russie et les Russes*.

In addition to the agricultural serfs, there was a still more
unhappy class who were really very nearly slaves, and who
were called personal serfs or *dvorovyé*. M. Tourguéneff says
of them: " On les appelle en Russie *gens* de cour (*dvorovyé*), et
pour ne pas donner aux courtisans la même denomination on
a inventé pour eux une variante, en les appellant gens prés
de la cour (pridvornvyé).

The idea of emancipating the serfs was not a new one.
The serfs of the Baltic provinces became freemen in name, if
in name only, under Alexander I.; and Nicholas during
the latter part of his reign bestowed much attention upon a
project which was to apply to the whole of the rest of the
country where servitude existed. It is said that the present
emperor was, when heir to the throne, by no means favourable
to the project, and that the Grand-duke Constantine was its
chief partisan in the imperial family ; while Count Kisseleff,
Count Bludoff, who died this year in honourable poverty after
having exercised enormous power for many years, and General
Bibikoff who had already introduced considerable improvements in the situation of the peasantry in Kieff, Volhynia,
and Podolia, were its principal supporters in their immediate
entourage. Prince Dolgoroukoff tells, in the first number of his

Review called *Le Véridique*, a curious story of the deathbed
of Nicholas, and traces what Alexander II. has done since
to the words of his father upon that occasion.

When the emancipation had been fairly determined upon,
the nobles were requested to send in their views as to the
way in which certain general principles, which the emperor
declared were to be the basis of his great reform, should be
carried out. Forty-six provincial committees laboured for
eighteen months to come to an agreement as to details, but
without arriving at any result very satisfactory to the government, which afterwards took the affair into its own hands.
Upon one point, and almost upon one only, were all parties
agreed, and that was that no indemnity was to be paid to the
proprietors for their personal rights over the serfs.

The state of feeling which prevailed during the transition
period which intervened between the announcement of the
intention of the government, and the production of its plan,
was well described to English readers in the pages of *Russia
by a Recent Traveller*, a small but very remarkable book which
was published at the office of the *Continental Review* in the
year 1859.* The situation was to the last degree uneasy, and
might have become dangerous. The government only obeyed
the dictates of common sense in at last determining to act for
itself.

The landed proprietors, by the testimony of one who had
perhaps a better right to express an opinion upon the subject
than any other man, showed in the whole transaction all the
defects and all the merits of the Russian character. While
the method of emancipation was still uncertain, they were
most unpractical and unsatisfactory in their suggestions.

* See also a paper by Aurelio Buddeus in *Unsere Zeit* for 1858.

When it was once settled, they threw themselves heartily into it, and have tried honestly to carry it out.

The whole number of serfs, male and female, in the beginning of 1861 was about twenty-three millions, but of these considerably more than half a million may be left out of account, as the arrangements which applied to them were special, and not those of the general measure of enfranchisement. The 22,500,000 serfs to whom that measure applied were scattered for the most part over forty-six governments of European Russia. The excepted governments were Archangel, where there were hardly any serfs; the three Baltic provinces, which, as we have seen, were under a different *régime;* and the district inhabited by the Cossacks of the Black Sea, where serfdom never existed. In Siberia there were in all only 3700 serfs. Out of these 22,500,000, about 1,300,000 were *dvorovyé*, the rest were ordinary peasants.

The proclamation of enfranchisement was issued on the 3d of March 1861. By that proclamation all the serfs instantly acquired personal liberty and civil rights, but it remained to regulate the relations between them and their former masters in respect to the land. For this a period of two years was allowed.

With a view to effect this purpose, the government created a new body of officials, answering somewhat to our Justices of the Peace, and taken from amongst the gentry of the country. On them was thrown the duty of arbitrating, upon certain fixed principles, between the serfs and their former lords, and of seeing that the deeds of agreement between these parties were correctly drawn up. The clearest and most succinct account of what has been done which we can recommend to the ordinary reader, is the pamphlet published by M. Milutine in 1863 in Paris, and which was originally read as a paper at the meeting of the French Politico-Economical Society, in May 1863. M. Milutine took a very active part in carrying out the government scheme, and no man is better entitled to speak about it.

In May 1863, when he read his paper before the Economists of Paris, nearly all the necessary agreements had been drawn up. Out of 112,000 which had to be concluded, 110,098 were already finished, besides a number of agreements between the very small proprietors and their serfs. Authentic details had only been received with regard to 99,420 agreements. These 99,420 agreements represented an equal number of communes, with a male population of 8,762,956 ; out of that number, 48,023 agreements were drawn up in consequence of friendly agreement between the parties, and they applied to a male population of 3,617,079 ; 51,397 agreements, applying to a male population of 5,145,877, were drawn up by the proprietors, and received the sanction of certain provincial commissions created for the purpose, and were afterwards accepted by the serfs, although not so freely as those in the other class. There were three kinds of agreements : the first, of which there were 30,368, reserved for the proprietors provisionally the right of *corvées* or forced labour, giving, however, to the peasants the right of compounding for that forced labour by an annual payment ; the second category, which consisted of 57,750, reserved only a rent and abolished all *corvées ;* the third category, consisting of 11,302, abolished all land relations whatsoever between the serfs and their former lords, so that the former became, for a consideration, subject of course to the rights of the commune, absolute owners of the soil, or of some portion of the soil which they had formerly cultivated as serfs ; or, in other words, arrived —except in so far as the commune still remains—at that position to which it is the object of the Russian government, by means of a complicated system of arrangement of advances made through the bank, eventually to raise the whole mass of the peasantry. It may be reckoned that already, in 1864, 15·5 of the Russian serfs had become proprietors, 50·8 paid the *obrok* or rent until they were able to acquire the fee-simple of their lands, and 33·7 remained provisionally subject to forced labour, which may, however, be commuted for rent.

The *dvorovyé* received their liberty on the same day as the others, but their obligations towards their masters were provisionally retained for two years. These obligations consisted either in household or farm service, or in payment of a rent. Many of these serfs appear by a legal fiction to have had their names inscribed on the rolls of the rural communes, and many in this way have become entitled to a share in the lands allotted to the communes of serfs *adscripti glebæ ;* others, however, were not so provided for, and in this way some think that a dangerous element of pauperism has been introduced. This does not, however, seem to be M. Milutine's opinion, and economists in the west of Europe will generally share his views. Russia, during the next generation, will be a battlefield in which the rival principles of individual property and socialism will contend for the mastery. We shall be well content to see the experiment fairly tried.*

---

* It is possible, as has been stated to us on very good authority, that M. Milutine took rather too favourable a view of the success which the measure in which he was so much interested had met with at the time when he read his paper ; but we have seen no figures which can claim equal authority with those given above.

Amongst other wholesome changes which may result from the enfranchisement of the serfs, we should give particular prominence to the great reinforcement which will accrue to the class of the resident gentry. Many persons who have hitherto neglected their estates, now find themselves obliged to go to look after them, and it seems probable that during the next twenty years necessity will cause the landed proprietors of Russia to learn how to make their diminished possessions more productive under a system of free labour than they ever were in the bad old times.

Many of the effects of serf-emancipation are, of course, extremely doubtful, and the ablest of those who have studied the question have probably in store for them not a few surprises. No one can say to what an extent the break-up of the old communal system may go, nor how far the love of wandering, which is characteristic of the half-nomade Russian, may ere long be carried. Then, again, is it certain that the peasant who has hitherto only communicated with the state through the commune and his lord, will very readily come to understand the allegiance which he now owes to the law? Will the district tribunal receive the same cheerful obedience as the patriarchal assembly of the village? Will not the tendency be ever more and more to forsake the country and to crowd into towns, to exchange the allegiance to the commune for the ever-changing, elastic combinations of the trades' associations or *artels*? Will, again, the proprietors try to use their power in the provincial assemblies for the re-introduction of serfdom in some form or other? Time only can answer these and other questions; but one thing is certain, the abolition of serfdom is the corner-stone of all real reform in Russia. If that corner-stone is displaced, it is impossible to foresee the consequences, but our anticipations, if anything of the kind occurs, cannot be too gloomy.*

In the spring of 1861 a large party was gathered together at the house of a well-known Russian in London to celebrate the emancipation of the serfs. It was a meeting of a kind not usual in our staid metropolis, for the whole of the exterior of the building in which it took place was illuminated, to the astonishment and confusion of the neighbourhood. The house would have been as gay within as it appeared to be without, if it had not been for intelligence which had reached London a few hours before, and had thrown a gloom over the festival.

It was the news of the first collision between the troops and the people at Warsaw. What the news of that tragedy was to the gathering in London, that the Polish insurrection has been to the reign of Alexander II. It has dimmed— nay, in the minds of many it has altogether blotted out— the glory which had accrued from the emancipation. And yet nothing can be more utterly false than the statement which is often made by those who arrogate to themselves the title of friends of the Poles, that they "were driven to revolt by the bad government of the last two reigns." What the Poles wanted, it cannot be too often repeated, was not better government, but national independence. National independence they had a perfectly good right to wish for, and to demand, if they thought they were strong enough to obtain it, at the sword's point ; but to say that they were driven by oppression to revolt, is simply to pervert history.

* Perhaps hardly enough has been said of the great sacrifices made by the Russian proprietors. They were, to be sure, inevitable, but not the less hard to bear.

Alexander I. returned to his own dominions after the great peace, full of the most generous intentions towards Poland. In early life, while his grandmother was still alive, he had knit the closest relations with Prince Adam Czartoryski, which began in a sort of stolen interview in the Taurida Gardens at St. Petersburg, and ended in a close friendship. At one time he even dreamt of re-annexing to Poland those western provinces of Russia which she won back in 1772 from her old enemy and former oppressor; but the strong feeling which was excited by this proposal, and which found a mouthpiece in the historian Karamsine, soon induced him to dismiss from his mind his half-formed purpose. The liberal inclinations of Alexander never hardened, so to speak, into liberal principles; they were *velléités*, as the French say, nothing more. He was ready to let everybody have the most perfect liberty, provided that that liberty was never used except just as he wished it. In Poland, as elsewhere, he was always halting between two opinions; and whilst with one arm he upheld the Polish constitution, with the other he upheld the authority of his half-madman, half-monster brother, Constantine. This *régime*, at once irritating to national pride, and stimulant of national hopes, gave rise to an extensive conspiracy, which was connected with that of Pestel, and would have broken out simultaneously with it, if a premature end had not been put to the designs of that enterprising man. After the failure of both the Russian conspiracies, the Poles determined to act alone, and broke into open revolution some years afterwards. As usual, they chose a most unlucky moment, and as usual they were utterly defeated. Nicholas, when once fairly their master, used his power without a thought of mercy, and every hope of Polish independence seemed for a moment to be for ever crushed, except in the hearts of those who had escaped over the frontier. Gradually, however, two tendencies began to manifest themselves amongst the Poles in Poland—for we leave the exiles, who were feeding on hope, as usual, out of account. When Nicholas was dead, and it became possible to breathe freely, these two tendencies showed themselves more openly, and their representative men in the early years of the reign of Alexander II. were the Marquis Wielopolski and Count André Zamoyski. The first of these, who had been the envoy of the insurrectionary government in England in 1831, was fully convinced that Poland had nothing to hope from the Western Powers ; that the time was come for her to resign all ideas of political independence, and to ask only for administrative independence. The other hoped, by improving the material prosperity of the country, gradually to make it strong enough to try another fall with its mighty neighbour. The views of these two men unequally divided the gentry of Poland ; the former having very few, the latter very many partisans. Between 1831 and 1861, however, a new power had grown up. Something like a middle-class had been called into existence. This middle-class was composed of the so-called lesser nobility (an absurd term which we use for want of a better, although the persons who composed it were chiefly in the position of the humbler portion of the middle-class in England), of the Jews, and of the Catholic clergy. These sections, from various motives, but above all from a very natural and laudable patriotic sentiment, were excessively anxious for national independence, and they kept up the closest relations possible with the democratic section of the emigration ; while what we may call the aristocratic section of the emigration was in equally close connection with the party of Count André Zamoyski. The rule of Alexander II. in Poland at the beginning of his reign was milder than anything that had been known since the death of his uncle; and encouraged by the comparative mildness of his government, and hopeful of great convulsions in Russia as the result of stirring the serf question, both the Zamoyski party and the democratic party prayed and worked.

The former had for their chief organ the Agricultural Society. The latter gradually wove a great secret conspiracy extending over the whole of Poland, and connected by invisible threads with the democratic party in most Continental countries. Presently demonstrations of a religious character took place. The government, at once afraid of being inhuman, and afraid of allowing the movement to get too strong for it, wavered and took half-measures. Things got more and more alarming, and at last unarmed multitudes were attacked in the streets of Warsaw, and the first blood was shed. Then began the period of which M. de Montalembert gave an account to Europe in the eloquent and sentimental pages of *La Nation en deuil*. Every day through 1861 and 1862 the excitement in Poland grew more intense, and the determination of Russia to hold her own more savage. It was perfectly clear that the breaking out of a deadly struggle was only a question of time. The beginning of the year 1863 saw the government of Poland in the hands of the Marquis Wielopolski. Holding the views which he held, there was nothing which he so much dreaded as the outbreak of a revolution. Standing aloof from the great mass of his countrymen, and thinking the Zamoyski party and the democratic party equally unwise, he fondly hoped to be able to save his country in spite of them both. Haughty to an excess, he was restrained by neither affection nor pity from doing what appeared to him to be abstractedly best. Clear-sighted and able, but destitute of political tact, he did not feel that it is impossible to save a nation against its will, and that his only proper course would have been to retire from a position where he could do no good, and to leave the sanguine Poles and the grimly-resolved Russians to the only arbitrament which they could accept.

He decided otherwise, and fancied that by a stroke of statecraft he would get out of his difficulties.

Since the close of the Crimean war there had been no conscription in Russia or in Poland, but a new one had been ordered for the beginning of 1863. Between the close of the Crimean war and the commencement of 1863, a new law had passed, by which the old system of conscription in Poland, under which the government had the power of taking any one it pleased, had been done away with, and a system like the French had been introduced. In order to carry this out, it would have been necessary to collect large bodies of men in the towns for the purpose of drawing lots, and Wielopolski saw clearly that if this was done, the revolution which he so much dreaded, as likely to prove absolutely fatal to the country, would immediately break out. He determined, therefore, deliberately to break the law, and to cause the conscription to be made after the old fashion, with a view to get into his power, and to draft off into the army, the persons whom he thought most dangerous. His secret was badly kept, and his *coup-d'état* utterly failed, for many of those, whom he most desired to seize, escaped, and getting into the woods, began the insurrection. The broad outlines of the history of what followed are sufficiently familiar to all readers of newspapers.

Through the whole of 1863 the hopes of the revolutionists
were buoyed up by expectations of assistance from abroad,
and more especially from France. When, however, Austria,
which had connived at the export of arms and munitions of
war across her frontier, changed her policy, and began to be
as severe in her repression as the Russians themselves, all
reasonable Poles saw that the game was up, a conclusion to
which less interested observers had come some months before.

Now that all is over, we do not care to criticise the conduct either of our own government or of any other, with
regard to the Polish question ; but we do wish to press upon
all serious political students the importance of coming really
to understand the difficulties of this question, so that when
next the affairs of Poland come up for discussion, they may
be able to give some advice which will be worth listening to
upon the subject. They will be met at the outset by one
great difficulty : there is no really good book about Poland,
answering, for example, to Mr. Paget's work on Hungary.
The late war has brought into existence several *livres de
circonstance,* of which far the best is Mr. Bullock's interesting
Polish Experiences, written from the insurgent point of view ;
with which may be compared Mr. O'Brien's book written
in the interest of the victors. A paper in Vacation Tourists
by the Cambridge Public Orator, two articles which appeared last autumn in the *Spectator* and the *National Review,*
and a series which appeared in *Blackwood's Magazine,* may
also be mentioned.* What we want, however, before we

* Since this was written, Mr. Sutherland Edwards has published his
Private History of a Polish Insurrection, a more valuable work than any of
the above. See also " Le Lendemain de la Victoire en Pologne," in the
Revue des Deux Mondes for November 1864. We want, however, to know
much more of Poland than we do. To how many readers will not the follow-

can form any very definite opinions about the future of
Poland, is a book of a quite different kind—a book which
shall sum up all the resources belonging to the one party and
the other, which shall point out the difficulties in the way of
Russia's assimilating Poland, the difficulties in the way of
Poland's becoming reconciled to Russia; and after having gone
minutely into all this, shall attempt to strike the balance and
say, Whether any future Polish insurrection will or will not
deserve the sympathies of the Liberal party in Europe? Do
those who struggle for Polish independence follow a reasonable instinct which will one day lead them to attain what
they desire; or has the time come when they must submit
for ever to that "inexorable necessity," the idea of which
enraged the emigration so much when that phrase was used
in January 1864 with reference to the war which was then
drawing to a close?

It is not only from sympathy for a brave and unhappy
race, but because we are anxious to see Russia far greater
than she is, that we long for some satisfactory arrangement
of her Polish difficulty. When, however, we ask, What is to
be done? a load of despondency settles down upon us. The

ing paragraph, which we take from *Man and Nature*, by G. P. Marsh, be new
and startling?—" There are still unsubdued sand-wastes in many parts of
interior Europe, not familiarly known to tourists or even geographers. ' Olkucz and Schiewier in Poland,' says Naumann, ' lie in true sand deserts, and
a boundless plain of sand stretches around Ozenstockau, on which there grows
neither tree nor shrub. In heavy winds this plain resembles a rolling sea,
and the sand-hills rise and disappear like the waves of the ocean. The heaps
of waste from the Olkucz mines are covered with sand to the depth of four
fathoms.' No attempts have yet been made to subdue the sands of Poland,
but when peace and prosperity shall be restored to that unhappy country,
there is no reasonable doubt that the measures, which have proved so successful on similar formations in Germany, may be employed with advantage in
the Polish deserts."

struggle which so recently ceased has left behind it embers
from which may burst forth a conflagration more terrible even
than itself.   Seven years ago many enlightened Russians
wished to give up the kingdom.   Few indeed would venture
to propose that now, for there flows between Warsaw and
Moscow a stream. of blood too wide and deep to cross.
Another generation will, however, soon grow up which has
forgotten the past.   That is the only hope ; but it is a faint
one.   The Russians have, as we shall presently see, under the
able guidance of M. Milutine, lately introduced into the kingdom a territorial arrangement highly favourable to the peasants.
Their intention has been partly, no doubt, to confer a benefit on
the country, but partly also to conciliate the sympathies of
that class which was least concerned in the insurrection.   Will
they succeed ?   It is more than doubtful.

The peasants did not take a very active part in the
national movement,—not because 'they liked the Russian
government,—not because they had any great dislike to the
gentry, but because they had not sufficient education to come
within the spell of Polish nationality.   Wealth, however,
will bring education, and with education that spell will come.
The year 1888 may find Russia face to face with an insurrection as much more formidable than that of 1863, as it was,
teste Mouravieff, more formidable than that of 1831.   We are
quite ready, nay, only too anxious to be convinced that there
is a happy future for Poland ; but nothing that we have ever
heard, either from the partisans of the insurrection or from
the partisans of Russia, leads us to hope that either are strong
enough to overcome the others, and so arrive at a state, so to
speak, of stable equilibrium.   Poland must remain, we fear,
the Ireland of Russia, as much more perplexing than our

Ireland as Russia is larger than Great Britain. The fathers
have eaten sour grapes, and the children's teeth are set on
edge. Well will that Russian deserve of his country who
can in any way rid her of this terrible embarrassment.

Of course it is more than doubtful whether it is not a
positive advantage to Western Europe, that Russia, for some
time to come, till she has transformed herself into a thoroughly-
civilised state, should have a joint in her armour through
which she can always be attacked with deadly effect. Nay,
looking only to the interests of the rest of Continental Europe,
it would probably be exceedingly desirable to have a small
state bitterly hostile to Russia interposed between Germany
and that country. The question is not, however, Is this desirable? but, Is it possible? and if so, is it worth the sacrifices
which Western Europe would have to make in order to obtain
it? We are far from disposed to answer that last question by
an absolute negative.

During the first debate which took place in 1863 in the
House of Commons about Poland, there was, if we remember,
only one person who alluded to the religious element in the
insurrection. For once, that monomaniacal horror of the Jesuits,
which makes him see the finger of Rome everywhere, led Mr.
Newdegate not right, but in a right direction. It is quite true,
that on that frontier-land between two civilisations, Rome and
Byzantium were "fighting the old quarrel out." There were
causes enough of a purely political kind to bring the war about,
but the venerable feud of the "Filioque" was not without its
influences. The pleasant lectures of Dr. Stanley, who always
seizes so well the picturesque aspect of a subject, have done
something to rouse our interest in those far-scattered and too-
much-forgotten communities which, in the words of Mr. Neale,

" extend from the icefields which grind against the walls of the Solovetsky Monastery to the burning jungles of Malabar;" but we suspect that, in spite of Dr. Stanley's vivid pictures, the reader must actually stand in the Kremlin and Troitza before he fully realises what a mighty, although latent power, the Greek Church still is, and how great a part it may have to play in the drama of human history. Inert, abject, superstitious, full of abuses, it undoubtedly is. It can hardly be said to have done anything for literature or for art, nothing at least that has become famous beyond its own frontier ; and yet a form of religion which has supported its adherents under the successive deluges of misery which flowed over Russia during the middle ages, and in spite of the dull weight of wretchedness which has weighed on the Russian peasant almost up to the present hour, has made him so gentle, so enduring, so tolerant, must have some not inconsiderable merits. Its education of a thousand years must have something to do with that inexhaustible gentleness which, in the words of Schédo-Ferroti, is the base of his character ; with "that incomparable sweetness of temper which causes his soul to reflect everything in a way different to that which we observe in the lower classes of other nations."

We have more than once asked lay and clerical members of the Russian Church, whether there was any book which could give us the same sort of glimpse into the influence of their communion upon the minds of its adherents, which Miss Sewell's novels do with regard to the Church of England at this moment, or the *Memoirs of Eugénie de Guérin* do with regard to the contemporary Church of France ? We have never received a satisfactory answer, and do not believe that anything of the kind exists.

The art of the Russian Church is, as is well known, essentially conventional ; but of late years it has become less purist than formerly, and some of the modern pictures are at least graceful. The exquisite music, a modification of the old Gregorian chant, has often been described, and can never be over-praised. It is amusing to observe that controversies of which we know something nearer home have agitated the Russian Church. Mr. Sutherland Edwards mentions that the Emperor Nicholas was anxious to introduce an organ into the Cathedral of the Assumption at Moscow, but that the Metropolitan Philaret threatened to resign if this sacrilegious innovation was attempted. The story may or may not be true, but there is no doubt that the dislike of the Russian peasant to the " kist fu' o' whistles"* would be quite as intense as anything to be found in Scotland.

The reforms necessary in the Russian Church, are, alas ! of a very rudimentary kind. Before any accommodation of its dogma to the existing state of human knowledge can be hoped for, the great mass of the clergy must be raised out of the state of abasement in which they now are. Some means of providing a decent subsistence for the secular clergy, who are obliged by the ecclesiastical law to incur the expense of a family, must be discovered. They must be better educated, and educated if possible, as Schédo-Ferroti proposes, along with those who are destined for other callings. At present the son of a priest usually enters an establishment in connection with the

---

* This "organ question" has been making the tour of Europe. The writer was visiting some months ago the great Calvinist church of Debreczin, in company with one of the professors of the neighbouring college. " Oh !" he said, " you have got an organ here." " Yes," was the reply, " it was introduced some twenty years ago, and caused some discussion at first, but all that has long passed away."

theological seminary at eight years old, and, until his education is finished, associates only with persons who are destined to take orders. Further, they must be freed from the abject subservience in which they are held by their bishops, who are taken from the regular or black clergy; and lastly, they must be taught that they have duties which are quite incompatible with their performing the functions of assistants of the police.

M. Golobensky, whom Haxthausen saw at the Troitza, is now dead. Such persons are of course quite exceptional, but it would be interesting to know how many priests there are in the whole of the Russian Church who have studied any of the more important works of theology or biblical criticism, which have been produced during the present century to the west of the Vistula. The theological seminary attached to the Troitza would be called in any country but Russia a truly wretched place ; and although the educated society at Moscow speak highly of the harmony and ability of its professors, we venture to doubt whether they apply to them a very high standard of excellence.

A reader would, we think, carry away too favourable an impression of the Russian Church if he were to trust only to the interesting sketch of Dean Stanley ; and perhaps if he were to take his ideas exclusively from the pages of *Russia by a Recent Traveller*, he might, on the other hand, rate its merits too low. The truth is, that a very strong line must be drawn between the clergy of high rank and the ordinary priests. The former are much looked up to, and a high position is favourable to the development of their best qualities. The latter, when not in the exercise of their sacred office, are thoroughly despised, and the contempt, with which they are regarded, reacts upon their characters and lives.

It is sad to think that even if the mighty improvements were carried out, to which we have alluded, the Russian priests would not be necessarily superior to some of those who are justly considered nuisances and obstructions in Western Europe ; but, bad as things are in some other countries, there is in Russia a lower deep still, and as—

" Die Weltgeschichte geht unendlich lang,"

it may well be a hundred years before even these changes come to pass.

The question of the Dissidents is one of the gravest with which Russia has to deal. Stated in a sentence it is this : There are some nine millions of subjects of the Czar who are for most purposes beyond the pale of the law. The government ignores their existence that it may not be forced to act up to its own detestable principles, and to persecute them accordingly. Every act which these people can perform from birth to death is performed on sufferance or in secret. They have neither family nor right of inheritance ; indeed they can hardly be said to have any civil existence at all. Through the mazes of this difficult subject the Western reader is fortunate in possessing the guidance of the admirably-informed and most sensible writer who masks himself under the *nom de plume* of Schédo-Ferroti.

It is constantly said in and out of Russia that great danger may one day arise to the empire from a rebellion among the Dissidents, and this is the reason why they are treated with so much harshness. Schédo-Ferroti, in a chapter which is simply a demonstration, combats this idea. His reasoning is in a few words as follows :—" There are two kinds of Dissidents, the 'Bespopowzi' and the 'Popowzi ;'" that is to say, the anti-hierarchical and the hierarchical : the first kind is divided into two classes—the *sectaries*, who have nothing in common with the Russian Church, and the *schismatics*, who have kept its creed and traditions. This religious subdivision corresponds to a political subdivision, so that we have not two but three different ways of thinking with regard to the state as with regard to the church. The wild sects who form the first subdivision, full of apocalyptic ideas madder than those of Dr. Cumming himself, dream either of the imperishable empire of Ararat, or of the return of Peter III., or of Napoleon, or of Christ. Not one of them cares the least for the Russia of to-day, and they all with one accord look to the East. If China were inhabited by a great and warlike people, and some barbaric conqueror marched from it through Siberia, proclaiming that he had found the Christ in that country, or if not the Christ, then some of the other expected ones, the result would no doubt be formidable enough ; but this is out of the question, and there is not the very slightest chance of any of these people joining an enemy coming from the West. Except the Napoleon sect, they all existed in 1812, and none of them joined the French army, or dreamt of doing so. The schismatics, who admit the priesthood on principle, but as a matter of fact have no priests, have nothing in common except their hatred to the church and government of to-day, and their love for those of the long ago. Bring back Ivan the Terrible, and his Boyards and his priests, and these men might rally around him ; but if no such miracle is worked, they are not to be feared. We come, then, to the noncon-formists—the still hierarchical old believers—peaceable, laborious, well off ; they disapprove of the church as it is, and long for the times before Nicon ; but they submit quietly to the state, are perfectly inoffensive, and conservative in their inclination. The position of the Dissidents in Russia is, we thus see, only so far dangerous as any frightful social injustice is dangerous. It retards her civilisation, it weakens her power; it must be speedily amended, but a rebellion amongst these oppressed people is not to be feared.

Of course, amongst the Russian laity, who travel so much, it is easy to meet with persons whose religious ideas are those which are common amongst the most educated classes in the West. The simplest and purest form of Christianity has no national colour, and belongs to a region far above the contentions of rival churches; but there is a being in Russia rarely seen in the West, who, thoroughly and intensely attached to what he calls the Orthodox Church, yet holds its tenets as an educated man. The typical instance of this was the poet Chamiakoff, now dead, whose works, published in French, we cannot too strongly recommend as giving an insight into the Russian Church.

So surely as an Englishman is introduced to a Russian priest of rank, he will hear some civil things about the possible future union of the two Churches. The name of William Palmer is familiar to many both in Scotland and England, and there now lies before us a pamphlet, called *Papers of the Russo-Greek Committee*, which show that the dreams which were once cherished by him still live both in England and in America. Those persons who dream of effecting a union between the Anglican and orthodox communion little know the signs of the times. They remind one of Philip de Comines, who, as Arnold so truly observes, wrote as if the idea had never crossed him that the knell of the middle ages had sounded. On the eve of carrying farther the great and glorious work of the Reformation, we have something else

to do than to coquet with the Eastern Church.   And yet
these men are doing an immense deal of good.   They are
multiplying the personal relations between England and
Russia ; they are increasing good-will and toleration by increasing knowledge, the mother of both.   We wish to speak
of them with the greatest respect, although we believe that
their efforts will have no direct effect at all, till the day dawns
for that general reconciliation of Christendom which lies away
far down the centuries, in a time that we shall not know.

Politically, we are convinced that England and Russia have
all to gain and nothing to lose by being better acquainted.
M. Hertzen, writing under the name of Iscander, asked, in
1858 : " Is it not time to destroy the delusion of a rivalry,
which has its foundation only in an ignorance of geography?"
Where is it that our interests and those of Russia are likely to
clash ?   Is it in Asia, is it in the Eastern Peninsula, or is it
in Central Europe ?

Sir Henry Rawlinson, at a recent meeting of the Geographical Society,* remarked upon the apathy with regard to
Russian aggrandisement in Asia which had succeeded to the

---

* The publication of M. Vambéry's work, shortly after the above was written,
recalled the attention of the English public to this interesting subject.   The
views of M. Vambéry himself, expressed at no great length, are a little
alarmist, but if any corrective is needed it will be found in an admirable
article upon his book which appeared last year in the *Quarterly*.   1865 also
brought us a work compiled or translated from Russian sources by the Messrs.
Michell, which contains much that is curious.   This publication was, in its
turn, also made the subject of an article in the *Quarterly* by another hand.   A
pamphlet, published in 1864 by the Rev. Mr. Long, of Nil Durpan memory,
should also be consulted ; but Mr. Long has, we think, been driven by a not
unnatural annoyance at the Russophobia of some circles with which he was
acquainted, to take too roseate a view of the great northern empire.   As our
temptation, however, in England, lies generally in an opposite direction, Mr.
Long's partiality will not bias any one who is once warned that he must not
take this pamphlet as an infallible guide.

panic of twenty-five years ago, and he pointed out that the frontiers of our empires are now much nearer to each other than they were then. To us it seems that the governments of England and of Russia, if directed by wise counsels, ought to be not rivals but a support each to each in Asia. Neither of us can hurt the other seriously, except by exciting insurrections amongst our respective subjects, or stimulating the hostility of the tribes conterminous to our borders. Such a policy must react against the power that uses it, for against both the cry of religion in danger, and the cry for independence, can be easily raised. If the statesmen of the two empires thoroughly understood each other, it could be nothing but a cause of rejoicing to us that Khiva and Bokhara received laws from St. Petersburg, and the reaction against barbaric invasion which was begun by Demetrius of the Don, had reached at length the ancient capital of Timur.

Much has been said about its being the destiny of Russia to renovate our decrepit civilisation. Our civilisation is not decrepit, and her mission is a nobler one. It is to take revenge on the countries which sent forth the hordes that ravaged Europe, by forcing them to submit to the arms and to learn the arts of Frangistan. Writers like M. Michelet, who have listened too exclusively to the prejudices and the "history made to order," by Duchinski and a certain school of Polish writers, think that the Muscovite, as they delight to call him, is incapable of civilising Asia. We entirely disagree with them, and looking to what has actually been accomplished, we may say of this problem, *solvitur ambulando.*

There are many in this country who think that the importance of Constantinople has been exaggerated, and some who even go so far as to say that that great and ancient city is in our days less really important than a mushroom growth like Chicago. This last is, we think, a very questionable proposition, and we are sufficiently anxious not to see the Eastern Rome added to the gigantic empire of Russia, to listen with satisfaction to any who tell us that Russia would not be prepared to make for its possession any very enormous sacrifices. Constantinople should, we think, become, when the Turkish Empire breaks up, a free city under the guarantee of all Europe. Haxthausen points out that the religious sentiment which draws the Russian people towards St. Sophia is one of the vaguest kind, and believes that if it were ever to lead to a successful attempt upon the Bosphorus, it would undo much of the work that has been accomplished since the accession of Peter the Great, and make Charkoff and Odessa, rather than St. Petersburg and Moscow, the centres of the Russian government. Doubtless, in case of any reconstruction of Turkey, Russia might with perfect justice insist upon obtaining considerable advantages ; but we should trust that, before that event arrives, Western Europe may have come to so good an understanding, with respect to her own interests in the matter, and public opinion in Russia may have been led to take so reasonable a view of what her government has a right to claim, that any renewal of the events of ten years ago may be quite impossible. We do not dream of a golden age, but the increasing amount of intelligence, which is every year brought to bear upon public affairs, can hardly permit nations to fight as fiercely for imaginary interests, as they doubtless will continue to do for real gains or to avenge wounded pride.

Are we then likely to be brought into collision with

Russia, in order to prevent an invasion of Central Europe by the "New Huns?" We confess that we think this to the last degree improbable. It may be presumptuous to disagree with Aurelio Buddeus, whose remarks upon this subject in *Russlands Sociale Gegenwart* should most certainly be read ; but we have been too much accustomed to the panic fear with regard to Russia, which prevails from time to time in Germany, to attach the same importance to his views upon this as upon other subjects. Germany is in some respects fifty, in some a hundred, years ahead of Russia, and if she has anything to fear from that country it is entirely her own fault. If Germany becomes united, or anything like united, round a free Prussia, she may laugh at the bare idea of peril from Russia. If there were any danger of her falling, for any length of time, into the hands of such rulers as Bismark and his friends, no reasonable human being need care how soon the Cossacks are encamped in the Mark of Brandenburg.

We have not very much respect for those Russians—a very numerous class, nevertheless—who still raise the Pansclavist banner, and urge their government to make reforms, chiefly that it may be more able to go to the rescue of oppressed Sclavonians everywhere, on its way to the conquest of Europe. Those who have not learnt by this time that Russia is weak for aggression, must be very unapt scholars. In these days there are two conditions without which real power cannot exist. They are wealth and knowledge, and Russia is deplorably deficient in both. Before she has gained wealth and knowledge, all classes will have come to see that they can do something better than to ape Attila, and the strong barriers of a German union, and a united Italy, will have been formed across their path.

We fully believe that the result of Russia's entering into the sort of retirement into which she entered when Gortschakoff said, "La Russie se recueille," will be that she will come forth stronger but less inclined to aggression. The Russian is naturally peaceful ; it is the German government that has made of the empire a great camp. Intensely true is the sentiment of that poem of Chamiakoff's which is quoted by Haxthausen :—

"A LA RUSSIE.

" Le flatteur dit : Courage, sois fier, oh pays au front couronné, au glaive invincible, toi qui disposes de la moitié de l'univers.

"Pas de frontières à ton empire. La fortune obéit à un signe de ta main. Le monde t'appartient et plie en esclave devant ta majesté.

" La steppe s'epanouit en champs féconds, tes montagnes élèvent dans les airs leur tête boisée, et tes rivières ressemblent à l'océan. Oh mon pays, dépose ta fierté, n'écoute pas les flatteurs.

" Et quand tes rivières rouleraient des ondes comme l'océan, et quand tes montagnes ruisseleraient de rubis et d'émeraudes, et quand sept mers t'apporteraient leur tribut,—

" Et quand des peuples entiers baisseraient les yeux devant l'éclat de ta toute puissance, depose ta fierté, n'écoute pas les flatteurs.

" Rome a été plus puissante, les Mongols plus invincibles : Où est Rome, que sont devenus les Mongols ?

" Ta mission est plus haute, plus sainte, c'est le sacrifice et l'amour, c'est la foi et la fraternité."

Of course the Russian people have *inclinations* of conquest ; what people have not ? This very Chamiakoff astonished a friend of ours by his minute knowledge about India, and the way in which his mind seemed dazzled by the possibilities of Russia's future there. Long, however, is the way from inclinations to acts. Let the Russian people once be the masters of their own destiny, and the seventh part of the land surface of the globe, with some moderate rectifications of frontier, will seem, we think, enough for them.

The chief question for us to ask is : Are reforms progress-

ing which may destroy for ever the artificial military organisation? Of some we have already spoken, of a few others we
must speak very briefly. Let it then be observed that the
army has no longer, as it had under the reign of Nicholas,
the precedence of all other services—that one of the results
of the Crimean war was to depress the German or Petersburg party, which is always thinking of Russia's position
in Europe, and to exalt the national or Moscow party, which
looks to improvement in Russia by means of local self-
government, and which, full enough of Pansclavic aspirations,
adjourns the commencement of its Pansclavic victories for a
long time. Again, the organisation of provincial assemblies
of a constitutional kind, which is already far advanced, will
tend to increase the interest in internal reforms ; while the
great judicial changes which are already carried, or about to
be carried, into execution, will entail others, and tend still
further to occupy the national mind with its own affairs. The
intense desire for increase in material prosperity, which burst
out after the Crimean war in so many bubble speculations,
has only been checked, not stopped, by the recent commercial
crisis. Vast educational reforms have been rendered more
necessary than ever by the emancipation which has created, so
to speak, many millions of persons in Russia, where before
these were only fractional parts *of*, or dependents *on*, persons.
Lastly, let it be remembered that a profound self-distrust may
be observed in the conversation of all Russians who know
anything of Western Europe, and we think we have accumulated reasons enough to show that it will not be a trifle that
will make Russia engage in an aggressive war, for many a day
to come.*

* The following passage, quoted in the *Echo de la Presse Russe*, of the 21st

For the purposes of a defensive war she is of course enormously strong, and is becoming stronger. Nor will it do too much to reckon upon joints in her armour. Finland already possesses a sort of constitution of her own, and although there is a Swedish party, consisting chiefly of persons of Scandinavian blood, the mass of the people is by no means inclined to separate from Russia. It will be the fault of the Czar himself if he ever loses that province. If it is decently governed, it will become in time as dependable as Livonia, Esthonia, and Courland, which are about as likely to break their connection with Russia as the Shetlands are to break theirs with Scotland.

of March 1866, pretty much represents what we believe to be the state of Russian feeling on this subject :—

"Nous empruntons à la revue politique de la *Gazette* (russe) *de l'Académie* le passage suivant :

"Le peuple russe, nous semble-t-il, n'a aucun motif de vouloir la guerre : il a beaucoup à faire en temps de paix. Il lui faut avant tout poser une base solide pour ses affaires intérieures ; et s'il faut accepter comme juste la sentence continuellement répétée par les journaux français soi-disant démocratiques, que la Russie et l'Europe occidentale sont deux mondes radicalement opposés ; si tôt ou tard une lutte ouverte est inévitable entre le Russe et l'Européen occidental, dont le genre de vie et la façon de penser ressemblent si peu à ceux du Russe, et qui continue opiniâtrément à envisager la Russie de son point de vue suranné et étroit ;—si cette lutte est inévitable, nous avons toute raison de désirer qu'elle soit remise à une époque plus ou moins éloignée. Mais cela ne veut pas dire que le peuple russe puisse tranquillement permettre aux autres puissances de se poser en maîtres dans les affaires qui intéressent immédiatement la Russie. Cela ne veut pas dire, par exemple, que le peuple russe puisse voir d'un œil indifférent l'Autriche occuper les Principautés danubiennes, et en général la voir s'agrandir aux dépens de la Turquie sans la participation de la Russie. Si cet événement venait à s'accomplir, si les bruits qui représentent cette éventualité comme possible venaient à s'accréditer, la Russie ne pourrait pas s'empêcher de s'opposer à ce qu'elle se réalisât. Ce ne serait pas seulement le gouvernement qui verrait dans un événement semblable un *casus belli*, mais le pays tout entier dans le sens le plus large de ces mots. Nous en sommes persuadé, tout comme nous sommes persuadé que la Russie ne désire pas faire la guerre sans causes très-graves, sans une nécessité absolue."

As to Circassia, we cannot do better than refer the reader to an article in a recent number of *Fraser's Magazine* for 1864, on the Russian side of the question, as compared with one in the *Quarterly* for the same year, which is vehemently hostile to Russia. Every humane person must regret the misfortunes of a gallant people, but for years it has been perfectly clear that the subjugation or expulsion of these brave barbarians was only a question of time.

The disorder of Russia's finances, as to which the reader should consult M. Wolowski's recent work, tells naturally more on her capacity for offence than for defence. It is much to be hoped that the disorder in her affairs may induce her, ere long, to revise her whole fiscal and commercial system. Fortunately the free-trade party is growing rapidly, and we do not think that Russia will be the last country in Europe to abandon false economical views.

Our hopes of Russia becoming a good, instead of what it has long been, an evil force in the world, depend of course entirely on the non-resurrection of the system which prevailed up to the death of Nicholas, and the success of the wiser portion of the Liberal party.

The Liberals in Russia, as elsewhere, are divided into several sections. Of these we may count four :—1. The bureaucratic Liberals; 2. The Constitutionalists; 3. The moderate Republicans; 4. The Socialists. The first of these is headed by the Grand-duke Constantine. It is relatively strong in men of ability, and is the party which at this moment has far more power than any other. Indeed it may be said just at present to govern Russia. The second has its centre at Moscow, and is strong in several of the provinces. The landed proprietors of Twer and of Toola, more especially, have shown themselves strongly in favour of its views. The Western reader is fortunate in possessing an excellent guide to these in the works of Prince Dolgoroukoff. The traces of strong personal resentment break out continually in his writings, but the very fact that these occur so often puts those who use them on their guard. In helping to complete the picture of Russia as it is, his books are most valuable, being full of matter which it is difficult to procure elsewhere, and they are characterised very often by sound sense and political knowledge.

A remarkable article in the *Quarterly Review* for January 1863 brings out into strong relief the too unfamiliar fact that, although we are accustomed to associate Russia with ideas of an almost Asiatic despotism, parliamentary government has been, in former ages, by no means unknown on these wide Eastern plains. Taking the courtly Karamsine and the more ultra-national Aksakof, with some other writers, chiefly Russian, for his principal guides, the author shows us how "the Sclave worked out his earlier civilisation very much like the Germanic races;" how, as early as 997, we hear of a Veché or Wittenagemote at Kieff; how, in 1219, the Veché of Novgorod the Great told their prince: "If you forget your oath, we will bow you out of the city." We follow the writer with interest as he points out how the great bells which summoned the citizens to deliberate on their common affairs, continued to sound, though becoming ever rarer all through the period of the Tartar domination, until in 1510 the liberties of Pskof were overthrown by Basil IV. Within a generation after this commenced the period of those assemblies, irregularly summoned, and varying from time to time in their character and powers, which may be called the Russian

States-General. These reached almost to the accession of Peter the Great, with whom began the period of purely autocratic rule, broken, but hardly broken, by the short-lived Commission of 1767, called by Catherine II. to draft a new code, consisting of 565 deputies, and "a parliament all but in name." From that time to the death of Nicholas, little indeed was heard of representative government. But the reader should bear these facts in mind before he too rashly concludes that a government like that which Prince Dolgoroukoff desires is not suited for Russia. The third or moderate Republican party desires to see Russia divided into several great federative republics, and this is the programme which would be generally supported by the revolutionary party in the rest of Europe. This section is not very strong in point of numbers, but it is increasing. The fourth or Socialist section is very strong amongst young men, much stronger than the preceding. Many of its adherents are, no doubt, persons of good intentions, but it comprises in its ranks a great many dangerous lunatics. A ridiculous and detestable document, proceeding from this section, may be read in *Le Véridique.*

It is, we presume, with the Socialists that we ought to class a man who has been long well known in England, and has done very great services to his country, though, of course, we do not for a moment suspect him of having favoured any of the wilder views of the party, and although he is utterly disclaimed by its most advanced members. M. Hertzen was long the severest and the most dreaded censor of Russian misgovernment. Not only has he, by publishing his memoirs, given the Western world a most curious picture of the difficulties which beset the man who was bold enough to think for himself under the rule of Nicholas. Not only has he printed the

secret memoirs of Catherine II., and traced the development
of revolutionary ideas in Russia, but he has, by means of his
newspaper, the *Kolokol** or Bell, kept up an unceasing warfare
against all those proceedings, either on the part of the government or of individual functionaries, which did not appear
to him to be politic or just. It has been said that the emperor himself was one of his readers during the earlier part
of his reign ; and there is no doubt that M. Hertzen's newspaper was, in spite of rigorous prohibitions, very generally
circulated in Russia. Since the commencement of the Polish
insurrection, however, his popularity has much diminished.
Before it broke out he was thought to be only a stern monitor
of his country. Of late he has been too generally considered
to be her enemy. The views of M. Hertzen, which, as we have
seen, are more or less deeply tinged with Socialism, have
shared his unpopularity, and since his name has ceased to be
one which it was dangerous to pronounce, and he has been
freely quoted and criticised by the Russian press, he has lost
that prestige which always attaches to what is forbidden and
mysterious. He is in some sort the Mazzini of Russia,
although differing in many and most essential particulars
from that remarkable man. We do not think that the views
which he advocates, and which will be most readily gathered
by the reader from his work, *Du Développement des Idées Révo-
lutionnaires en Russie,* are likely to prevail either in Russia or
elsewhere, but his name should always be mentioned with
respect.

The antiliberal party is by no means large, chiefly because
the Czar has put himself at the head of reforms, and partly

---

* The *Kolokol* has now been transferred from London to Geneva, and only,
we believe, just contrives to exist.

because an immense number of the landed proprietors, who were no friends to the emancipation of the serfs, have since that event determined to try whether, in return for their loss of material advantages, they could not obtain greater political rights, and have in consequence joined the Constitutionalists.

No attempt to cast the horoscope of Russia will succeed, if we fail to remember that that great empire rests on a democratic basis. The middle class is altogether insignificant. We doubt whether there are half-a-million of people who could be with propriety included in it. The nobility is a body utterly different from our own, and just as different from that of Germany. Primogeniture is recognised neither by law, nor by custom, except in a very few families. The extraordinary wealth of certain great houses, and the recklessness which makes many Russians of moderate means appear very rich when they travel, because they are spending their capital, deceives the nations of "the old civilisation." We suspect that out of St. Petersburg and Moscow £2000 a-year is a large fortune for Russia. The attainment of a very low *tchin* or rank in the government service gives personal nobility. The higher ranks give hereditary nobility, which before the emancipation carried with it the right of possessing serfs.

The so-called Russian nobility, in the widest sense of the term, consists, according to Buddeus, of more than three million persons, but of these not much more than 100,000 were owners of serfs, and even in this class an enormous number were extremely poor. Very many, again, of the members of old families have hardly any property at all. Of the 120 Prince Galitzins, for example, a large proportion are princes only in name. It is unlucky indeed that the word *Kniaz* cannot be translated by some word less hopelessly misleading to English ears.

The venality and incapacity of the *tchinovniks* or functionaries, all of whom above a certain class are, as we have seen, noble in virtue of their offices, does scant credit to their order, and is one of the greatest difficulties in the way of the empire. The organisation of this powerful body, introduced by Peter the Great, but much modified since, has been often explained, and is found in all the common books about Russia. It was borrowed from countries whence it has long disappeared, and the sooner it is improved off the face of creation the better. "Who is the devil?" said a Russian peasant's child to his father. "The chief of all the *tchinovniks*," was the ready reply. A considerable check to the unrighteous gains of this class has resulted from the abolition of the brandy farming.

Without entering the government service, nobility is not retained for more than three generations. Those who desire to inform themselves about the few families amongst the Russian nobility which have anything like historical illustration to boast of, will find a full account of them in a book by Prince Dolgoroukoff, which has been translated. They are, however, few and far between. "The only aristocrat in my dominions," said the Emperor Paul, "is he to whom I speak while I speak to him." It must be said, to the credit of the Russian nobility, that, while it reckons amongst its ranks the worst enemies, it contains also the warmest friends of liberty, and this is true of all its fractions. Almost a nation in point of numbers, it is divided into as many parties as divide the nation at large.

One of the first acts of Nicholas was to entrust to the eminent jurist Speranski the codification of the Russian law. A full and interesting account of the circumstances which led to this measure, and the manner in which it was carried out, will be found in Schnitzler's* *Histoire intime de la Russie,* a book which deserves to be better known in England. Although, however, Russia is more favourably situated than our own country in respect of the form of her law, her code must be completely remodelled before she can be called by any enlightened man a thoroughly civilised state. It has been well observed, that it would be an immense boon, not only to England, but to mankind, if this country, which has incomparably the best system of law in the world, could only point to some series of volumes, not requiring the study of a life, from which that law could be learned. It sounds like a paradox, but we do not hesitate to say, that the codification of the English law would do more to advance good government in Russia and over the whole of the Continent, than any other measure that occurs to us.

The censorship has been of late relaxed, and in truth a great deal of latitude is allowed, provided certain limits are not transgressed. For a history of Russian literature

---

* This writer, whose Herodotean *naïveté* often makes his readers smile, knows probably more about the *larger* or *Russian* portion of Europe than any inhabitant of the smaller or historical portion of it, although, in some departments of research, M. de Bernhardi, M. Bodenstedt, and others, are doubtless superior to him. Up to this time, France and Germany have done most to make us acquainted with Russia. We much want a good American work on that country, to bring out the analogies between it and the United States. Railways, that greatest material blessing of the future to the empire of the Czar, will no doubt give us this. Scotland, at least, has done her duty, as the names of Gordon of Auchleuchries, of his namesake who wrote the Life of Peter the Great, of Bell of Antermony, of Wylie, of Bremner, and last, not least, of Murchison, sufficiently prove.

in recent times, in its bearing on politics, the reader should compare the work of the absolutist Gerebtzoff upon Civilisation in Russia,* with M. Hertzen's book on the Growth of Revolutionary Ideas, to which we have already alluded. Mr. Sutherland Edwards—whose *Russians at Home* is, for the Englishman who wants to read only one book on Russia, far the best we know—gives much interesting information about Russian newspapers and reviews. M. Katkoff, editor of two very important periodicals at Moscow, is perhaps at this moment one of the most popular persons in the whole empire.

One of these periodicals is a newspaper, the *Moscow Gazette*, which has taken the lead in the anti-Polish and patriotic crusade of the last three years. In its eyes the Grand-duke Constantine is what " Clemency Canning" was during the Indian mutiny to the Calcutta press. It has exalted Mouravieff into a national hero, and fostered the enthusiasm which reached its culminating point when his admirers presented him with a statue of the Archangel Michael! Before we too severely condemn this effervescence of patriotic savagery, let us reflect how we should feel if there was a serious insurrection in Ireland. Those of us who most fully admit that there has been, in times past, much atrocious injustice there, and that all is not, even now, as it should be, would, we fear, be hardly as humane as Cromwell, who at least offered his enemies the alternative of " Hell or Connaught." And the Irish, it should not be forgotten, have never invaded England, while the Poles perpetrated the most frightful cruelties in the very heart of Russia, only 252 years ago. Yet, in spite of all this, we

---

* A great deal of useful information is collected in F. R. Graham's *Science and Art in Russia*, published by Blackwood.

think that ere long the conductors of the *Moscow Gazette* will feel that they went too far, and will acknowledge that men like Walouieff and Suvaroff, who did not quite wish to "eat up the Poles alive," were wiser than they.

Another remarkable figure amongst Russian journalists is M. Aksakoff,* who, since the death of his brother, has been the most conspicuous of the Sclavophiles. The student of contemporary history may compare with great advantage the Oxford movement of 1833 with that of which he is the Coryphæus. As that was an attempt to fall back upon old English, so this was an attempt to fall back upon old Russian ideas. What William III. was to our Tractarians, that Peter the Great was to the Sclavophiles. The liberalism which Dr. Newman hated so heartily was closely allied to those "Western ideas" which were the bugbears of his representatives in "Moscow the Holy." The beautiful description of that sacred city, which is quoted by Mr. Sutherland Edwards from the *History of the Russian Church*, by the brother of the terrible Dictator of Lithuania, is conceived in the very spirit of Faber's sonnets about Oxford.

The oldest Russian University has only existed for about a century. In the 22d volume of the *Statistical Journal* will be found a paper upon the Russian Universities, which we recommend, not only because it contains a concise and intelligible account of those institutions, but because its tone represents extremely well the current views of the best class of young men in Russia. Its author, M. Koloomzine, would certainly have been *inter primos* amongst his contemporary Oxonians. We learn from him that in 1856 the whole number of students at the Russian Universities was over 4000;

* His journal has, we believe, this year (1866) ceased to appear.

thus divided :—2634 sons of nobles and employés ; 181 sons
of priests ; 316 sons of merchants ; 797 sons of persons above
the rank of serfs.   " The freedom of speech of the professors in
their lectures," says M. Koloomzine, "and the perfect freedom
of the students, causes their general spirit to be very high and
liberal."   It should be observed that this paper was written
before the disturbances at the University of St. Petersburg,
which attracted some attention in England, and which gave
an opportunity to the reactionary clique to try to alarm the
emperor.*   Since those events, the Russian University system
has been in confusion, but plans have been considered for its
re-organisation, and it is hoped that these, under the management of M. Golownine, the present Minister of Public Instruction, who is a man of ability and liberal inclinations, will
soon be in thorough working order.

The education of the higher classes in Russia is conducted
to a great extent at home, a custom of which Nicholas naturally enough disapproved.   Their proficiency in modern languages
has often been remarked.   This arises much more from the
fact that they travel a great deal, and are accustomed from
their earliest years to speak several languages, than from any
peculiar aptitude.   It is said, and probably with truth, that
their attainments are somewhat superficial ; but we are inclined to think that a Russian of good family at twenty-two
will in general be more really educated, as well as more ac-

* These disturbances were mainly traceable to the measures introduced by
Admiral Putiatine, a worthy man, much respected by his private friends, and
much at home on the quarter-deck, who had been made Minister of Public
Instruction.   The notion of an admiral being placed in such a position is, of
itself, sufficiently ridiculous; but Admiral Putiatine was peculiarly ill-fitted
for his place, because he had added to the fanatical prepossessions of an
orthodox Greek some of the special delusions of the Tractarian party in
Oxford.

complished, than an Englishman who has gone through Eton and Oxford with no more than the usual knowledge of those who only aspire to take an ordinary degree. It is later in life that an Englishman, who has been an idle boy at school and idle man at college, is forced by the pressure of competition, or by the duties that are thrown upon him, to become fit for something; while the young Russian, hampered by a vicious political system, too often sinks into a lounger or a debauchee. It is English public and professional life which reflects light on our wretched English education.

The dark side to all this progress, and to all those inclinations towards improvement, does not reveal itself till we know how brilliant was the promise of the years from 1815 to 1826, and how terrible was the period which succeeded to that premature spring. Liberty has hardly yet struck roots in the Russian soil. Let but the Autocrat give the sign, and many of the wise words which we now hear will cease to be uttered. Luckily, humanity has a hostage in the interest of those in power, no less than in their good-will. A return to the system of Nicholas means political ruin. It means a period of insolent triumph at home, and lowered influence abroad, followed by conspiracies, outbreaks, and revolution.

Buddeus mentions that the Czar constantly repeats the words, "Better from above than from below." If so, he is, as Cavour once said to the writer of this paper, when speaking of Louis Napoleon, "*Un homme habile qui connait son peuple et son temps.*" We hope everything for Russia; but our hopes are mingled with fears, which the reader who has accompanied us through the preceding pages will hardly think unreasonable. What Custine said is, we fear, still true :—" Russia is the country in Europe where men are most unhappy." Before she reaches the point at which we in England have arrived—great as are the still uncured evils of our society—she has many a difficult crisis to traverse. Will she ever succeed in reconciling Poland to her sway, or in cutting adrift and converting into a peaceful and friendly neighbour so much of that country as she cannot assimilate? Will she be able to substitute for her communal organisation, so unfavourable to individual enterprise, a system like that of the West, without creating a mass of pauperism worse than that with which we are struggling? or, if not, will she succeed in a new experiment, and reconcile the commune with advanced agriculture and civilisation? Will the empire hold together under one central authority? or, if not, will its surface be covered by independent communities, which will keep the peace, and do no hurt each to the prosperity of each? Will the Russian Church shake off those unnumbered superstitions, and rise from that abasement which makes it, for all purposes of influencing human conduct, far inferior to Rome, although it has never committed itself to the worst Roman absurdities? Will, in short, the high and pure form of Christianity, which is held by the best minds in Germany and England, be substituted in any reasonable length of time for the delusions which now prevail? Will the universal venality of the functionaries be gradually amended? Will the army be reduced within reasonable limits, and military service cease to be a curse and a scourge to the population? Will justice and law be soon substituted for the arbitrary decisions of power? Will the Russian government, while asserting its fair claims as a European power, more especially in the Eastern Peninsula, learn that its true field of fame is Northern and Central Asia? Will the experiments we are working out teach Russian statesmen that nothing is gained by fostering branches of industry which have no real affinity for the country? Will a succession of wise and moderate rulers inaugurate and watch over the commencement of constitutional government; or will Russia have to win her liberties, as others have won them, with blood and toil? Who can answer these questions? and yet, while they remain unanswered, how uncertain must be the future of this mighty empire, and of the political state-system of which it forms so important a part!

*   *   *   *

The period of twenty months which has passed since the preceding paragraph was originally published, has not, we need hardly say, given any answer to the questions contained in it. Under the calm surface of official Russia there is still a vast ocean heaving under contending winds, and agitated by opposing currents. What the end may be it is impossible to say; but we may safely assert that no generation of Englishmen, except that which saw the first French Revolution, has ever assisted at so remarkable a spectacle as is likely to be presented between this and the end of the century in the vast dominions of the Czar. Amongst the more satisfactory symptoms, we may note the gradual carrying out of the arrangements between the peasants and their landlords, which are every year placing a larger number of *ci-devant* serfs in the position of free proprietors. Another favourable circumstance is the continuance in office of several ministers who are, at least relatively, liberal and enlightened. The most important of these are, the Minister of War, General Milutine, brother of the administrator of that name, of whom we have already spoken, and M. von Reutern, who manages the finances. M. Golownine has just, we regret to say, retired, but the ministry of the Interior remains under the control of M. Walouieff, a man of much ability and very liberal tendencies, against whom we have never heard any reproach, except that he is said by some to be over-conciliatory, whence his Russian nickname of " Vilaieff," *the Tacker.* All these men are understood to share the views of the Grand-duke Constantine, and they are, in consequence, bitterly detested by those who think that the system of Nicholas was perfection, and by the would-be ultra-patriotic party. As there is no solidarity in the Russian Council of Ministers, which is in no sense a cabinet, it is not surprising that several of the colleagues of the persons, whom we have mentioned, should have quite other views.

The great fires which occurred in the heart of St. Petersburg in the summer of 1862, following as they did the disturbance at the University already noticed, were connected in the language, and perhaps in the minds, of the reactionary party, with the designs, not only of an extreme anarchical faction, but with the liberal feeling which was generally abroad. It is, however, more than doubtful whether they would have succeeded in making political capital, out of these events, if the great moral conflagration of the Polish insurrection had not speedily followed. The friends of the old order were, of course, not slow to attribute this to the encouragement given in high quarters to the political heresies of the times, nor can it be denied that their explanation was to a great extent correct. If the system pursued by Nicholas in Poland had been continued by his successor, the same results would have attended it, and the Polish insurrection, instead of breaking out in 1863, would have been deferred to the moment when an enlightened ruler found the process of slowly strangling a nation incompatible with his ideas of right. But it was not the reactionary party alone that was carried away by its anti-Polish rage. M. Katkoff was, as we have seen above, some few years ago, by no means a reactionist. Far from it, he was an ardent advocate of self-government, and more than suspected of Anglomania. No one, however, has been more furious in his denunciations of anything approaching moderate measures since the suppression of the Polish insurrection. No one has attributed more sinister political meaning to the fires* which have raged so much of late years in Russia. No one has been more defiant towards Western Europe. No one has been so quick to discover separatist tendencies in Georgia, or in the Baltic provinces. No one has gone such lengths in attacking the Grand-duke Constantine, and indeed every other human being who has ventured to think that a Pole had a right to live, or a Russian to differ from the *Moscow Gazette*. If this was to be attributable merely to the insanity of an individual, it would be of no great importance, but it means more than this. It means that the Polish insurrection has reacted unfavourably on vast numbers of people in Russia, and has thrown back the advance of enlightenment in that country for some years.

The death of the heir to the crown in the spring of 1865 cast a gloom over the whole of Russia. All accounts combine to represent his character as a singularly attractive one ; and he seems to have been entirely devoid of that passion for soldiering which is so great a snare to Russian rulers. About the same time took place an event which had

---

* In 1864 there were 13,000 fires, attributable partly, no doubt, as in Turkey, to political discontent, but largely also to the great increase of drunkenness, to the careless use of lucifer matches, and to the innumerable accidents to which wooden houses are always liable in a climate where great artificial heat is a necessary condition of human life.

been long looked for and ardently desired—the recal of General Mouravieff. We wish we could say that the sway of his successor had been as much milder as the moderate party desired. In the kingdom General Berg seems to have been relaxing the rigour of his reign as far as the "res dura et regni novitas" permitted, which is, perhaps, not saying a great deal ; but in the western provinces an effort is being made to get rid of the Polish proprietors altogether and to replace them by Russians. It may be said, of course, that this is a just retribution for the foolish attempt of the Poles to wrest these wide districts from their mighty neighbour ; but the doctrine of the "væ victis," carried out to all its consequences, is shocking to the nineteenth-century mind, at least in this part of Europe. Nor does it appear to us at all very clear that Russia will attain her object ; and if she does not, the amount of "misery in waste," as Bentham would have called it, will be tremendous. A fierce polemic upon this subject has been raging in the Russian press—the leading champions being the *Moscow Gazette*, which represents, we need hardly say, the Pole-devouring party, and the *Wiest*, a journal directed by M. Skariatine, and established chiefly for the purpose of opposing the high-handed system of dealing with property, which the changes necessitated by the emancipation of the serfs have made dangerously familiar to this generation of Russians. The varying fortunes of the strife between these journals, and indeed the whole play of Russian political thought, may now be followed with the greatest ease by all educated persons in this country. For nearly a year there has appeared twice a-week in Brussels, under the editorship of M. Schédo-Ferroti, a journal called *L'Echo de la Presse Russe*. The editor makes it his business to examine all the principal Russian newspapers, and to select from them the more important articles, wholly irrespective of the opinions advocated. Most of the extracts are of course in Russian, but some are in French and German; and a careful French *résumé*, filling generally about two columns of large print, is prefixed to the whole.

So excellent a means of acquiring information about what is passing in Russia, being now, so to speak, brought to the very doors of our political writers, we trust that they will take advantage of it, and not content themselves with information filtered through Central European newspapers, which are often accidentally and often intentionally incorrect in their Russian information.*

A circumstance which happened in connection with M. Schédo-Ferroti in 1864 curiously illustrates the state of parties in Russia. In the summer of that year he wrote a singularly moderate and sensible little book, called *Que fera-t-on de la Pologne.* It reflected very exactly the kindly and conciliatory views with respect to that unhappy country,

---

* On the history of Russia during the last two years, an article by M. C. de Mazade, in the *Revue des Deux Mondes* of the 15th March 1866, should be consulted. This paper has been furiously attacked by the *Moscow Gazette,* which attributes it—we believe without the slightest shadow of foundation— to the object of that journal's especial aversion, M. Schédo-Ferroti. One would think that that gentleman, instead of being, as he is, a Courlander—a native, that is, of one of the provinces most faithful to the Imperial House— was a Pole or a Frenchman, so fierce is the animosity of the crazy party of which M. Katkoff is the mouthpiece.

A valuable addition to our knowledge of Russian commerce has been made by the report on the present state of the trade between Great Britain and that country, which was drawn up by Mr. Michell, one of the secretaries to Her Majesty's Embassy at St. Petersburg; and we believe it is to the same gentleman that English travellers are now indebted for a handbook which has replaced the miserable performance which, up to last year, disfigured Mr. Murray's list.

which the most extreme provocation does not seem to have banished from the mind of the Grand-duke Constantine. This book was sent by the Minister of the Interior and by the Minister of Public Instruction to many establishments of which they had the official superintendence. Amongst others it was sent to the University of Moscow, but was returned unopened by that body, while a perfect storm burst upon the heads of the unlucky ministers, and a howl of execration, led of course by M. Katkoff, reached the quiet study of the enlightened publicist at Brussels, who had dared to counsel moderation and common sense. The violence of the *Moscow Gazette* became so intolerable that the two insulted ministers attempted to restrain it, but all in vain. Opinion was too strong, and the struggle ended in the majority of the imperial advisers taking the side of the journalist.

The rigour of the censorship has been of late relaxed in favour of the newspapers of the capitals, and a system of *avertissements* on the French plan to some extent substituted for it. This indulgence is not, however, extended to the provinces, and we witness at this moment an amusing result. The *Moscow Gazette* may abuse the system on which the relations between the Esthonian or Lettish peasantry and the German landowners of the Baltic provinces is founded, and the *Riga Gazette* is not allowed to say a word on the other side.

With regard to the re-organisation of Poland, which has been proceeding steadily since the close of the insurrection, we do not feel ourselves qualified to speak. The views of the Polish proprietors have found eloquent expositors in the French press, and those who desire to know them will find no difficulty in informing themselves; but we make no

apology for laying before our readers the following extract
from an unpublished work by M. Nicholas Tourguéneff, a
man not likely to take a violent or prejudiced view of this or
any other subject, and who has lived for more than forty
years far away from "Muscovite" influences, in the very centre
and focus of the civilisation of the West.

Speaking of the arrangements introduced by M. Milutine,
he says :—

"Préparée sagement, honnêtement, justement, la grande œuvre a
été accomplie de même. Nous ne dirons pas que nous sommes fiers
mais on nous permettra bien de dire que nous sommes heureux de ce
qu'elle a été accomplie par un tzar Russe et par des Russes.

"Ceux dont les intérêts ont souffert peuvent être mécontents—cela,
se comprend ; mais ce qui est incompréhensible c'est que des hommes
désintéressés matériéllement, des hommes professants des idées libérales,
n'aient salué cette réforme que par des déclamations sur le socialisme,
etc. ; ne se donnant pas, et ne voulant pas se donner la peine d'appro-
fondir tant soit peu la question.

"La réorganisation de l'état des paysans dans le royaûme de Pologne,
nous l'appelons émancipation, quoique ces paysans fussent dejà en possession de la liberté personelle ; en réalité leur position ne différait
guère de celle des paysans serfs. Jadis les paysans polonais comme les
paysans russes, étant serfs, possédaient quelque chose : le bétail, les
instruments de travail, la maison qu'ils habitaient, tout cela ils le con-
sidéraient comme leur bien et ce n'est que très-rarement qu'on voyait
les propriétaires les en priver ; mais bientôt apres le décret de Napoléon
et l'introduction du code civil qui octroyaient aux paysans la liberté
personelle, parut un édit du Roi de Saxe, Grand-duc de Varsovie, qui
déclara tous ces biens des paysans appartenant aux propriétaires. La
fameuse 'juridiction patrimoniale' qui existe encore de nos jours en
Mecklenburg, s'établit dans le duché de Varsovie, puis dans le Royaume.
Le propriétaire était en même temps voït ou administrateur de la commune, juge de premiere instance et maître de police, avec le droit
d'infliger aux paysans des punitions corporelles. Peu à peu, les propriétaires, trouvèrent avantageux de diminuer ou de supprimer les lots
de terre occupés par les paysans, transformant ainsi les hôtes ou fer-
miers en simples ouvriers ou prolétaires.

"En 1846, un dècret de l'Empereur Nicolas interdit aux propriétaires de priver les paysans de leur terres ou de les renvoyer. Ce dècret ne fut jamais exécuté. L'administration polonaise à force de ruses et d'interprétations, fit de cette ordonnance une lettre morte. quoique la volonté de l'Empereur fut claire et précise. A la tête de cette administration se trouvait le vice-roi russe, mais les employés qui l'entouraient etaient des Polonais dévoués aux interêts non des paysans, mais des propriétaires. Les paysans continuèrent à être privés de leur terres et sur trois millions et demies ils en trouva 1,300,000 privés de toute propriété territoriale, des prolétaires enfin.

" L'émancipation des paysans en Pologne dans ses bases principales, correspond à l'émancipation des paysans en Russie.

" Comme en Russie, les paysans polonais réçoivent en toute propriété la terre sur laquelle ils vivent et qu'ils cultivent pour leur propre compte. Le pouvoir administratif municipal et le pouvoir judiciaire de premiere instance sont confiés à des hommes élus par les paysans euxmêmes. Les propriétaires réçoivent pour la terre acquise par les paysans des obligations rapportant 4°/₀ et amortissable en 42 ans. Mais dans l'application de ces principes fondamentaires il y a un différence importante entre l'émancipation en Russie et en Pologne.

" En Russie la somme entiére du rachat des terres données aux paysans tombe sur les paysans eux-mêmes et cela les oblige à un très lourd impôt pendant 49 ans. En Pologne on a augmenté pour ce rachat les impôts directs sur la propriété immobiliére à l'exception de la propriété des paysans. En outre une partie des biens de la couronne doit être vendue, et le produit de la vente employé au rachat. Quant aux paysans, ils auront à payer comme impôt le double de ce qu'ils paient à présent, soit au gouvernement, soit à la commune. De cette maniére les paysans contribueront aussi au rachat.

" Un autre différence existe dans l'application du principe de l'administration communale (self-government). Les propriétaires russes en perdant leur anciens droits seigneuriaux, ne perdent pas leur autres droits et privilèges de caste. La noblesse est restée caste, avec ses marèchaux élus, ses assemblées et toutes les attributions d'une classe privilégiée et l'administration communale et les tribunaux communaux ne peuvent avoir d'action que sur les paysans.

" Dans le royaume, les droits et privilèges des propriétaires ne consistaient que dans leur droits seigneuriaux ; en perdant ces droits, ils doivent nécessairement faire partie de la commune, comme les autres habitants. Ils ne peuvent en être détachés.

" De toutes les objections à l'émancipation, deux seulement nous paraissent dignes de mention."

*　　　*　　　*　　　*

Here follow some remarks about the rights allowed to the peasants in the woods of the proprietors, and the power given them, under certain circumstances, to reclaim lands taken from them contrary to the ukase of 1845.

" Le Comité Constitutif ne manquera pas de trancher avec son équité habituel, ces difficultés. Malgré toute la bonne volonté du gouvernement, il ne peut pas espérer de donner des terres à tous les prolétaires, il laisse beaucoup d'entre eux dans leur situation actuelle, ceux surtout qui ont été privés de leur maisons et logés dans une espéce de casernes construites par les propriétaires ; mais autant que possible les prolétaires seront établis sur les terres de la Couronne.

" Si l'on reproche au gouvernement d'avoir favorisé les paysans contre les propriétaires, nous répondrons par les chiffres d'estimation des prestations personelles des paysans, chiffres qui ont servi de base à l'evaluation due de l'indemnité aux propriétaires : en Galicie un jour de travail d'un ouvrier a été évalué à 3 kops. d'argent et un jour avec attelage de deux bœufs ou de deux chevaux à 15 kops. ; dans le royaume, une journée est fixée de 7½ à 12 kops. et une journée avec attelage 30 à 45 kopecks.

" La somme du rachat, capitalisée d'apres une évaluation aussi modérée était divisée en Galicie en trois parts dont une part tombait sur le paysan qui était obligé de la payer au propriétaire. La seconde a été payée à ce dernier par le gouvernement ou la province, et la derniére tombait sur le propriétaire lui même, c'est à dire qu'il la perdait. En Posnanie, comme dans toute la Prusse, les paysans reçurent gratuitement leur maisons, et la moitié, dans certains cas les deux tiers, de la terre occupée par eux, avec le droit de racheter l'autre moitié ou le tiers restant. Cela prouve jusqu'à l'évidence que sous le rapport de l'appropriation des terres aux paysans, les propriétaires du royaume de Pologne se sont trouvés dans une position plus avantageuse que les propriétaires de la Galicie et de la Posnanie.

" Il était impossible de compter sur la sympathie des nobles Polonais dans cette affaire et l'éxécution dut en être confiée à des Russes. Des hommes connus par leur valeur morale et intellectuelle, de jeunes officiers pleins de zèle et de dévouement contribuèrent par un travail acharné au succès de l'entreprise. ' Marchez au travail,' disait à ces hommes de bonne volonté celui qui les dirigeait, ' marchez au travail, et faites en sorte que dans la posterité la plus reculée, quand il n'y aura peut-être plus de Russes en Pologne, on ne souvienne encore parmi le peuple, qu'un jour le tzar de Russie envoya des Russes qui donnérent aux paysans la terre et la liberté !'

" De telles instructions pourront paraitre ètranges à ceux qu déclament avec tant de complaisance contre la Russie. Elles diffèrent sans doute des instructions données généralement en des occasions semblables, des conseils, par exemple, que donnait,—dans des sphères sans doute incomparablement plus hautes,—l'Empereur Napoléon à son frère Joseph roi de Naples.

" Le fait est que tout ce qui a été accompli en Pologne pour l'émancipation des paysans l'a été honnêtement, sagement et jusqu'à présent avec succès. Les paysans temoignent une confiance illimitée aux Russes chargés d' introduire le nouveau règlement. Les elections faites par les paysans ont été en général satisfaisantes. Ils ont nommé comme maire (voit), quelques un des anciens propriétaires on de leur intendants ; le plus souvent, sans doute, des paysans jouissant de la considération générale.

" On peut assurément considérer cette émancipation des paysans Polonais, en la detachant de toute circonstance environnante, comme une grande chose, juste et equitable, et contribuante au bien de l'humanité. Peut-être dans l'avenir apparaitra-t-elle aux Polonais plus bienfaisante qu'ils ne le supposent à present.*

" Néanmoins la situation générale du pays est triste, douloureuse et nous ne nous serions jamais décidés à parler en ce moment de la Pologne et de son avenir, si son sort n'était intimement lié à celui de la Russie, et c'est uniquement sous ce rapport que nous pouvons et que nous voulons parler de la Pologne.

" Les Polonais ont évidemment sur leur pays leur manière de voir, leur désirs, leur espérances ; pour nous, desirs et tendances ne vont pas au delà de la Russie.

M. Tourguéneff believes that Russia and Poland, which it has been found impossible to weld together under a despotism, might be bound to each other by a common constitution, and a common parliament. In his ardent attachment to constitu-

---

* A présent même, quelques Polonais éclairés en reconnaissent l'utilité. Au procès de Berlin, un des prevenus, Monsieur Niègolewski, membre de la Chambre des Députés Prussienne, dit dans son interrogatoire : " Je me félicite d'avoir pris part à cette lutte qui a amené, en fin de compte, l'émancipation des paysans du royaume de Pologne et de la Galicie, reclamée en vain depuis tant d'années par la noblesse." — Le Temps, 8 Septembre 1864. Nous ne savons si c'est un erreur du traducteur qui mentionne la Galicie, ou l'émancipation avec la terre a en lieu dès 1849. Quant à l'ancien désir de la noblesse, nous nous bornerons à dire : Tant mieux !

tional government, even for Russia, he differs at once from
reformers like M. Milutine, and from reformers like M. Schédo-
Ferroti, but he has with him a large and increasing party
amongst the educated class in Russia.　Hitherto, the government of the Czar has shown itself singularly impatient of any
hints at a desire for a central representative government, and
the nobles of Moscow, in 1865, were rebuked almost as sharply
as those of Twer and Toola in 1862.　Nor does it appear that
there is for the present the slightest chance of anything being
done in this direction.　The best that we can expect, is the
gradual introduction, from above, of judicious measures of
improvement, many of which will look better on paper than
they will work ; but by which, nevertheless, a vast amount
of evil will be swept away.　After all, the rule of the present
Czar has lasted only ten years, and yet how much has been
effected !　To say nothing of the emancipation of the serfs, and
the gradual creation of an enormous mass of free proprietors—
surely one of the greatest changes for good which has ever been
effected by a single act—we have the relaxation of the censorship, the reduction of the price of passports from £80 to a figure
which permits any one to travel, the abolition of several atrocious methods of punishment, the institution of representative
bodies for local matters, an amnesty which restored to their
country many of the victims of Nicholas, a humaner system in
the navy, improvements in the Universities, increased facilities
for communication, and a generally gentler and more civilised
spirit in the administration.　When we reckon up the gains
and the losses of the Crimean war, do not let us omit to remember that these were amongst the things which it procured.
Nothing less violent than that catastrophe would have sufficed
to break up the system of Nicholas.　We know that there are

many dark shades which must be filled in if we would complete the picture. We appreciate, to the full, the horror of the Polish tragedy. We know that people, writing of the rule of General Kauffmann in Lithuania, speak of "le bon vieux temps de Mouravieff." We know that the Russian nobility has suffered severely, to the extent often of a fourth or more of its income. We know that there is a violent anti-social faction, and a faction which thinks that the system of Nicholas was perfection. We know that many of the improvements which we have instanced are merely beginning to work, and that Russia is only commencing the race of civilisation ; but after making every deduction, we still think that, unless the policy of Alexander II. very materially alters, he is likely to take a high place amongst the benefactors of mankind. The atrocious attempt to assassinate him which has just startled Europe will, we fain hope, turn out to have been the act of a man of impaired intellect. Certain it is that nothing more unfortunate for the cause of the liberal party in Russia could possibly have occurred. It has been taken advantage of by the most savagely "National" section of the press to call for vengeance upon all Poles and revolutionists, while the government, we regret to see, has confided the conduct of the investigation to General Mouravieff, an officer whose iron rule in Lithuania at a time when the stamping out the rebellion in that district was a matter of life and death for Russia, can be readily explained, but who is surely the last man in the world to be entrusted with an investigation which requires great tact, complete absence of prejudice, and a judicial mind.

CHAPTER III.

MR. BONER, in the first chapter of his very agreeable book on Transylvania, tells us that he went one day into a bookseller's shop at Vienna, and asked for a map of that country. On examining the one which was handed to him, he observed to the bookseller, " that the different divisions of the districts were not marked." " That is no matter," said the man, quite gravely ; "in a week perhaps all may be changed. If I were to give you the map you want, before you reached Transylvania very likely everything might be altered."

The answer was a sensible one enough, and the bookseller's words hold good not only of the boundaries of Transylvanian districts, but of almost everything in the Austria of to-day, except the natural features of the land. All is in a state of chaos,—a chaos out of which we ardently hope that a new and fairer empire may arise, but a chaos which no one would attempt to describe in detail, and the ultimate outcome of which no wise man would attempt to predict, except in the broadest of most general terms. It can hardly be doubted, however, that all through 1866 the affairs of Austria will engage the earnest attention of those for whom European politics have any interest ; and in this belief we have thought it not undesirable to lay before our readers such a sketch of recent Austrian history as may enable them to judge for themselves as to the bearing of the events which will follow each other in that country, through the successive months of a year, which can hardly fail to determine whether Austria is, or is not, during the remainder of the nineteenth century, to have any claim to her traditional epithet of " Felix."

We shall not, of course, shrink from expressing our opinions upon the most important questions relating to the empire, which are now demanding, or will soon demand, solution ; but we shall express those opinions with the utmost diffidence, and in the fullest conviction that the statesmen who shall conduct Austria happily through the next two decades of her history, will have to deal with a succession of problems as difficult as any which have ever called forth political genius and administrative ability.

An attempt to sketch the recent history of Austria has been much facilitated by the publication of the *Geschichte Oesterreichs seit dem Wiener Frieden*, 1809, by Professor Springer of Bonn, the second volume of which appeared a few months ago. This elaborate and most able work terminates with Görgei's surrender at Világos in August 1849, and we have used it as our guide down to the revolution of 1848. The period from 1849 to the ᵉ present day is hardly yet historical, but there is, of course, no lack of information with regard to it in pamphlets and articles, to some of the best of which we will refer in the proper place. Upon Hungary, which is at this moment the most interesting part of the empire, the English reader is fortunate in possessing two works, written by no common men, from very different points of view. These are the travels of Mr. Paget and of Mr. Paton. The first of these books was published in 1839, and the author looks at the politics of that period like a Hungarian Whig, if indeed we can properly apply a term, taken from our own party warfare, to that of a country so dissimilar. Numerous and important as are the events which have occurred in Hungary since Mr. Paget's volumes were given to the public, they still deserve to be read ; and it is strange that so useful a work should not have sold more extensively than we have reason to believe it has done.

Mr. Paton, so well known for his travels in the Eastern Peninsula, visited Hungary immediately after the surrender at Világos, and remained a considerable time in the country. His book is extremely useful as a corrective to the one-sided accounts which were so freely supplied to our press by the Kossuthian propagandists in London. He is by no means disposed to justify the violent measures of centralisation which were introduced under the auspices of M. Bach ; but his sketches of that politician, as well as of Schwartzenberg, appear to us much too favourable. At the same time, we think that no one who attempts to form an opinion about recent Austrian history, exclusively from English authorities, would do at all wisely to neglect a careful perusal of what this most intelligent, painstaking, and well-informed author has to say upon the unpopular side.

Mr. Boner writes rather as a traveller and observer of manners than as a politician, but in all that he says about politics he evidently desires to be thoroughly impartial, and his observations must be taken as " evidence to go to a jury," in favour of the system which prevailed from 1861 till last September. Great insight into the real wants of the Hungary of to-day is given by the work of Dr. Erasmus Schwab, of which, so far as we are aware, only the first volume has ap-

peared. This gentleman was for eight years a schoolmaster
in Northern Hungary, during which period he not only came
to know intimately the district in which he was settled, but
travelled on foot in various parts of the country, and became
familiarly acquainted with all ranks and classes. The book
is full of conversations, which bear the stamp of truth, and is
a most valuable contribution to our knowledge.

The modern history of Austria may, for our purpose, be
considered to commence with the reign of Joseph II. The
imperial philosopher had drunk deep and long at the foun-
tains of eighteenth-century enlightenment, and hastened, as
soon as he became the sole ruler of his hereditary dominions,
to carry his revolutionary ideas into effect. He saw around
him an array of provinces connected with each other by their
common allegiance to himself, and by the influence of long
habit or artificial arrangements. Scattered across Europe
from the English Channel to the half-barbarous regions where
the Crescent and the Cross carried on a ceaseless warfare, the
possessions of the House of Austria were bound to each other
by few of those links which usually hold together a body
politic. The critical eye could distinguish only one feature
which was common to them all. They were all behind the
age ; they were all governed rather by custom than by right
reason. Everywhere there was a clergy, always obscurantist,
always jealous of the civil power, and but too often inclined
to persecute. Everywhere there was a nobility, penetrated
sometimes by rays from the sun of Paris, but for the most
part thinking of little except the preservation of its own
privileges. Everywhere there was a peasantry, oppressed and
unhappy—subject in some districts to feudal exactions, and in
others bound by customs different from, but not less unjust than,

those of feudalism. Into this world of unreason and of wrong the emperor determined to introduce regularity and common-sense. That he may have been influenced to some extent by personal motives, we do not care to deny ; nay, rather, we have no doubt that he expected his own position to be materially improved by the change. Still his motives, although mixed, were mainly good, and he has hardly yet received from his countrymen, or from Europe, as much praise as he merits. In laying his plans, however, Joseph II. characteristically omitted to allow for the disturbing influence of two forces,—the blind attachment of ignorance to old usages, and that regard for traditional rights, even when they work ill, which is one of the best features of half-civilised communities. These two forces were quite enough to break up the whole of his elaborate scheme for the reconstruction of Austria, the former acting chiefly in the Germanic and Germanised provinces, the latter in Hungary.

In that country the fierce and intractable spirit of the ruling class showed itself immediately, but in the other crown lands the storm did not burst in its full fury until the emperor was in his grave, although he had to recal most of his acts. It was left for Leopold to receive from all the assemblies of the Germanic or Germanised provinces earnest representations as to the ruinous consequences which would follow, if the peasants were not replaced in their old state of vassalage ; if the privileges of the nobles were not extended and increased ; if the Jews, Freethinkers, Protestants, and foreigners were not once more oppressed ; if pilgrimages were any longer discouraged; if the schools were not again put under the control of ecclesiastics, and if the old privileges in matters of taxation were not immediately restored.

To some of these representations the government listened with pleasure, to others it turned a deaf ear, and in all cases it acted on the principle of keeping as much as possible of the Josephine legislation, when that legislation was favourable to the central authority, but surrendering as much of it as it well could, when what it surrendered was favourable to popular rights and the freedom of opinion.

The movement in Hungary was far more serious, for here the government had to do, not with discontented nobles, but with an angry nation. The popular belief as to the relations between the king and the people of Hungary was summed up in the phrase—"*Princeps est, qui jurat, qui jurata servat et qui coronatus est.*" Now Joseph II., intending to introduce great changes in Hungary, and not wishing to incur the charge of perjury, had never taken the oaths, and had never been crowned. Many of the changes which he had introduced were excellent, but in introducing them he had not only altogether exceeded his powers, but had given a fair colour to the assertions of those who maintained that, under the circumstances, it was no longer necessary that the Hungarian crown should rest on the brow of a prince of the House of Hapsburg-Lorraine. The emperor wisely yielded on most points, and agreed even to the assembling of the Diet in 1790. Before it came together, he had breathed his last. His two successors had much to do to calm the agitation which he had caused, but they succeeded for a time, and the real results of the reaction from his centralising legislation did not appear till the winds were loosed in the days of the Emperor Ferdinand.

The liberal innovations of Joseph II. had been the result of his personal convictions, and these were by no means shared by the councillors who surrounded his successor. It did not

suit them, however, to allow the nobility to reap the full advantage of the reaction, and to get into their hands a large
share of the power which had been hitherto vested in the high
officials.   They fell back accordingly upon the venerable
Austrian maxim, "*Divide et impera*," and checked the rising
ambition of the Provincial Estates by favouring the pretensions
of the peasants.   By this policy they contrived to bring back
things to a state of stable equilibrium ; and to careless observers, the empire, when it passed into the hands of Francis,
in 1792, did not appear materially different from that which
had acknowledged the sway of Maria Theresa.   Those who
could look deeper saw that the legislation and the general
principles of government were full of inconsistencies and con-
tradictions, the Josephine maxims and ideas coming into
perpetual collision with the state traditions.   It was not till
the days of Schwartzenberg and Bach, that, as we shall see
hereafter, a consistent and logical attempt was made to expel
the liberal poison which had been introduced by Joseph II.
Leopold, Francis, and Ferdinand all lived upon expedients ;
and the more intelligent of their servants saw, every day more
and more clearly, that sooner or later a crash would come.
The time, however, was not yet, and the echoes of the first
French Revolution in Austria were not very loud or long-re-
sounding, while the war which followed afforded ample excuse
for letting internal reforms alone.

The policy of Leopold, as might have been expected from
his antecedents in Tuscany, only seems illiberal when compared with that of his immediate predecessor ; but it was
succeeded by a policy, consciously and intentionally illiberal
in the highest possible degree.   During the first eighteen years
of his long reign, the Emperor Francis was, perforce, obliged

to entertain the plans of military or other reform, of which the Archduke Charles was at one time the conspicuous advocate. But his reasonable distrust of his brother was not likely to predispose him to favour any of the Archduke's views ; and after the treaty of Vienna in 1809, and still more conspicuously after the pacification of Europe, the political wisdom of the rulers of Austria inclined them ever more and more to the maintenance of that state of things which was known to friends and foes as the SYSTEM.

But what was the SYSTEM ? It was the organisation of do-nothing. It cannot even be said to have been reactionary : it was simply *inactionary*. About the contemporary proceedings of the restored tyrant in Piedmont, when he sent for a copy of the old court almanac, and had everything arranged on the pre-revolutionary model, there was, it must be admitted, a certain foolish vigour ; but in Austria there was nothing of the kind. ' Mark time in place ' was the word of command in every government office. The bureaucracy was engaged from morning to night in making work, but nothing ever came of it. Not even were the liberal innovations which had lasted through the reign of Leopold got rid of. Everything went on in the confused, unfinished, and ineffective state in which the great war had found it. Such was the famous SYSTEM which was venerated by the ultra-Tories of every land, and most venerated where it was least understood.

Two men dominate the history of Austria during this un-happy time—men who, though utterly unlike in character and intellect, were nevertheless admirably fitted to work together, and whose names will be long united in an unenvi-able notoriety. These were the Emperor Francis and Prince Metternich. The first was the evil genius of internal politics;

the second exercised a hardly less baneful influence over foreign affairs.

The Emperor Francis was born at Florence in 1768. His slender natural abilities received little aid from education during the first sixteen years of his life, but in 1784 he was summoned to Vienna, to be trained, under the eye of Joseph II., for the great office to which his birth had destined him. An account of his hopeful pupil, by the emperor's own hand, still remains to us ; and it would be difficult anywhere to find a more pungent satire. The selfishness, the falsehood, the dislike of intellectual exercise, the love of all things mean and trifling —which are the principal features in the imperial portrait, as traced by the hands of his guardian—grew with his growth, and were not corrected by his misfortunes. True it is, that whereas in youth he shunned all public business, he worked in age with the assiduity of a laborious *employé,* but this was only because he had discovered that public as well as private affairs have their trifling side. In later life he liked to have as many documents as possible accumulated in his cabinet ; but it was always the important ones which lay for weeks upon his table, and the unimportant ones to which he attended. In every part of his empire, as in his own *entourage,* he loved to repress whatever was vigorous or noble, to promote what was common-place and insignificant. " I want," he said to the professors at Laybach, " obedient subjects, and not men of learning." " *Totus mundus,*" he declared at Pesth, " *stultizat et vult habere novas constitutiones ;*" and although this sally was coupled with a compliment to the ancient franchises of Hungary, his conduct amply showed that he hated them as heartily as the bran-new charters of Cadiz or of Paris. His natural love of what was vulgar led him to prefer the Vienna dialect ; and he was cunning enough to see that he could, by indulging this taste, obtain no little popularity in the capital. His fancy for busy idleness made him delight in giving audiences; and during a single journey in Italy he is said to have received 20,000 people. This habit gained him the approbation of the unreflecting, who forgot that the time spent in this useless activity was stolen, not from the amusements or pageants of the court, but from the real duties of the monarch—duties which, had he honestly sought to discharge them, would have overwhelmed a far abler man ; for he had concentrated in his hands the management, or mismanagement, of the whole of the Home Department, and of the Police. This last was his favourite branch of administration, because the reports of his agents supplied him with all the gossip of the empire, a pleasure which he purchased, as all rulers do who have similar tastes, by becoming a puppet in the hands of the vilest of mankind. Such a character and such a system of government naturally resulted in driving the best men far away from court, and in giving a premium to worthlessness and servility. Some idea of the state of things may be formed from the fact that one of his prime favourites was the infamous Kutschera, who, when in the height of his influence, got into trouble with the police, for appearing, of course in the most primitive of all costumes, at one of the so-called Adamite balls in Vienna—a proceeding which was passed over by his master, with a remark which had rather the character of a jest than of a reprimand. Yet the private life of the monarch was correct, and he may be not unreasonably suspected of having encouraged the prevailing vices of those around him with the express object of degrading them.

The father of Prince Metternich had left the service of

the elector of Treves for that of the emperor, and had been
employed in various diplomatic missions, chiefly amongst
the small courts of the Rhineland. His son, born at Coblentz
in 1783, won in his earliest days the character which he preserved to the end, and was "*fin, faux,* and *fanfaron*" before
he passed out of boyhood. Throughout life he preserved the
impress of the gay and joyous life which characterised the
capitals of the small potentates, whom the revolutionary period
swept away ; and long as he lived in Vienna he never became
an Austrian, or understood the vast and heterogeneous empire
with which his name is so closely connected. Neither at the
University of Strasburg nor elsewhere does he seem to have
received more than a superficial culture, and his first success
was gained while acting a part in the ceremonial of the imperial coronation at Frankfort, rather by the elegance of his
manners and his good looks, than by any more solid acquire-
ments. He soon passed into the imperial service, and was
sent as Minister to the court of Dresden, when only eight-
and-twenty. Here there was little to do, but Berlin, to which
he was presently removed, offered a wider field for his fine
powers of intrigue. He managed so dexterously to recommend himself to his French colleagues, that it was soon intimated at Vienna that his presence as Austrian minister in
Paris would be agreeable to Napoleon, and immediately after
the battle of Wagram he took, as the supposed representative
of French interests, the reins of the Foreign Department,
which he held till they dropped from his hands in the grand
overturn of March 1848. His relations to his suspicious
master must have been at first extremely difficult, but his
great tact soon enabled him to make himself indispensable,
and the pair thoroughly understood each other. "*Sinere res*

vadere ut vadunt," was the motto of the emperor in internal affairs ; and for the external policy of Prince Metternich, the first and most necessary condition was, that Austria should give to Europe the impression of fixed adherence to the most extreme Conservative views.   So for many years they worked together, Prince Metternich always declaring that he was a mere tool in the hands of his master, but in reality far more absolute in the direction of his own department than the emperor was in his.   For Prince Metternich, although by no means a man of very great intellect, or deep and broad culture, was at least "*par negotiis* ;" while his master, potent in details and inefficiently active, was constantly being led, in important matters, by men who appeared to be the humblest of his creatures.   Prince Metternich had the power of making the most of all he knew, and constantly left upon persons of real merit the impression that he was a man of lofty aspirations and liberal views, who forced himself to repress such tendencies in others because he thought that their repression was a *sine quâ non* for Austria.   The men of ability, who knew him intimately, thought less well of him.   To them he appeared vain and superficial, with much that recalled the French noblesse of the old *régime* in his way of looking at things, and emphatically wanting in every element of greatness.

With the outbreak of the Greek insurrection in 1821, began a period of difficulty and complications for the statesmen of Austria.   There were two things of which they were mortally afraid—Russia and the revolution.   Now, if they assisted the Greeks, they would be playing into the hands of the second ; and if they opposed the Greeks, they would be likely to embroil themselves with the first.   The whole art of Prince

Metternich was therefore exerted to keep things quiet in the Eastern Peninsula, and to postpone the intolerable " *question d'Orient*." Many were the shifts he tried, and sometimes, as just after the accession of Nicholas, his hopes rose very high. All was, however, in vain. England and Russia settled matters behind his back ; and although the tone which the publicists in his pay adopted towards the Greeks became more favourable in 1826-7, the battle of Navarino was a sad surprise and mortification to the wily chancellor. Not less annoying was the commencement of hostilities on the Danube between Russia and the Porte. The reverses with which the great neighbour met in his first campaign cannot have been otherwise than pleasing at Vienna. But the unfortunate success which attended his arms in the second campaign soon turned ill-dissembled joy into ill-concealed sorrow, and the treaty of Adrianople at once lowered Austria's prestige in the East, and deposed Metternich from the commanding position which he had occupied in the councils of the Holy Allies. It became, indeed, ever more and more evident in the next few years that the age of Congress politics, during which he had been the observed of all observers, was past and gone, that the diplomatic period had vanished away, and that the military period had begun. The very form in which the highest international questions were debated was utterly changed. At Vienna, in 1814, the diplomatists had been really the primary, the sovereigns only *secondary* personages ; while at the interview of Münchengratz, between Nicholas and the Emperor Francis, in 1833, the great autocrat appeared to look upon Prince Metternich as hardly more than a confidential clerk.

The dull monotony of servitude which oppressed nearly the whole of the empire was varied by the agitations of one of its component parts. When the Hungarian Diet was dissolved in 1812, the emperor had solemnly promised that it should be called together again within three years. Up to 1815, accordingly, the nation went on giving extraordinary levies and supplies without much opposition. When, however, the appointed time was fulfilled, it began to murmur, and very soon the government discovered that, instead of dealing with a single Diet assembled at Presburg, it was engaged in the still more hopeless task of attempting to coerce a miniature Diet in every county of the kingdom. The inhabitants of more civilised portions of the monarchy—the Viennese themselves, for example—could be amused and kept in good humour without thinking of politics; but to the Hungarians the excitement of political life was a necessity. It was as hopeless to try to eradicate from their minds the desire for free political discussion as it has been found, in many districts of Western Europe, to root out the attachment to particular forms of religion which were not to the taste of the ruling powers. Year by year the agitation went on increasing, till at last the breaking out of the Greek revolution, and the threatening appearance of Eastern politics, induced Prince Metternich to join his entreaties to those of many other counsellors, who could not be suspected of the slightest leaning to constitutional views. At length the emperor yielded, and in 1825 Presburg was once more filled with the best blood and most active spirits of the land, assembled in parliament.

Long and stormy were the debates which ensued. Bitter was, from time to time, the vexation of the emperor, and great was the excitement throughout Hungary. In the end, however, the court of Vienna triumphed. Hardly any griev-

ances were redressed, while its demands were fully conceded.
The Diet of 1825 was, however, not without fruit. The discussion which took place advanced the political education of
the people, who were brought back to the point where they
stood at the death of Joseph II.—that is, before the long wars
with France had come to distract their attention from their
own affairs. The hands of the party which, while it wished to
preserve the old constitution as against Austria, saw that
that constitution required amendment, were greatly strengthened, and France and England were taught for the first time
to sympathise with the liberal aspirations of a country which
had most truly, up to that time, been " Terra Incognita."

Sharp as was the contest between the government and the
people in Hungary, it caused little excitement in the provinces
on the western bank of the Leitha. The tranquil surface of the
public mind was, however, rippled by the Greek revolution.
There was too little classical knowledge in Austria to call forth
such enthusiasm as was excited in England, or even in North
Germany ; but some memories of the Turkish wars remained,
and in Prague the Czechish population, which was beginning
to awake from a sleep of two centuries, did not forget that in
Bosnia, in Servia, and in other districts of the Eastern Peninsula,
men, of blood and language nearly allied to their own, were
suffering under a yoke from which they had themselves only
been saved by the exploits of a Sclavonic hero—the gallant
John Sobieski. There were not wanting, also, in the Germanic provinces, persons of a conservative turn of mind,
who dreamt of compensating the losses of the mediatised
princes by cutting up Roumelia, Bulgaria, and other such
outlandish districts, into little principalities for those injured
potentates ; while others, who thought that the only two

things which the well-disposed in Central Europe wanted
were "the Word of God and a navy," fancied that both those
good things might be brought to them if only the Turk
could be driven back "to his old Asian seats." For the first
four years of the war the Austrian government spared no
pains to show its contempt for these illusions. Ypsilanti
was shut up in Munkacs. No phil-Hellenes were allowed to
pass through Austria to the scene of the conflict, and
Austrian subjects were protected against the Greek cruisers
in carrying contraband of war to their enemies; while the
utmost publicity was given in the official organs to every
piece of news which was calculated to influence public opinion
against the Greeks. All this, as we have seen, was slightly
modified in the last years of the struggle, but the general result was, that the Greek revolution had very little effect in
stimulating a desire for liberty in Austria.

Far more formidable was the wave of sentiment which
was propagated over the country by the Polish struggle of
1831. In Hungary the storm rose very high, and the county
meetings offered large supplies in men and money to the
government if it would take the field on the side of the
insurgents; but Hungary did not stand alone, and more
especially in Bohemia the public mind was very deeply stirred.
In that province the successes of the Poles were considered
as national glories by a population which, while it dreamt of
a great Pan-Sclavic future, amusingly enough forgot that this
was, from a Pan-Sclavic point of view, only a civil war—one
portion of the illustrious and high-destined family cutting
the throats of the other. The Austrian government secretly
encouraged the revolution of 1831, just as it encouraged the
more recent revolution which we have so lately witnessed.

So good an opportunity of weakening the Colossus which overshadowed the empire it was not in human nature to lose; but even if it had not wished well to the movement, it would have found it difficult openly to take the side of Russia. The hopes and sorrows of the Poles touched a chord in Austria which no other revolution had struck there. We see in this the first great political result of that spirit of nationality which was evoked in many of the provinces by the essentially German legislation of Joseph II. Of this we shall have more to say hereafter. For the present the effect was only a wave of sympathy which rolled across the empire. The slumbers of Austria were not yet over. The SYSTEM dragged its slow length along. Little or nothing was done for the improvement of the country. Klebelsberg administered the finances in an easy and careless manner. Conspiracies and risings in Italy were easily checked, and batches of prisoners sent off from time to time to Mantua or Spielberg. Austrian influence rose ever higher and higher in all the petty courts of the Peninsula ; and even Nicholas, in his hatred of revolution, was induced, contrary to the old traditions of Russia, to aid the advance of Austrian garrisons further and further towards the south. In other regions Russia or England might be willing to thwart him, but in Italy Prince Metternich might proudly reflect that Austria was indeed a " great power." The French Revolution of 1830 was at first alarming ; but when it resulted in the enthronement of a dynasty which called to its aid a " cabinet of repression," all fears were stilled. The Emperor Francis continued to say, when any change was proposed, " We must sleep upon it," and died in 1835 in " the abundance of peace."

The mob of Vienna, when they raged against Prince "Mitternacht" in 1848, were under a great mistake—a mistake which they shared with their betters in most countries. They fancied that he was the pivot round which the whole state machine revolved, and that without him it could not exist. In truth, however, the period of Prince Metternich's highest influence in European politics extends from 1814 till the rising of the twin but adverse stars of Canning and of Nicholas. The liberal policy of the one, and the purely *bayonet* policy of the other, were both fatal to the ascendancy of a system which was based upon diplomatic intrigue. As far as Austria herself was concerned, Prince Metternich's influence was unimpaired, within his own department, up to the death of the Emperor Francis in 1835; and although the testament in which that monarch recommended the veteran statesman to his successor as the most faithful of his adherents turned out to be a forgery, it doubtless expressed his real opinions.

It was no secret in Vienna that the harmless and amiable Ferdinand, who, at the age of forty-two, succeeded his imperial father, was quite unequal to the duties which absolute power imposes upon him who wields it. The necessity of providing some substitute had been long foreseen, but had, characteristically enough, not been provided for, as anything seemed better than agitating the minds of men by a premature announcement to all the empire of the sovereign's weakness. After many months spent in discussion and intrigue, Prince Metternich, Count Kolowrat, and the Archduke Louis, were formed into a triumvirate, and became for a time the virtual rulers of Austria. Kolowrat had long been the right-hand man of the Emperor Francis in the manage-

ment of internal affairs, and the imagination of the multitude
had quite erroneously invested him with a halo of liberalism,
so that he passed for the antithesis of Metternich, whose name
had been long a byword for his opposition to all reform. In
truth, Kolowrat, although more educated than his master,
shared the narrow views of the emperor, and was little better,
as far as his *public* character was concerned, than the civil
equivalent of Kutschera, the notorious adjutant, whose name
we have already mentioned. The Archduke Louis had no
higher idea of governing than to take care that everything
should be done as it had been done in the time of his brother,
whose passion for inefficient activity in the details of administration he fully shared. It was under the auspices of these
three personages that the old order in Austria dragged itself
towards its doom. The SYSTEM, which two of them had done
much to create, they kept to the end. Day by day it became
less suited to the wants of the time, and day by day the gulf
between the people and their governors became wider and
wider. As years passed on, it seemed as if the noisy but
wholly ineffective clatter of the state machine had lulled those
who managed it into sleep. Metternich, more especially after
his diplomatic mishaps in the year 1840, became quite super-
annuated, and the real business of his office passed into the
hands of Ficquelmont and other secondary persons.

Meanwhile dissatisfaction, and even insubordination, were
spreading in the most diverse shapes over every province.
In the Tyrol it was the clergy who felt themselves sufficiently
strong to force the government to come to terms. The Emperor Francis, it must be remembered to his honour, had,
while he professed, and doubtless entertained, highly orthodox
opinions, walked in the paths of Joseph II., so far as the re-

lations of the church and the state were concerned, and asserted
his own supremacy with sufficient sternness. The reins were
now somewhat looser, and the wary ecclesiastics soon saw
their advantage. It was in 1837, two years after the death
of Francis, that the eleven years' contest about the Protestants
of the Zillerthal ended in those unfortunate persons accepting
the hospitality of the king of Prussia, and leaving their own
beautiful valley to seek an asylum in Silesia, after undergoing
a long course of molestation, which was equally opposed to
the Josephine laws and to the federal obligations of the
Austrian empire. The conduct of the government in this
matter was determined rather by weakness than by evil will,
and it showed itself almost equally powerless in dealing with
opponents of a very different kind.

Long before the death of the Emperor Francis the national
spirit in Hungary had, as we have seen, become thoroughly
roused ; but in the Diet—which assembled in 1832, and continued to sit till 1836—symptoms of a far more serious kind
became visible than any which had been seen in 1825. The
old patriotic party, which had only thought of defending the
ancient constitution, with all its merits and abuses, against the
encroachments of the Kaiser, was now pushed aside by a new
party, which aimed at procuring for Hungary a series of reforms which should make her a liberal state after the western
model. It was in this Diet that the grievances, which had
been formulised by the Diet of 1790, first came on for serious
debate. These were, according to Paget, who was himself in
Hungary at this time—

" That Dalmatia, Transylvania, Galicia, and Lodomeria should be
re-incorporated with Hungary ; that the military frontiers should be
placed under the command of the Palatine, and governed by Hungarian
laws ; that the duty on salt should be reduced ; that the edicts of go-

vernment to officers of justice should be discontinued ; that the laws respecting the taxes on the clergy should be observed ; that the Hungarian chancery should be made really, not merely nominally, independent of the Austrian chancery ; that the coinage should bear the arms of Hungary, and that the exportation of gold and silver should be prevented ; that the paper money should be abolished, and a return made to a metallic currency ; that the Hungarian language should be used in all official business ; that the fiscal estates, such as have fallen to the crown on the extinction of the families to whom they were granted, should, as the law directs, be given only as the reward of public services, and not sold, as at present, to the highest bidder; and, lastly, that spies should not be employed and trusted by the Austrian government."

But the discussion of grievances was not all. New names and new projects appeared. It was now that Kossuth first made himself conspicuous, not by his speeches—for his subordinate position, as the mere delegate of a magnate's widow, did not give him the right to vote, and hardly the right to speak—but by the system of reporting which he organised. It was in this Diet too that the good Stephen Széchenyi first proposed the building of a chain-bridge to unite Pesth with Buda—a proposal which, unimportant as it appears at first sight, contained the germ of a complete political and social revolution. Some of our readers may remember the long bridge of boats which in the summer of 1847, and perhaps for some time later, connected the two halves of the Hungarian capital. If so, they must have observed that while most of the persons whose dress and appearance showed that their position in society was a humble one, paid toll as they passed the bridge, most of those who appeared to belong to the higher ranks passed without challenge. The immunity which the Hungarian *nobilis*, who was in ninety-nine cases out of a hundred in no respect what we call a noble, but merely a freeman, or member of a privileged class, and indeed often a pauper, enjoyed at this bridge, was a type of the immunity which he boasted from all dues and taxes whatever, which were borne by the *misera contribuens plebs*. Széchenyi proposed that, with a view to defray the expense of the new bridge, the nobles should abdicate, as far as it was concerned, their special privilege ; and it was clear that when such a privilege was abandoned in any one instance for the sake of the public weal, its final abolition was only a matter of time. The proposition was carried, as were also several other measures of reform, and with this Diet the preparation for the Hungarian revolution may be considered to have begun. The flowing tide of liberal sentiment in Hungary was soon aided by an agitation, chiefly amongst the Magyar population of Transylvania, which in 1834 forced the government to convoke the Transylvanian Diet, which had, contrary to law, been left unsummoned for twenty-three years. The leader of the patriotic movement in Transylvania, the impetuous Wesselyeni, the true son of his father, who had been shut up for four years in Kufstein for storming the castle of an obnoxious neighbour, soon passed beyond safe limits, and was imprisoned by the government, a fate which also befell Kossuth, and some young men who had tried to walk in his steps. But these measures only tended to increase the unpopularity of the ruling powers, and to sow disaffection wider. The lead in the movement was taken by the Magyars, who comprised a very much larger portion of the privileged class than any of the other numerous nationalities which inhabit Hungary. Unfortunately for them, their pre-eminence was too undisputed, and day by day the agitation assumed more of a Magyar character, while it became evident that the victory of the movement party would be anything but a triumph for the Sclave, or the Rouman population. A national revival which had taken place amongst the Sclavacks, or Sclaves of north-western Hungary, had taken the form partly of a passive resistance to the exaggerated claims of the Magyars, partly of a controversy with the Czechs of Prague, as to the respective merits of the Sclavack and Czechian dialects. But the linguistic enthusiasm of the Croats, another branch of the great Sclave family, soon became more formidable. For generations there had existed a party in Croatia which resisted what it considered the exaggerated claims of the Presburg Diet, and aimed at giving greater power to the minor Diet which assembled at Agram. A long controversy had been waged about the relations to Croatia and Hungary respectively, of the district between the Save and the Danube, which is usually known as Sclavonia, and about the port of Fiume in the Adriatic. These, and other ancient matters of dispute, were of course called into new life when the Magyars proposed to abolish the use of the Latin, which had for ages been the language of business in Hungary, and to oblige every one who wished the smallest possible public office throughout the whole of Hungary to speak Magyar, thereby confining in practice the use of all other languages to the family circle. It is possible that the reaction in favour of their own nationality among the Croats might not have reached a dangerous height if it had not been for the efforts of Louis Gai, a journalist of great talent, who, after having been brought up at a German university, returned to Croatia, and started a newspaper, with the view of advocating the claims of his countrymen to become the leaders of a great Illyrian movement, which was to embrace not only Dalmatia, Croatia, and Sclavonia, but also a large portion of European Turkey. Increased

experience of the world soon showed Gai that his dreams were
at least premature, but he roused an enthusiasm which was
artfully taken advantage of by men who were looking nearer
home, to excite the Croats to resist the encroachments of the
Magyar majority in the Presburg Diet.   When, therefore, that
majority succeeded, in 1844, in getting the Vienna authorities
upon their side, and in making Magyar the official language
of the whole of Hungary, the irritation of the Croats became
very bitter, and they were in consequence a ready instrument
in the hands of the Austrian government, some years later,
in opposing the ultra-Magyar party, by force of arms, although
there is no evidence to show that, at the moment of which we
are speaking, the policy of Vienna was dictated by any views
about the use to which the Croats might be put, if the worst
came to the worst, in Hungary.   Indeed, the evidence is all
the other way.   The men of the SYSTEM followed their wonted
habit, and thought of nothing but keeping things quiet.   " If
the Hungarians were to ask for the moon," it was truly said
at this time, " I verily believe that the Austrian government
would not refuse their request, but would only say that the
matter required mature consideration."

While the linguistic controversy was inflaming the passions of the Magyars, and exciting anti-Magyar feelings
through all the non-Magyar populations of Hungary, a number
of other irritating questions were being discussed in successive
Diets, in the county meetings, and in the press, which last,
chiefly through the instrumentality of Kossuth, had suddenly
grown into a great power.   There was the question of the religious education to be given to the children of mixed marriages—a most important matter in a country where the
Protestants are so numerous.   This subject of dispute, after a

long struggle with the Ultramontanes, was settled in a liberal sense. There was the question of the abolition of the immunities of the *nobiles* in matters of taxation, of the increase of the political power of the urban communities, of the better ordering of the counties, of the criminal law, of improving the material condition of the country, with many others. Discussion gradually opened the eyes of nearly all politicians to the necessity of making vast changes in Hungary, and three parties slowly separated themselves and fell into rank. These were—(1.) the Conservatives, led by the Chancellor Apponyi, who wished for a strongly-centralised government of the absolutist kind, the driving-wheel of which should be in Vienna ; (2.) the Liberals, led by Deak, who wished for a government of the constitutional kind, based on a reform of the old institutions of Hungary, the driving-wheel of which should be the Diet ; (3.) a party whose views were as yet indeterminate, but which became, in 1848-49, the revolutionary and democratic party, and which, in the Diet of 1847, was led by Kossuth. Count Stephen Széchenyi became a little before this time identified with the Conservative party, much in the same way in which we have seen M. Michel Chevalier gradually become an out-and-out imperialist, because he thought that through the Conservatives and the Vienna government his plans for the material amelioration of the country would best be carried out.

An important section of the second party was led by Baron Joseph Eötvös, who, possessing a far deeper knowledge of political science than most of his countrymen, and entitled, from his wide and varied knowledge, to take rank among the best of his contemporaries, looked with impatience on the many follies and atrocities of the old Hungarian system, which he has satirised in *The Village Notary*, and would have desired to govern Hungary on a more centralised system, the driving-wheel of which should be the Diet, amended and made into a parliament after the English manner.

These parties met in the Diet of 1847, and in its discussions were being gradually shaped and moulded. What forms they all, and especially the third, might ultimately have taken, if the Revolution had not, in February 1848, broken out in Paris, it is impossible to say ; but that event acted in Hungary, as in so many other places, like a torch in a powder magazine. On the 1st of March 1847, Kossuth rose and said : " There are moments when the legislature must not only demand reforms, but also ward off dangers." With these words the curtain fell upon the old party contests.

The interest which attaches to all that is passing in Hungary at the present moment has induced us to trace the course of events in that country at far greater length than it will be necessary to do those of the rest of the empire.

The assemblies of the nobles in the provinces on this side the Leitha, more especially in Bohemia and Lower Austria, began also during this period to show symptoms of discontent. Their efforts were, as was perhaps natural, chiefly directed to obtain greater liberty, and some substantial share of political power, for their own class ; but their members were by no means unaffected by the liberal aspirations of more advanced countries. Many of them were more or less familiar with French and English literature, or had travelled in Western Europe ; and their efforts, if barren of immediate political advantage to themselves, nevertheless cast further discredit upon the SYSTEM, by showing not only its inapplicability to modern exigencies, but, in some cases, its distinct opposition to still unrepealed laws.

The nobility was the only class which could give voice to its complaints, but the professional and commercial classes suffered at least equally. The SYSTEM had succeeded in repressing, but not in crushing, the intelligence of the empire. There grew up after the year 1815, very slowly and gradually, a race of men to whom the articles of the court journalists and the verses of the court poets were wholly intolerable. There was a time when the self-satisfied saying—

" s'ist nur a Kaiserstadt s'ist nur a Wien,"

represented the creed of all the German-speaking subjects of the kaiser; but that delusion had hardly outlived the Emperor Francis, and by the year 1840 had quite vanished away. The censorship was now felt to be an evil which was only endurable because it was so constantly evaded. It had become, indeed, to a great extent inoperative; for so surely as a work was pronounced harmless by the censor, the public refused to buy it, and so surely as a work printed in Leipzig or Hamburg obtained the distinction of a " damnatur," it was sure to be smuggled in scores over all the northern frontiers. Instead of the literature of the Romanticists, some of whom had looked lovingly to Austria, and had even selected it for their habitation, there were the spirit-stirring verses of Count Auersperg (Anastasius Grün), whose *Spaziergänge eines Wiener Poeten* attacked the existing state of things in no measured way. The government itself was obliged to call in the assistance· of strictly-prohibited journals, if it wished to defend itself with effect; for to the statements of the authorised organs no credence at all was attached. The schools were

everywhere in an utterly wretched condition; and the few
Austrian subjects who could boast of any superior acquire-
ments had either obtained them abroad, or only after a
laborious course of study at home, the first step of which was
to blot out from their memories nine-tenths of what they had
acquired from their teachers.

The last blow was given to the tottering edifice by the
events which took place in the Polish provinces in 1846.
For some months it had been manifest to all who had eyes to
see, that the Poles of the emigration were about to make a
new attack upon their enemies. Warsaw was their principal
object, but they proposed to begin operations in Posen and
Galicia. The little independent republic of Cracow, the last
remnant of ancient Poland which had not been seized by the
spoiler, was the centre of their patriotic but foolish machinations; and the 21st of February 1846 was destined for the
outbreak of the insurrection. The Austrian government,
although quite aware of what was intended, took its measures
so badly as to allow General Collin, who had marched into
Cracow at the request of the representatives of the three
partitioning powers, to be overwhelmed and driven out,—
the honour of the Austrian flag being only saved by the
courage and conduct of Benedek, whose name became
then for the first time famous. The same carelessness
which the rulers showed in not sufficiently strengthening
the hands of Collin, led them to neglect giving specific
orders to the officials who were scattered through the Polish
provinces. The result of this was, that when the insurrection
broke out, and the Ruthenian peasants came to ask what part
they should take, they were too often, it is to be feared,
directed by men who were in panic-fear for their own lives

to secure the persons of their disaffected Polish landlords, living or dead.

How far the Vienna authorities were accessories before the fact to the hideous massacres which followed, it is very difficult to decide. Certain it is, that after the insurrection had broken out, rewards were paid by Austrian *employés* to the men who were engaged in the massacres. And on the heads of those whose culpable negligence permitted such things to happen, must rest an amount of reprobation but little inferior to what would have been their due if, as was loudly asserted by the Poles, and very generally believed throughout Europe, they had deliberately planned out for the assassins their bloody and terrible work.

Before the end of the year 1846 Cracow was seized by Austria, in spite of the hostile attitude of France and England,—a proceeding for which there is but one excuse, and that is, that Prince Metternich knew perfectly well that if Austria hesitated to do the deed, Russia was determined not to be so scrupulous. The massacres had excited the people against Austria all through Western Europe. The incorporation of Cracow was not less successful in alienating statesmen. By that act Metternich stultified his whole life, threw ridicule upon the treaty of Vienna, and illustrated once more the true words of the poet—

"Quam temere in nosmet legem sancimus iniquam,"

by affording an admirable precedent to be followed in the case of Lombardy.

Such were the effects of the occurrences in Austrian Poland upon the foreign relations of the empire, but they were hardly less momentous in their influence upon its internal condition. The detestation with which the Ruthenian

peasants regarded their Polish landlords was the result not
only of differences of race and of religion, but of long ages of
oppression. It was quite clear that the relations between the
owners and cultivators of the soil in those provinces must be
materially altered ; but no sooner was the idea of an important alteration *anywhere* introduced, than the leading idea of
the SYSTEM was shown to be unsound.   From the moment
that changes began to be made in the landed tenures of the
Polish provinces, partial and ineffective though those changes
were, the desire for change seized the one class which had
hitherto been on the side of the government, from Bodenbach
to Orsova. The stupid Conservatism of the peasants was at
an end, and one more element of confusion was introduced.

Those who were politically or pecuniarily interested in
Austria, will not soon forget with what anxiety they watched
for the first news of the effect which should be produced in
that country by the news of the February revolution in Paris.
No one could have visited any part of the empire, during the
course of 1847, without perceiving that everywhere a most
dangerous spirit was at work.   The question which no
stranger who had not enjoyed very exceptional opportunities
could answer, was, How far will it be in the power of the
government to put down firmly and finally any troubles that
may break out ?   For as to the certainty of troubles breaking
out there really could be no doubt, unless, indeed, in the
minds of Prince Metternich and his friends, who seem to
have foreseen nothing, and provided against nothing.

The first effects were seen in Presburg, but the echo of the
words of Kossuth, to which we have alluded above, died
away before they reached our shores, and Englishmen first
learned that a storm was about to burst when they heard of

the disturbances in the Austrian capital upon the 13th of March, followed, as they soon were, by the resignation and flight of Prince Metternich.

The words of Kossuth on the 1st of March marked, as we have seen, the end of " the old order." From that moment the great agitator abandoned himself to the impulses of the moment, and, partly acted on by events, partly exercising a reflex action upon them, hurried along his strange and meteoric course, till the day when, in the great church at Debreczin, amidst the plaudits of a multitude which had gone wild with excitement, he proclaimed the dethronement of the house of Hapsburg-Lorraine and the independence of Hungary.

The events of the 1st of March 1848 at Presburg were followed by six weeks ^ crowded with events of the most exciting and important character, the array of which was closed by the emperor's going in person to that city, and formally sanctioning a series of resolutions of a highly revolutionary character, which had been passed under the influence of the orator who had attained in a few days a worldwide reputation. These are the laws of 1848, about which. we have heard so much. We give a *précis* of them, taken from a work called *Hungary and its Revolutions, with a Memoir of Kossuth*, which affords, on this head, more detailed information than the work of Professor Springer :—

" The substance of the resolutions passed in this Diet, and confirmed by the king, was as follows :—That the executive power should be exercised through the ministry alone. That the palatine, in the absence of the king, should be invested with all royal power, excepting the appointments of the dignitaries of the church, officers of the army, the high barons of the kingdom, and the disposal of the army when out of Hungary. That every member of the cabinet should be responsible for his official acts, liable to impeachment by the Chamber of Deputies, and to be tried by a committee from the Chamber of Magnates. That the sessions of the Diet be held at Pesth, and the laws sanctioned during the session by the king. That perfect equality of rights, as well as of public burdens, should be established among all the people of Hungary, without distinction of class, race, or denomination. That the franchise should be extended to every man possessing property to the value of three hundred florins, or an income of one hundred ; to every one who had received a diploma in a university ; and every artisan who employed an apprentice. That with the concurrence of both countries, Hungary and Transylvania, and their Diets, should be incorporated. That the number of representatives sent by Croatia to the Diet should be increased from three to eighteen, and the internal institutions of that province remain the same as before. That the military frontiers of Hungary, or border troops, should be placed under the authority of the Hungarian Minister of War."

We do not propose to enter into any detail as to the events of the revolutionary period, which occupied nearly the whole of 1848 and 1849. The direct influence of the transactions which then occurred upon the history of Austria, during the last sixteen years, has not been so great as might have been expected ; and if we were to attempt to describe with any minuteness the elements which then came to the surface, and which may be expected to work in various ways during the years that are coming, we should be carried far beyond the limits to which even the longest article can be extended. Through the complications of the eventful months which followed the flight of Prince Metternich we know no more sober guide than Professor Springer, and for no period of recent history is a sober guide more wanted. Greater issues were decided before Sebastopol, far larger masses of men were hurled against each other in the American civil conflict, but no war of our time has ever approached in romantic interest that which was waged in 1848 and 1849 upon the plains of Hungary.

The English public was plentifully supplied, from 1850

to 1854, with the narratives of rival generals, and with the pamphlets, sometimes disguised in the form of history, of the contending parties; but we know no narrative and no political treatise in English, referring to these events, which we could venture to recommend, without advising the reader to follow up its perusal with that of a work of diametrically opposite tendency.

The two great gains which the moral earthquake of 1848 brought to Austria were, that through wide provinces of the empire, and more especially in Hungary, it swept away the sort of semi-vassalage in which the peasantry had been left by the Urbarium of Maria Theresa, and other reforms akin to or founded upon it, and introduced modern in the place of middle-age relations between the two extremes of society. Secondly, it overthrew the policy of do-nothing—a surer guarantee for the continuance of abuses than even the determination, which soon manifested itself at head-quarters, to make the head of the state more absolute than ever.

After the taking of Vienna by Windischgrätz, the National Assembly had, on the 15th of November 1848, been removed from the capital to the small town of Kremsier, in Moravia. Here it prolonged an ineffective existence till March 1849, when the court camarilla felt itself strong enough to put an end to an inconvenient censor, and in March 1849 it ceased to exist. A constitution was at the same time promulgated which contained many good provisions, but which was never heartily approved by the ruling powers, or vigorously carried into effect—the proclamation of a state of siege in many cities, and other expedients of authority in a revolutionary period, easily enabling it to be set at nought. The successes of the reaction in other parts of Europe, and above all the *coup d'etat* in Paris, emboldened Schwartzenberg to throw off the mask ; and on the last day of 1851 Austria became once more a pure despotism.

The young emperor had taken " *Viribus unitis*" for his motto ; and his advisers interpreted those words to mean that Austria was henceforward to be a state as highly centralised as France—a state in which the minister at Vienna was absolutely to govern everything from Salzburg to the Iron Gate. The hand of authority had been severely felt in the pre-revolutionary period, but now advantage was to be taken of the revolution to make it felt far more than ever. In Hungary, for example, which had, as we have seen, always proved intractable, even when the Germanic provinces were living in contented servitude, it was fondly imagined that there would be no more trouble. The old political division into counties was swept away ; the whole land was divided into five provinces ; and the courtiers might imagine that from henceforth the Magyars would be as easily led as the inhabitants of Upper Austria. These delusions soon became general, but they owed their origin partly to the enthusiastic ignorance of those who were at the head of the army, and partly to two men, about whom we must say a word. The first of these was Prince Schwartzenberg, the son of the generalissimo of the allied army in the campaign of 1814. Bred to diplomacy, he was the Austrian minister at Naples when the revolution broke out in that capital, then served for a short period under the imperial flag in Northern Italy, and shortly afterwards returned to the centre of affairs, to animate the drooping spirits of the court. Several of his sayings will be remembered, and they show a certain amount of shrewdness and insight ; but there is nothing recorded, either of his words or actions, which bears evidence of a high capacity for statesmanship, to say nothing of wisdom or matured political ability. He had energy and power of will, nor would it be difficult to draw a parallel between him and Count Bismark, although we are bound to say that the latter has given much greater proof of talent. In audacity, however, there is little to choose between them ; and in the "Systole and Diastole" of German politics the Prussian statesman played in 1865, to the disadvantage of Austria, just the same part which the Austrian statesman played in 1850 to the disadvantage of Russia. Those who are tempted to attach too much importance to such triumphs of audacity should remember how much easier it is to cut knots than to unravel them, and wait to see the end.

Whether Prince Schwartzenberg might have developed any higher powers if his life had been prolonged, we cannot say. He died suddenly in April 1852.

More space to develop his energies, we might almost say "more rope to hang himself," was given to Alexander Bach, who succeeded the conservative, but able, and by no means bigoted Stadion, when the health of that statesman broke down in 1849. Bach was born in 1813, and was the son of a provincial *employé* under the department of Justice, who, however, eventually removed to the capital, where he established a thriving business as an attorney. His son began life as a clerk in his father's office, studied the law with success, and became a *Doctor Juris.* He then travelled, and ultimately succeeded his father. Before 1848 he was so conspicuous, both as a jurist and as a reformer, that he was called to take the portfolio of Justice in the ministry which came into power in May 1848. His behaviour in this office gave much offence to the extreme revolutionary party ; and during the disturbances which marked the month of October in that year, his life was in some danger. Whether it was that the experiences of that stormy time cooled his reforming ardour,—or whether it was that the temperature of that ardour had been always exaggerated,—or whether, as his enemies assert, he distinctly changed sides to further his own purposes,—or whether again he was gradually led further than he meant to go down the slope of reaction,—we need not here inquire ; but certain it is, that after the first successes of the court he soon became one of its most trusted agents. His two leading ideas were to cover the whole empire with a German bureaucracy, and to draw closer the ties which connected the court of Vienna with that of Rome. In his view, and in that of the ecclesiastics who worked with him, much of the evil that prevailed in the empire could be traced to the anti-religious influences which had acted on the mind of Joseph II. ; and it was under his auspices, and those of Count Leo Thun, that Austria made that extraordinary retrograde movement which was announced to Europe by the conclusion of the Concordat. If absolutism in Austria had a fair trial from the 31st of December 1851 to the Italian war, it is to Bach that it was owing ; and if it utterly and ludicrously failed, it is he more than any other man who must bear the blame.

Already, in 1849, the bureaucracy had been reorganised, but in 1852 new and stricter regulations were introduced. Everything was determined by precise rules—even the exact amount of hair which the *employé* was permitted to wear upon his face. Hardly any question was thought sufficiently insignificant to be decided upon the spot. The smallest matters had to be referred to Vienna, if their settlement had not been provided for in the instructions previously issued.

The higher officials were directed to keep an accurate record of the political dispositions of their subordinates, and the non-official citizens were subjected almost as completely to the despotism of these subordinates as *they* were to that of their superiors. The result of all this was, that in spite of many improvements upon the pre-revolutionary system in matters of detail, and a greatly increased vigour at head-quarters, the internal affairs of the empire soon fell into hopeless confusion. The finances, which had been thrown into terrible disorder by the events of the revolution, and by the expenses attendant on the menacing attitude adopted towards Prussia in 1850, showed no tendency to recovery. The new communal organisation was put off from year to year, and was at last promulgated in 1859, only to be found absurd and unworkable. The new criminal code, which was one of the few things actually accomplished during this period, revived obsolete punishments, was particularly severe upon the press, and in all respects disgraceful. The same may be said of the Concordat concluded in 1855, of which the best that can be told is, that it has never been so fully carried out as its promoters desired, and that it was a most efficient instrument in exciting hatred against the party to which it owes its origin. The best thing between the pacification of Hungary and October 1860 was the remodelling of the system of public instruction by Count Leo Thun,—a statesman who, although his opinions led him to promote the views of the Ultramontane party, had yet sufficient firmness not to let it drag him further than he wished to go, and sufficient enlightenment to see that the state of the Austrian schools and universities was simply disastrous and intolerable. In general, however, the politicians of the reactionary period showed themselves singularly incapable of translating their ideas into accomplished facts, partly, perhaps, from want of ability, but much more because the task which they had set themselves was absurd and impossible. It was a time of great activity in the public offices, of endless instructions, counter-instructions, revised counter-instructions, and so forth ; and when we learn that between 1849 and 1860 the medical department of the army was reorganised four times, the artillery and engineers three times, the Judge-Advocate's department three times, and the War Office at least four times ; when we learn, further, that the same spirit prevailed in other branches of the administration, we can hardly be surprised that the great ruin of the Italian war brought down with a crash the whole edifice of the reaction.

While the internal affairs of the empire were going from bad to worse, its external affairs were by no means prosperous. All those who understood the German question saw that the triumph gained at the expense of Prussia in 1850 could only be of temporary importance. There were fewer who were aware that Louis Napoleon had been on the very point of declaring war against Austria, immediately after the news of the battle of Novara had reached Paris, or who felt certain that the day would ere long arrive when France would break with a strong hand the web of treaties which Metternich had woven around the limbs of Italy. A quarrel with Switzerland, and another with Piedmont, came to embitter public opinion in Europe against the cabinet of Vienna, already roused by the exaggerated but eloquent declamations of Kossuth, as well in the New as in the Old World. The mission of Count Leiningen to Constantinople on the subject of Montenegro was by many supposed to be a diversion in favour of Russia ; and although this has never been proved, and is in itself improbable, it did not tend to make Austria more popular either in France or England. Her uncertain attitude during the Crimean war alternately flattered and dashed the hopes of the West ; and although the diplomatist can hardly blame her, the opinion of intelligent Europe was not gained to her side, while she became to Russia the object of the most deadly hostility. Thus, at the table of the Congress in Paris she had hardly a single real friend, and men began to watch, with all the pleasures of malevolence, the struggle between her and the wily Genevese-Italian, who was destined to rob her of all she had won in the Peninsula by the labours and the crimes of more than forty years.

The isolated position in which Austria was placed after the conclusion of the Russian war had a very unfavourable influence upon her internal politics. The watchword of the new system was, as we have seen, " *Viribus unitis*," but now the wielders of these " united forces," the ministers at Vienna, at length thoroughly awake to the fact that their system was a failure, began to throw the blame upon each other. Bruck, the one man of real insight amongst them, occupied his high position as Finance Minister solely in virtue of his merit, and had none of those powerful connections which are necessary to one who would carry through great reforms without popular support. He passed his time making one concession here, another there, in the vain hope of getting something useful done. It was all in vain. From the beginning of 1849 to the end of 1858, the public debt rose from 1200 million florins to 2292 million florins, and every source of taxation had in the meantime been strained to the uttermost. The years 1857 and 1858 passed in peace, but without producing any important improvements in the state of things; and at last, in 1859, the long-deferred retribution came.

There was no violent outbreak of disaffection, and although Kossuth accompanied the emperor in his Italian campaign, ready to do what he could to raise Hungary as soon as the French flag appeared on Hungarian soil, he prudently insisted upon its appearance there as a condition precedent. It is of good augury for the non-resurrection of absolutism in Austria that it was not overthrown, but died a natural death. Bach was dismissed in August 1859, and was succeeded by Count Goluchowski, a man of much inferior ability, who had been governor of Galicia, but who did not do anything as minister to justify the respectable reputation which he brought into the government. M. de Hübner became at the same time Minister of Police, and showed, during his short tenure of office, far more consideration for the press, and far more desire for reform, than his predecessor. Both he and the Foreign Minister, Count Rechberg, are believed to have seen, even at this period, that concessions to Hungary had become absolutely necessary. Indeed, M. de Hübner is said to have resigned his portfolio in consequence of the rejection of his plans for effecting something in this direction.

It must be borne in mind that all through the reactionary period the so-called "Old Conservative party" (whose name, be it remembered, has nothing now to do with the sort of questions which divide our Liberals and Conservatives) amongst the Hungarian magnates, had been protesting as ardently against the system of M. Bach as they had protested against the ideas of Kossuth in 1848. Those who would follow the outs and ins of their long struggle—and no one, we are persuaded, can follow them without having his impression of the political capacity of the Magyars considerably raised—should read the earlier pages of the work called *Drei Jahre Verfassungsstreit*, the author of which is well known, and is a person whose possession of the best information can be relied upon.

The resolution to break with the system of M. Bach was not, however, taken in a day ; and even after his dismissal things went on for a time in the old fashion. Numerous commissions were called into life charged to advise the government, but nothing decisive was done except by a Hungarian commission, which refused to report, and reminded the rulers that if they wanted advice about Hungary, the best plan would be to obey the laws and summon the Hungarian Diet. Abroad, the Austrian diplomatists fought hard to recover the ground which they had lost in Italy, and are said to have arranged the preliminaries of a grand Catholic league, which they fondly believed would replace them in their old position, and which would perhaps have given serious trouble if it had not been for Garibaldi's timely landing at Marsala. At home, the reactionists obtained a triumph by driving Bruck to commit suicide—not, however, before he had publicly pointed out that the whole system of government in Austria was rotten to the core.

The first step in advance was made in the end of May 1860, by calling together the assembly which was known as the "Verstärkte Reichsrath" (strengthened Council of the Empire). Ever since 1851 there had existed a Reichsrath ; but this was a mere governmental board, remarkable for nothing, unless it were that it was a shade more illiberal than the other public departments. The new Reichsrath was an assembly of notables from all parts of the empire, chiefly, but not exclusively, composed of men of very high rank. What the government expected from the Reichsrath was advice as to what was to be done in the dire perplexity into which want of money, Hungarian disaffection, and its other misfortunes, had thrown it; but of specific advice it succeeded in getting very little. On the other hand, the Reichsrath thoroughly condemned the existing state of things, and begged the emperor, in his omnipotence, to find out and apply a remedy. Nothing was further from its views than to make an energetic demand for a constitution ; and the Saxon Transylvanian M. Maager, who ventured to pronounce that dreaded name too loudly, was no doubt thought by the majority of his colleagues a very dangerous person. The chief difference of opinion which was manifested in the Reichsrath related to the amount of centralisation and de-centralisation to be maintained in the reorganised empire. The opinion of the de-centralising or federalist party prevailed, and the government proceeded, a week or two after the four months' session of the "strengthened Council of the Empire" came to an end, to issue the diploma of the 20th October 1860. The broad difference between the system of M. Bach and that inaugurated by the October diploma was this—that while in the Bach system everything was, as we have seen, regulated down to the minutest detail by the government offices at Vienna, acting under the pressure of unmitigated despotism ; in the system inaugurated by the October diploma a broad distinction was drawn between those general concerns of the empire which had to be regulated at Vienna, and those particular concerns of the provinces which had to be regulated by the provincial

assemblies. Further, a sort of modified system of representation was introduced, by the creation of a new sort of
Reichsrath, consisting of one hundred persons, whose members were to be selected by the emperor from the provincial
assemblies.

This was well, so far as it went, but it did not go far
enough. Hungary, indeed, had her Diet, which could immediately be called together, and could, if the nation were so
minded, proceed to take its share in working this new system.
Hungary, however, positively refused to do anything of the
sort, and the measures taken to enable it to elect members
to the Diet, in the manner customary before the revolution,
wholly failed to lead the country to give up its determination
to stand firm in its legal position, and to have the laws of
1848, or nothing. The difficulty in the Germanic or Germanised provinces was different, but not less great. In them
there were no provincial assemblies at all adequate to modern
necessities, and when Count Goluchowski was rash enough
to publish the scheme of provincial assemblies devised by
M. Bach, in the height of the reaction, retaining as it did
many of the worst features of the pre-revolutionary period,
he was met with a shout of derision, and soon afterwards
retired from office, having made himself " impossible " on
both sides of the Leitha.

His successor was M. Schmerling, of whom we shall have
more to say presently, but in the meantime we may observe
that it was in the winter of 1860-61 that the two parties
which at this moment divide the empire began to take a
definite shape. The nucleus of these two parties, respectively, were the Hungarian advisers of the court, who thought
that if Hungary could only be fully conciliated, other things

would in the end come right of themselves, and those German
advisers, who thought that if the Germanic or Germanised
provinces could be fully conciliated, Hungary might be
coerced, and obliged to take its part in working a new
system, the driving-wheel of which should be a parliament
at Vienna, acting under *moderate* pressure on the part of the
sovereign,—a parliament in which the non-Germanic provinces should indeed be fairly and liberally represented, but
in the eye of which even Hungary should be merely a province like the Vorarlberg, and not a kingdom connected with
the rest of the empire by the link of the Pragmatic Sanction.

One of the most important incidents of this period was
the summoning to Vienna of Baron Nicholas Vay, the leader
of the Hungarian Protestants, in their struggle against the
encroachments of the central authorities, which was one of
the many results of the unlucky policy which was inaugurated by M. Bach.   Vay had been three times tried by
Haynau's military commissions ; twice he was acquitted,
but at last convicted, and imprisoned for two years in There-
sienstadt.   At this moment he was the most popular man in
Hungary ; for the religious contest had been really a political
one, and had engaged the sympathies, not only of the Protestants, but of other confessions also.   This man was now
made chancellor of Hungary, and exerted a most important
influence, until he was obliged to retire in the summer of
1861.   He is understood to have been one of those most
instrumental in raising M. Schmerling to power, probably
because, knowing his ability, and miscalculating the strength
of his Germanism, he thought that he would understand and
be equal to the situation.

It soon became clear, however, that it was not to the

views of Baron Vay that M. Schmerling would give his support.

There ought, indeed, as it seems after the event, to have been little doubt as to the scale into which the new minister would throw his influence. Born in 1805, of a family which belonged originally to the Rhineland, but which settled last century in Lower Austria, he had passed his early manhood and middle life in the bureaucracy, and is before all things a bureaucrat—liberal in the ends he pursues, not liberal in the means by which he would compass them. A decided opponent of the SYSTEM, he had made himself observed in the provincial assembly of Lower Austria before 1848, and had been sent in the spring of that year to represent Austrian interests at Frankfort. There he took a conspicuous place in the ranks of the Gross-Deutsch party, and combated with all his might the idea of the Prussian Hegemony. On his return to Vienna he became a member of Prince Schwartzenberg's ministry, but retired from it when it began to move fast down the steep of reaction.

A man with these antecedents was not likely to yield without a struggle to the pretensions of Hungary. If the Hungarians could make good their claims, farewell for ever to the idea of a great united Germany, to which Vienna should give the word of command! The views of the new minister were no secret to his colleagues, and the breach between him and those who represented the interests of Hungary in the government became every day wider and wider.

The first result of M. Schmerling's activity was the Patent of February 26, 1861. This document was in form an addition to the Diploma of October 1860, but in reality it amounted to a new constitution. Instead of the Reichsrath of a hundred members, sitting in one chamber, it created a much larger Reichsrath, sitting in two chambers ; and whereas the Diploma of October contemplated a federalist organisation, the Patent of February contemplated a centralised organisation, worked by a real Parliament, which might eventually grow to be as powerful as our own. There is nothing in such a conception that can be otherwise than agreeable to an Englishman. But that is not the question. The question is, Are the circumstances of Austria such as to make it possible to create and to work such an organisation? The events of the last five years have answered that question for us, but in the early spring of 1861 it was not so easy to answer. The experiment was of course to the last degree hazardous ; but one can hardly blame a statesman who held M. Schmerling's views with regard to Central European politics, if he determined to make a fight for it.

The first thing to be done was to call together the Hungarian Diet, which had not met since the Revolution, and to try whether it could not be induced to come to terms. The next step was to summon the new Reichsrath, in the constitution of which an arrangement was introduced for turning it into a "special or restricted Reichsrath," for the discussion of the affairs of the German and Germanised provinces, so that its activity would not necessarily be suspended, even if the Hungarians were to prove obstinate.

The Hungarian Diet met upon the 6th of April ; at first in Buda, and immediately afterwards in Pesth. Some time was occupied with the verification of the elections, and then the struggle of parties commenced. The point debated was whether the Diet should reply to the Crown by an address or by a resolution. The Moderates, lead by Deak, preferred an address; the extreme party, led by Count Teleki, preferred a resolution, taking their stand upon the undoubted fact that the emperor was not, according to the laws of the pre-revolutionary period, *de jure* king of Hungary; for, as we have already seen, according to the old view, "*Princeps est qui jurat, qui jurata servat, et qui coronatus est.*" Just at this crisis Count Teleki committed suicide, having found himself in a position from which he thought he could not escape without either being false to his political convictions or breaking a promise which he had given to the emperor. The views of the "address party" in the end prevailed, but they made some concessions to the views of their opponents, and amongst other things omitted the title of "Imperial Royal," in addressing the emperor. This was objected to at Vienna, and the address was finally voted unanimously in the form in which it was originally proposed by Deak.

It is far from impossible that, if the government had shown itself disposed to make concessions to Hungary, it would have got better terms than it is now likely to have to put up with; but concession was the last thing of which it thought. The jurists in the service of M. Schmerling answered the Hungarian address, and showed, at least to their own satisfaction, that Hungary had no shadow of right to stand upon, that the revolution had swept away all her old franchises, and that she was in no better position than any other province of the empire. Between parties so diametrically opposed as those of Deak and Schmerling, it was evident that there could be no *rapprochement*, and so in August the Diet was dissolved, and the Cabinet of Vienna determined to break the spirit of the nation, by reinvigorating, for the countries beyond the Leitha, the worst maxims of M. Bach.

The day will come, we hope, when the story of the stern resistance of Hungary, during the period of four years which intervened between the dissolution of the Diet and the issuing of the Patent of the 20th of the last September, will be fully told to Western Europe. There would, we think, be material in it for many pages like the best of those in Baron Eötvös's *Village Notary*. We are far from wishing to assert that such a record would contain only pages creditable to Hungary. At the county meetings, held previously to the meeting of the Diet in 1861, much appears to have been said and done which was quite unjustifiable ; but the Hungarians were right in the main, and we must forgive, in a people which has been so misgoverned, many excesses which would be unpardonable if the ordinary march of affairs had not been broken by revolution and counter-revolution. M. Boner's chapters on Transylvanian politics show the effect that the vehement one-sidedness of the Magyars produced on the mind of a friendly observer, who was not persuaded of what we believe to be true— that, viz., the system attempted to be carried out in Hungary after the dissolution of the Diet could lead to no good result.

We may now return to Vienna, where the Reichsrath assembled a week or two later than the Hungarian Diet, and was opened by a speech of great vigour, in which a breach with the old absolutist system was distinctly promised. The place of meeting was but badly filled, for neither Hungary, Croatia, Transylvania, Galicia, Venice, nor Istria had sent deputies, and of the three hundred and forty-three members who ought to have attended, only some two hundred were there. It soon became clear that of these two hundred about two-thirds were distinctly centralist and governmental in tone, altogether opposed to the ideas of the Federalist, or, as they have been called, State-right party. In the Upper House, too, the governmental majority was decisive. The tone of these majorities, as shown in their first debates, had a bad influence, it would seem, upon ministers, or, if this was not the case, the traditions of the Bach system and of the pre-revolutionary period, were too strong to be overcome, for certainly very little was done during the years in which M. Schmerling enjoyed power, even for the Germanic and Germanised provinces. Trade was still in fetters, the transgressions of the press were punished by long and cruel imprisonments, no right of association for political purposes could even be dreamt of, and societies formed for non-political purposes were always in danger of being suppressed, if they strayed at all too near the charmed boundary. During its later period the Reichsrath showed itself far less complaisant to ministers, and they had to endure very sharp criticisms ; but a dispassionate observer will hardly consider that the re-sults of the working of the February Patent in Austria were such as to make him very much regret the suspension of the sort of constitutional life which was enjoyed under it.

Ever since the dissolution of the Hungarian Diet and the retirement of Vay and Szechen, close relations had been kept up between the Hungarian "Old Conservatives" and the Federalist section of the Reichsrath. They showed, on the other hand, great attention to Deak, and endeavoured to come to an understanding with him, as the leader of the moderate Hungarian Liberals. At last, about Easter 1865, a highly-conciliatory article appeared in his organ at Pesth, and that was speedily followed by three letters from Pesth, which appeared in the *Debatte*, laying down authoritatively the programme of the moderate Hungarian Liberals. The *Debatte*, acting in the in-

terest of the "Old Conservatives," claimed for these most remarkable letters a careful and candid perusal, which they obtained
in very wide circles, nor can we doubt that they contributed
materially to prepare the way for a good understanding.

The principal points laid down in these letters are, that,
without the retirement of M. Schmerling, no good understanding between Hungary and Vienna could be dreamt of; that
Deak was in the habit of speaking in the most friendly terms
of the Lower House of the Reichsrath ; and that his friends
were generally in favour of a conciliatory policy.   They then
go on to point out that the Hungarians take their stand upon
the Pragmatic Sanction, and that to leave so firm a standing-
ground would be impossible.   Looking, then, to the Pragmatic
Sanction as the ultimate authority on all questions between
Hungary and its monarch, the writer asks—

1. Are there any affairs which are common to all the lands
of the Austrian empire ?

2. If so, what are they ?

3. How should they be managed ?

The first of these questions was answered by the laws of
1848 and the addresses of the Diet in 1861.

*There are affairs which are common to all the lands of the
Austrian empire.*

The answer to the second question can easily be deduced
from the Pragmatic Sanction, if we suffer ourselves to be
guided by the principle, that all affairs which are common
to all the lands of the Austrian empire, are so only in so far
as their being treated as common affairs is *necessary to the safety
of the monarchy.*

The Pragmatic Sanction, then, contemplates all the
Austrian lands as belonging to one common ruler.   The first

common affair is then the *keeping up the position and dignity of the common ruler.* Next, the Pragmatic Sanction binds the several lands to *mutual support.* That mutual support must be of a twofold kind, peaceful and warlike—that is, diplomatic and military. *Hence the management of foreign relations and of the army are common affairs.* The management of foreign relations must necessarily be entirely common, and guided by one hand. Not so the army. The command of the army, and all that relates to its internal management, must belong to the emperor; but the right of determining all matters relating to Hungarian troops, which it is not necessary to the *idea of a common army should belong to one hand,* must belong to the Diet. This relates to such matters as time of service, recruiting, amount of force, billeting, and so forth. Of course there is nothing in this demand to exclude common deliberation as to the quota of troops to be furnished by Hungary.

Another common affair *is the providing of money for all common affairs,* and it would be the duty of the Hungarian Finance Minister to furnish to the Imperial Finance Minister Hungary's proper quota; but he would at the same time manage the finances of the nation, in so far as they were not common affairs, according to the pleasure of the Diet. So, too, *the highest and broadest questions of commercial policy* must also, in the nature of things, be common affairs, and a good understanding about them can hardly be difficult to arrive at, when we remember that the tendency of the age is in all countries towards uniformity.

The answer to the last question is more difficult, and the writer speaks, when he comes to deal with it, with more diffidence. His leading principles are : That a central parliament is impossible ; that a separate Hungarian ministry is

indispensable ; and that the countries east and west of the
Leitha must be considered as two aggregations of lands, having
a *parity* of rights.   Into his other suggestions we need not go,
for they have, to a considerable extent, been already left behind by the progress of events ; but we have analysed his first
two letters in some detail, because they form the very best
answer which we have met with to the question—What is it
precisely that the Hungarians want ?

We ought, perhaps, to say something of the man to whom
all Hungary was now looking, and whose views are supposed
to be embodied in these letters.

Francis Deak was born in the year 1803, on an estate belonging to his father in the county of Szalad.   He studied at
Raab, and, like most of the Hungarian gentry, began to attend
the county meetings as soon as he was of age.   There he soon
became conspicuous, and acquired the goodwill of the Cortes,
or electors, in so high a degree, that he had no difficulty in
succeeding his elder brother as their deputy to the Diet, which
sat from 1832 to 1836.   By 1840, his position as the leader
of the Liberal party was acknowledged, and he had become
known beyond the limits of his country, for his profound
acquaintance with her laws, as well as for his wisdom, political tact, and conciliatory temper.   He was not a member of
the Diet of 1847, but held a portfolio in Count Louis Batthyani's first cabinet, in 1848.   This he resigned when Kossuth
and his immediate supporters seemed bent upon pushing
matters to extremity ; and his last public appearance during
the revolutionary period was as a negotiator in the camp of
Windischgrätz, when that commander was marching upon
Pesth.   After the revolution, the government of Prince
Schwartzenberg tried to induce him to aid them in their plans

for re-arranging the institutions of Hungary. Although, however, the changes which he had proposed to introduce as
minister were very great, their leading ideas were so utterly
different from those which were entertained at this period in
Vienna, that he declined the advances made to him, and lived
as a private citizen, till the events of 1861 brought him, as
we have seen, once more into prominence. And now, again,
" the wheel has come full circle," and he stands before Europe
as the first man of his people. If his wise · and moderate
policy succeeds, no one now living will better deserve the title
of "*pater patriæ.*"

Even before the reconstruction of the cabinet last summer,
the royal visit to Hungary, which has been so well described
in the *Revue des Deux Mondes*, the retirement of M. Schmerling, and other symptoms, showed that a change of system
was in contemplation. Of the new ministers who were
gathered under the wing of Count Mensdorff-Pouilly, whose
importance is not in connection with the internal affairs of the
empire, Count Belcredi became Minister of the Interior for
all the provinces not linked with the crown of Hungary. Of
Italian descent, he has property in Moravia, has been Statt-
halter of Bohemia, and is favourably known as a good administrator, averse to the "Zopf" of the old bureaucratic
system ; Count Larisch, a nobleman of good intentions and
liberal views, but by no means a Gladstone, took charge of
the finances ; while George von Majláth, an extremely
able man, became Chancellor of Hungary. The name, however, which has been chiefly mentioned in connection
with the overthrow of the Schmerling policy, is that of
Count Maurice Esterhazy, who has been in the government ever since the retirement of Baron Vay. His name,

it must be admitted, associated as it is with intrigue and
Jesuitry, has been anything but a tower of strength to his
colleagues.

The overthrow of the Schmerling policy was finally announced to the empire by the imperial manifesto of the 20th
September 1865. Whether we agree or disagree with the views
which dictated it, it is impossible to read that document without
feeling that the intentions of those who framed it were honest.
By it the emperor declares his intention of falling back upon
the Diploma of 20th October 1860, suspending the effect of
the Patent of the 26th February 1861, with all its consequences. In fact, he admits, in effect, that the system of
centralisation by which M. Schmerling had attempted to work
out and to modify the ideas of the October Diploma, had been
an utter failure, and that upon the foundation of that Diploma
a new system must be erected, carrying out its ideas without
any modification, at least in a centralist sense.

The effect produced upon public opinion in Vienna by this
proclamation was of course very great ; and those who, like
the writer of this paper, chanced to be upon the spot, heard
the most diverse opinions. "The situation," said one, " is as
triste as possible. The ministry stands alone, and has really
no party, except in Hungary." "Why do you come here at
present?" said a second ; "you can learn nothing now. All
that was has disappeared, and nothing has been put in its
place." "The present position of affairs," said a third, "is
very puzzling, and the Germans are not unnaturally irritated ;
but the change of system having been once announced, there
is nothing for it but to help it to work. The new ministers
are honourable men—men of the world, aristocratical in tendency, and hence unpopular with the German party, which is

essentially of the middle class." "Talk of governing Austria by the Hungarians!" said a fourth; "talk of governing England by the gipsies!" Some there were who thought that the irritation of the emperor against certain members of the Reichsrath had had much to do with the suspension of its powers. Others, again, looked at the whole matter from a very different point of view. "Of course," they said, "for Liberals to rejoice at the suspension of a constitution has an ugly look; but if that constitution is only laid aside in order to put something better in its place, they are surely right in rejoicing. The recent change was the only thing possible."

This chaos of opinion* still continues, and will continue; and while we range ourselves on the side of the new ministers, we do so with the full consciousness that some of the most impartial and best informed observers of Austrian politics have taken the other view.

To our thinking, then, it would be infinitely desirable that the idea of that Austrian Guizot, M. Schmerling, should be carried out, and that there should be in Vienna a Parliament whose decrees on all subjects should be as much respected in Essek and Sissek, in Debreczin and Kronstadt, as those of

---

* About a month after this paper originally appeared, an extremely interesting article upon the "Situation in Austria" was published in the *Westminster Review* of April 1866. It should be read in connection with another article, evidently by the same hand, which enriched the pages of the same periodical about three years ago. Both are the productions of one who had a good right to interpret to England the views of the party most opposed to the September Patent, more especially the Bohemian section of it. The following paragraphs, which we quote from this well-informed and able writer, express with very great clearness the views taken by the various provincial assemblies, of the lands unconnected with the Hungarian crown, about the great change of last autumn :—

"All the Diets of the countries on this side the Leitha, seventeen in number, met towards the end of last November. We give below, in a tabular

our own are from London to Unst or St. Kilda; but that seems
to us just one of the many desirable things which are simply

form, the votes for and against the present government in the different Diets,
with the population of the countries represented, the number of members in
such Diet, and their quotas of deputies to the Reichsrath, according to the
Patent of February 1861:—

Countries and Seats of Diets.	Population represented.	In respect to the Sep. Patent; Votes for and against the Ministry.		Number of Members in the	
				Diet.	Reichs-rath.
Galicia—Lemberg	4,612,000	149	1	150	38
Bukowina—Czernowitz	462,000	30	—	30	5
*Moravia—Brünn	1,887,994	51	42	100	22
*Carniola—Laibach...	451,941	18	12	37	6
Görz—Gradiska—Görz	195,000	13	6	22	2
Istria—Parenzo	235,000	30	—	30	2
Trieste—Trieste	95,000	36	4	40	2
Dalmatia—Zara	404,499	32	3	43	5
Bohemia—Prague	4,705,525	118	97	241	54
	13,038,959				
Lower Austria—Vienna ...	1,681,697	10	46	66	18
Upper „ Linz ...	707,450	12	34	50	10
Styria—Gratz...	1,056,773	7	50	63	13
Salzburg	146,769	—	26	26	3
Silesia—Troppau	443,912	1	30	31	6
Carinthia—Klagenfurth ...	332,456	7	28	37	5
Vorarlberg—Bregenz	102,000	2	18	20	2
	4,471,057				
†Tyrol—Innspruck	774,000	—	—	68	10
		513	393		

It will be seen in the above table that seven of the Diets, representing a
population of about four and a half millions, have, either in resolutions or
addresses to the Throne, expressed more or less dissatisfaction with the September Act. It has been most decidedly pronounced in the addresses of Lower

---

* Although, as regards confidence in the present ministry, the votes in
these two Diets were as above, yet in neither were motions of addresses to the
Crown, to express thanks or dissatisfaction, carried. That for the expression
of gratitude for the September Act was lost by a majority of three in the Diet
of Moravia; that to express dissatisfaction was lost by a majority of nine.

† The Diet of Tyrol did not enter into any discussion of the September
manifest. It was received in silence. The Diet is not satisfied with the
present ministry on the Protestant question. It never, however, approved of
Schmerling's policy.

impossible. We can well understand how painful it is to the
members of the "Great-Austrian party" to be obliged to give
up a brilliant and cherished dream ; but they must learn, we
fear, to recognise the limitation's of existence, and to say, with
the philosophy which distinguishes their race, "Es ist nun
einmal so." There may be a time far off when their dream
shall become a reality ; but it must be at a time so remote as
to lie quite beyond the ken of the politician.

It is but too true that even if the question which now
divides opinions in Austria were settled in the most satisfactory manner, and if the Hungarian Diet and the Central
Assembly at Vienna were working side by side, with most of
the minor provincial assemblies, from the Lake of Constance
to Cattaro, following suit, the empire would still be an object
of considerable anxiety to all politicians. It is hardly possible that such a state of concord can be perpetual ; nothing,
at least, has ever occurred in the world's history to entitle us

Austria and Vorarlberg. That of the latter little province was couched in
language so violent and disrespectful to the Crown that it has not been received.
In this land, as in Tyrol, the greater portion of the country population has
always been opposed to the policy of the late government; and it has been
owing to the influence of the Protectionist wealthy German manufacturers
and the people in their employ (most of them immigrants from Switzerland
and Southern Germany) that the action of the Diet has been decided.

The Diets of Galicia, Bukowina, Bohemia, and of the coast-lands (Istria,
Trieste, etc.), have acted in a direction contrary to the above, and have presented addresses to the Throne expressing deep-felt gratitude for the September manifest, and the change of policy involved therein. The Diet of Dalmatia
likewise voted an address approving the manifest, but at the same time
regretting the suspension of the lesser Reichsrath. This clause was introduced
through the influence of the officials, too many of whom, owing to Schmerling's election manœuvres, have seats in this assembly, greatly to the dissatisfaction of the Slavonic population of that country. If we include
Dalmatia, the Diets which, in addresses to the Throne, have expressed
approval of the September Act, represent a population of upwards of ten and
a half millions."

to cherish so bright a hope. The best, perhaps, to which we can look forward is, that some day or other, under circumstances different, and far more favourable than the present, it may be given to some statesmen to turn the *personal* union which Deak now conceives to exist between Austria and Hungary ; or the *real* union which Wheaton and other publicists see in their connection ; or the *unnamed union between a real and personal* union, for which the author of *Drei Jahre Verfassungsstreit* contends, into an incorporative union like that which exists between England and Scotland. The increase of railways and other means of communication may make this come quicker than seems possible at present, but it must still be very far away.

There is in this mighty empire the strangest intermingling of society as it was in the seventeenth century with society as it is now in the most highly-advanced nations. How difficult it is to believe that the scenes which Mr. Boner describes in the Transylvanian Saxon-land are going on at this moment ; or that in the Rouman nation, which is called to equal rights with the most civilised populations of the empire, there should be only about 150 educated men !

The difficulties which have been entailed upon the present rulers of Austria by the follies, crimes, and neglects of many generations, are so great, that we ought to judge particular acts, if they continue as now to be clearly animated by honest intentions, with the greatest forbearance, and give much weight to what such writers as Mr. Paton and Mr. Boner have to say about the doings of Austrian *employés*, even at the worst and most painful moments of recent years. We hope that if the questions which at present agitate the empire can be in any way tolerably arranged, the next few years will be given, as much as possible, to material improvement. Much, even since we first saw Hungary, nineteen years ago, has been done for the improvement of that magnificent country ; but millions of capital must still be expended before her resources are even half developed ; and we cannot help thinking that Mr. Boner is right in pointing to Transylvania as a very profitable field for English enterprise.

A most wise beginning has been made by the present ministers of Austria in the commercial treaty with England— a measure which, as has been truly said, marks a turning-point, not only in the policy of their country, but in that of ours ; in the policy of their country, because they give up the prohibitive system in which they have so long delighted ; in that of ours, because, far more decidedly than in the French treaty, we come forward as the assertors of the principle that for a nation to refuse to exchange with us those commodities which can be exchanged with mutual advantage by both nations, is an unfriendly, semi-hostile act, and because we give it distinctly to be understood, that far from thinking it necessary to buy " concessions" by " concessions" on our part, we think that by persuading the Austrians to make these " *concessions* " we are conferring at least as great a benefit upon them as on ourselves. The " concessions " which we make with regard to the timber duties, and to the duties on wines in bottle, are really no equivalents at all for their " concessions," for not only are they trifling in themselves, but we should very soon have made them for our own purposes. In fact, their being treated as " concessions" at all, is only an accommodation to the weakness of half-converted neophytes.

The history of this treaty is a curious one. Springing out

of the anti-French sympathies of a small knot of English politicians, becoming complicated with questions of a loan and the private arrangements of capitalists, it gradually slipped into the hands of the two men most fitted to carry it to a successful issue—Mr. Morier, one of the ablest of that not too numerous class of diplomatists who take *au serieux* their noble profession, and Mr. Mallet of the Board of Trade, whose great knowledge of mercantile affairs, wide sympathies, and high political ability, are known and appreciated by all who have watched our commercial progress in the last ten years. Great credit is also due to Mr. Somerset Beaumont for having originated the idea of a treaty with Austria, and for having paved the way for it, at the cost of infinite time and trouble—efforts which have as yet by no means been, in our opinion, sufficiently appreciated. These three gentlemen should divide between them most of the praise which accrues to England from this transaction, although other figures flitted across the negotiations, and were sometimes helpful enough. On the Austrian side all credit is due to Count Mensdorff and Baron Wüllerstorf, especially to the former, whose conduct was loyal and honourable in the highest degree.

The direct effects of the treaty in promoting trade between Austria and this country will not be very great or very immediate, although we need hardly say that the average of the new duties will be far below the maximum of 25 per cent. A very large trade between Austria and Switzerland, and Austria and Italy, may presently be expected to arise, and when any impulse is given to the general trade of Europe, we shall not be long without reaping great indirect advantage.

The finances of Austria may be expected to improve under this judicious change of system, and we may trust that in twenty years the least advanced of Austrian economists will look back with astonishment on the fact which Count Larisch lately announced to the world, that the state lotteries brought into his coffers more than half as much again as the customs.   Still we must not expect to see the fruit of all this late wisdom ripen too soon.   Austria is terribly poor, and it will be long before she feels in all her members the vivifying influence of a just commercial legislation.

It must not be forgotten that, even if the relations of the lands of the Hungarian crown to the rest of the empire were definitely settled, much tact and good sense would be required on the part of Hungarian statesmen to prevent the outbreak of those jealousies of nationality which proved so fatal to Hungarian aspirations in 1848 and 1849.   Doubtless, the tyranny of the Bach period, by showing all the nationalities that they had a common enemy in the centralisers of Vienna, did a good deal to destroy the memory of old feuds.   " The Croat," said a man in the neighbourhood of Agram to the writer, in 1851, "put down the Hungarian, but he will take uncommonly good care not to do it again."   A very little manifestation, however, of the old ultra-Magyar spirit would soon make the Roumans or the Ruthenians more unwilling to take laws from Pesth than even from Vienna, if, indeed, the former will not be hostile to any Magyar ascendancy, however beneficent.   Baron Eötvös, who shows in his recent pamphlet, *Die Nationalitäten-Frage*, that he thoroughly understands the force, while he does not estimate too highly the wisdom, of the nationality cry, takes a hopeful view of this subject, and thinks that many of the difficulties which are involved in the question of Hungarian nationalities will be got over, if only the state will leave as much play as possible to individual

liberty; and without pronouncing any opinion upon a question about which no one who has not lived long in the country,
and transacted business in many parts of it, has a right to
speak, we would fain accept the views of one who is at once
a patriot and a man of enlightenment.*

The question of Venetia is extremely difficult—far more
difficult than it appears at first sight to most of our countrymen. In the first place, The military reasons which have been
so fully stated in England by Mr. Bonamy Price in favour of
the retention of the Quadrilateral, deserve serious attention;
secondly, The pride of the Austrian army appears to be engaged
in favour of not surrendering this piece of Italian soil without
a struggle; thirdly, The emperor is himself understood to feel
very strongly on the subject; fourthly, A very large number
of persons in the Germanic provinces would consider the
abandonment of Venetia as a heavy blow and a great discouragement; fifthly, There is no evidence that the Hungarians, if their own demands were satisfied, would not be
willing to fight against Italy.

To these various considerations we may reply, first, that
if Italy becomes reasonably powerful, there is little chance of
French armies repeating against Austria the tactics of Napoleon's Italian campaigns, while it is hardly probable that the
Italians, if once they have Venetia, will allow themselves to
listen to those zealots who would teach them to clamour for
Istria and other such *revendications*. The second and third
objections are serious, and we confess we do not see how anything but the *ultima ratio regum* is likely to overcome them.

* For a more formal statement of the views of Hungarian Liberals on this
subject, see the translation of the Second Address of the Diet of 1861 in Mr.
Horne Payne's Collection of Documents illustrative of Hungarian history in
that year.

To the fourth we answer that we do not believe the majority of persons in the Germanic provinces would allow, when it came to the point, their passions to overcome their interest in a matter which is capable of being translated into a question of figures. We have heard a prominent member of the most essentially German section of the Reichsrath admit that the question of Venetia must one day be settled against Austria, although not without a war. To the fifth objection we hardly see what to reply, but trust that the argument of the purse might, at the critical moment, not be without its influence on the other side of the Leitha.

When we balance these considerations, we may well doubt whether Austria is at all likely to sell Venetia, but hold it to be more than probable that, if she does not do so, she will ere long lose it by war. Much depends on the course that things take in Italy. If the new kingdom becomes gradually consolidated, if its miserable finances are put in order, if the brigandage which makes people almost long for the rule of the Dukes and the Bourbons is effectually put down, if the Roman question is solved, and the country begins to be respected rather than patronised—public opinion in Europe, and common-sense at home, may possibly become too strong even for the pride of the House of Hapsburg-Lorraine, and the susceptibilities of that devoted army to which it owes so much. In one way or another, however, we cannot doubt that Italy must eventually possess Venetia, and that Austria must make up her mind to the loss, if loss indeed it be.

The future position of Austria with regard to Northern and Central Germany is another question of even greater difficulty. The relations of Austria to Germany have been treated at great length in a very interesting work by Baron

Eötvös. His thesis is that the unity of Germany is necessary to the peace of Europe, and that the legislative separation of Hungary, and her connection with the rest of the empire by a merely personal union, is a necessary condition of German unity. Unlike Baron Eötvös, we should prefer to see Austria altogether divorced from her connection with the Bund, although we are, of course, not insensible to the grand features of the so-called Gross-Deutsch idea, and to the maimed and truncated appearance which Germany would present, if she lost all the fair and historic German-speaking lands which are politically connected with Austria. Looking, however, not to what is abstractedly desirable, but to what is not wholly impossible, we pronounce for the view which finds favour in Prussia. So vast, however, are the difficulties which lie in the way of any such solution of the German question, so much has the popular sentiment in the Middle States been damped by the succession of follies which have characterised the reign of the present king of Prussia, so fiercely will a hundred menaced interests fight each for their own hand against the Klein-deutsche solution of the problem, that, it may well be, several decades may pass before any revolution in Germany comes about. German patriots pray for sages on the throne of Prussia, and fools on all the minor thrones ; but as yet their prayers do not meet with any very satisfactory answer.

There are some who say, and we can well believe them, that the Austrian dynasty will give up anything rather than its hold upon Germany. Venetia may go, Hungary may go, anything and everything, rather than the old recollections of Frankfort. Nothing is more natural than that the kaiser should think the felicity of reigning over any given number of Roumans, Bulgarians, or Bosnians, would be dearly bought by the loss of even a single German province ; and if we look at the latest information from Northern Turkey in Europe—the little work lately edited by Mr. H. Sandwith for two enterprising English ladies—we shall see great reason to doubt whether the prospect of only exchanging Turkish for Austrian rule, would excite any particular enthusiasm on the southern side of the Save. If this be so, however, and if it be true, as we fear it is, that the Austrian occupation of the Principalities has left behind it more bitter recollections than either the Russian or the Turkish, what is the idea of an Austria whose centre shall be Pesth, and which shall extend all down the Danube valley, but a pleasant dream? We say this with sorrow, and should like nothing better than that some one might prove to us that we are too desponding ; for since the resignation by the Emperor Francis of the imperial German crown, with all its shadowy and sublime prerogatives, this has seemed the natural and logical solution of many of the great difficulties of Central Europe.

We do not wonder, then, that the policy of the modern statesmen of Austria with regard to Turkey should be, and has been, a Conservative one. They have quarter-barbarians enough of their own to manage without the addition of a few million semi-barbarians from the spoils of Turkey ; and considering the powers of national deglutition and digestion which Russia has shown, they may well fear that the death of the Sick Man would add far too largely to her inheritance.

The views which any one will form about the Polish question in its bearings upon Austria, will of course depend upon his views of the far larger question as to the future of Poland, of which we have elsewhere spoken.

Ever since the famous prophecy of Maria Theresa, Austria

has been more favourably disposed to that unhappy country than either of the two other partitioning powers ; and it is not surprising that she should have thought it far more important, at more than one period of her recent history, to have a strong barrier between herself and Russia, than to possess the, after all, not very extensive territory which was her reward for the part she took in the evil transactions for which Europe has paid and will still pay so dearly. The hopeless and inextricable difficulties with which the Polish question is surrounded have, however, up to this time, wholly prevented anything definite being done. Some little-known details will be found in a recent article by M. Klaczko in the *Revue des Deux Mondes.*

When we remember how bitterly hated the Austrian government was in this country only a few years ago, it is satisfactory to see with how much good feeling our press has recognised the efforts which it has recently made to improve the institutions of the empire. There are, however, still persons among us who can only look at Austria through Italian spectacles, and who believe that out of her no good thing can come. We are, we need hardly say, of a very different opinion. There is no country of the Continent for whose prosperity we feel more anxious. This Europe in miniature—comprising in itself more contrasts of climate, of scenery, of race, of language, of religion, of civilisation, than any other region of equal extent in this quarter of the globe—can hardly fail to excite the interest and conciliate the goodwill of every one who makes a study of her affairs. We cannot name any country which affords so many facilities for experiments of living, under unfamiliar but not unfavourable conditions. That out of her disorder may come a many-sided order, that out of her

discouragement may come cheerfulness, and out of her errors
wisdom, is our fervent hope; but as we close the review of
her recent history—by no means the darkest portion of her
annals—we cannot help counting up the sins of her rulers, and
asking ourselves whether it is not but too possible that for
those sins there may yet come a day of reckoning, even worse
than that of 1848. How often, during the period through
which we have been conducting our readers, must not the
wisest observers of what was passing at Vienna have been
tempted to exclaim with the poet,—

> " Aber sie treiben's toll ;
> Ich fürcht ? es breche ?
> Nicht jeden Wochenschluss
> Macht Gott die Zeche."

*   *   *   *

The three agitated months that have passed since this
paper was first printed have not, we think, very materially
altered the situation in Austria. The negotiations between
the Hungarians and the government still drag their slow length
along, and impartial observers can hardly help fearing that
in their desire to get as much as they can for themselves,
each party runs the risk of putting off a settlement until some
sudden event may force them to accept one, which may be
anything but agreeable. Sometimes we even doubt whether
they really wish to come to terms, and whether each does not
hope more from the chapter of accidents than from their long-
continued parley.

Since we wrote, great clouds have gathered, both on the
south and north of the empire, and the German and Italian
questions have alike become threatening. If an appeal is made
to force, no one can venture to say what may be the issue ;
but if things are left to take their natural course, we do not,

on reconsideration, feel inclined to change much that we have said, although perhaps our view of the Hungarian question was a little too hopeful.

It is hard to see how war, should it unfortunately break out, can materially alter the relations of Austria either to the Bund or to Italy,—always supposing that Austria continues to exist in anything like her present shape. Once let war break out, and even that becomes uncertain, for who can say what unforeseen circumstances may arise? Whatever may be the strength of their armies, Prussia is a natural, Austria an artificial body. We have already said that it seems to us, in the necessity of things, that the German and Venetian questions must be eventually settled in accordance with the views of Berlin and Florence. Even if Austria were for a time signally victorious, it would make no very material difference in the end. Should war not arise, it is possible that the discussions which have been and are taking place may, on the other hand, pave the way for us to arrive more speedily at a settlement of the affairs of Central Europe, which may have some chance of being permanent.

Of the internal events of the empire, not the least curious which has occurred within the last few weeks, is the fresh outbreak of Czechish agitation at Prague. Nothing could better illustrate the extraordinary and quite exceptional difficulties of Austria.

CHAPTER IV.

THE politics, no less than the scenery of North-eastern Germany, are by no means attractive. The interminable marshes of the Havel, the dreary sand-waste which surrounds the capital, the rich but unlovely plain of Magdeburg, have all their antitypes in the history of Prussia. From time to time some enterprising English newspaper sends a correspondent to Berlin ; but the editor soon discovers that not one reader in a thousand pays any attention to his letters, and the veil once more descends upon those confused struggles, of which, even more truly than of the pictures of Wouvermans, it may be said that it is difficult to make out "which is plaintiff and which defendant."

But Prussian politics have a meaning after all, and sometimes, as at this moment, very grave issues are depending on the decisions of Prussian rulers and the good sense of the Prussian people. We propose, accordingly, to set down a few notes, which may save those who wish to have a tolerably clear idea of what has of late been passing at Berlin, some trouble in turning over books and newspapers.

In the recent history of Prussia it is easy to distinguish four well-marked periods.

The first of these extends from the accession of Frederick William IV., in June 1840, to the opening of the " Vereinigte Landtag," in April 1847.

The second commences with that event, and terminates with the dissolution of the National Assembly and the proclamation of the new Constitution on December 5, 1849.

The third begins with the proclamation of the new Constitution, and extends to the assumption of the regency by the prince of Prussia.

The fourth opens with that occurrence, and is still in progress.

To the three first of these periods we may with confidence assign the names of the period of *expectation*, the period of *revolution*, and the period of *reaction ;* but he who could with confidence give a distinctive name to the fourth would know the secret of the future of Germany.

In June 1840 Frederick William III. closed his long and chequered career. Tried by both extremes of fortune, he had shown few great qualities in either, and the numerous expressions of regret which followed his decease, proved only the loyal sentiments of his deceived and long-suffering subjects. The advent of his successor was heralded by many hopes. The Crown Prince was not very well known ; but those who had been admitted to his society spoke highly of his accomplishments, his learning, and his liberal opinions. His good disposition had not, people said, been changed by his altered position. He had remarked, it was reported, to Alexander von Humboldt, that as Crown Prince he was necessarily the first noble of the realm, but that as king he was only the first citizen. The new reign opened with a series of gracious and popular acts. A general amnesty for political offences ; the recal to high office of Schön, the illustrious and beloved fellow-labourer of the deeply-venerated Stein ; the advancement of Boyen, who was regarded as the inheritor of the traditions of Scharnhorst and of Gneisenau, cheered the hearts of all enlightened and liberal Prussians, and excited no little alarm at Vienna and St. Petersburg. The morning which dawned so brightly was not, however, destined to be long unclouded. The first untoward event was the answer given by the monarch to the states of East Prussia, when, on the occasion of the *Homage* ceremonial at Königsberg, they ventured to express their hopes that the long-promised constitution would at last become a reality. Somewhat later an order in council appeared, which left no doubt on the minds of reflecting men as to the real intentions of the king. It was clear that the sort of change which he contemplated was not that which the nation wished. Some half middle-age, half lower-empire organisation might take the place of the old order, but of a constitution founded on the abstract ideas of what was right and just, or on the actual necessities of the nation, there was no chance whatever. The appointment of Eichhorn, a member of the ultra-pietistic and absolutist party, to the important office of minister of public instruction, in the room of the wise Altenstein, the one man of enlightenment who had contrived to the last to retain the favour of the old king, further increased the uneasiness of the public mind. The advancement of this mischievous tool* of obscurantism was the signal for a series of coercive and ill-conceived measures, many of them attributable to the king himself, which had their natural result in the antagonistic follies and excesses of 1848. The censorship grew ever stricter and stricter ; numerous press prosecutions took place, the most famous of which was that

---

* Eichhorn was no worse than some of his colleagues, but the king took more interest, and did more mischief, in his department, than in any other.

of which Dr. Jacoby of Königsberg was the victim, on account of his pamphlet *Vier Fragen beantwortet von einem
Ost-Preussen,* and which ended in the acquittal of the accused
by the High Court of Berlin, much to the disgust of the king
and of the government. Eichhorn extended his mischievous
activity into all departments. Students were encouraged to
denounce the religious or political heresies of their professors;
the books in the libraries of schoolmasters were carefully in-
spected ; the standard of elementary education was intentionally lowered ; men were advanced in the various gymnasia
and universities, not on account of their attainments, but on
account of their attachment to the views of the pietists. The
régime of the most literary of contemporary monarchs seemed
destined to result in the same hostility to all real learning
which was openly avowed by the Emperor Francis. It was,
however, too late. In vain Hengstenberg and his crew
tried to bring in a Prussian if not a Roman popery ; in
vain Eichhorn travelled from university to university,
suspending here, denouncing there; in vain successive
ministers of the interior seconded him with all their power,
ordering domiciliary visits, turning Liberals from other German states out of the country at two hours' notice, suppressing newspapers, and so forth. In vain the king himself, for
seven long years, scolded now this city and now that—
Breslau one day and Berlin another; in vain he speechified
and in vain he cajoled ; in vain he dismissed petition after
petition, which the provincial state assemblies addressed to
him; in vain he tried to make the Prussian people content
with a representation formed of an agglomeration of committees, chosen from the different provincial state assemblies,
and possessed merely of a deliberative voice. The pressure

from without grew too strong, and at length, after mature consultation with confidential advisers, the "patent" of February 3, 1847, was given to the world.

The king was a most ardent, as he was certainly a most influential, disciple of the "historical" school of publicists and of jurists. It would be difficult to speak too highly of the merits of Savigny and his fellow-labourers, as long as they confined themselves to explaining the present by the past ; but unfortunately these same men, when they came to be ministers of state, made an altogether improper use of their own researches. They were justly proud of having shown how baseless were the speculations by which their immediate predecessors had attempted to account for existing phenomena in the domain of politics. They hated the *à priori* verbiage which had been the cant of the day during the French Revolution, and they jumped to the conclusion, that all the state arrangements which were historically explicable, and which had once been reasonable, should still be kept unimpaired, or at most should be developed. They forgot that for more than half-a-century the people for whom they had to legislate had been sitting at the feet of those often-mistaken but still effective teachers against whom they had made war.

The "Vereinigte Landtag," which was called into being by the "patent" of the 3d of February, was a masterpiece of learned reconstruction ; but it was not a body likely to be of much use in a world of hard realities.* It met on the 11th of April, and sat through a considerable part of the summer. The king had told it that the last thing in the world which he wished

---

* This was not the fault of its members, many of whom showed great talent and most remarkable firmness ; but its position was an " impossible " one.

its members to do, was to represent the feelings of the people—
" The rôle of so-called representatives of the people" was an
object of supreme contempt to the royal *savant.* Nevertheless, the one good result which it produced was to give vent
to the popular uneasiness. Already the names of Vincke and
others, who have since been famous for their advocacy of
liberal opinions, began to make themselves familiar to the
public ear. The king talked theocratic nonsense : " Never,
never, will I allow a piece of written paper, like a second
providence, to force its way between our Lord God in heaven
and this land, to rule us with its paragraphs, and to supersede
by them the old holy loyalty." No wonder, then, that he
was embittered by the language held by some of the deputies,
and that he closed the session in no good humour. It is
difficult to say how long the farce might have lasted, if events
had not occurred beyond the frontier which changed altogether
the aspect of affairs.

The news of the outbreak in Paris came to Berlin on one
of those sunny February days which cheer the long cold spring
of the great German plain. Groups were soon gathered on
the Linden, and the exciting intelligence, passing from mouth
to mouth, soon reached the remotest quarter of the city. The
tidings of the flight of Louis Philippe, and of the fall of the
monarchy of July, followed in quick succession. On the 6th
of March the first public meeting took place in the Thier-
garten. The events of the 13th at Vienna brought the revolution nearer, and on the 18th Berlin was in full revolt.
No little mystery still shrouds the occurrences of that day
and of the one which followed it. Thus much is, however,
clear : the impulse to actual violence came from abroad.
Poles and Parisian builders of barricades were in the city by

hundreds. In the palace the greatest indecision prevailed.
The king lost his head, and his nearest relatives were more occupied in intriguing for their own advantage than in taking
measures to insure his triumph. At length, while the contest
was still undecided, when the military were in full possession
of the principal streets and squares, and the insurgents had
fallen back into the side streets and suburbs, the order went
forth from the highest authority that the troops should be
withdrawn. Withdrawn they were, to the annoyance of many
moderate Liberals, who felt that either the conflict should have
been avoided altogether, or the insurrection should have been
effectually crushed.

With the withdrawal of the troops began eight uneasy
months, in which no party, and hardly any public man, in
Prussia, gathered any laurels. The first scene was the deep
humiliation of the king, who was made to stand with uncovered
head before the bodies of those who had fallen in defence of
the barricades, while a hymn, composed by his ancestress, the
wife of the great Elector, "Jesus meine Zuversicht," was sung
by the immense crowd which had gathered under the windows of the palace. In the beginning of April the "Vereinigte
Landtag" was called together, but merely for the purpose of
preparing the way for the National Assembly, which was to
succeed it, and which was opened on the 22d of May. This
body, which ought to have fulfilled the functions of a constituent assembly, proved itself curiously incapable of useful
work. The king, whose imaginative and excitable tempera-
ment had been impressed by the "Grossartigkeit" of the
popular movement, seems really at first to have wished to
deal honestly by his people ; but he was pushed further and
further towards the reactionists, partly by the blunders of the

national representatives, and partly by the growing insolence and atrocity of the mob. The plundering of the arsenal on the night of the 15th of June—the outrageous attack on the hotel of the Liberal minister Auerswald in the month of August—the revolutionary harangues of such wretched demagogues as Held and Müller of the Linden—the assaults which were made upon unpopular journalists, showed that the lower classes of the population as little understood the difference between liberty and licence as the reactionary coteries among the nobles, the clergy, and the military, understood the distinction between order and servitude.

The National Assembly was divided into unnumbered cliques and fractions of cliques ; but we may distinguish in it four very well marked shades of opinion. First, there was the " extreme left," the foremost names of which were Waldeck and Jacoby ; the former an impetuous and able speaker, who united strong Romanist religious sympathies with extreme popular opinions—the other, the author of that famous pamphlet of which we have spoken above, and which had been to the Prussian revolution what the tract of the Abbé Siéyès on the Tiers Etat had been to that of France. This section leant to republican ideas.

Next to it, but separated by a real though narrow division, stood the " left centre," which was led by Rodbertus, and was distinctly antirepublican, although determined to carry out to their fullest logical consequences the concessions made by the king in the month of March, and to turn the old absolutist Prussia into a limited monarchy, governed on advanced liberal principles. To this section also belonged Schultze-Delitzsch, of whom we shall have something to say hereafter.

The true " centre" was led by Von Unruh, who was for

some time Speaker, and whose name was associated with the last adventures of the short-lived and unfortunate body over which he presided.

The "right" numbered amongst its foremost names the gifted Catholic lawyer, A. Reichensperger, well known as a passionate lover of Gothic architecture, and the celebrated Protestant preachers Jonas and Sydow, both names to be had in honour, and the last of whom is still closely connected with the liberal *Protestantische Kirchen-Zeitung*, and represents the traditions of Schleiermacher in the pulpit of Berlin.

On the whole, however, there was less ability in the Assembly than might have been expected, and, above all, there was a deplorable want of political experience and tact. The successive ministries which had to deal with it were not more skilful. The so-called "transition" ministry of Camphausen, which was called into existence on the 29th of March, gave way in the course of the summer to the Hansemann cabinet, which called itself, somewhat self-consciously, the "ministry of action." When the king had begun to despair of any good results being attained by the National Assembly, and had cast his eyes on Wrangel and his battalions, whom he regarded as the destined means of restoring the old state of things, the Hansemann ministry was succeeded by that of General von Pfuel, and that again in a few weeks by the ministry of Count Brandenburg, who on the 9th of November announced to the assembled deputies that their sittings were adjourned to the 27th, and that their next meeting was to be held, not at Berlin, but at Brandenburg. We need not follow the Assembly through its last inglorious days. On the 11th the National Guard was

disbanded ; on the 12th the state of siege was proclaimed at
Berlin; and on the 5th of December the National Assembly
was dissolved, and the new constitution announced.

Arrived at the end of the revolutionary and at the
opening of the reactionary period, we may pause, and ask
whether the Prussian people had gained anything by the
agitations and losses of 1848. The answer must be in the
affirmative. The constitution of the 5th of December was
not by any means perfect, and some of the modifications
introduced into in the year which followed, were far from
being improvements; but the step in advance was not the
less great and real. It was more than worth the blood which
had been shed, and the property which had been wasted.

The dissolution of the National Assembly had been
pronounced by M. Manteuffel ; and as it was his influence
which was in the ascendant during the whole of the reaction,
this is the proper place to say a few words about him. The
Freiherr Otto von Manteuffel was born in Lusatia in 1805,
and belongs to an ancient family. He entered the Prussian
bureaucracy early in life, and rose rapidly through all its
grades, giving ever new proofs of his diligence, his attorney-
like acuteness, and his knowledge of administrative detail.
In the Landtag of 1847 he defended the bureaucratic method
of government against the advocates of the parliamentary
system ; and when he came into power in the end of 1848
he lost no time in showing that he regarded himself simply
as a servant of the crown, and that he was absolutely
indifferent to the opinion of the parliamentary majority.
Those who have read the *Gespräche aus der Gegenwart* of
Radowitz—which is, we may remark in passing, one of the
best helps to understanding the state of things in Germany

on the eve of 1848—will remember the character of Œder. M. Manteuffel was the spokesman of all the Œder class ; the bureaucrat *par excellence.* He is a man of few illusions and of no high aims. He was clear-sighted enough to understand that the Kreuz-Zeitung party was an anachronism, but he could not reconcile himself to an honest constitutional policy, His favourite weapon was intrigue, and his favourite department was the police. To keep his own place and to advance his own fortune was his first object ; to prevent sudden changes and to keep things quiet was his second aim.

The first parliament elected under the new constitution assembled in the beginning of 1849 ; but the Second Chamber was dissolved in the month of April, chiefly on account of its vote against the maintenance of the state of siege. Before allowing the elections to proceed, a new electoral law was enacted by the simple process of a royal edict ; and the democratic party, seeing that it had no chance of success, retired from the contest, and brought forward no more candidates till 1861.

When the new Chamber met in August, it was found that the ministers had not been mistaken in their calculations. The reactionists were in a decided majority, and immediately proceeded to revise the constitution in an anti-liberal sense. When their labours were finished, the revised constitution was laid before the king. In the first days of 1850 he replied by a message, in which he asked for further concessions. The Chambers took the royal proposals into consideration, accepted some and rejected others. At last a compromise was arrived at, and the king, with much solemnity, swore to the constitution in the palace at Berlin. In a speech which he delivered on the occasion he explained the reason which had led him to proclaim the much more liberal constitution of December 1848.   He then thanked the Chambers for having revised his own work, and diminished its dangerous liberalism.

The "German question," in the meantime, grew ever more important.   Prussia, which had definitively broken with the Frankfort Parliament, and had given up all hopes of obtaining the hegemony of the whole of Germany, had been trying plan after plan for a smaller federation, in which she might have the undisputed lead.   Alliances quickly made and as quickly broken, a congress of princes and a college of their plenipotentiaries, a parliament at Erfurt, and what not, the affairs of the Germanic Confederacy in 1849 and 1850 are not a labyrinth into which our readers would thank us for conducting them unawares.   Suffice it to say, that in December 1850 the question presented itself—thanks to the Hessian complication—in the form of submission to the dictates of Austria and peace, or adherence to the Germanic pretensions of Prussia and war.   The conciliatory Brandenburg died.   The more determined Radowitz* was dismissed. Manteuffel was not the man to play double or quits ; he hurried to Olmütz, and gave up everything.

---

* The feelings at this period of this noble and highly-gifted man, whose mystical views and false political position cannot prevent our feeling a deep sympathy for him, are well shown in a letter addressed in the very first days of 1851 to Mr. Hayward, and quoted by that gentleman in not the least pleasant and instructive of his many pleasant and instructive essays :—

" Ces reflexions avec lesquelles vous finissez votre article, sont à très peu pres les mêmes qui se sont presentés à moi lors de la revue retrospective que j'ai faite le dernier jour de l'an.   J'ai dû en faire une application toute personelle.   'Triste du mal que je prévois, impuissant pour le bien que je désire, je voudrais finir par un peu de repos une vie que je n'ai point epargnée, mais que je n'ai pu rendre utile.'   *Ces temps actuels sont difficiles—je dois dire plus, ils sont impossibles.*"

The disaster of Olmütz soon led, by way of the Dresden Congress, to its natural result,—the re-establishment of the federal relations which had been overturned in 1848, and the revival of that ill-contrived body, the Frankfort Diet, which one of the most rising of German statesmen, M. de Roggenbach, has aptly called "the contradiction of thirty-five wills." In internal as well as external affairs the party of reaction grew ever bolder. M. Manteuffel declared in so many words, in the first days of 1851, that the government meant to break finally with the revolution. M. von Westphalen, who represented in the cabinet the feudal section of the Conservative party, called once more into life the old provincial assemblies, which all Europe had thought finally laid to rest by the legislation of the previous year. The journey of the king to meet the Emperor Nicholas at Warsaw added to the uneasiness of the Liberals, and the *coup d'état* of the 2d of December in France encouraged the pamphleteers of M. Manteuffel to call loudly for a new revision of the constitution. The year 1852 brought no change for the better, except in so far as it showed more distinctly the diversity of opinion between the two halves of the dominant party; Manteuffel and the bureaucratic Conservatives looking across the Rhine for a line of conduct to imitate, and the Feudalists vehemently denouncing the French ruler, and reserving their sympathies for the emperor of Russia, who visited Berlin in the month of May. The elections, which took place in the autumn, were so managed by the government that very few Liberals were returned ; and the power of the reactionists, from this time to the end of 1857, was modified only by their internal dissensions, and by the presence in the lower house of a powerful body of Catholic representatives, who frequently voted with the opposition, to subserve the special interests of their co-religionists.

The negotiations which preceded the Russian war, and that war itself, diverted for a considerable period the attention of Prussian Liberals from their internal affairs. They had given up all hope of a speedy change for the better at home ; but they trusted that if the government could be forced into siding with the Western powers, a new turn would be given to the fancies of the king. The nation was soon divided into three parties,—the Liberals of all shades desiring an alliance with France and England ; the feudal faction urging the government to assist Russia ; and Manteuffel's adherents determined to uphold the neutrality of Prussia at any sacrifice.

The name of the Kreuz-Zeitung party became now for the first time familiar to Europe. This name was given to the Feudalists in consequence of their having for their principal organ the newspaper started to assist the reaction, and called the *Neue Preussische Zeitung,* but which, in order to show its orthodoxy and patriotism, bore the Prussian Landwehr Cross of 1813 on its first page. The leaders of this party were Stahl and Gerlach. The former, who died in 1861, was originally a Jew, but changed his religion at seventeen. He was born in 1802 at Munich, and studied chiefly at the small Bavarian university of Erlangen. In time he became a professor there, and was summoned thence to Berlin in 1840 by Frederick William IV., for whom his biblico-juristical mysticism had a great fascination.* From first to last

* Of the many things that have been said and written with regard to Frederick William IV., nothing has, we think, so well hit the mark as the following observations which we extract from the extremely remarkable little book, which was published in 1862, by Dr. Strauss, upon H. S. Reimarus, who is now known to have been the author of the once mysterious and celebrated

Stahl's influence was simply mischievous : intolerant and obscurantist, he would, if he had appeared earlier on the scene, have been a most dangerous counsellor ; but the cause of religious liberty was virtually gained in Prussia before he arose. As it was, he and his friends did infinite evil.

The President von Gerlach, and his brother the general,

Wolfenbüttel Fragments. Some of our readers may recollect that many years ago Dr. Strauss published a *brochure* about the late king of Prussia, which, under the name of " Julian the Apostate, or the Romanticist on the Throne of the Cæsars," was more talked about in England than German pamphlets usually are—as, indeed, it well deserved to be.

" Ein Berliner Philosoph hat neulich Friedrich Wilhelm IV. einen historischen Geist genannt. Mag ihm der Geist der Geschichte eine solche Lästerung vergeben ; aber so viel ist richtig, jener Fürst war recht eine Verkörperung dessen, was das neunzehnte Jahrhundert ist, sofern es das achtzehnte verleugnet. Ueberfluss an Geist, aber Mangel an Meuschenverstand ; Gefühl nur gar zu viel, aber Charakter doch gar zu wenig ; mehr Edelmuth als Rechtlichkeit ; Andacht ohne Ernst der Gesinnung ; vornehme geschichtliche Liebhaberei ohne gesunden geschichtlichen Trieb, ohne die Lust und die Kraft, von dem Blättern in dem Bilderbuche der Vergangenheit hinweg einen männlichen Schritt in die Zukunft hinein zu thun. Und kann man denn einen Geist historisch nennen, der eben die nächstliegende Vergangenheit aus dem Buche der Geschichte streichen möchte ? der zwar das Mittelalter zu verstehen und zu lieben meint, aber das Zeitalter Friedrich's und Joseph's, der deutschen Vernunftkritik und der Französischen Staatsumwälzung verkennt, ja selbst an einem Luther und Calvin eigentlich nur von ihrer rückwärts dem Mittelalter zugekehrten Seite sich angesprochen findet ?

" Es gehört zu den unwillkürlichen Verdiensten, deren der romantische König sich manche erworben, selbst der blödesten Fassungskraft thatsächlich gezeigt zu haben, wohin unser Jahrhundert mit solcher Verleugnung der Errungenschaften des achtzehnten kommt. Verdumpfung und begonnene Fäulniss in allen Gebieten, in Staat und Kirche, Schule und Wissenschaft war das Erbe, welches die jetzige Regierung Preussens vor drei Jahren antrat. Und auch jetzt sind noch lange nicht genug Fenster dem freien Luftzuge geöffnet, noch lange nicht alle faulen Reste der vorigen Wirthschaft beseitigt. Es gilt immer noch entschiedener an das Jahrhundert der Aufklärung und Humanität, der Volks und Menschenrechte anzuknüpfen, noch offener anzuerkennen, dass jeder Fortschritt über dasselbe hinaus durch Aneignung seiner Ergebnisse, durch Weitergehen auf seinem Wege, nicht durch Umkehr von demselben bedingt ist.

were devoted to the same cause. The name of the latter was mixed up with the disgraceful intrigues by which the Kreuz-Zeitung faction tried to support their influence at court, and of which so much was said in the papers of the day, in connection with the names of the spies Lindenberg and Techen. The President von Gerlach is a man of great although misused ability. He was born in 1795, and is sprung from a respectable family, but one which by no means belongs to the old gentry, whose cause he has always supported. He served in the war of independence, and after its conclusion entered the magistrature. Unlike Manteuffel, his nature is not bureaucratic. Nay, rather, he is the enemy of centralisation, the friend of local government. The government which he prefers is not, however, self-government, but that of an infinite number of petty despots—a parish and county government, administered by squires and parsons. From the first he has been consistent. Already, more than forty years ago, he contributed to a newspaper which took for its motto, "Not counter-revolution, but the contrary of revolution ;" and before 1848 he got into great trouble with the *bourgeoisie,* for maintaining that only men of noble birth should be permitted to be officers in the army. He would have the nobles gathered into chapters, the citizens gathered into guilds, and all things as like the golden days of the German middle age as they well can be. He is a friend to England, but it is the old church-and-king England of which he thinks. He dislikes the autocratic system of Russia, but leans to her as an exponent of the divine character of kingship, and sympathised with her during the Crimean war. A ready and powerful debater, he was ever at the breach attacking the constitution, and holding aloft the banner of "Deutsches Recht und Evangelisches Christenthum."

The Liberals at this time were led by Vincke, one of whose speeches made a great sensation in England in 1854. The descendant of an old Westphalian house, the Freiherr von Vincke was born in 1811. His father and most of his ancestors had been in the bureaucracy, and the young Vincke, after studying at Göttingen and elsewhere, pursued for some time the same career. Perhaps, however, his most valuable training was gained in the provincial assemblies, and when he appeared in the Vereinigte Landtag of 1847 he was already an orator. He spoke in favour of a real constitution, of the liberty of the press, of the Polish nationality, against the disabilities of Jews and Christian dissenters, and connected himself with all the best movements of the time. In 1848 he sat on the right, and opposed revolution as strongly as he had opposed absolutism. So great was his influence over the Moderate Conservatives and Liberals at Frankfort, that the Club Milani, to which Radowitz, Count Schwerin, and Bruck, who was afterwards finance-minister in Austria, belonged, was called "The fortyfold-repeated voice of Vincke." He has since been accused of being sometimes too fond of fighting for his own hand, and preferring the fame of a daring guerrilla to that of a wise general. His oratory would seem to have something of the character of Mr. Bright's, but his political sympathies and his party connections are quite different. He is more of a Whig, or Liberal Conservative, than a Radical ; though perhaps we can hardly use these terms in relation to Prussian affairs without giving rise to confusion and misunderstanding.

The most remarkable result of the differences of opinion about the Russian war was the breach between the prince of Prussia and the government. The heir to the throne had no

great liking for the Emperor Nicholas, who was by no means
over-cautious in his treatment of his Prussian relatives.   Nor
did he believe in the success of the imperial system of repression.   On one occasion, after Nicholas had been expressing
himself with more than his wonted violence against coquetting
with liberalism, the prince asked a Russian who stood high
in the favour of his master, whether he thought that revolutionary notions had been effectually kept out of Russia.
"So far am I from thinking so," was the answer, "that I do
not believe my head, or the head of any of the emperor's
advisers, is worth ten days' purchase after his eyes are
closed."

The prince represented the old Prussian military spirit,
which never forgave the emperor for telling the officers of the
royal guard at Berlin, as he had the want of tact to do, that
they were his advanced posts ; and the feelings of the high-
spirited soldier grew more and more bitter as Prussia sank
lower and lower in the estimation of Europe.

During these years, the various sections of the Conservative party maintained their ascendancy in the internal
politics of Prussia.   The long-adjourned question of the
definitive organisation of the Upper House was settled in
October 1854 in a manner which, although it did not entirely
meet the views of the Feudalists, was at least far more favourable
to them than they had any right to expect.   The provincial and
communal legislation of 1850, which was redolent of the modern
theories of 1848, was seriously modified in 1852, but rather in
the sense of the bureaucratic than of the feudal faction.*   This
last, however, succeeded in giving the name of "Herrenhaus"

---

* The local police was, however, restored to the landowners.   Every proprietor of a *Rittergut* is now, as before 1848, *de jure* his own head-constable.

to the First, and that of "Abgeordneten-Haus" to the Second Chamber, a trifling matter which it had much at heart. The elections of October 1854 were extremely unfavourable to the Liberals, in spite of the strong support of the Catholic clergy, who, for reasons relating to their own church affairs, were opposed to the government, and more especially to the High Lutheran and Kreuz-Zeitung zealots who presided over the ministry of the interior and that of public instruction. Vincke, who had been the great orator of the constitutional opposition in the two preceding parliaments, declined to stand, and his friends in the Lower House were led by Count Schwerin and by M. Patow. The Kreuz-Zeitung faction was very strong, and was commanded as usual by Gerlach. As well without as within the walls of parliament, it asserted itself in a very offensive way, and the adherents of M. Manteuffel were almost forced into the position of Liberals. The bad feeling between the two Conservative factions reached its height in 1856, and was made notorious to all Europe by the duel between the bureaucratic Hinckeldey, the director-general of the police, and M. von Rochow, a young man of landed property, and a member of the Kreuz-Zeitung party in the Herrenhaus.

So complete, indeed, was the reaction that many have wondered why the victorious party permitted even any traces of constitutionalism to continue, and have ascribed its forbearance sometimes to fear of conscientious scruples on the part of the king, sometimes to his vacillation. There was a league of the bureaucracy, the orthodox clergy, and the small provincial noblesse, supported by a section of the proletariate, against all the intelligent classes in the nation. That a portion of the proletariate should have joined a party whose interests are so opposed to its own, is not surprising, when we remember the gross political ignorance and the uncultivated condition in which the Prussian countryman lived in many districts before 1848. By the legislation of 1850 no less than twenty-four feudal obligations were swept away, which had up to that time remained in vigour; nor must it be forgotten that the grandfathers of the men who were ready to march with their flails against the democrats of the towns had some of them themselves been almost in the position of serfs.

But how are we to reconcile this political ignorance and want of cultivation with all we have heard about the excellence of Prussian popular education? The following sentences, quoted by Mr. Pattison in his report to the Education Commission which was presided over by the late Duke of Newcastle, from a work by Mr. Horace Mann, who travelled in 1843, may afford a satisfactory answer to this question :—

"A proverb has obtained currency in Prussia which explains the whole mystery of the relation between their schools and their life : ' The school is good ; the world is bad.' The quiescence or torpidity of social life stifles the activity excited in the school-room. Whatever pernicious habits and customs exist in the community act as antagonistic forces against the moral training of the teacher. The power of the government presses upon the partially-developed faculties of the youth as with a mountain's weight. . . . When the children come out from the school they have little use either for the faculties that have been developed, or for the knowledge that has been acquired."

We recommend this passage to the consideration of those who think that the reason why the Prussians do not make greater exertions to obtain the management of their own affairs, is, that they have been over-educated by a too zealous government.

That elementary instruction in Prussia is in an advanced state is indisputable. It is now said that of the recruits from the Saxon Province only 4 in 1000 are unable to read, write, and cipher ; but before 1848 the stagnation of the peasant's intelligence was indescribable. He did nothing with his elementary instruction when he had got it—at least in many districts.

In Prussia, as elsewhere, it was too little, not too much, light, that made the reaction possible, and the reactionary party well knew its enemy, for on no class did its hand fall more heavily than on newspaper-writers and men of letters ; nor would it be impossible to darken our pages by stories of their persecutions, which almost recal the atrocities of the Neapolitan Bourbons.

No material change took place in the situation of parties until the king's illness in October 1857. It was clear that if the prince of Prussia should succeed to the regency, the days of the Manteuffel ministry were numbered. Nevertheless, the friends of the future ruler observed a wise silence, and made no sign. The Kreuz-Zeitung faction at court did what it could to prevent the heir-presumptive succeeding to the regency with full powers, as provided by the constitution. Their efforts were, however, in vain, and a royal ordinance of October 1858 put an end to the exceptional state of affairs, and conferred the regency upon the prince, who summoned the Chambers to meet him upon the 20th of that month.

The first change was the retirement of the detested

Westphalen, who had been deeply concerned in all the intrigues against his new master. On the 26th the regent swore to the constitution, and on the 6th of November the Manteuffel ministry was dismissed. The leading spirits of the new cabinet were the Prince of Hohenzollern-Sigmaringen, MM. von Schleinitz, Patow, Bethmann-Hollweg, and Auerswald.

The prince of Hohenzollern, the head of the new cabinet, was, up to 1849, an independent prince. In that year he concluded a treaty with Prussia, by which he surrendered all his sovereign rights, retaining only the title of Hoheit and the position of a younger son of the royal house. His mother was a niece of Murat, and one of his daughters married the late king of Portugal. He is a Catholic; and his appointment had a good effect upon the Rhenish populations. For the rest, he is a man of wide political knowledge, and of moderate and enlightened ideas, while his practical adhesion to the views of those who think that the position of the smaller princes is becoming impossible makes him acceptable to all who desire the reform of the Germanic Confederation.

The Freiherr Alexander von Schleinitz was born in 1807, and belongs to the Brunswick branch of his family. He has been employed chiefly in the home and foreign departments of the diplomatic service, and owes his political importance principally to the friendship of the prince regent, whom he had sheltered on the memorable night of the 19th March 1848, when the life of the unpopular heir to the throne was in considerable danger. He is said to be too fond of pleasure, and though not without ability, he made only an indifferent minister for foreign affairs.

The Freiherr von Patow was born in 1807. Possessed of considerable property, and in the position of an English country gentleman, he has spent nearly his whole life in the bureaucracy, and up to 1848 was understood to belong to the "Œder" section of administrators, to which we have alluded above. Summoned to take the place of minister of commerce and public works in the Camphausen cabinet, he had the sense to recognise the signs of the times, and has ever since been a good constitutionalist. His qualifications for the post which was given him in the Hohenzollern cabinet—that, viz., of finance minister—are unquestionably very great.

A far more interesting, though not more useful personage, is M. Bethmann-Hollweg, to whom was assigned the delicate task of inaugurating the new system in the management of religious and educational matters. He was born in 1795 at Frankfort, and was the son of a M. Hollweg, who married a daughter of the wealthy house of Bethmann. His private tutor was the great geographer Karl Ritter, and his early education — conducted partly at home and partly at the Frankfort gymnasium, where Schlosser and Matthiæ then taught—was as careful and thorough as admirable management and large means could make it. He became professor of jurisprudence at Berlin after a distinguished university career. Thence he went to Bonn, where he held a similar position. In 1840 he entered the service of the government, and has ever since been an important public character in Prussia. Like the late king, he has been influenced very strongly by the romanticists ; but he possesses a better head and a deeper culture. In church matters, to which he has ever given great attention, he belongs to the "mediation" school ; and his tall figure and grave countenance might some years ago often be remarked at Nitzsch's sermons. He is a great patron of the Evangelical Alliance, which has at least the merit of being bitterly hated by the zealots who follow Hengstenberg, and which should hardly be judged by the names of the persons who are connected with it in this country. M. Bethmann-Hollweg is the much-to-be-envied proprietor of Rheineck, which he has restored with great splendour.

Rudolf von Auerswald was one of several brothers belonging to an excellent family at Königsberg, who were brought up in close intimacy with the present and the last king during the residence of the royal house in East Prussia. All of them had the good sense not to wish for the position of court favourites, but worked, each his own way, by surer although slower methods. The eldest, a distinguished officer, was murdered with Prince Lichnowsky at Frankfort. The youngest sat in the Camphausen cabinet, and the second in that which followed it. It was he who again appeared as an important actor in 1858. He was for some time in the army, but his chief training was that of a county magnate and a provincial administrator. All the Auerswalds belonged to the school of East-Prussian Liberals, of which Schön was so great an ornament, and in which the influence of Kant, and the hated neighbourhood of Russia, tempered the old aristocratic and exclusive traditions.

Conservative influences were not entirely unrepresented in the cabinet. Von der Heydt kept his place as minister of commerce, and M. Simons remained for a time as minister of justice. Later, too, General von Roon superseded the Liberal General von Bonin.

Flottwell, who took for a time the department of the interior, is an enlightened bureaucrat, who had been much employed under Schön, and Count Schwerin, who soon succeeded him, is a strong constitutionalist, who belongs to the family of the celebrated general of Frederick the Great, and has, as the son-in-law of Schleiermacher, always taken a strong part on the liberal side in Prussian ecclesiastical affairs. Perhaps he is most in his place as president of an assembly.

The regent lost no time in issuing a manifesto, in which, while making many reserves, he acknowledged the necessity of amending the communal legislation—much altered, as we have seen, since 1850—and pronounced strongly against the mixing up religion with politics, which had been so characteristic of his brother's rule.

The new elections completely changed the balance of parties. The Feudalists who, thanks to the zeal of M. de Westphalen, had been so successful in 1852 and 1854, were reduced to 62 ; while the ministerial Liberals counted 236— 38 Catholics and 18 Poles made up the Assembly.

It may be asked by those who remember 1848, how it was that the accession of the prince of Prussia to the regency excited the hopes of the Liberals, and was followed by the advent of a Liberal ministry. In that year it is notorious that the absence of the heir-presumptive from Berlin was considered necessary to his personal safety ; and if we turn to the political writings of the time, or even to so impartial an authority as the remarkable article on Prussia in the *Revue des Deux Mondes* of October 1847, we shall see that he was regarded as anything but a friend to popular rights.

The answer to this question will throw some light on the occurrences of the last few years. The prince of Prussia

was in one respect radically different from the king. He had
not a particle of his religious mysticism ; nay, rather his
" Hausbackener Rationalismus" was revolted by the maudlin
follies of his brother's court. When, then, the reactionary
party began to be all-powerful, and such advisers as General
von Gerlach ruled the day, the prince made no secret of his
annoyance and disgust. The attitude of Prussia during the
Russian war, as we have seen, irritated him excessively, and
led to something very like a breach between him and his
brother's ministers. The influence of his wife, a woman of
talent, the granddaughter of Karl August, was exerted in a
liberal direction, as well from choice as from policy ; and,
above all, his experience of Kreuz-Zeitung rule in the Rhineland, and his personal quarrel with Kleist-Retzow—a prominent member of the feudal party, who occupied part of the
same palace at Coblentz—tended effectually to open his eyes.
Subsequent events have shown that his liberalism did not go
very deep.

The first mistake of the new reign was the coronation at
Königsberg. That unlucky ceremonial was not even historical, for nothing of the sort had taken place since, in 1701,
the elector of Brandenburg first turned himself into a king.
It was a compromise between the Liberal ministers who
thought that quite enough had been done, when the king had,
in presence of the Houses, taken the oath to the constitution,
and the Junker or feudal party, which claimed the right for
a portion of the noblesse, or rather squirearchy, to do homage
after the old feudal fashion. In so far as this celebration
refreshed in the mind of the king those divine right fancies
which he had naturally imbibed from his absolutist education, it did of course some harm ; but the harm would not

have been abiding if the military question had not soon come to make a gulf between the well-meaning monarch and his people.

The Prussian military organisation, which had served its purpose for some time extremely well, and was popular with the nation from the recollections of 1813, had in 1850 and 1856 given signs of breaking down, and when the Italian war of 1859 again required the Landwehr to be put on a war footing, the symptoms became still more alarming. The king, who had all his life made a study of military matters, and looked at everything from an adjutant's point of view, saw clearly all the defects of the old system and not a little underrated the sacrifices which the changing it would impose upon the country. Fully supported then by those military counsellors in whom he most trusted, he devised a new and very large scheme, the object of which was, in one word, immensely to increase the strength of the regular army and to diminish proportionately the importance of the Landwehr. The king had, no doubt, only one purpose, and that was the good of the country, but some of his advisers may well be suspected of having had other views. The officers of the regular army have always been very closely connected with the Junker party, and that party knew that if the number of officers was multiplied its power would be largely reinforced. The Liberal ministry, unwilling to offend the king, persuaded that he was to a great extent right from a military point of view, but fearing, also, to throw on the shoulders of a poor country a burden of taxation greater than it could easily bear—knowing too that the great mass of the people was wedded to the old system— attempted, as was their wont, a compromise. How far they might have succeeded if no third party had come upon the scene, it is difficult to say ; but things did not so turn out. The so-called democratic or advanced-liberal section, which had disappeared from practical politics, as we have seen, in 1849, feeling that it had now a large portion of the population behind it, once more put forth a programme, relying partly upon its opinions on internal matters, and partly on the vast impulse that had been given to national feeling in Germany by the Italian war of 1859. Very wisely, however, it now changed its name, and called itself the " German party of Progress," to show that it desired at once internal reforms and the settlement of the German question.

The principal aims of the *Fortschritts Partei*, as set forth in its address, were as follows :—

1. Reform of the Upper House.

2. A liberal system, conscientiously carried out in all the details of the administration, with a view to avoiding the scandals now of frequent occurrence, when an obstinate or bigoted official sets at defiance the liberal initiations of the government, trusting to backstairs influence.

3. Ministerial responsibility.

4. An easy method of bringing to justice guilty officials, who are at present, as in France, in all conflicts with simple citizens, like men armed *cap-à-pie* fighting with the defenceless.

5. The abolition of all disqualifications on account of religious opinion.

6. An improved system of national education, which has, since the victory of the reactionists, been deliberately, and of *malice prepense*, lowered and corrupted, with the express purpose of subjecting the minds of the young to the yoke of the feudal and fanatical party.

7. The abolition of certain privileges of the landowners, such as the appointment of their own police.

8. A revision, in a liberal sense, of the laws relating to trade.

9. Economy in the management of the army, maintenance of the *Landwehr*, physical training of the youth of the country.

10. The adoption of a firm line of policy, with a view to place Prussia at the head of a united Germany.

Parliament met on January 14th, 1862. The Lower House was constituted pretty nearly as follows :—

Ministerialists	156
Party of Progress and Fraction Harkort . .	100
Roman Catholics	50
Poles	18
Feudalists	16
Doubtful	12
	352

The cry which the party of progress had raised most loudly at the elections was the cry of economy. In the former parliament the ministry had brought forward a proposal, to which it was understood the king attached the greatest possible importance, relative to the organisation of the army. Of this we shall presently give some account; but before doing so it may be well to state a few particulars as to the principal persons who had seats in the new Chamber.

The leading man of the Fortschritt party was perhaps Waldeck, surnamed the Bauern-König, from his constant advocacy of the cause of the Westphalian peasants. His tall commanding figure and striking countenance do not

bear so many traces of political persecution as might have
been expected in one who suffered so much at the hands of
the reactionaries. Close beside this white-haired leader, but
differing from him on several points, notably on the German
question, is Schultze, called from his birth-place Schultze-
Delitszch, a man still in the prime of life, who is best known
as the apostle of coöperative associations in Germany, but is
also honourably distinguished as an orator, a poet, and a
magistrate. Waldeck is " Grossdeutsch ;" that is, he wishes
for a united Germany including Austria. Schultze wishes for
a narrower confederacy, exclusive of Austria ; he is, in other
words, " Kleindeutsch." Virchow, a most eminent medical professor at Berlin, was another active member of the Fortschritt
party, and soon achieved considerable success in debate, in
spite of a certain dryness of expression and perhaps a touch
of pedantry.

We have reckoned along with the Fortschritt party the
section known as the Fraction Harkort ; so called from M.
Harkort, an old man who was wounded at Ligny, and has
since led a most active and useful life, promoting the material
prosperity of his native Westphalia and other districts,—
advocating railways and steam-navigation, enlightening the
peasantry, and fighting in Berlin, now the mob and now the
reaction.

The chief persons of the less advanced Liberal party were :
—Grabow, who was chosen president, and Simson, an ex-
professor of jurisprudence at Königsberg, who is celebrated
in Prussia as one of the ablest of her orators and as a model
president. His imprudently over-loyal behaviour at the time
of the coronation festivities lost him his old seat, and he was
returned for a small place too late to be chosen president,

although he was thought to be better fitted for that office than the excellent Grabow, who is somewhat deaf. Vincke declined to stand, and remained watching events.

The great point at issue was of course the military question, and that grew ever more and more embittered. The king was determined not to yield ; the moderate Liberals were no longer masters either in the Court or in the Lower House. The Fortschritt deputies were numerous and uncompromising, and ere long a motion brought forward by one of their number led to the resignation of the ministry and the dissolution of the second branch of the legislature.

In May the elections took place, and in the same month the deputies found themselves again in Berlin. Things looked worse for the king than ever, for the Fortschritt party had gained considerably. The new ministry was very inferior to the old. Its more prominent members, in addition to Von der Heydt, were—M. von Jagow, a man much hated for his annoying and arbitrary measures when he was director of police ; Prince Hohenlohe, a member of one of the less violent sections of the Kreuz-Zeitung party ; M. Mühler, who, as the author of the excellent Bacchanalian song " Grad' aus dem Wirthshaus," deserved some reward, but for whom a place more suitable than that of Minister of Instruction and Public Worship might possibly have been found. He is said too, by his enemies, to atone for the merriment of his youth by the fanaticism of his age. Von Roon kept his place, and Bernstorff, well known in England.

These were not the men to meet and manage such an assembly as that with which they had to deal. Most of the leading Fortschritt politicians had come back fiercer than ever ; and the moderate Liberals, although they tried to prevent the last extremities, were not by any means friendly.

The principal speakers of the moderate Liberal party in the new parliament were Vincke, who again appeared on the scene, and Professor von Sybel, the well-known and popular historian.

Heinrich von Sybel was born at Dusseldorf in 1817. He studied at Berlin, and became a passionate admirer of Ranke, whose method he has adopted, and his most important historical works relate to the Crusades and to the French Revolution. He was the youngest member of the Parliament at Erfurt, by which Prussian statesmen hoped to arrive at some satisfactory settlement of the German question ; and, in a speech which excited great attention, he urged Prussia to fulfil her great mission, and to raise up anew a German empire. His ideas on this subject did not prevent his being called to Munich by King Maximilian ; and he remained there in great favour till the events of 1859 resuscitated the hopes of the Gotha party, which had slumbered since the disaster of Olmütz. Munich then became too hot to hold him, and he accepted the chair at the university of Bonn, left vacant by the death of Dahlmann. He was elected in 1861, but was prevented by illness from taking his seat. In 1862 he was again returned, and became from the first one of the most important figures in the left-centre, or Bockum-Dolffs party, which included far the largest portion of the moderate Liberals.

The recognition of the kingdom of Italy brought some goodwill to the government, and they carried the ratification of the commercial treaty with France by a large majority ; but the fatal question of the military expenditure could at last no longer be postponed, and an unusually fierce debate ended, on the 20th of September, by the absolute rejection of the demands of the government, with regard to the money required for the reorganisation of the army. Bernstorff and Von der Heydt had the wisdom to retire, and M. von Bismarck-Schönhausen took the unenviable post of president of the council.* His first act was to withdraw the budget of 1863, which was about to meet the fate of its predecessor ; his second, to send to the Herrenhaus the budget of 1862, and to have the military part of it, which had been eliminated by the representatives of the tax-payers, reintroduced and authorised by that imprudent assembly ; his third was to prorogue the Second Chamber, which had protested against the unconstitutional proceedings of the other House, until January 1863.

But who was this new minister, then so little known, now so notorious ? M. von Bismarck-Schönhausen was born at Brandenburg in 1813. Already as a very young man he connected himself closely with the ultra-conservative party in the district assembly of the Saxon province of Prussia, in which he has property, and in 1848 he pursued the same course at Berlin, making himself particularly conspicuous, when the German national enthusiasm for the first Schleswig-Holstein war was at its height, by speaking of the Prussian intervention in that struggle as—" Ein höchst ungerechtes frivoles und verderbliches Unternehmen zur Unterstützung einer ganz unmotivirten Revolution." He was a member of the

* We all cheat him of his full designation, and very often of one letter of his name. Let it stand here in full for once—Otto von Bismarck auf Schönhausen und auf Kniephof ! ! Why has no one translated the exhaustive article about him in the eighth volume of *Unsere Zeit ?*

assembly of the Conservative party to which the name of the
Junker-Parlament was given, and was one of the founders of
the Kreuz-Zeitung.   He was present at Erfurt, and was a
secretary of the assembly, getting there also into a quarrel
with the press by way of prelude to more serious attacks upon
it in after years.   His good services to the reactionary party
gained for him in 1851 the post of First Secretary of Legation
at Frankfort, an appointment which was all the more remarkable because he had never before been in the diplomatic
service.   Three months afterwards, however, he was promoted
to the first place as Prussian representative to the Diet, and
this post he occupied until he was succeeded by a much
better man, Baron von Usedom.   This was in the early days
of the present king ; before his failure to obtain the approval
of the people for his scheme of army organisation had driven
him from the right path—the happy time which German
Liberals too hastily called the *Neue Æra*. In that happy
time M. Bismark was sent off to St. Petersburg, and it is
indeed unfortunate that he did not remain in a country for
which he is far better suited than his own.   The destinies,
however, had other work in store for him ; for, after a short
period of duty in Russia and France, he was summoned to
Berlin, and in September 1862, on the very day, as it happened, upon which Lord Russell's famous Gotha dispatch
began a new phase of the Schleswig-Holstein question, he
became first minister.

The time has not yet come for attempting to pass judgment upon a man who is still in the midst of his career ;
but it is not too much to say that his action upon the
affairs of Europe has hitherto been simply evil. His worst
enemies do not deny that he has great readiness, a strong

will, and audacity almost amounting to genius. The ground-tone of his character, it has been truly said, is ὕβρις, but that ὕβρις, which takes in public life so offensive a form, does not seem incompatible in his case with much geniality in private life, and it would not be difficult to cite instances of the ease with which he obtains influence over persons who are brought across him. Many stories are current which show that his conservatism does not go really so deep as that of many men who make less parade of their anti-liberal views ; and we think it far from impossible that as the drama of German politics unfolds itself we may be destined to see this unscrupulous politician in more than one unfamiliar character.

That, however, is a matter of speculation ; for the present we have before us a sort of composite being—half French-Imperialist, half disciple of M. Gerlach—"making," to use his own expression, "Junker-Politik" in the face of an angry but powerless nation.

The new session of the Lower House was opened on the 14th of January 1863, by a very decided and manly speech from President Grabow, but the real fighting did not commence till the 27th, when the address came on for discussion. All fractions were represented on this occasion, but the majority of the deputies supported the draft address, to which the names of Dr. Virchow and M. Carlowitz, asking for a return to a constitutional state of things, were attached. Of the former of these we have already spoken. The latter, a Saxon by birth, and long a member of the Dresden Chambers, as also of the short-lived Erfurt Assembly, has in recent years bought property in Prussia, and become an active Liberal politician in that country. One of the incidents of the debate was a telling speech by M. Waldeck against the new president of the council. To this the latter replied very vigorously, contesting the right of the Lower House to exercise a paramount control over the budget, as well as accusing that body of a desire to take from the House of Hohenzollern its constitutional rights, and to transfer them to a Parliamentary majority. The views of the Liberals were supported after a long discussion by 255 votes to 60.

The secret convention with Russia, which was concluded on the 8th of February, afforded a further ground of quarrel; the Lower House insisting upon absolute neutrality, while the government, supported by the Upper House, wished to play into the hands of the Czar.

The hostile feeling of the ministers and the representatives of the people went on increasing, till at last, on the 11th of May, they came to an open rupture. The immediate cause of this was the refusal of M. von Roon,* the Minister for War, to recognise the authority of the chair; a proceeding which would in this country be simply impossible, but in which he was supported, not only by his colleagues, but by the king, who, finding the House determined not to yield, prorogued it on the 27th of May.

Five days after this, M. Bismark, being now more at

---

* General von Roon, whose name is probably chiefly known to those of our readers who glance at the news from Germany, as a rough, coarse soldier, is really a man of more merit than his doings in the Chamber would lead people to believe. Like all his class, he was brought up in one of the cadet-schools; but his abilities were sufficient to entitle him in very early life to be made an instructor there, and he was an enthusiastic admirer and follower of the great geographer Karl Ritter. His own works are chiefly upon geography, especially as seen from a soldier's point of view, and their success has been such as to entitle him to take a respectable rank amongst the pupils of his illustrious master.

his ease, persuaded the king to issue an illegal ordinance restraining the liberty of the press, an act against which not only the principal newspapers of the capital protested, but which was condemned in the strongest terms by the heir to the crown, in a speech delivered on the 5th of June at Danzig.

The high-handed proceedings of M. Bismark with regard to the press were very naturally resented by the municipality of Berlin, which presently sent an address to the Crown, remonstrating with it for such an abuse of power. The example of the capital was followed in various provincial towns; and it is not impossible that, if the municipalities throughout the country had stood firm, they might have so bombarded the king with addresses, as to make him sacrifice his obnoxious minister. The Prussians, however, as a people, showed on this occasion a certain want of that political tact which tells those nations which possess it when to fight and when to give way, just as their Liberal leaders have shown a certain want of statesmanship. The government threatened, and in many places the municipalities allowed themselves to be intimidated. The victory of this passage of arms remained, not with right, but with might.

The summer passed on, without in any respect changing the state of affairs, but in the autumn the king dissolved Parliament, in the hope of finding himself better supported by the nation at large than by the authorised exponents of its wishes.

The demands of the Liberal party, as set forth in the Fort-schritt address, which was issued on this occasion, were :—

1. Freedom of the press, and the setting aside of the press ordinances of the 1st of June.

2. The passing of a law of ministerial responsibility, as promised by the Constitution.

3. Acknowledgment in fact of the control of the Lower House over expenditure.

4. Reform of the Upper House.

5. An army on a popular basis with two years' service.

6. A German Parliament, freely elected by the people.

These demands were supported by a majority of the electors. M. Bismark had misunderstood the situation, for while the most moderate or Vincke section of the Liberals lost, the party of progress and the left-centre or Bockum-Dolffs party—so called from their leader, a Westphalian gentleman of considerable property, much independence, and great power of work—were largely recruited. The Kreuz-Zeitung, however, gained a little, counting in the new House 37 as against 11 in the old one. The new Parliament was opened on the 9th of November, and the true colour of the Lower House was soon apparent, even to the sanguine minister. M. Grabow was re-elected president, and M. von Unruh and Bockum-Dolffs vice-presidents. M. von der Heydt, who was supported by the government as their candidate for the presidential chair, was beaten by 224 to 37.

A more friendly House than that which had been collected would have been provoked by the proposal which the government soon made, that, for the future, in cases where the ministry and the Lower Chamber could not agree about the budget, the last budget voted should be considered as the legal budget for the ensuing year.

The formidable turn which was given by the death of Frederick VII. of Denmark to the Schleswig-Holstein question, was a new embarrassment to ministers, and brought out new points of dissension between them and their opponents. It would be unprofitable to attempt to follow their skirmishings in detail; but we may safely say that the end of the year 1863 saw the contending parties no nearer a reconciliation than they were at its commencement.

They did not, indeed, long remain in presence of each other, for a fresh prorogation took place before the end of January 1864 ; not, however, till M. Bismark had defined in the most offensive manner the position of the Prussian government with regard to the Bund, by stating that "political questions were questions not of law and right but of might ; that Prussia could not allow herself to be out-voted by a majority in the Diet, which might only represent some two millions, and that the two German great powers acted as a greenhouse in protecting the Bund from the cold blasts of the winds of Europe." Not less offensive was his attitude with regard to the Parliamentary opposition as set forth in the speech by which he closed the session in the name of the king ; for he accused it of a desire to increase the importance of the Lower House, at the expense of the other bodies of the state, condemned its dealings with the budget, its opposition to the army organisation, and contrasted with its hostility the loyal and friendly behaviour of the Upper House. A week or two after, the resolution of the government to govern without a budget was openly announced, and a detailed explanation was given of the course which it proposed to adopt in dealing with the public expenditure.* The whole real interest

---

* Unfortunately it must be admitted that the present detestable government of Prussia manages the finances extremely well. Nothing makes the action of the Liberal party against abuses so difficult as this.

of Prussian history for the last eleven months of the year 1864 centres in the Danish war, or the negotiations which sprang out of it; and the general course of what occurred is in the recollection of all. It would be unfair to deny that the large land and the scanty sea forces engaged on the part of Prussia behaved with considerable spirit, and that officers and men acquitted themselves very creditably. The raptures into which the good Prussians went over their victories may well make Englishmen smile; but then we are hardly ever without a war going on in some portion of our dominions, while to the Prussian of 1864 a real war was quite a new excitement. Nor must it be forgotten that the Prussian army is recruited from all ranks of society, and the interest with which the tidings from Düppel were looked for, was more of the kind which we should expect if a large number of our volunteer regiments were engaged in foreign service, than anything with which we are familiar. Upon internal politics the result of the war was utterly mischievous. It gained a certain amount of prestige for M. Bismark, and it roused to such an extent the passion for territorial aggrandisement that before the end of the year nearly all the principal newspapers of Prussia had declared in favour, either of the annexation of the Duchies to their own country, or at least of a very exceptionally close union between it and them. Meantime, the Prussian government proceeded to injure the state in the most fatal way that could have been devised. They set to work every means to influence the tribunals in all political trials, thus striking a blow at a system of administration of justice, which had been for many years reputed to be singularly pure and upright.

No advance of much importance was made by either

party with regard to the constitutional question in 1865. The conduct of M. Bismark was more defiant and outrageous than ever ; but the general features of the situation remained unchanged. Prussia gained a kind of triumph over her great rival by the terms of the convention of Gastein, and acquired amongst the unthinking a certain amount of prestige; but the violent and illegal proceedings which filled the long recess only stored up new difficulties, so that the session of 1866 opened under even gloomier auspices than its immediate predecessors. The stopping of the Cologne banquet in the summer, the high-handed proceedings with respect to Lauen-burg, and the decree which a section of the Supreme Court at Berlin, carefully packed for the purpose, had pronounced in limitation of the liberty of speech guaranteed to all deputies by the constitution, had embittered men's minds to a great degree. These events, and the dealings of the government with the Cologne and Minden Railway, were the principal subjects of discussion during the short and agitated session which was closed before the end of February, on the pretext that the Lower House was acting unconstitutionally. The speeches during this session appear to have been of a very high order of excellence ; and that of Dr. Gneist, on its last day, of very exceptional merit.

It is difficult to see how even the form of constitutional government can be kept up if the present ministry remains in power; and the leader of the Kreuz-Zeitung party avowed, in answer to Dr. Gneist, that what he and his friends were aiming at was the alteration of the constitution. Meanwhile, in spite of the deep disapproval with which the conduct of the government is viewed, public order has nowhere been disturbed; and in consequence no excuse has been given to

M. Bismark—now, by the way, raised to the rank of a Count—
to tell the king that violent measures are necessary.

The sneers which are constantly directed by a portion of
our press against the Prussian Liberals for not resorting to
those methods of resistance by which our English liberties
were preserved during the seventeenth century, betray either
the strangest misconception of the present state of Europe, or
a spirit of the most reckless mischief. The task which was
performed by Hampden, Cromwell, and the other heroes of
the great rebellion, was mere child's play in comparison with
the task to which many English journalists invite the people of
Prussia. In the seventeenth century the central government
was extremely weak, and any robust countryman or citizen
was speedily turned into a soldier quite as good as any whom
the king could oppose to him. In our days all governments
are indefinitely stronger than they were, as long as the armed
force remains true to them ; and in no country can the
government more implicitly reckon upon the armed force
than it can in Prussia. The reason of this is to be sought in
the national history and in the geographical position of the
land.

The Prussians feel that for them a large and powerful
armed force is absolutely necessary. That is a point upon
which all parties are agreed. The difference between the king
and the people turns upon the character of the armed force to
be kept up, not upon the question as to whether Prussia
should or should not be preeminently a military state.
Whatever glory she has to boast, other than that which accrues
to her from a certain number of learned men, is military
glory. In Prussia every man has been a soldier for a part of
his life, and he retains, with some of the virtues, also some of

the weaknesses of the military character. The officers belonging, for the most part, to a class hostile to the great body of their fellow-citizens, use every endeavour to instil into the minds of their privates a contempt for every one who does not wear uniform, and with this view they are not only permitted but encouraged to use their arms in case of any quarrel with the civilians. Similar efforts are made to cause the men to attach an altogether absurd importance to the military oath, which they are carefully trained to consider a far more sacred bond than that which engages them as citizens to uphold the constitution. That there are far more officers in the Prussian army who take liberal and reasonable views than is generally believed, we well know to be the case; but still they form so small a minority and are so carefully watched, that little can be hoped from them. There are few things more melancholy than to talk to an average Prussian officer, and to see how little his thoughts have travelled beyond his narrow, old-fashioned, poverty-stricken, little world. Indeed, it is this same poverty that meets one at every turn in dealing with Prussian affairs. If the class from which the officers are recruited were a real aristocracy, with wealth and wide-reaching European connections, their sons could not be half so wedded as they are to antiquated pretensions at which their foreign associates would only smile.

The Junker or feudal class, out of which the Prussian army is principally officered, corresponds to nothing which exists in this country. It can by no means compare in wealth or cultivation with our landed gentry, while it advances claims which are not advanced by our nobility. Some names there are in it which go far back in German history; many more which are connected with the short, though creditable military annals of Prussia; but a large portion of it can boast no historical illustration at all.

An aristocracy might be a very good thing in Prussia, as in other countries, if it had existed for a long time; but to patch up a bran-new aristocracy out of a handful of mediatised princes, whose recollections, if they have any, are German-Imperial, not specifically Prussian recollections, reinforced by proprietors of estates which have remained a hundred years in their family, was a hopeless design, and like too many other proceedings of the romanticist Frederick William IV. has much of gingerbread Gothic about it. The Herrenhaus of 1854 is not, we may be sure, destined for long duration, even as improved by the first ministry of the present king. There seems no particular reason why the mediatised princes of whom we have spoken should *not* continue to sit in it, although there is really none why they should; and the nominated life members might be a valuable element; but, on the whole, the Belgian senate forms perhaps the best model of a Second Chamber for such a country as Prussia.

The result of the measures which the Kreuz-Zeitung party would fain introduce is well shown in Mecklenburg, which has long enjoyed the unenviable distinction of being the worst governed district in Germany, and is managed to this day upon strict Kreuz-Zeitung principles. There the landed proprietors, after 1848, did everything in their power to encourage emigration, hoping to get rid entirely of the unruly spirits who chafed against the truly mediæval order of things which they kept up upon their estates. Now, however, the tables are turned; emigration has gone so far that their own personal interests are grievously threatened; and they are making convulsive, but perfectly ineffectual efforts to throw difficulties in the way of their people leaving the country, or trying by foolish little palliatives to make their native land less intolerable to them. There are to be found, we think, in this Mecklenburg affair, some hints for people nearer home ; and we much wish that some Englishman who has eyes, ears, and a good knowledge of German, would turn his tourist steps towards that little-visited region, and tell us something about the doings of the Schack-Basthorsts, and Pentz-Gremmelins, and the Klockmann-Hoppenrades, and all the rest of them. This kind of folly is only possible in an out-of-the-way country which has little communication with its neighbours. When any institutions come directly in contact with the spirit of the time, they may resist for five years, or ten, or twenty, but down they must go in the end. And so we can afford to contemplate the position of Prussia at this moment with tolerable equanimity, and share to the full the indignant confidence of a recent speaker at Berlin, who said, with reference to the tampering with the courts of justice : "For a time even the impossible is possible, but only for a time." Nothing would more complicate the situation than the resort of the Liberal party, under the advice of half-informed sympathisers, to anything like violence.

One French writer at least, we mean M. Forcade, understands the state of the case much better than some of our instructors ; and we find in the *Revue des deux Mondes*, for February 1, 1865, amidst much judicious praise of the conduct of the Lower House at Berlin in the beginning of last year, the following remarks, which are worth quoting as showing that the good example of the Prussians gives comfort to their less fortunate brethren on the other side of the Rhine. After commenting on the dignified speech of President Grabow at the opening of the session, M. Forcade says : "Les peuples européens ont de notre temps une faculté merveilleuse ; ils ont l'air de dormir, ils dorment même solidement, et ils se reveillent, comme la belle au bois dormant, sans avoir rien perdu de leur jeunesse. Nous retrouvons la chambre Prussienne comme nous l'avons laissée, et nous nous figurons que le jour ou la France couronnera l'édifice, on la retrouvera aussi libérale qu'il y a vingt ans, et qu'il n'y aura de vieux, de laid et de décrépit parmi nous que les absolutistes."

The simplest and most satisfactory, but, alas! the least probable solution of the present difficulty would be the king's abdication. Public opinion forced Louis of Bavaria to resign, and placed the Austrian diadem on the head, not of the rightful heir, but of his son the young Francis Joseph. There is everything to be said for, and nothing to be said against, this plan. William I., junior to his brother by only seventeen months, was an ensign at ten years old, and never till comparatively lately contemplated his accession to the throne as a probable event. He is simply incapable of comprehending the position of a monarch with a real constitution. His views are analogous to those of an old French legitimist duke who remarked to Niebuhr, when asked whether he had not had a hand in framing the *Charte :* "Oh, yes, I had ; but, good God! do you suppose I ever imagined that the king was not to do what he liked in spite of it ?"

In the event of his abdication, his son would be able gracefully to retire from an untenable position, and the state-machine might at length be got into good working order. We only fear that such a course is too wise a one to have any chance of being adopted. True it is that the brood of " court theologians, missionary deaconesses," and the like, who enraged Alexander von Humboldt, no longer flit about the palace. The king is in the hands of a military clique—of the " Ungeist in uniform" as the Berliners say ; and the policy which it is likely to recommend will hardly be one of concession. What, then, is to be the remedy ? Much, we think, may be hoped from a new reign, which, in the nature of things, cannot be very far distant. It will be said that this is a hope which always rises up in Prussia, and is always disappointed. We do not think that that statement is quite fair. The advance made from reign to reign has not been so great as was expected, but still there has been an advance; and the Prussia of 1866, unfortunate as its condition is, need not envy the Prussia of 1820. Undoubtedly the present Crown Prince has, to say nothing of his English marriage, been brought up under infinitely better influences than his uncle, whose mediæval dreams ruined, for the practical purposes of life, a very fine intelligence, and all Germany looks with great confidence to his succession. At the same time it cannot be doubted that the influences brought to bear in an opposite direction will be very powerful ; and the proceedings of the Fortschritt party during the earlier part of the present king's reign do not lead us to expect any extraordinary development of political tact upon its part. However this may be, we look with absolute confidence to the gradual spread of enlightenment even amongst the Prussian Junkers, and above all to the increase of the wealth and position of the middle class. If any one were to take a list of the Prussian Lower House at present, and to run through the names with the aid of some one who knew well the circumstances of the persons included in it, he would be surprised to find upon how many of them the government can put a very serious pressure. These men are, however, the most spirited of their order ; and for one who ventures to come forward boldly to back his opinion, there may well be ten who do not do so. Every day, however, the power of the middle class is growing ; if, indeed, we might not almost say that a new upper class is rising up which may push the present conventional upper class out of its place by the sheer weight of greater real importance. It is reserved, perhaps, for the sons of the men who are now making fortunes to build up on a thoroughly satisfactory basis the edifice of Prussian freedom. When Germans tell us, as they often do, that their country is only just recovering the ravages of the Thirty Years' War, we are at first tempted to smile ; but if we examine into the matter closely, we shall find that their statement is literally and perfectly correct. It is only in this century that Prussia has become anything more than a court, an army, and a bureaucracy. The real wonder is, not that she is so far back, but that she has made so much progress. Those who would realise what the Thirty Years' War really was, and who cannot turn to M. Freytag's *Sketches*, may look at a useful little book, *Gustavus Adolphus*, partly founded on them, by the archbishop of Dublin, which will explain to them very clearly how the effects of that great struggle have been so lasting ; and it need hardly be said that the wars of the Great Frederick and of Napoleon, although comparatively slight visitations, helped very much to retard the natural progress of the country.

Sooner or later, we do not in the least doubt that the existing confederation must break up, and that a large part of the middle states must, in one form or another, be grouped round Prussia ; and as well for the tranquillity of Europe as for the internal progress of Germany, we think it desirable that it should be so. But this may be done in two ways : either, as M. Bismark and his friends desire, by fraud and force—that is, by the old methods of "Il Principe,"—or by a natural but slower process. The feeling in favour of German unity had been growing so powerful for many years previously to the accession of the present king of Prussia, that if he had adopted a frankly constitutional and progressive course, being content to be king in the sense in which Leopold was king in Belgium, or Her Majesty is queen in England, the force of attraction which would have been exerted by Prussia, over all the smaller states, would have been so great that we cannot doubt that for all diplomatic and military purposes they would in a few years have become mere provinces of Prussia. Now, however, Count Bismark has succeeded in bringing about so great a reaction that everything has again become uncertain, and the satisfactory solution of the German question seems indefinitely postponed.

Those who, like the writer, were in Prussia just before and soon after the conclusion of the Schleswig-Holstein war, cannot have failed to perceive that a very disagreeable change had taken place in the views of a large portion even of the Liberal party. Before the struggle, they were content to look at the Schleswig-Holstein question from the point of view which was maintained by the Diet through the whole of 1863. After it they had allowed themselves to be seduced by the prospect of direct advantage to Prussia, and talked of nothing but annexation, thus drawing a broad line of demarcation between the internal and external policy of Count Bismark. We are far from saying that all the Prussian Liberals thus bowed the knee to Baal, but the number which did so was far too great. Many Englishmen, irritated by the conduct of Prussia in the Danish war, so far forgot themselves as to desire that France should avenge Denmark by seizing the Rhine. That there is, even amongst highly-intelligent and well-informed French politicians, an ardent desire for the frontier of the Rhine we know too well, but a wilder dream never entered into the imagination. Any attempt to realise it would bring about such a union of Germany as few have ever hoped for. Those who, in answer to this, would point to the French feeling which existed for some years after 1815, in the Rhineland, probably forget what was the condition of things to which the French domination there put an end. If so, they will find the real state of the case extremely well summed up in an address delivered last summer at Bonn, by Professor von Sybel; but they may rest assured that, in spite of M. Bismark, the Rhinelanders have no desire whatever to return to the imperial fold.

The conclusion which we have formed, and which we should wish our readers to form, from a study of the last twenty-five years of Prussian history, is this: Through all that time the country has been steadily advancing. It is on the whole well governed and prosperous, nor are there any elements out of which a really reactionary system of policy can be created. M. Bismark himself has a liberal side—as, for instance, in commercial matters—and admitted, in so many words, the other day in the Lower House that, sooner or later, a Liberal ministry must come into power. The present situation is only temporary, and a Liberal party, composed of the best of the landowners and the best of the bourgeoisie, will have it all its own way in the end. It may be a question of one decade or two, or even of a generation, though we do not expect it to be nearly so long ; but the " Ungeist" in uniform, which rules the present king, no less than the " Ungeist " in priestly garb, which ruled the late king, are both doomed to give way.

CHAPTER V.

AMONGST the states of which the European political system is composed, there are three which, although having, as regards their fellows, all the attributes of individual political existences, are really groups of two or more states connected mechanically, but not, so to speak, chemically united. These are :—1. Norway and Sweden ; 2. Switzerland ; 3. Germany. The first-mentioned is a unique example of a confederation with a common hereditary sovereign ; the second is collected under an elective president, and is ruled by a Federal Council of seven, which forms the executive, by a States-Council or Senate of forty-four (two for each canton), and by a National Council or Lower House, in which each member represents a certain amount of population. It forms thus an organisation closely akin to that of the United States of America, and is a perfect example of what German political writers mean by a Bundes-Staat or Federative State. The third is the much looser political organisation of which we propose to give in this paper a somewhat detailed account, and with regard to which we wish, first and foremost, to impress upon our readers that it is emphatically *not* a Bundes-Staat, but a Staaten-Bund ; or, in other words, not a *federative state,* but a *confederation of states.*

The Holy Roman Empire, powerful once, but always much more dignified than powerful, invested as it was with certain vague attributes which had descended from the days when there really were Cæsars,* had come in the eighteenth century to be a shadow of its former self, and to deserve the taunt of Voltaire, that it was neither " Holy, nor Roman, nor even an Empire." It is not by organisations of this kind that powerful shocks from without are successfully resisted; and so in 1806 it crumbled to pieces.† The Emperor Francis assumed the title of Emperor of Austria, surrendering his infinitely more dignified position ; and in the room of the old order Europe saw a chaos of unequal, unconnected states, and the Confederation of the Rhine. That body, more celebrated than honoured, was called into existence in the month of July 1806, by the document styled " L'Acte de la Confédération du Rhin, ou traité entre sa majesté l'Empereur des Français Roi d'Italie, et les membres de l'Empire Germanique dénommés dans ce traité." It consisted at first of sixteen members, varying in importance from the king of Bavaria down to the Prince von der Leyen. Within the next three years, however, twenty-three other members adhered to it, so that in the beginning of the year 1810 it comprised a population of fourteen and a half millions, although this number was soon after diminished. It was a purely international union. The central authority of the Confederation had nothing whatever to do with the internal

---

* Mr. Bryce, of Oriel College, Oxford, has lately traced for English readers the history of this wonderful institution, in an extremely interesting work. His treatise grew out of an essay written for the Arnold prize—a fact which makes us sigh to think how much might be effected for learning in this country, if only our great universities would devote a larger portion of their revenues to the encouragement of manly as distinguished from boyish studies.

† The best authority on the present constitution and recent history of the Confederation is Kaltenborn.

regulations of the various states of which it was composed. Napoleon was its hereditary protector, and reserved to himself the power of summoning the Federal Assembly; of initiating all discussions in it through its prince-president, the duke of Dalberg ; the right of naming the prince-president, and the right of commanding it to make war or peace. The Federal Assembly was composed of ambassadors accredited by each state, and was divided into two colleges—the Royal Grand Ducal and the Princely. The Confederation of the Rhine had hardly time to develop itself, or to show what were likely to be the results of French influence acting upon a German body-politic ; but its tendencies, so far as they showed themselves, were unfavourable to individual and local liberties—despotic and bureaucratic.

The fortunes, however, of the Confederation of the Rhine were destined to be "of hasty growth and blight." Germany, which had been at first paralysed by the success of the French arms, gradually recovered her consciousness, and began to plan a rising when a suitable occasion should present itself. Ere long the disasters of the Great Captain in Spain and in Russia, the successes of Kutusoff and of Wellington, made Leipzig possible, and the allied armies of Central and Eastern Europe rolled across the Rhine. Paris fell, and with it the prestige of the conqueror. The Confederation of the Rhine did not even wait for the final decision of the struggle to dissolve itself; nay, it did not even die by any formal diplomatic act. It melted gradually away, one member after another falling off, and joining the victorious march of the avenging hosts.

Germany was now utterly disintegrated. The Holy Roman Empire had ceased to exist ; the Confederation of the Rhine had followed it ; and from the Black Forest to the Russian frontier there was nothing but angry ambitions, vengeances, and fears. If there was ever to be peace again in all these wide regions, it was clearly necessary to create something new. What was to be created was a far more difficult question ; but already, on the 30th of May 1814, the powers had come to some sort of understanding, if not with regard to the means to be pursued, at least with regard to the end to be attained. In the Treaty of Paris we find these words : " Les états de l'Allemagne seront indépendants et unis par un lien fédératif." But how was this to be effected ? There were some who wished the Holy Roman Empire to be restored. This was naturally enough the view which found favour with most of the mediatised princes ; and many individual thinkers, whose interests were not affected, had come to the same conclusion. Of course neither Prussia, Bavaria, nor Wurtemberg, could look kindly upon a plan so obviously unfavourable to them ; but not even Austria really wished it, and indeed it had few powerful friends. Then there was a project of a North and South Germany, with the Maine for boundary ; but this was very much the reverse of acceptable to the minor princes, who had no idea of being grouped like so many satellites, some around Austria and some around Prussia. Next came a plan of reconstruction by circles, the effect of which would have been to have thrown all the power of Germany into the hands of a few of the larger states. To this all the smaller independent states were bitterly opposed, and it broke down, although supported by the great authority of Stein, as well as by Gagern. If Germany had been in a later phase of political development, public opinion would perhaps have forced the sovereigns to consent to the formation of a really united Fatherland with a powerful executive and a national parliament—but the time for that had not arrived. What was the opposition of a few hundred clear-sighted men with their few thousand followers, that it should prevail over the masters of so many legions? What these potentates cared most about were their sovereign rights, and the dream of German unity was very readily sacrificed to the determination of each of them to be, as far as he possibly could, absolute master in his own dominions. Therefore it was that it soon became evident that the results of the deliberation on the future of Germany would be, not a federative state, but a confederation of states—a Staaten-Bund, not a Bundes-Staat. There is no doubt, however, that much mischief might have been avoided if all the stronger powers had worked conscientiously together to give this Staaten-Bund as national a character as possible ; to gratify as far as they could the natural desire of most active-minded Germans, that their country, which covers so large a space on the map of Europe, should play a part in Europe somewhat commensurate with its vast extent ; and that the internal arrangements of the different states should, as regards commerce, justice, postal communications, and many other matters, be one and the same. Prussia was really honestly desirous to effect something of this kind, and Stein, Hardenberg, William von Humboldt, Count Münster, and other statesmen, laboured hard to bring it about. Austria, on the other hand, aided by Bavaria, Wurtemberg, and Baden, did all she could to oppose such projects. Things would perhaps have been settled better than they ultimately were, if the return of Napoleon from Elba had not frightened all Europe from its propriety, and turned the attention of the sovereigns towards warlike preparations. It was perfectly natural that the labour necessary to perfect the new machine should be grudged when all men's thoughts were directed towards the new struggle which had commenced.

The document by which the Germanic Confederation is created is of so much importance that we may say a word about the various stages through which it passed. First, then, it appears as a paper drawn up by Stein in March 1814, and submitted to Hardenberg, Count Münster, and the Emperor Alexander. Next, in the month of September, it took the form of an official plan, handed by Hardenberg to Metternich, and consisting of forty-one articles. This plan contemplated the creation of a confederation which should have the character rather of a Bundes-Staat than of a Staaten-Bund ; but it went to pieces in consequence of the difficulties which we have noticed above, and out of it, and of ten other official proposals, twelve articles were sublimated by the rival chemistry of Hardenberg and Metternich. Upon these twelve articles the representatives of Austria, Prussia, Hanover, and Wurtemberg, deliberated. Their sittings were cut short partly by the ominous appearance which was presented in the autumn of 1814 by the Saxon and Polish questions, and partly by the difficulties from the side of Bavaria and Wurtemberg, which we have already noticed. The spring brought a project of the Austrian statesman Wessenberg, who proposed a Staaten-Bund rather than a Bundes-Staat ; and out of this and a new Prussian project drawn up by W. von Humboldt, grew the last sketch, which was submitted on the 23d of May 1815 to the general conference of the plenipotentiaries of all Germany. They made short work of it at the last, and the Federal-Act (Bundes-Acte) bears date June

8th, 1815. This is the document which is incorporated in the principal act of the Congress of Vienna, and placed under the guarantee of eight European powers, including France and England.

Wurtemberg, Baden, and Hesse-Homburg, did not form part of the Confederation for some little time—the latter not till 1817 ; but after they were added to the powers at first consenting, the number of the sovereign states in the Confederation was altogether thirty-nine. The outward and visible sign of their unity was the presence in Frankfort of representatives from each state forming the Diet, of whose powers and method of conducting business we shall have more to say when we have traced the history of the Confederation to our own times, but which, we may observe in passing, has always been thoroughly inefficient for any good purpose.

The following are the chief stipulations of the Federal Act. The object of the Confederation is the external and internal security of Germany, and the independence and inviolability of the confederate states. A *diète fédérative* (Bundes-Versammlung) is to be created, and its attributions are sketched. The Diet is, as soon as possible, to draw up the fundamental laws of the Confederation. No state is to make war with another on any pretence. All federal territories are mutually guaranteed. There is to be in each state a " Landständische Verfassung"—" il y aura des assemblées d'états dans tous les pays de la Confédération." Art. 14 reserves many rights to the mediatised princes. Equal civil and political rights are guaranteed to all Christians in all German States, and stipulations are made in favour of the Jews.

The Diet did not actually assemble before the 5th of November 1816. Its first measures, and, above all, its first words, were not unpopular. The Holy Allies, however, pressed with each succeeding month more heavily upon Germany, and got at last the control of the Confederation entirely into their hands. The chief epochs in this sad history were the Congress of Carlsbad, 1819—the resolutions of which against the freedom of the press were pronounced by Gentz to be a victory more glorious than Leipzig ; the ministerial conferences which immediately succeeded it at Vienna ; and the adoption by the Diet of the Final Act (Schluss Acte) of the Confederation on the 8th of June 1820.

The following are the chief stipulations of the Final Act :— The Confederation is indissoluble. No new member can be admitted without the unanimous consent of all the states, and no federal territory can be ceded to a foreign power without their permission. The regulations for the conduct of business by the Diet are amplified and more carefully defined. All quarrels between members of the Confederation are to be stopped before recourse is had to violence. The Diet may interfere to keep order in a state where the government of that state is notoriously incapable of doing so. Federal execution is provided for in case any government resists the authority of the Diet.

Other articles declare the right of the Confederation to make war and peace as a body, to guard the rights of each separate state from injury, to take into consideration the differences between its members and foreign nations, to mediate between them, to maintain the neutrality of its territory, to make war when a state belonging to the Confederation is attacked in its non-federal territory if the attack seems likely to endanger Germany. The constitutions of the respective states are made expressly as little inconvenient to the sovereigns as possible : " der Souverän kann durch eine landständische Verfassung nur in der Ausübung bestimmter Rechte an die Mitwirkung der Stände gebunden werden." The liberty of the press is restrained.

No very material event in the history of the Confederation between 1820 and 1834, when there were again ministerial conferences at Vienna, in consequence of the revolutionary agitation which had been called forth by the fall of the elder branch of the Bourbons. Frederick William IV. of Prussia was really anxious for a change in the constitution of the Confederation, and many plans were agitated, but nothing came of them.

On the 1st of January 1848, Prince Metternich assembled the diplomatists who were then in Vienna, and made, according to his usual custom, a statement with regard to the position of public affairs. With a sagacity truly worthy of himself and of the school of statesmen to which he belonged—a school unfortunately not yet extinct—he assured his listeners that never was Austria so tranquil, nor the peace of Europe more assured. Within three months he was on his way to the frontier, and Vienna and Berlin were in insurrection. The news of the Paris revolution worked not less powerfully in the valley of the Rhine than on the Danube and the Spree. Before the first symptoms of insubordination had been observed in either of the two great capitals, upon the 5th of March, fifty-one political writers, professors, and other persons of importance, had assembled in Heidelberg, and had summoned all who were or had been members of German constitutional assemblies to meet in Frankfort. Many responded to their call, and the body thus got together, which

was called the Vorparlament, and the committee which succeeded it devised the electoral law under which the assembly
of the German people was presently convoked. The sovereigns neither did nor could attempt to resist the movement,
and very soon the deputies of Austria, Prussia, and the minor
states had gathered in the Paul's Kirche. On the 12th of
July the Diet formally resigned its powers into the hands of
the Reichsverweser or Vicar of the Empire, the Archduke
John, and the laborious work of the diplomatists of 1814 and
1815 seemed to have finally disappeared. Already, however,
there had risen in the minds of the Frankfort legislators the
terrible question, What is this Germany for which we are to
devise a constitution? and very soon the assembly fell into
two bitterly hostile sections. These were the since celebrated
Klein-deutsche and Gross-deutsche parties. The first of these
wished to exclude Austria from the Confederation, and to
group the smaller states around Prussia. The second desired
to retain in the Confederation all the German provinces of
Austria, and to throw the hegemony into her hands. The
former party was embraced by the most thoughtful and truly
constitutional deputies, and was supported as a matter of
course by the great bulk of the Prussian people. The latter
was strong in Southern Germany, strong in the support of
the ultra-democrats, who saw, in the constitutional leanings
of their adversaries, a most dangerous obstacle to their designs,
and was aided by all the power and prestige of the Haps-
burgs. The opponents were well matched. The struggle was
long and doubtful, but in the end of 1848 the Klein-deutsche
party prevailed. Heinrich von Gagern, the son of the man
whose name we have mentioned in connection with the first
conferences about the Federal Act, succeeded M. Schmerling;

and on March 28th, 1849, the crown of the resuscitated German Empire was decreed to Frederick William of Prussia. The feeble monarch after some hesitation declined it, making, as an English publicist of that day remarked, "il gran rifiuto" of our times. He wrote to Arndt, the author of the famous song, "Was ist des Deutschen Vaterland?" in these characteristic words : " Is this offspring of the revolution of 1848 really a crown ? It has no cross on it. It does not mark on the brow of him who wears it, the seal of the grace of God. It is the iron collar which would reduce to the position of a slave the descendant of twenty-four electors and kings, the chief of sixteen millions of men, and of the bravest and most devoted army in the world."

The refusal of Frederick William was a death-blow to the Frankfort Parliament. It lingered some time longer, but at last transferred itself to Stuttgardt, where it was dispersed by the police—a fate akin to that of the great river of the Fatherland, "which streams forth from the glaciers of the Adula, and ends in the sluices of Katwyk."

The king of Prussia had too little courage, or perhaps too tender a conscience, to "play at the gold table ;" but the advice of some of his best friends, his own ideas of what was right, and his personal ambition, combined to make him put himself, on the 26th of May 1849, at the head of the so-called "League of the Three Kings," his colleagues being the rulers of Hanover and Saxony. Round these three were grouped twenty-four minor states ; and the whole was formed into the body known for some time to the politicians of Germany as the "Union," or the "Engere Bundes-Staat" (restricted confederation). After reading the explanation of Radowitz, it is difficult not to believe that the king of Prussia was really anxious to meet to some extent the aspirations of the people. Not so their majesties of Hanover and Saxony. They merely bowed to events. The real supporters of the "Union" were the men of the "party of Gotha"—so named from the assembly which took place in that town in June 1849 ; and their ranks included many of the best patriots in Germany.

Of course, this *Sonderbund* was anything but agreeable to Austria. She, however, in May 1849, was too hard pressed to make an effectual resistance. She "bided her time," and had not to bide long. The first advantage which she gained was the treaty of the 30th September 1849. By it Austria and Prussia arranged for an *interim* management of the affairs of the Confederation in the room of the Reichsverweser, who was about to abdicate ; and henceforward two Austrian and two Prussian plenipotentiaries sat at Frankfort.

The reaction, however, was growing ever stronger and stronger. In the month of August the surrender of the Hungarian army at Világos materially improved the position and prospects of Austria. No sooner had this occurred than Saxony and Hanover began to draw off from their close union with Prussia and to gravitate towards her rival. They had associated themselves, they maintained, with their northern neighbour, not because they liked her projects for a reconstitution of Germany, but because they, equally with the reactionary party in Prussia, cared above all things for the suppression of revolution in their respective territories. Prussia, however, unwilling to sacrifice the advantage which she had gained from the temporary weakness of Austria, insisted upon holding them to the alliance of the three kings, and to the re-

stricted confederation. Hanover broke away before the end
of 1849. Saxony showed an unmistakeable intention of doing
so; but even in the spring of 1850, when she opened the
assembly of Erfurt, Prussia affected to regard them as still
bound to her. A significant answer to the Prussian summons
to Erfurt was given, only a few days before the assembly met,
by the king of Wurtemberg, who made a speech, in which he
withstood the pretensions of Prussia from the point of view
of the so-called league of the four kings—Saxony, Bavaria,
Hanover, and Wurtemberg—who naturally enough inclined
to the opinion of those who thought the future constitution
of Germany should be based upon a parliament, to which
Austria, Prussia, and the united smaller states should each
send a hundred members ; and a directory of seven, in which
Austria, Prussia, Bavaria, Saxony, Hanover, and Wurtemberg
should each have a voice, while Electoral and Grand-ducal
Hesse had each half a voice. The Prussian star was evidently not in the ascendant when Radowitz first addressed,
in the name of his sovereign, the great council of the restricted confederation, the Assembly of Erfurt.* The project
of a reconstituted Germany, with a less democratic constitution than that which had been elaborated at Frankfort, which
he laid before that assembly, was adopted in its entirety, after
much discussion. Nothing more embarrassing to Prussia
could have occurred ; for even that project was a great deal

---

* We have called attention on a former page to the first series of *Gespräche
aus der Gegenwart*. What it is to the period before 1847, that the second
series is to the years 1848, 1849, and 1850. To the general reader the second
work will be less interesting than the first ; but to those who wish to understand the politics of Germany it is even more important, because Radowitz,
the Waldheim of the conversations, was an actor of first-rate importance
through the whole of the revolutionary period.

more democratic than what her rulers really wished for. The Duke of Coburg came to their assistance with a proposal for a congress of princes. The congress met, not in Gotha, but in Berlin, and was composed of the states most favourable to Prussia. The majority of these unfortunately were only of a third or fourth rate importance, and neither it nor the college of plenipotentiaries, from these various princes, which followed it, came to any result. The game, however, now became more exciting. Austria replied by convoking the old Plenum at Frankfort; and before the autumn was out the kings of Bavaria and Wurtemberg had met Francis Joseph at Bregentz and exchanged toasts and promises of the most warlike character. Where so many causes of estrangement existed, it was easy to find a pretext for quarrel. That pretext was furnished by the affairs of the most typically misgoverned of German countries, Electoral Hesse. We need not go into the details of the constitutional struggle in that ill-starred district: suffice it to say, that the Elector appealed to Frankfort and to Vienna; the people appealed to the restricted confederation and to Berlin. Troops marched from north and south. Shots were exchanged between the Austrian and the Prussian outposts. The situation was almost precisely what it was in the first days of April 1866. In 1850, however, the Emperor Nicholas was at the height of his power. He had poured, in 1849, a vast force into Hungary, and had apparently, with the greatest ease, restored that country to the House of Hapsburg. He had kept revolution far away from his own borders, and in the intoxication of success he almost believed himself something more than a man. Strong in his yet unbroken prestige, strong in the personal ascendancy which he had established over the court of Berlin, he threw his whole influence into

the scale of peace—not because he disliked war, but because
he identified the cause of Austria with the cause of order.
Other influences, and above all the temper of the king, made
the position of Radowitz untenable. He was, as we have seen
in the preceding article, driven from power, and with him
went down with a crash the whole fabric of the " Union."
With him too passed away for a time all hopes of Prussian
hegemony.

Deep was the humiliation and bitter the wrath of all the
best men in Germany, but on that we must not dwell. So
elated with his victory was Prince Schwartzenberg, that at
the Dresden conferences which presently assembled he had
actually the assurance to propose that Austria should enter
into the Germanic Confederation with all her non-Germanic
provinces. Luckily France, England, and Russia came to the
rescue. Baron Brenier, in a remarkable dispatch, pointed out
that this was altogether inadmissible, and perfectly opposed to
the views of the three great non-Germanic powers who had
guaranteed the order established in 1815. So Prussia had,
after all, a sort of poor little triumph wherewith to console
herself for the disgrace of Olmütz ; and, in less than three
years after its disappearance, back came the old Frankfort Diet
again, with all its lumbering and unsatisfactory machinery,
and German hopes and aspirations once more slumbered, if
they did not sleep.

What, then, is the constitution of this most unloved
assembly ? We have seen that the Confederation originally
consisted of thirty-nine sovereign states. Of these, six have
ceased to exist. Gotha has been divided between Coburg and
Meiningen ; Anhalt-Cöthen has merged in Anhalt-Dessau; so,
within the last few years, has Anhalt-Bernburg ; while the

two Hohenzollerns—Hechingen and Sigmaringen—have been ceded to Prussia, and only a month or two ago Hesse-Homburg fell to the grand-duke of Darmstadt. * There are now, therefore, only thirty-three states included in the Germanic Confederation. These are—1, Austria ; 2, Prussia ; 3, Bavaria ; 4, Saxony ; 5, Hanover ; 6, Wurtemberg ; 7, Baden ; 8, Hesse-Cassel ; 9, Hesse-Darmstadt ; 10, Schleswig-Holstein ; 11, Luxemburg and Limburg ; 12, Brunswick ; 13, Mecklenburg-Schwerin ; 14, Nassau ; 15, Weimar ; 16, Meiningen ; 17, Altenburg ; 18, Coburg-Gotha ; 19, Mecklenburg-Strelitz ; 20, Oldenburg ; 21, Anhalt ; 22, Schwarzburg-Sondershausen ; 23, Schwarzburg-Rudolstadt ; 24, Lichtenstein ; 25, Waldeck ; 26, Reuss-Greiz ; 27, Reuss-Schleiz ; 28, Schaumburg-Lippe ; 29, Lippe-Detmold and the four free towns ; 30, Lübeck ; 31, Frankfort ; 32, Bremen ; and 33, Hamburg. Of these states the 1st is ruled by an emperor ; the 2d, 3d, 4th, 5th, and 6th, by kings ; the 7th, 9th, 11th, 13th, 15th, 19th, and 20th, by grand-dukes ; the 8th by an elector ; the 10th is in an exceptional position ; the 12th, 14th, 16th, 17th, 18th, and 21st, are ruled by dukes ; from the 22d up to the 29th inclusive, the rulers are princes ; and the four others are small republics.

The executive power of the Confederation, and its legislative power, in so far as any such exists, are vested in the body which is popularly called the Diet (Bundes-Versammlung), so styled from *dies*, as meeting from day to day. That name, however, although accurately applied to the old assembly of the empire, has no such fitness when applied to the existing directory of the Confederation. This directory appears in two

* This potentate has now become Grossherzog von Hessen und bei Rhein und Souveräner Landgraf zu Homburg !

forms—1, as a Plenum, or extraordinary convention'; 2, as a
committee (Engere Rath, or Conseil Restreint). In the former
of these assemblies each of the thirty-three states has at least
one vote, while Austria and the kingdoms have four ; Baden,
the two Hesses, Luxemburg and Limburg, each, three ; Brunswick, Mecklenburg-Schwerin, and Nassau, each, two. In the
smaller assembly all the estates which have three or four voices
in the larger, have one ; while all the rest have only fractions of
a voice, being classed together for this purpose in "curie," or
colleges, whence the distinction between virile and curial voices.
The sixteenth college is composed of no less than six small
states; those namely, which are marked above from 24 to 29 inclusive. As a general rule, all matters not specially withdrawn
by the Federal and Final Acts from the control of the Engere
Rath are decided by it, and by a simple majority. In the Plenum,
on the other hand, a majority of two-thirds at least is always
necessary. To the Plenum are referred—1. Questions about
changes in fundamental laws ; 2. Questions about changes in
organic institutions ; 3. Proposals as to the admission of new
members ; 4. Affairs of religion. No discussion takes place
in the Plenum ; but in the Engere Rath every subject may be
fully discussed. When it is proposed to change a fundamental law, a unanimous vote must be first taken in the
Plenum in favour of entertaining the question, after which
the details are worked out in the Engere Rath. Decisions
about the admission of a new member also require unanimity.
It is obvious that in the larger assembly the influence of the
smaller states is much greater than in the other.

Everything which is within the purview of the Federal
and Final Acts is within the competence of the Diet. For
greater clearness we may give the following summary :—1. It

watches over the international relations of Germany, the maintenance of internal peace, and of all the fundamental laws which regulate the existence of the Confederation. 2. It settles all quarrels between members of the Confederation, either by mediation or by a complicated judicial process, known as *un jugement austrégal*, from *Austrag*, a decision (a subject on which a perfect literature has accumulated in half-a-century). 3. To it belongs the settlement of disputes between sovereigns and their subjects, when all constitutional methods have failed. (We need hardly say that this power has been frequently abused.) 4. The duty of taking care that each state in the Confederation should have, in accordance with the Federal Act, a " Landständische Verfassung," was originally imposed upon the Diet, and it was also directed to provide that no constitution once given should be modified except by constitutional means. Further, it was directed to prevent any constitution being so worked as to make it impossible for the state in which it existed to fulfil its Federal obligations. (Here was a field opened for infinite oppression, and under this head the action of the Diet has always been very unsatisfactory.) 5. The Diet watches over the rights of the mediatised princes, and of private individuals who may have a *locus standi* to appeal to it. 6. The Diet receives ambassadors, and has the power of sending them if it pleases. 7. It regulates all things relative to the military force of the Confederation.

All the resolutions of the Diet which have an executive character, and are taken constitutionally, become at once valid for all purposes. Not so decisions which have a legislative character. These must be first approved by the respective Chambers of the confederated states.

The Engere Rath meets every Thursday, but may adjourn for not more than four months after concluding its discussion on any subject. It has no power over its members, who are only responsible to the governments which they represent. A decree of the 8th of March 1860 permitted the publication of its proceedings.

Eight committees—permanent or renewable—attend each to some specified department, and report to the Engere Rath on finance, general political affairs, commerce, military matters, the publication of its proceedings, upon the 14th article of the Federal Act, which relates to the affairs of the mediatised princes, upon cases which arise for federal execution, and upon petitions. The funds of the Confederation are under two different systems of management, according as they are applicable to mere routine matters—such as the support of the Federal chancery ; or to great enterprises—such as war, and enforcement of Federal authority. The Federal army consists of 503,072 men, of which Austria contributes 158,037, Prussia 133,769, and the small states all the rest. Five great fortresses—Landau, Luxemburg, Mayence, Rastadt, and Ulm—are garrisoned by Federal troops.

Austria has the largest area in square miles protected by the Confederation and controlled by the Diet, but Prussia has the largest amount of population in the same position : Austria having 75,822 square miles to 71,698 of Prussia, and Prussia having 14,138,804 inhabitants to 12,802,944 of Austria, according to the census of 1861. More than twenty-two millions of Austrian subjects are not under the protection of the Confederation, which extends only to the archduchy of Austria, Bohemia, Styria, Tyrol, Moravia, and part of Illyria ; whereas little more than four millions of Prussians are beyond its limits. 6,860,000 Austrians protected by the Confederation are not Germans, and 825,000 Prussians. Lichtenstein, with 64 square miles, is the smallest of the sovereign states ; and Frankfort, with 43 square miles of territory, is the least considerable in extent of the free cities ; its population is, however, much larger than that of Lübeck, which rules over a district nearly three times as large.*

* A few words as to the political life of some of the German States, considered not in their corporate but in their individual capacity, may not be out of place here.

The patronage bestowed upon artists by King Louis of Bavaria has diverted attention from the narrow-minded and bigoted character of his rule. No similar consideration detracts from the credit due to the efforts of his son to collect round him men of letters and enlightenment. Possessed of good but not brilliant abilities, he played no remarkable *rôle* in Germany; but he steadily carried out what he thought right, and kept faith with his people. The character of the present king is probably still immature, and is criticised in the most opposite ways. The kingdom to which he has succeeded is the only member of the Germanic Confederation—except the leviathans of the south and north—which could ever do more than dream of playing an independent part. Internally, it is fairly prosperous and contented ; and the Bavarian has rather to complain of a teazing care for his welfare on the part of the government than of any intentional oppression. In the last three chapters of Mr. Wilberforce's *Social Life in Munich* will be found a clear account of the infinite leading-strings which shackle him, more especially of the restraints on marriage and upon trade, both of which produce the most disastrous results.

Wurtemberg lost in her late sovereign a man who, if he had been the prime minister of a large state, not the king of a small one, would have left in all probability a great name to history ; but the chief importance of this part of Germany, in our generation, has been theological rather than political. The university of Tübingen was the university of Strauss, the publication of whose *Leben Jesu* in 1832 is the epoch with which the history of recent theological movements in Germany commences. Here, too, a few years ago, died F. C. Baur, whose scholars, scattered over all German-reading countries, have given to the Tübingen school so great a renown.

Saxony has fallen from her high estate, and her capital is now far more remarkable for its collections of art than for its political significance or the resort to it of learned men ; but the industrial life of some Saxon districts

Among the seventeen plenipotentiaries who form the ordinary council of the Bund, there is only at this moment one man of very great eminence. He is the representative of

is unusually active, and trade has been freed within the last five years from many antiquated shackles. The accident of the royal family being attached to a very rigid school of Catholicism is an unfortunate circumstance, but has had more influence upon the foreign than the internal politics of the country. The king is a highly-cultivated man, has translated the *Divina Commedia*, and is, strange to say, a very excellent jurist. A natural distrust of Prussia, and perhaps the personal ambition of M. von Beust, has made the Saxon government very active in trying to raise up a third power in Germany ; and during the Schleswig-Holstein controversy these same influences—aided, it is said, by the personal convictions of the king—have had the good effect of keeping this little state thoroughly true to the German, as distinguished from the Austrian or Prussian, view of the question.

The Hanoverian government has adhered with but too much persistence to the evil course which was given to its politics by our own notorious Duke of Cumberland. Obliged to yield for a time to popular demands in 1848, it felt itself strong enough to make a long step backward in 1855 ; and although the king is not personally unpopular, his advisers have rarely shared his good fortune. In 1862 the attempt to substitute a catechism strongly tinged with neo-Lutheran views, in the place of the comparatively reasonable one which had been in use for some seventy years, brought about disturbances which might easily have taken a serious turn ; and it is characteristic of the state of chronic opposition in which the bulk of the population lives, that the idea of the *National Verein* should have been first developed in the brain of the leader of the Liberal party in Hanover, M. von Bennigsen.

The peaceful *laisser faire* of Brunswick contrasts advantageously with the efforts which are made by antiquated parties in the neighbouring states to maintain a power which events have undermined. Both here and in Oldenburg the rulers are decidedly popular ; and in those two districts, as well as in Weimar and Coburg-Gotha, the year of revolutions was followed by no reaction.

The Grand-duchy of Weimar, containing only about 270,000 inhabitants, and not quite so large as Sussex, has attracted to itself a greater amount of attention than many much larger countries. What is still better, it contrives to be extremely happy. The present ruler is a grandson of Karl August, and has inherited much of his love for art, and other good qualities. In the present circumstances of Germany it would be impossible even if any Göthes or Schillers were to be found, to connect them with a small court after the fashion of the great days of Weimar. The pleasant little town, however, has been

Baden, Robert von Mohl, one of that family of distinguished brothers, amongst whom M. Jules Mohl, the professor of Persian at the Collège de France, is probably the best known in

chosen as a place of residence by several men of letters and painters of some distinction. Nowhere has the practical morality which was inculcated by Röhr and his school produced better results than amongst the poor but honest population of the Grand-duchy, and in no country have the principles of religious toleration been better carried out.

The Grand-duke of Hesse-Darmstadt has thrown his influence very decidedly into the scale of the Middle State policy, a proceeding which is natural enough on his part, but has by no means tended to increase the popularity of his family, which has been at various times involved in disagreeable discussions with the representatives of the people about the Civil List. Hesse-Darmstadt, though by no means a model state, shows to great advantage by the side of Electoral Hesse, where for two generations the ruled and the rulers have been in a state of war. Their quarrel, which from time to time has seemed on the point of setting all Germany in a blaze, has made itself but little talked of since 1862 ; but when so wayward a personage as the Elector Frederick William is in the case we shall never be surprised at hearing that it has broken out again with more violence than ever.

It is gratifying to turn from Hesse-Cassel to a country in every respect its antithesis—to the Grand-duchy of Baden, which, under the rule of an enlightened prince, may fairly be said to lead the Liberal movement in Germany. Whether we look at its constitution, at its ecclesiastical condition, or at the line which it takes in the affairs of the Confederation, we shall see much that is satisfactory.

Post lucem tenebræ.—The two Mecklenburgs, ruled by sovereigns of Sclavonic race, of which Mecklenburg-Schwerin is about five times larger than the other, although the titles of their rulers are the same, are the most backward states of the Confederation. There are no districts in which the life of Germany, as Germany was before the Napoleonic wars, could be better studied.

The Grand-duke of Oldenburg rules over three small patches of territory : Oldenburg proper, the principality of Lübeck, and Birkenfeld. The former lies between Hanover and Holland, and is a flat unlovely strip cut out of the great northern plain, very similar in character to the adjoining province of Friesland. The second is surrounded by Holstein, and the third lies in the hilly region along the Nahe, on the left bank of the Rhine ; Oberstein, so famous for its agate-cutting, is the best known spot in it. The Grand-duke is a man of high cultivation and good abilities. Up to 1848, his territories were under one of the least liberal governments in Germany ; but the reverse is now the case. He is nearly connected with the imperial family of Russia, and

England. The other two, Hugo and Moritz, have made themselves famous, the one as a microscopic botanist, and the other as a very active member of the parliament of Wurtemberg.

has been accused of being too friendly to the European policy of his powerful relatives.

The dukedom of Anhalt-Dessau, which has now swallowed up its kindred dukedoms of Zerbst, Cöthen, and Bernburg, is remarkable chiefly for its fertility. The revolutionary shock of 1848 was felt here with unusual intensity, and the reaction was proportionably greater than in most parts of Germany. Hence the reigning house is very far from popular.

The two small principalities of Schwarzburg-Sondershausen and Schwarzburg-Rudolstadt divide unequally between them the highland district called the "Upper County," amid the Thuringian hills, and the "Lower County," which lies considerably to the north of the other, within the edge of the great northern plain. The former contains 318, and the latter about 340 square miles.

Lichtenstein is situated on the left bank of the Rhine, between Switzerland and the Tyrol. Its capital is the little town of Vaduz, over which rises the old castle, which is the "Stammhaus" of its princes. The ruler of Lichtenstein, although the least of sovereigns, now that Kniphausen is merged in Oldenburg, is one of the greatest of nobles, possessing estates in Austria thirty-four times larger than his principality. He draws no revenue from Lichtenstein, and the only grievance of which his subjects have recently complained is his absenteeism. Even this is now remedied, for he has agreed to spend a portion of every year at Vaduz.

Waldeck contains in all 466 square miles, of which 32 belong to Pyrmont, and the rest to Waldeck proper. The latter, a picturesque and hilly country, lies out of the path of tourists, and is very rarely visited, although not far from the town of Cassel, which is upon one of the great lines of communication. The well-known mineral springs, and the usual attractions of a watering-place, make Pyrmont, which is separated from Waldeck proper, and considerably to the north of it, much better known. The reigning prince, George Victor, was born in 1831, and came to the throne, after a long minority, in 1852.

This small country has given in very recent years three names to Germany, without which her contemporary annals would be much poorer. These are Rauch the sculptor, Kaulbach the painter, and Bunsen, to whom not Prussia only, but also England, owes so much. Since 1848 the system of government in every department has been remodelled, and although great questions—such as one about the price of firewood—sometimes shake it to its centre, and call forth the sternest patriotic resistance in its parliament

Robert von Mohl was born in 1799. He studied at Tübingen, and was afterwards professor of political science in that university. He was then for some time a member of the Cham-

of fifteen members, it must be pronounced to be one of the best governed portions of the Fatherland ; and it will be a happy day for the Prussians when they enjoy *la liberté comme en Waldeck*. It appears, indeed, to suffer under no evils except those which are necessarily incidental to so tiny a state—viz. a superabundance of public functionaries and a superfluity of public establishments—the former badly paid, and the latter poorly kept up. Then there is, of course, an absence of all object for ambition—a want of many institutions for which large means are indispensable, and a relaxed, sleepy mode of life. What we say of the evils of Waldeck holds equally true of all the German states below those of the second rank, if indeed we might not include those of the second rank also.

The elder or Greitz branch of the ancient house of Reuss rules over a territory which is smaller than the county of Rutland ; but the younger or Schleitz branch has succeeded to the possessions of the now extinct lines of Gera, Lobenstein, and Ebersdorf, and possesses a district more than three times as large as its rival. The scattered patches which belong to them lie partly in the Thuringian uplands, partly in the Erzgebirge and the richer lowlands of Saxony. The family custom of calling each succeeding head of the house by the name of Henry, and distinguishing him by some number between one and a hundred, is well known. The present sovereign of Reuss-Greitz is Henry XXII., and of Reuss-Schleitz, Henry LXVII. The elder branch counts up to one hundred ; the younger begins a new reckoning with the century.

The little principality of Lippe-Detmold lies close to Pyrmont, and is about the size of Waldeck. It contains about 445 square miles ; or, in other words, is about three times the size of the Isle of Wight. It is a rugged and much-wooded country, and is saved from insignificance by the fact that it witnessed that famous defeat of the Romans under Varus, which Arnold, perhaps not unjustly, considered to be one of the turning-points of history. A statue of Arminius, the Hermann of the Germans, has been erected at Detmold, the town which is the residence of the prince.

Schaumburg-Lippe, which is close to the other, is not quite half so large, and in every way unimportant.

The fate of Schleswig-Holstein still trembles in the balance ; nor can we consider, in the face of the opposition of the Prussian Lower House, that the *status* of Lauenburg is definitely settled.

Luxemburg and Limburg belong to the king of the Netherlands. The old Grand-duchy of Luxemburg, which was part of the possessions of the House of Austria, in the Low Countries, was joined to the Germanic Confederation at ber, but in 1847 was called as professor to Heidelberg. He took a conspicuous part in the proceedings of the Vorparlament, was closely associated with the policy of Heinrich von Gagern through the eventful years of 1848 and 1849, and is a partisan of the Prussian or Klein-deutsche theory of German reconstruction.

This article would be even more incomplete than the difficulty of compressing so large a subject into narrow limits renders almost necessary, if we were not to give a brief account of the various plans which have recently been suggested for the reconstruction of the Germanic Confederation. The present system has been condemned by all parties. Its extreme complication, the opportunities for obstruction which it affords, and the fact, that as long as it exists Germany can never really take its place as a great power beside France and England, irritate beyond all bearing a people which, satisfied with its achievements in literature and science, is passionately desirous of political renown.

The years which immediately succeeded the revolutionary period of 1848, 1849, and 1850, were marked in Germany rather by the successful prosecution of industrial enterprises than by political combinations. The reaction had triumphed

the Congress of Vienna, but nearly the whole of it revolted in 1830; and it was only in 1839, after the Dutch had made up their minds to accept the basis of the treaty of the Twenty-four Articles, that about half the country was handed back to its old allegiance. So violent was the feeling in Belgium at this time that M. Gendebien, in voting against the surrender, said: "No! 380,000 times No! for the 380,000 Belgians whom you are sacrificing to fear," and resigned his seat then and there. That was one side of the question, but on the other the king of Holland thought that half Luxemburg was a poor exchange to offer to the Germanic Confederation for the whole of it, so he added Limburg, which became thus, *de jure*, Federal territory. It has never, however, become so *de facto;* and thus, perhaps, room is left open for a *querelle Allemande* on some future day.

in Prussia, and it soon became clear that nothing could be done so long as Frederick William IV. dragged on his unhappy life. The commencement of the reign of his successor brought some glimmerings of hope, soon to be overcast ; but, on the whole, things went on at Frankfort very much in the old way until the Italian war of 1859. No sooner had it broken out than all Germany went mad with fear of France, and the results were similar to those which were observed in 1813, 1840, and 1848. A violent desire for German union became once more developed. In some parts of the country the people would have hailed with delight a declaration of war, and were quite ready to subscribe to the marvellous doctrine that the Mincio is the true frontier of Germany. In Bavaria, more especially, the warlike excitement was intense. In Prussia and the north, although there was a strong war party, the passions of the nation were, so to speak, driven inward, and the result was the formation of the great society called the *National Verein*, which adopts the ideas which found favour at Frankfort and Gotha ten years before. To this same impulse from without was owing, in a great measure, as we have seen in the previous article, the renewed activity of the democratic party at Berlin.

The most conspicuous names which are connected with the *National Verein* are those of politicians who belong to the Fortschritt section in the Prussian Chamber. We should perhaps make an exception in favour of one remarkable man, who seemed inclined for a time to cast in his lot with that section, and may very probably do so again. We allude of course to the brother of the late Prince Consort. The names of the twin duchies of Coburg and Gotha are more familiar to English readers than those of most of the small states of

Germany, and will one day probably be even better known than they are now, as Prince Alfred is heir-presumptive to both of them. The two together are but little larger than Worcestershire, and have a population of about 160,000 ; nevertheless, they are governed by separate Chambers, which, however, combine for the transaction of common affairs every second year. The duke resides part of the year in each, but his establishment in Coburg is the more important of the two which he maintains. His relations to his subjects have not always been of the happiest, owing rather to the old-world notions of the ruled than to the shortcomings of the ruler. Few stranger political pamphlets have appeared in recent years than that which, under the title of *Der Herzog von Coburg-Gotha und sein Volk*, was put forth in 1861 by Ernest II. Amongst all the minor princes of Germany, he is the most conspicuous figure; his character presents a striking contrast to that of his brother—the one is as impetuous as the other was prudent. He has been well described by one of his intimate friends as a Husaren-Natur, and he was in some sort for a brief period the leader of the Liberal party in Germany. Within the last few years his politics have been Prussian, Austrian, and Middle State; so that, thanks rather to circumstances than to any change of ultimate aim on his own part, he has boxed the compass of opinion upon the affairs of the Fatherland. His range of accomplishments and information is very great, and his position as head of that fortunate family which has arrived at such great destinies in Portugal, Belgium, and England, has mixed him up with the *grande politique* to a very great extent. His life, passed under the shadow of his ancestral fortress, which rises over Coburg, or in his cheerful capital on the other side of the Thuringian range, varied by frequent journeys, and enlivened by a constant stream of society, is about as pleasant as the life of a potentate without real power can be; yet he obviously thirsts for a larger, if less dignified, sphere of action, and incarnates the vain longing for more real national life, which is felt by the subjects of all the dukelets and princelets within the limits of the Confederation.

The most important official steps which have been taken for the reform of the Confederation since 1859 have been :—

1. The proposals of the Duke of Saxe-Meiningen, in 1860, for a personal interview of the sovereigns, with the view to arrange the establishment of a directory of three, in which one member, elected by the smaller states, should sit by the side of the representatives of Austria and Prussia.

2. The declaration of Saxe-Coburg-Gotha in 1861, made formally in the Diet, that if the monarchical principle was not to be sacrificed, German unity could only be brought about by an individual will, resting on a general representation of the German people.

3. The proposal of M. de Beust, the Saxon minister, in October and November 1861, the chief features of which were the retention of the *Engere Rath* as it now stands, but with the proviso that it should sit one month in the year in North Germany, under the presidency of Prussia, and one month in the year in South Germany, under the presidency of Austria ; that in the intervals the affairs of the Confederation should be managed by a directory of three, on the Meiningen plan ; and that from time to time the Engere Rath should be assisted by an assembly of 128 delegates, selected from the several German Parliaments.

4. The proposal of M. Bernstorff, in the name of Prussia,

which had in view the creation of a smaller Prussian Confederation within the great Confederation, of which Austria formed part.

5. The project brought before the assembled princes of Frankfort, in the month of August 1863, by the great Kaiser himself. He proposed that Germany should henceforth be governed : *a.* By an executive directory of five—that is, by Austria, Prussia, Bavaria, and two representatives elected by the minor states ; *b.* By a Federal Council, which was to consist of twenty-one representatives, and which was to have very considerable powers ; *c.* By a Chamber composed of the princes, who were to have the right of accepting, rejecting, or modifying all the proposals which were brought before them. *d.* A General Assembly of 300, of whom 200 were to be elected by the Lower, and 100 by the Upper Houses of the Confederation. Austria was to send 75 members ; Prussia, 75 ; Bavaria, 27 ; Hanover, Saxony, and Wurtemberg, 15 each ; and the smaller states from 1 to 12 each. The effect of this plan would have been to throw the preponderance into the scale of Austria, and to have formed the princes into a sort of league of mutual assurance against their subjects. Its warmest supporter was the king of Saxony.

The first of these projects was overthrown chiefly by the opposition of Bavaria, because it might well have happened that its sovereign should not have been the third member of the directory. The Duke of Coburg's proposal coincided with the desires of the great mass of the German people, but was eminently distasteful to most of the sovereigns, and was used by his enemies to give colour to the report that he aspired to be emperor of Germany. The idea of Baron Beust was strongly opposed by Prussia and by Baden ; while that of Count Bernstorff brought half the Confederation about his ears, and threatened another Olmütz. Prussia had her revenge most amply in 1863 at Frankfort ; putting, so to speak, a spoke in the wheel of her old enemy with eminent success.

As these sheets are going through the press, we learn that Count Bismark has proposed to checkmate Austria by calling together at Frankfort a German Parliament elected by universal suffrage. Up to the time at which we write, little favour has been shown to this proposal, a fact which is not to be wondered at when we know that as far back as the 22d of August 1862, it was announced by the *Grentzboten*, before, it will be observed, Count Bismark had become minister, that one of his plans was to win over the democracy by summoning a German Parliament ; to get rid of that German Parliament when it had done as much work for Prussia as Count Bismark desired ; next to reintroduce the absolute *régime* at Berlin, and to extend it by military demonstrations to all the states which had accepted Prussian hegemony. " Surely in vain is the net spread in the sight of any bird."

No feasible scheme for the reconstruction of the Confederation has yet been presented to the world. Are we, therefore, to join in the cry which is so often heard, that Germany is incapable of reasonable political action ? This would, we think, be most unjust. No political sagacity which has ever yet been exhibited in this planet, would be sufficient to bring order out of the chaos of German politics, as long as the throne of Prussia is occupied by a weak or unworthy man. Cavour himself could have done nothing if his lot had been cast in Modena.

All the plans which have been suggested have been modifications of three ideas. The largest and most imposing (for we leave the idea of Austria's entering the Bund with all her non-Germanic provinces on one side as being utterly out of the question) would be the union in one confederation, like the Swiss Confederation, of all really German lands.

That is the Gross-deutsche Idée, far the most striking, most poetical, and least political of all. To it there are two great objections—objections so great that all the smaller ones fall into the shade.

First, it is impossible that Prussia should ever consent to subordinate herself to Austria in the way which would be necessary, if this idea were to be carried out.

Secondly, such a Germany as would thus be created would have no internal principle of cohesion.

The most unobservant traveller can hardly fail to remark the difference of Northern and Southern Germany. The scenery, the vegetation, the climate, the mode of life—everything but the language of the middle or upper classes is dissimilar; and a Bavarian transplanted from Munich to Berlin, or a Suabian banished to Bonn, is very apt to feel like a fish out of water. Hence a vague dislike, which sometimes almost passes into antipathy, and does not go for nothing amongst the influences which make a close union of Germany, in its widest sense, nothing better than "a pious wish."

Of even greater importance is the difference of religion. There are, of course, wide Protestant districts in Southern Germany, and wide Catholic districts in Northern Germany; but speaking broadly and generally, the first is distinctly Catholic, and the second as distinctly Protestant. There can be no doubt that the dogmatic decomposition which is going on alike amongst the Lutherans, the Reformed, and the adherents of the old religion, will at some distant period unite the vast majority of those who are now kept asunder by distinctions of creed in attachment to the same ideas; but the process which is bringing this about is a very slow one, and no political results will flow from it in our days. Nay, for all calculations as to the near future of Germany, it is more needful to regard the tendencies which are adverse to this tendency towards unity. The philosopher may think of the bigotry of Maintz, and its allied phenomena, as mere back-waters which tell nothing about the set of the main current, but to the politician they are of great moment. During the last few years the distinctions between Catholics and Protestants have been drawn sharper in many districts, and men never meet each other, whose fathers were accustomed to live together in the same clubs altogether oblivious of confessional differences.*

Next come plans, founded on the so-called *Trias-Idée*, which contemplate the reform of the Confederation by raising up a third power out of the middle states to balance Austria and Prussia. Against these we think that the same objections may be brought which are urged against the

---

* To those who wish to know as much of the history of modern theological movements in Protestant Germany as is necessary to a clear understanding of Prussian and German politics, we recommend with great confidence the *last* edition of the *Geschichte der Neuesten Theologie*, by Dr. Carl Schwartz, Court preacher at Gotha. We say emphatically the *last* edition, because, in the interval between the publication of the second in 1856 and the third in 1864, the whole aspect of Germany altered. The reaction had done its worst, and the tide of liberal opinion flowed again.

Much valuable information upon Catholic as well as Protestant affairs in the most recent times is also to be found in the fifth volume of F. C. Baur's *Church History*, but we cannot say that it is conveyed to the reader in so agreeable a manner. Dr. Schwartz is one of the best prose writers in Germany.

present Confederation. We do not see any device by which the real strength of the smaller states could be made equal to that of either of the two German great powers ; and as long as this is so, any such arrangement would want all real guarantees of stability.

Last, and least poetical, but most political, is the humbler Klein-deutsche Idée, which merely contemplates something like the " Union" of 1849 around Prussia, a union which it might be hoped would gradually grow closer and closer until the minor princes became merely great German nobles, and all Northern and Central Germany was gradually fused into one country. If this came about in our time, and if Austria became more and more an *Ost-Reich*, or Empire of the East, finding her centre of gravity not in Vienna but in Pesth, there is no reason why such a Germany might not attract to itself all German lands ; but that is a mere matter of speculation. Nothing of the sort could now be brought about except by force, and Prussia has nothing like the force necessary to bring it about, to say nothing of other difficulties which we have pointed out elsewhere.

If a war were to break out now between Austria and her, the very best that could happen would be that at the end we might see, by evil and violent means, some such a fusion of Northern and Central Germany in Prussia, or of Prussia in Northern and Central Germany, as can, we believe, be arrived at by patience and fair means ; but a war would put everything on the hazard of the die, and no information exists anywhere, to enable the acutest statesman to guess when and how such a war would end ; because, even if we knew with the utmost accuracy the exact distribution of forces in Germany, no one can form even a guess as to the views and intentions of more than one non-German power.

The problem of German unity would be sufficiently difficult, if, in order to solve it, it were only necessary to compel the wavering wills of the people, and to break the obstinate wills of some of the sovereigns. Even for this a revolutionary period is a necessary condition. There are, however, other influences to be taken into consideration, and above all the opposition of France. It is perfectly natural that no French statesman of any political party should particularly approve the creation of a vast new power beyond the Rhine, more especially as that new power, although for the most part pacifically inclined, would be uncomfortably desirous to rectify its frontiers. One thing, however, is certain, and that is, that German unity has no terrors for this country. We may not be very enthusiastic for it; we may feel to the full what Montalembert has so well insisted on—the superiority of small and happy little states, like Weimar, to a few centralised despotisms; we may acknowledge all that *Particularismus* has done for mankind— the vast intellectual treasures which have been accumulated in the universities of Germany, the works of genius which have been produced under the enlightened patronage of her too-much-reviled princes :—Still the Germans know what is best for themselves ; their hearts are set upon more real political life, and the hopes of nations, "like all strongest hopes," generally fulfil themselves.

How they will be fulfilled no one can venture to prophesy; but the most favourable conditions for their fulfilment would, as it appears to us, be the coincidence of some sudden agitation, like that of 1859, with the occupation of the Prussian throne by a thoroughly constitutional, English-minded ruler, who, not desiring to injure his small brother-potentates more than was necessary, nevertheless fully recognised the truth that kings and princes exist only for their people. All beyond this must, we think, be little better than guess-work. Very striking are the words with which Radowitz, speaking in the character of Waldheim, closes the second series of his *Conversations :—*

"What, you get angry at an idea which others only find silly ! My dear old friend, as once at the turning-point of the world's history it befel the everlasting verity that some thought it foolishness and others a stumbling-block, so it is now with an earthly verity. That the German nation should desire to rise out of its confusion and abasement to a true corporate existence ; that by this means, and only by this means, can the revolution be ended ;—this to some is foolishness, and to some a stumbling-block ; but ' fata viam invenient :' farewell —' the rest is silence.'

It is unfortunate that a natural sympathy for the weaker party has combined with much ignorance of the real merits of the question, to create during the last few years in England a very strong feeling in favour of Denmark in her quarrel with Germany. There are many persons in this country at present, who would willingly see Austria and Prussia fall out, to the desolation of half the Continent, merely to gratify their feelings, which were wounded so deeply by the events of 1864. We, who have been all along strongly opposed to the conduct of these two states, and partisans of the German, as distinguished from the Austro-Prussian view of the question, may be permitted to remind these unwise friends of Denmark that if our view of the matter had prevailed—if a strong pressure had been brought to bear in time upon the Danes, causing them to give up Holstein and Southern Schleswig, and uniting these two districts into a separate state under the much-abused Augustenburg, but in the closest union with Prussia compatible with the rights of their inhabitants—not only would the demands of justice have been fulfilled, but much blood, treasure, and heart-burning would have been saved to Europe.

Far from having the slightest vestige of dislike to Denmark, we have the greatest respect and admiration for that country; and we only wish that the Tory party here, which took up its cause so eagerly, would advocate some of its institutions. If we suffered ourselves to be guided merely by feeling, we should have been decidedly in favour of leaving everything as it was before 1846 ; but feeling has nothing to do with the matter.

We are far from denying that a great deal of absurdity has been mixed up with the contests of the rival languages and nationalities in the Cimbric peninsula ; but, after all, who have so good a right to go mad upon the question of nationalities as those very people of Holstein, amongst whom was bred the man who first originated the nationality mania—the illustrious, but not, as we venture to think, politically-sagacious Niebuhr ?

The question having been once stirred between Denmark and Germany—legal right being, as we venture to think, on the side of Germany, the enormous superiority of material force being also on the side of Germany ; the modern passion for nationality—the desire, as has been said, "that those who *resemble* should *assemble*," pointing to a division of Schleswig into two parts—we cannot understand why all statesmen who were biassed neither by Eider-Dane nor Schleswig-Holstein sympathies should not have combined to force upon both parties a solution so conformable to common-sense.

However this may be, the results of the Schleswig-Holstein war have left England and Germany, who ought to be united in the bonds of the closest friendship, somewhat estranged from each other. All this, however, is merely temporary. Increased knowledge of each other's language, and increased personal intercourse, must continue to draw closer and closer two countries whose interests can never clash, and who are peculiarly fitted to act and react upon each other with infinite advantage to the development of each.

CHAPTER VI.

HOLLAND.

TEN hours' sail from the mouth of the Thames lies a long low line of coast—"a bare strand of hillocks, heaped from ever-shifting sand." These—more desolate than the Lido, and beat by a wilder sea than the Adriatic—are the famous Dunes of Holland.

Behind them stretches to the frontier of Germany on the east, to the hills which border the upper and middle valleys of the Meuse, upon the south-east and south, a country which is one of the least inviting and most remarkable on the globe. It comprises the whole of what we now call Holland, and the northern or Flemish part of Belgium.

"The ocean there," says a Roman author, "pours in its vast tides twice every day, and makes it a matter of uncertainty whether the country is to be considered a part of the land or of the sea. The miserable inhabitants establish themselves upon such slightly-raised pieces of ground as they can find, or in huts built upon piles, so as to be out of the reach of the highest tides. When the waters advance, they look like navigators at sea; when these recede they seem as if they were shipwrecked. And yet," he goes on a little later to tell us, "these people, if they fall under the dominion of Rome, complain of their hard fate, and speak of being reduced to servitude."

Could Pliny revisit now the country which he thus described, he would see strange changes. The wretched huts of which he speaks have grown into stately houses, and multiplied into great cities.   An immense network of canals connects the most remote villages with the centres of trade and civilisation ; huge dykes prevent the overflowing of the rivers; others, even more gigantic, keep out the sea.   Nowhere has labour encountered such difficulties, and nowhere has it obtained such triumphs ; lakes have been turned into rich pasture-fields, and wastes of sand have become provinces of gardens.

The children of those miserable fishermen who starved upon their mud-banks, but clung nevertheless to their unhappy independence, have earned themselves a name which history will not willingly let die.   They have fought, not unsuccessfully, with three great empires—they have won and lost wide possessions from which they are separated by half the world—they have sailed far into the Arctic Sea—they have colonised Southern Africa—they have opened a commerce with Japan and the islands of the Indian Ocean.   They have numbered amongst them, scholars and jurists, statesmen and warriors, theologians and philosophers.   They have filled their country with works of art—pictures and painted glass, noble organs and noble churches.

But Holland has quite another side.   Indeed Europe has been laughing at the Dutch for the last three centuries.

One English writer says—

> "They built their watery Babel far more high
> To reach the sea, than those to scale the sky ;
> Yet still his claim the injured ocean laid,
> And oft at leapfrog o'er their steeples played ;
> The fish ofttimes the burgher dispossessed,
> And sat not as a meat, but as a guest."

Another tells us—

"In Holland the laws of nature seem to be reversed ; the

sea is higher than the land ; the lowest ground in the country is 24 feet below highest water-mark, and when the tide is driven high by the wind, 30 feet! In no other country do the keels of the ships float above the chimneys of the houses, and nowhere else does the frog croaking from among the bulrushes look down upon the swallow on the house-top."

These and similar jests, duly reproduced by Murray, remain in our memories, and are not wholly without their influence on our mental attitude when we enter Holland. We go thither expecting to find the quaint and unusual, and we are apt to come away after we have run through the usual list of sights and oddities without discovering that there is anything worthy of our attention in the social or political life of the people. That is perhaps one of the reasons why there are so few links of connection between Dutch and English society. Let any one, after a long experience of London, count up how many Dutchmen unconnected with the diplomatic service he has met here, and the number, we suspect, will not be very great. Our countrymen, again, after a glance at the canals and the pictures, hurry on to Germany and the Rhine, disgusted with the badness of the hotels, the expense of living, and the harshness of the language.

Till lately, there have been no good books about Holland in any of the widely-read languages of Europe. Now, however, there are two, from either of which a great deal is to be learned. The first of these is *La Néerlande et la Vie Holland-aise*, by that same M. Alphonse Esquiros who has done so much to make England better understood in France. It consists of only two small volumes, is most agreeably written, and in every respect to be recommended. The second is a somewhat larger work, entitled *Die Niederlande, Ihre Vergangenheit und Gegenwart*, by Dr. Albert Wild, constructed mainly on the basis of Esquiros and Baedeker, but with some additional information derived from personal knowledge. It is a vulgar and unpleasant, but certainly a useful, guide.

Referring to these works for a vast amount of miscellaneous information about Holland, and to the agreeable volume recently published by M. Émile de Laveleye upon its agriculture, which has become of late years so extremely remarkable, we propose to confine ourselves to some observations upon the politics, the ecclesiastical affairs, and the education of the country.

The earlier history of Holland has, thanks to the labours of Mr. Motley, become familiar in many English and American households, but of its recent history few of us know anything, and we were not surprised to be told some years ago, by a Dutch gentleman at the Hague, that a person of some position in London had asked him the name of the present stadtholder.

The modern life of Holland dates from the French Revolution. In 1795, Pichegru entered Amsterdam with his mob of gallant and ragged followers. William V. sailed for England. The friends of the old order escaped as well as they could over the frontier, and the Batavian Republic was proclaimed. The constitution of 1795 lasted till 1801, but was changed in that year, and again in 1805. In 1806 Louis Bonaparte, the father of the present emperor of the French, was made king, and bore rule for four years, not without many rebukes from his domineering brother for his too great attachment to the special interests of the people over whom he had been made satrap. In 1810 a celebrated and characteristic proclamation announced the incorporation of Holland with the French empire; but in 1813 " the wheel had come full circle," and the son of the fugitive stadtholder, returning amidst the acclamations of his partizans, once more established himself in the possessions of his ancient. house, and having received, by the will of united Europe, the fair provinces which lay between them and the French frontier, assumed in 1815 the title of King of the United Netherlands.

Since that date Dutch history falls into four very well marked divisions.

The first extended to 1830, and was entirely occupied by attempts, sometimes judicious, but oftener the reverse, to weld together into one state the countries which we now know as Holland and Belgium. The motto of the second may be said to have been " Perseverance." It extended to the final negotiations with Belgium, and to the accession, in 1840, of the late king, who was so well known in England as Prince of Orange. This period was characterised chiefly by the obstinate determination of the court to recover the territory which had been lost—a determination which was at first seconded by great zeal on the part of the nation, but which, during its later stages, was not looked upon with the same favour by public opinion. The third period extended from 1840 to 1848, and was chiefly occupied by preparations for the great, peaceful, and eminently salutary change which took place in the last-named year.

The fourth period has been illustrated by carrying out in every department of national life the maxims which influenced that mighty reform.

The reign of the present king falls entirely within the last of our four periods, having commenced on the 17th of March 1849. He has kept faith with his people, and has been rewarded by their loyal attachment—an attachment which was much increased some years ago by his courage and self-sacrifice in one of the great inundations. He married Sophie, the daughter of the late king of Wurtemberg, who, as we have elsewhere said, would probably, if he had been placed in a less brilliant and more really influential position, have left a great name in European history. The same fate seems to attend his descendants; for if anything shall prevent the present queen of Holland being remembered with the most remarkable of those women who shed a lustre over the great days of French society, it will only be the accident of her royal birth.

When the history of this great period comes to be written, one name will be found peculiarly prominent, the name of a personage whose lot it has been to be a great statesman in a small country, in a time which has been singularly prolific of small statesmen in great countries. The fame of M. Thorbecke has reached, we suspect, but few persons amongst us. He was born in the year 1796 at Zwolle—the home of one whose work in the world, though not less noble, was strangely different—the home of Thomas-a-Kempis, once believed to have written, but now more generally thought to have first made widely known to Europe, the *Imitation of Christ.**

* M. Renan, in his *Études d'Histoire Religieuse*, decides in favour of Gersen, abbot of St. Stephen's at Vercelli. The reader will hardly blame us for reminding him of one passage in M. Renan's paper which is worthy to be treasured as a companion picture to Mr. Ruskin's Fra Angelico or to the St. Jerome in the National Gallery:—

"Il ne sortit jamais de sa cellule de Verceil. Il ne lut d'Aristote que la première ligne, *omnis homo naturaliter scire desiderat*, et il ferma le livre tout scandalisé: 'A quoi sert, dit-il, de savoir des choses sur lesquelles nous ne serons point examinés au jour du jugement?' (liv. i. ch. ii. iii.) C'est par là qu'il est incomplet, mais c'est par là aussi qu'il nous charme. Que je voudrais être peintre pour le montrer tel que je le conçois, doux et recueilli, assis en son fauteuil de chêne, dans le beau costume des bénédictins du Mont-Cassin! Par le treillis de sa fenêtre, on verrait le monde revêtu d'une teinte d'azur, comme dans les miniatures du XIVᵉ siècle: au premier plan, une campagne parsemée d'arbres légers, à la manière du Perugin; à l'horizon, les sommets des Alpes couverts de neige. . . . Ainsi je me le figurais à Verceil même, en feuilletant les manuscrits maintenant déposés au Dôme, et dont plusieurs peut-être ont passés par ses mains."

M. Thorbecke graduated at Leyden in 1820, then passed two years in Germany, applying himself chiefly to the study of philosophy. When he returned to his own country he found that he was thought not "practical" enough for Holland, and so, for a time, he went back to the land of students, and lectured as "privat-docent" at Giessen and Göttingen. Eventually he was named professor of history, statistics, and political economy at Ghent; became, in fact, one of those too-liberal Dutchmen whose intrusion into the hallowed seats of superstition was so hateful to the Belgian episcopate, and had so much to do with the revolution. Driven over the frontier by that event, he obtained a chair at Leyden, where he gave lectures, first on Roman and commercial law, and later on the history and constitution of his country. He entered the Chamber in 1844 as deputy for the provincial estates of South Holland. The effect of his vigorous mind and strong political convictions was soon visible; and on the 10th of December 1844 he took a leading part in submitting, in common with some other members, a detailed project for the reform of the constitution. The movement, then begun, resulted in the constitution of the 3d of November 1848, by which the Upper House became substantially what the Lower House had been before—a representation of the wealthiest and most highly-taxed portion of the community, while the Lower became a true popular assembly.

M. Thorbecke has twice for a considerable period been at the head of affairs, and even when not in the cabinet, as at present, he exercises great influence.

If he at all resembles any English statesman, it is the late Sir George Lewis. Perhaps if Mr. Mill had entered the House of Commons twenty years ago, he might have been the English

Thorbecke. Perhaps, on the other hand, the forces of evil are still so strong in this country, that no Englishman of our generation, even if he had had all the gifts and more than the opportunities of the illustrious member for Westminster, could have been to England what Thorbecke has been to his native land.

Since 1848 not a year has passed without bringing to Holland some new good law or wise alteration of an old one. The provincial and communal legislation was presently remodelled according to the spirit of the constitution, and the antiquated state of things in which Old Dutch, French imperial, and post-revolutionary Dutch arrangements struggled for the mastery, was superseded by a system instinct with the modern spirit. Trade soon felt the benefit of the new impulse. The navigation laws fell in 1850, and improvements were rapidly made in taxation and the tariff; railways were pushed forward, a geological survey of the whole country was made, and the judicial system was reorganised.

In 1853 a storm suddenly gathered in a clear sky. The Vatican, following up the same policy which led to our Ecclesiastical Titles Bill, converted Holland, which had been hitherto a mission, into a country regularly provided with an episcopate. This it had, no doubt, a perfect right to do, for in modern Holland the state has nothing to say to the internal arrangements of the various churches which it recognises and pays.

It was not surprising, however, that a people whose history was so deeply coloured by hatred of Rome should have taken alarm at such an exercise of power, and there was nothing about the manner of the proceeding to make the matter of it more palatable. The ministry itself, while it could not take exception to what had been done, was justly provoked by the way in which it was done. M. Thorbecke, however, did not think himself justified in throwing himself into the first ranks of the agitation against this papal aggression. The tide, nevertheless, of popular feeling was too strong for him, and, deserted by the king, he and several of his colleagues left the cabinet. The issue of this agitation—the April movement, as it was called—was a bill regulating the relations of the state and the religious communities, which obtained the support of the more moderate Liberals, and the storm passed by without doing any serious damage to the free institutions of Holland.

The terrible inundations of 1855, and the anxieties which a small neutral state not unnaturally felt during the Russian war, checked for a little the political advance, but did not prevent the Dutch manufacturers showing at the Paris exhibition that they had made most remarkable progress in the four years that had elapsed since they contended in London.

The next great question that came on for solution was that of primary education, which was settled, we trust finally, in 1857. How it was settled we shall have occasion presently to state.

This done, the next subject which was taken in hand by the reformers was that of West Indian slavery, which was soon satisfactorily disposed of by a measure of emancipation. Then the completion of the network of railways became for a time the matter which was uppermost in the public mind; and now, again, it is the reform of the system under which the Dutch possessions in the Eastern Archipelago are managed, which is the all-absorbing topic of the day.

We have said enough to show that, since the great change of 1848, Holland has been adopting one after another all those steps which have made the glory of our own legislation during the last five-and-thirty years. In some of these reforms she

has followed in our wake; but there are two departments of
national life in which, thanks not least to Thorbecke, she is
far in advance of ourselves, as of every other European nation.
These are—1. Her ecclesiastical system; and 2. Her elementary education. Into both these subjects we must enter at
some length.

The waters of Dutch theology, which had been violently
agitated by the storms of the sixteenth century, congealed in
the first quarter of the seventeenth into an orthodoxy as icy
as that which about the same time overspread North Germany. There was this difference, however: the orthodoxy of
Holland was Calvinist, while that of her eastern neighbour
was Lutheran. The indigenous form of Protestantism, best
represented in the Netherlands by Wessel Gansfoort of Groningen, but which has also left its traces in the life and writings of the great and of late too-much-decried Erasmus, failed
to hold its own against the sterner system which, taking its
rise in the northern provinces of France, and counting as its
chief apostle the fierce and resolute Calvin, was brought into
Holland by the Walloon immigrants, and was eagerly embraced
by men who were engaged in a death-struggle with the old
religion. It was then not unnatural that the narrow theology
of Gomarus should be preferred by the uneducated masses to
the doctrines of the more liberal Arminius. In 1610 the followers of the latter presented their celebrated remonstrance to
the States of Holland. In November 1618 the Synod of Dort
assembled after years of debate and trouble; and on the 29th
May 1619 it rose, having condemned *in toto* the Arminian
opinions. The unscrupulous Maurice of Nassau, who cared
as little for counter-remonstrants as for their opponents, saw
clearly that the fanaticism of the masses was his best means

of combating the aristocratic party, which leant to the Arminian teaching; and the judicial murder of Olden-Barneveld,
as well as the persecution of Grotius, had his full and entire
sanction. Science fled the field, and fanaticism was victorious
along the whole line.

About the middle of the century the influence of the
Cartesian philosophy began to show itself in the writings of
theologians ; and Balthasar Bekker, who died at the age of
sixty-four in 1698, maintained in his *Enchanted World*
opinions in some points analogous to those afterwards
defended by the famous Semler. It was Cocceius, however,
a professor at Leyden, who had the honour to give his name
to the Liberal party of his day ; while Voet of Utrecht, his
opponent, became the idol of all those who thought that
religion was most honoured by a morose exterior and an
intolerant spirit. Friends to Greek and Oriental studies,
though misled by false principles of exegesis, the Cocceians
were, as may readily be guessed, attached to the aristocratic
or republican party ; while their enemies, who thought that
all truth was summed up in the canons of Dort, and hated
biblical criticism as the mother of novelties, relied on the
stadtholder and the mob. In 1677 their disputes had
become so fierce that the magistrates of Amsterdam were
obliged to interfere and to force them to agree to a compromise, by which each party was to have a right to an
equal number of representatives in the city pulpits. This
happy device was imitated elsewhere ; and when a third
school—that of the Lampians, which may be defined as a
reform of the Cocceians—came to add itself to the older
factions, it took its place quite naturally by their side, and
enjoyed its share of church accommodation. Lampe, who

gave his name to this section, was a professor at Utrecht, and died in 1729. Contemporary with him were Vitringa, whose harmonious Frisian name is, we should imagine, more familiar to the present generation than even his work on Isaiah, but who was really a man of eminence ; and Witsius, who took for his motto, " In necessariis unitas, in minus necessariis libertas ; in omnibus sapientia et charitas." Through the efforts of such writers as these, the old asperities of Cocceian and Voetian theology were worn down, and practical religion was naturally a gainer. The person who has the credit of having finally laid their differences to sleep was a clergyman of eighty years of age, who bore the, to our ears, appropriately soporific name of Mommers. The work by which he effected this excellent object appeared in 1736.

When the violence of debate had calmed, theologians began to devote themselves to studies really more congenial to their profession, although perhaps less exciting than those which had been too long in vogue; and the names of Venema and of Albert Schultens became famous throughout Protestant Christendom. It was not till about 1790 that the Latin language began to yield to the vernacular as a medium for theological exposition—a change which, while it contributed to the fame of Dutch writers in their own country, sadly diminished it abroad. The Voltairian ideas never had any great influence in the Netherlands, although even to this day individuals may be found amongst those advanced in years, whose religious notions are of the Ferney type. The writings of the early rationalisers of Germany, and of the Rationalists, properly so called, had a wider influence ; but the tendency which found most favour in the beginning of this century was perhaps that which bears the clumsy but expressive name of rational-supernaturalism, and which, in its Dutch variety, is best represented by the writings of Van der Palm (1762-1838), whose translation of the Bible, with notes and introductions to the several books, has long enjoyed an immense reputation in the Netherlands, and has formed the basis of the religious life of a large portion of the community.

The same wave of reaction which brought about the conversions of F. Schlegel and the Stolbergs, and which showed itself in our own country, first in the religious excesses of Methodism, then in the Clapham school, and at length in the more graceful pietism of the Oxford movement, early extended itself to Holland, and had as its leading champion the poet Bilderdyk.

This remarkable man was born in 1756, and was educated for the bar, which, however, he soon abandoned, in order to devote himself to science and literature. He followed the last stadtholder into exile, and passed some time in England as well as in Germany, but returned to his own country during the reign of Louis Bonaparte, and was received with much favour. When, however, Napoleon thought proper to put an end to his brother's rule, Bilderdyk lost his pension, and was once more obliged to live by literature. The restoration of the House of Orange was hailed by him with all the eagerness of one who had a personal as well as a political quarrel with France, and he it was who invented, or at least revived, the Orangiolatry which forms so remarkable a feature in the modern ultra-conservatism of Holland. His religious views were in conformity with his political prepossessions, and he used all the resources of his vast knowledge and of his great poetical genius in trying to turn back the current of the times. Bilderdyk died in 1831, but his work was continued by two remark-

able men—M. da Costa, and M. Groen van Prinsterer. M.
da Costa, who died very recently, was the son of a wealthy
Portuguese Jew, and was converted to Christianity under the
influence of Bilderdyk. The form of our religion which he
adopted, or rather constructed for himself, was a very strange
one. The present dispensation was only, in his eyes, the
church of the Gentiles, and would ultimately give way to a
new order of things, in which the chosen people should be restored to more than their old pre-eminence. Some of M. da
Costa's historical and theological writings have been translated
into English, and have no doubt done their part in spreading
the wild ideas about the past and future of Israel which prevail among certain religious cliques in this country. M. da
Costa owed his influence in Holland partly to his poetical
power and partly to his undoubted eloquence, the remem-
brance of which is cherished by many who detest his ideas,
and think but little of his *written* prose.

M. Groen van Prinsterer is a man who, if providence had
assigned to him a wider stage, would perhaps have been no
less famous than De Maistre. As it is, we dare venture to
guess, that of those who will read these lines, not one in ten
has ever heard of him. Neither in the English work called
Men of the Time, nor in the German *Männer der Zeit,* nor in
the huge French *Dictionnaire des Contemporains,** do we find
him alluded to. In his own country, however, his name is as
much a household word as that of Lord Derby is in England.
His enemies usually speak of him as the Stahl of Holland,
and to a certain extent they are justified in doing so. That
remarkable person was, however, too much of an adventurer.
The Bavarian Jew was too oddly out of place as the leader of

* His name does not appear even in the new edition of this useful book.

the squires of the Mark, the teacher and spokesman of the ultra-Lutheran fanatics who clustered round the late king of Prussia, to form a good *pendant* to the Dutch statesman. Shall we be intelligible to our readers if we call him a Stahl-de-Bonald—half-professor and half-cavalier? If we are not, we must refer them to a pamphlet by M. Groen himself which gives a very full and clear account of the views of the party which he leads and inspires.

Le Parti Anti-Revolutionnaire et Confessionel dans l'Eglise Reformée des Pays-bas is an elaborate reply to some strictures passed upon the conduct of the religious and political connection to which M. Groen belongs, by a writer whose point of view was that of M. Vinet. It is divided into three chapters, of which the first explains the character, objects, and tendencies of the confessional party, and points out that it is not strictly correct to say that it represents exactly the theologians of Dort; nay, rather that the influence of modern foreign writers, and of the Methodist movement, which is spoken of in France, Switzerland, and elsewhere, as the Réveil, have had much to do in shaping its course. In the second chapter he explains at great length what he means by "*Le principe anti-révolutionnaire.*" The revolution, he says—

" C'est dans sa source et ses resultats, la doctrine qui, librement développée, détruit l'Eglise et l'Etat, la société et la famille, produit le désordre sans jamais fonder la liberté ou retablir l'ordre moral, et, en matière de religion, conduit immanquablement ses consciencieux adeptes à l'atheisme et au désespoir. Le principe anti-révolutionnaire, c'est le contraire de la revolution ; c'est l'Evangile et l'Histoire qui résistent à l'anarchie, au nom de la religion, du droit, du progrès, et de la liberté."

M. Groen's opinions were formed as far back as 1831, in which year he published a sketch of the course of events since 1789. There is nothing very original in his political views. Haller is apparently one of his favourite teachers; but he has affinities with Montalembert, with Guizot, with Burke, and with Mallet du Pan—in so far, at least, as these writers are the enemies of the Revolution. In one respect his ideas are diametrically opposed to those of the first-named politician, for M. Groen thinks that Catholicism is unable to cope with the tendencies of 1789, and that the churches of the Reformation have alone that power:—

"On parle souvent des analogies de la Révolution et la Réforme; tâchons de les résumer. La Révolution part de la souveraineté de l'homme; la Réforme de la souveraineté de Dieu. L'une fait juger la révélation par la raison; l'autre soumet la raison aux vérités révélées. L'une débride les opinions individuelles; l'autre amène l'unité de la foi. L'une relâche les liens sociaux et jusqu'aux rélations domestiques; l'autre les reserre et les sanctifie. Celle-ci triomphe par les martyres, celle-la se maintient par les massacres. L'une sort de l'abîme et l'autre descend du ciel."

M. Groen is no absolutist:—"Personne n'a mieux que moi désiré les réalités du gouvernement représentatif, developpements naturels de la glorieuse histoire de mon pays;" but he feels towards the Dutch constitution of 1848 as Stahl felt towards the Prussian constitution of 1850, and would gladly change it by all legal means. In the third and concluding chapter of his pamphlet he details the very spirited struggle of himself and his handful of friends against the Liberals and the Liberal Conservatives—efforts which received a heavy blow and great discouragement when, in 1857, the excellent

Dutch school law of 1806 was still further amended, and all sectarian influences were banished from the schools supported by the state.

M. Groen is not only a very able political leader, and a most eloquent speaker, but a very voluminous and much admired historian. Many think that it would have been well for his fame if when, in 1833, he stepped back for a time from the political scene, he had remained for the rest of his life occupied in the tranquil investigation of past ages. Any one who glances at the notes to Mr. Motley's works, will see under what heavy contributions he has been laid by that popular writer. M. Groen, however, was thinking of the politics of the nineteenth century while he was writing the annals of two hundred years ago, and was trying to undermine the liberalism of the Netherlands, by exalting the party of the House of Orange and decrying the party of the States. The religious and political opinions of this excellent man are not shared in their entirety by any very considerable number of his countrymen. His following is chiefly drawn from two very different strata of society—from a portion of the higher class, and from amongst the uneducated masses. It seems hardly probable that his ideas are destined to be largely represented in the ensuing generation.

The theology of one who, like M. Groen, believes that Christianity and the anti-revolutionary principle are identical, is of course of the narrowest description. All the wealth which modern biblical criticism and the enlightened study of ecclesiastical antiquity have brought to the religious inquirer, is to him of no avail. He is a Protestant Christian, not of the nineteenth, but of the sixteenth century, although we have heard it whispered that even he would be judged unsound on the question of predestination, if he stood before the bar of Professor Gomarus.

Amidst the motley company which poetry, politics, and the influence of the Réveil have collected under the banners of the past, M. Groen is the most distinguished; and some very eminent politicians share his religious views. The party is not, however, strong in theologians.

M. Oosterzee, who was some years ago transferred from a parochial charge at Rotterdam to a professor's chair at Utrecht, is famous for his eloquence, which gives pleasure even to those who most dissent from the principles which he seeks to enforce; but he is not remarkable for learning. Professor Doedes, a very erudite biblical critic and expositor, belongs to the extreme left of the party; and so does M. Beets, the poet and novelist. Separated from the orthodox fraction by a very distinct line of demarcation, but sympathising with it to a considerable extent, are the friends of the late M. Trottet, and of M. Chantepie de la Saussaye. Both these writers have given, in French, an account of their relations to the school of M. Groen van Prinsterer, and of the condition of Protestantism in the Netherlands. M. Chantepie de la Saussaye was till recently a pastor attached to the Walloon churches, of which we shall speak hereafter; but he is now connected with the Dutch Church proper, and is settled at Rotterdam, where his great talents as a preacher make him extremely popular. No one who has sufficient interest in the subject of which we write to care to pursue it beyond the limits of this paper should fail to read his pamphlet—*La Crise Religieuse en Hollande* (Leyden, 1860). He looks at the situation from the point of view of a disciple of Vinet, which is not ours; but he expresses himself with great moderation, and puts his ideas before the reader in a very attractive way. He has not escaped, at the hands of his opponents, the criticism to which the great professor of Lausanne, no less than his followers, is by many considered to have laid himself open—that, viz., of want of clearness.

Of the once very important and still much-followed school to which we must next call attention, M. Chantepie de la Saussaye observes : " L'école de Groningue a fait son temps. Elle ne fait plus d'adeptes. On peut en dire de bien, sans craindre de se voir enrôlé sous sa bannière." Some people would hardly agree with him, if we may judge by a work which now lies before us—*Die Gröninger Theologen, dargestellt, von Dr. P. Hofstede de Groot (aus dem Holländischen übersetzt)*, Gotha, 1863.

This brochure, which forms a goodly volume of two hundred pages, gives at great length, and with a minuteness and rigour of arrangement which might be called pedantic if it were not so perfectly in place, the fullest possible account of the mental history, the labours, and the aspirations of its author and his associates. Most earnestly, and with obvious sincerity, does he disclaim the wish to be the leader of a party or to form a school.

Van Heusde, of Utrecht, celebrated as one of the most enthusiastic modern followers of Plato, was the person who, acting first on his pupils at Utrecht, and then indirectly upon a contemporary circle of thoughtful students at Groningen, gave the impulse to the new way of thinking. He did this not only by his Platonic lectures, but also by his constant reference to the old history of the Netherlands, to the stirring of religious thought in Wessel Gansfoort, and in the " Brethren of the Common Life." To this was added the influence of

Schleiermacher and other German writers. C. L. Nitszch, the
father of the well-known ecclesiastic at Berlin, would appear
to have arrived, by an independent route, at much the same conclusion as the Groningen theologians ; and more recently the
"mediation" divines of Germany, more especially Ullman,
have exercised great influence over them.   Of their own
number—in addition to Hofstede de Groot—Pareau, Muurling,
and Van Oordt, are perhaps the most famous.   Their leading
and all-pervading idea is that the most important feature of
Christianity is the "revelation and education" which, in the
words of their apologist and leader, "God has given to us in
Jesus Christ, to make us more and more like unto God."
This notion of the education of the human race by God recurs in
almost every page of Professor Hofstede de Groot's work, and is,
of course, not original—nay, is as old as Lessing ; but we are not
aware that it has ever before formed the keystone of a whole
system of theology.   The Groningen doctors deny the equality
of the Father and the Son, or, in the words of our author,
"Wir halten den Sohn für den Sohn, nicht aber für den
Bruder Gottes."   Again, with regard to the Third Person of
the Trinity : "Der Heilige Geist ist uns, der Geist, das
Leben, die Wirksamkeit und Kraft Gottes, die von Gott durch
Christum der Menschheit mitgetheilt wurde;" and in opposition to the comparatively modern doctrine which has been
widely accepted in Christendom, they attach as much importance to the life and teaching as to the death of Christ.   They
have ever taken a peculiarly active share in the charitable
works so characteristic of the Netherlands.   Their learning,
although obscured by various prepossessions, is respectable for
Holland, and would be eminent in England.   Above all, their
whole way of looking at things is remarkable for its extreme

amiability and gentleness. The last few pages of Dr. Hofstede de Groot's pamphlet upon the future of the work in store for himself and his followers, are beyond all praise—full of wide sympathy, apostolic fervour, and forgetfulness of self in the advancement of those objects in which all religious men are agreed. An account of the views of the Groningen doctors, in a very agreeable form, will be found in the *Pastor of Vliethuizen* (Trübner, London), a novel which has been translated into English by M. Marquard, the editor of a Dutch liberal newspaper at the Cape of Good Hope, which does very good work in that colony.

We may, it will be seen, characterise the Groningen school, very roughly and generally, as Unitarians, without any of that hardness which has been often attributed to the followers of that sect in this country ; and as mystics, without any of that contempt for learning which has often characterised the mystical writers, as well of Protestant as of Catholic Christendom. The doctrines of Groningen, although well calculated to form a bridge between the easy-going biblicalism of Van der Palm, and the system which will satisfy an age which does not shrink from raising questions, were evidently not fitted for a long existence. The reader will not, therefore, be surprised to find that, like the widely different views which began to be current in England about the same date, they have ceased to influence the majority of younger men. We have heard it said that even in Groningen many of the students are more acted upon by other teachers than by those of their own university. The school which is now in the ascendant is more philosophic in its method, more deeply learned, and more ready to break with the forms of the past, while retaining what was good in its spirit. The teachers of the school of

Leyden have had the advantage of the years of theological debate which have taken place in Germany, since the daring private tutor of Tübingen threw his sword into the scale. They have studied not only the destructive process of Strauss, and of those who thought to equal his fame by surpassing his audacity, but have entered into the labours of Baur and his numerous pupils. Last, but not least, between the rise of the school of Groningen and of its successor was interposed that great political change which has given to Holland a leading position amongst free and constitutional states.

The head of the school of Leyden is Professor Scholten, a man who may be now about sixty years of age. He has laboured chiefly in the field of dogma, and has attempted to form a system which shall be as strict and logical as the old system of Dort, without in any way shocking the reason or the feelings of enlightened men.*

Professor Kuenen, whose domain is exegesis, is an author whose writings are perhaps more adapted to the wants of the English mind at the present conjuncture. †

Professor Rawenhoff, who is still a very young man, and teaches ecclesiastical history, is also likely to sustain the credit of the school of Leyden, and the other acting professor, Dr. Prins, holds similar views. The aged Van Hengel, now "Emeritus," was famous in his day for his labours on the text and grammar of the New Testament ; and still, on the extreme verge of life, is full of encouragement to those of the younger generation who are serving the cause of sound learning and true religion with other arms. The whole faculty of theology, in

* Professor Scholten's *History of Religion and Philosophy* has been translated into French, and published by Treuttel and Wurtz of Strasburg.

† The whole of Professor Kuenen's great work on the Old Testament has now (1866) been translated into French, and a part of it has appeared in English.

short, in the noble and ancient university, which is perhaps
the grandest memorial of the rise of the Republic and the
overthrow of the Roman Church in the Netherlands, is
thoroughly pervaded with the liberal spirit, and sends the
" fresh blood from it year by year," into the remotest districts
of the country, even into those sleepy and old-world corners
which are described in the novel lately translated, called *The
Manse of Mastland.*

The theologians of Leyden hardly form the extreme left
of the Dutch Church. Beyond them is ranged a group of men
who are ordinarily spoken of as the followers of the " modern
theology ;" but the distinction is not very clear, and perhaps
something too much has been made of it. It is against the
dogmatic theology of Professor Scholten that the movement
may be considered as directed, but the amount of agreement is,
after all, very much greater than the amount of divergence.

This "modern theology" counts its most distinguished
champions in the ranks of the Walloon churches. These
communities, which are to be found in all the principal
cities of Holland, form one of the most interesting portions of
the Dutch Church. They date from the end of the sixteenth
century—from the days of William the Silent, and of his
friend Marnix de St. Aldegonde, who carried that restless
energy which is immortalised in his famous motto, " Repos
ailleurs," as well into the theological and literary, as into the
military and political arena.

In 1685 they were largely reinforced from France by
the refugees who left that country when the edict of Nantes
was revoked. To this day they have their own synod and
manage their internal affairs, although they have the same
confession of faith as the much larger division of the church

which carries on public worship in Dutch, and they take part in
the general synod.   The service in the Walloon churches has
many points of resemblance with that which is usual amongst
French Protestants.   They have always been remarkable for
the excellence of their preachers ; and the names of Jurieu,
Saurin, and Basnage will not be strange to any eye.

These Walloon churches form the principal link between
the Protestants of France and those of the Netherlands.   In
the year 1855 the commission which regulates their affairs
put forth a report upon the state of their own body and of
Dutch Protestantism generally, which is a perfect model of
good sense, moderation, and christian charity, and which we
most strongly recommend.   Its full title is, *Exposé historique
de l'etat de l'eglise réformée des Pays Bas, pour être presenté
de la part de la Réunion Wallonne aux Eglises réformées
étrangères, spécialement aux Eglises de la France et de la Suisse
Française.*   This admirable paper is perhaps rather too long
for the general reader, and might possibly escape the attention of those whose interest in the subject had not been
already excited.   It was then a fortunate circumstance for
the Protestants of the Netherlands that, thanks to the
organisation of the Walloon churches, they chanced to number in their ranks a Frenchman whose general literary ability
was such as to entitle him to become connected with the
Revue des Deux Mondes, and through it to speak in their name
to all educated Europe.   The appearance of M. Albert
Réville's article in 1860, upon *La Théologie Contemporaine en
Hollande,* revealed to many the existence of a powerful liberal
movement in the Dutch Church, and gratified to a certain
extent the curiosity which had been excited in others by the
brief notices of Dutch ecclesiastical affairs in those charm-

ing volumes of M. Esquiros which we have already mentioned.

M. Réville was born at Dieppe, and was brought up by his father, who shared the moderate opinions which were so common among French Protestants before the *Réveil*. His progress, however, to a clearer and higher view of theology was brought about chiefly by German influences. Although he is for the present established in Holland, he keeps his eye stedfastly fixed upon France, and labours, by his numerous writings, to awaken in that country an interest in biblical studies and in religious thought. His chief organs of communication with the public are the *Revue de Strasbourg*, which is edited by Colani, and ought to be better known in this country, and, as we have already seen, the *Revue des Deux Mondes*. A number of his contributions to various periodicals have been collected into a volume, and are published under the title of *Essais de Critique Religieuse* (Paris, Cherbuliez, 1860). The excellent paper on Nero as Antichrist will give to those who have not time to read the whole book a sufficient idea of M. Réville's manner,* and of the direction in which his influence is exerted.

A little to the left and on the extreme limits of *theological* as distinguished from philosophic liberalism, is M. Busken Huet, of Haarlem, a member of the Protestant branch of the family which gave to the see of Avranches its most famous and learned occupant. M. Busken Huet has written *Letters on the Bible*, and is considered to be a master of Dutch prose. His style does not appear to be conciliatory ; and M. de la Saussaye describes him as " le véritable bouc Azazel de la

---

* In 1863 M. Réville published a very interesting *Manuel d'Instruction Religieuse :* Cherbuliez, Paris.

théologie positive." He himself, however, while entirely disagreeing with the views of M. Huet, speaks of his abilities and of his character with great respect.

To such of our readers as are acquainted with modern German theology, we may perhaps best convey a clear idea of the tendencies of the school to which M. Réville and M. Huet belong by mentioning that their views are very analogous to those which are maintained in the *Geschichte der Neuesten Theologie*, by Dr. Karl Schwartz of Gotha, court preacher to the elder brother of the late Prince Consort, and the hardly less interesting work of Lang, *Ein Gang durch die Christliche Welt*.

In classing M. Réville and M. Busken Huet together, and separating them from the school of Leyden, we rather mean to point out that they form part of a sort of group, connected by their relation to the Walloon churches, than to draw any strong line between them and the followers of Scholten. All of them would speak of that great divine with profound respect, and would acknowledge the greatest obligations to him. All of them would acknowledge having felt the influence of another teacher, who starts from a point very different from that whence M. Scholten starts, and has at various times come into collision with the great doctor of Leyden.

This remarkable man is not a professional theologian, but a philosopher, and he speaks from Utrecht,* where the pinched but not unpleasant features of old Voetius must meet his eye whenever he enters the council-room of the professors. M. Opzoomer has been formed by Comte or J. S.

* Utrecht is now much tamed. Her theology is, says Réville, of the *Whateleian* cast.

Mill; shall we not add, to some extent by Renan? His system is defined by Réville as "spiritual empiricism." He rejects the à priori reasoning of the Hegelian school; and, commencing with facts, observes, classifies, criticises them; thus drawing the materials of his system from every science. The great influence which he exerts is owing, not to any body of doctrines which he teaches, but to his method. He thinks that the empirico-critical investigation of Christianity is the chief business of the theologian, and considers that the system pursued by the great masters of physical science is that which the student of divine things ought also to follow.

In addition to the three forms of liberal opinion which we have been characterising, it must be remembered that the school which we have connected with the name of Van der Palm has still very numerous adherents amongst the older clergy, but they are divided into various groups, according as they have been most influenced by Groningen or Leyden, or by the modern theology. Nay, some of them would appear to be, in their dislike to recent innovations, more inclined to fraternise with the "confessional" section than with any of the newer forms of liberalism. If we take all shades of this party together, we shall perhaps be not very wrong in saying that they stand to the more active and stirring fractions of the church, as our own High and Dry do to our Tractarians, Broad Churchmen, or Evangelicals.

Vinke of Utrecht, who died a few years ago, was perhaps the most eminent representative of the views of the respectable but rather arriérés theologians of whom we are speaking; and as his chair has, as we have seen, been filled by a professor who has grown up under other influences, it is

improbable that they will be further represented in the Dutch
universities.

Some readers will doubtless be surprised that we have
not, in speaking of Dutch theology, found it necessary ere
this to introduce the great name of Spinoza. The truth is,
however, that he produced no appreciable effect upon the
course of religious thought within the Dutch Church. He
came far too early. Men were in his day occupied, as we
have seen, in disputing about the inferences to be drawn
from certain premises which they never dreamt of disputing.
They were far from being prepared to listen to the still small
voice which asked if these premises were indeed themselves
indisputable. The Dutch intellect, to say the truth, is not
very much inclined to philosophy proper. In this respect,
perhaps, it stands about half-way between the Scotch and the
English, but nearer, we should say, to the latter.

A word or two as to the various sects of Holland which
are not connected with the Reformed Church. Of these the
Roman Catholics are far the most numerous, amounting to
about thirty-eight per cent of the population, and forming a
political power which has exercised a great influence on the
recent history of the country. The small Roman Catholic
community called "the Old Church," and sometimes improperly,
the "Jansenist Church" of Holland, ought to be better known
than we suspect it is in England. Mr. Neale has written an
account of it, and a still more accurate one has been lately
published in Latin by M. Gerth van Wyk.

The Protestants number amongst them Lutherans, who are
largely recruited from Germany ; Mennonites, the peaceable
and well-to-do descendants of the once fierce Anabaptists;
about 5000 Remonstrants, now less liberal than the Calvinist

Church, from which they seceded ; a few Moravians, and a rather large body of Dissenters, who broke off from the Reformed Church some thirty years ago, and belong to a deeper shade of Calvinism than even the most extreme section which remains within its pale, but are, as may be supposed, without social or intellectual importance. The largest of these sects is the Lutheran. In most of them there is some movement of mind—chiefly, perhaps, amongst the Lutherans and Mennonites. The Jews number about 65,000, but there is not amongst them any theological school which calls for remark.

About fifty-four per cent of the population belong to the Reformed Church, which consists, according to the most recent statistics we have seen, of considerably more than 1,800,000 adherents, and, speaking roughly, about 1500 clergymen. Of these perhaps three-fourths belong to one or other of the four liberal sections which we have mentioned, and of the remaining *fourth*, which will fall to the " orthodox," not a few would pass for Broad Churchmen in England.

Up to the revolution of 1795, the Reformed Church was established and dominant. Since that date it has ceased to have an exclusive pre-eminence, although its clergy, like those of all the other denominations, which do not object to state aid, are paid by the government. Its organisation is on the old Presbyterian model which prevailed in France before the revocation of the edict of Nantes, but it has been much modified during the present century, especially in 1816 and 1851. The clergy are supposed to be elected by their flocks, but as a matter of fact the election is really in the hands of the consistories—bodies closely resembling the Scotch kirk-sessions. This variation between the theory of the ecclesiastical constitution and the actual practice causes a certain amount of discussion. The salary of a clergyman in the country is very small, say about £70 a-year. In the large towns it ranges from £150 to £200, but these small figures are augmented by various funds, though they never rise beyond a very modest amount. The more credit does a church deserve whose pastors surpass so generally in theological learning their wealthier brethren in this country.

When thirty years have passed away, we may trust that some forms of opinion which we have described may have nearly ceased to exist, and a more general community of object may be attained. Peace is, we fear, not the lot of this generation. In the admirable words of the writer of a paper on Dutch ecclesiastical affairs, which is worthy to be put by the side of M. Réville's, and is to be found in Geltzer's *Protestantische Monatsblätter* for June 1861 :—"With regard to all differences, in all times and in all places, one truth holds good, that to every form of opinion, even the most highly praised and celebrated, is that saying of Hase's applicable— ' It is but an attempt to grasp the Infinite, which is revealed to us as a secret.'" Every theologian now alive who loves truth will at the end of his career have to apply to himself the words of De Wette—

> Ich fiel in cine wirre Zeit,
> Die Glaubens-Eintracht war vernichtet ;
> Ich mischte mich mit in den streit,
> Umsonst, ich hab'ihn nicht geschlichtet.

But even strife and trouble are better than a sleepy acquiescence in falsehood, and we are not without hope that some of those who are fighting the battle of religious freedom in this country may be cheered by the report which we have brought back from the other side of the North Sea. When shall we be able to say that three-fourths of the English clergy belong to some shade of liberal opinion ? *

*   *   *   *

People in this country are, it would seem, just beginning to find out that a battle is being fought in Holland which well deserves to attract the attention of the whole Protestant world, and we see from time to time in various periodicals accounts of Dutch books or notices of Dutch ecclesiastical affairs. In an article of the *Contemporary Review* we find the following wise and noble reply made by the General Synod to some zealots who asked it to interfere after the good old persecuting fashion :—

" It is clear that the true source of the—in many respects —distressing and confused condition of our church lies in a scientific strife. The amazing progress of the natural sciences, and the rich discoveries of history, have given rise to a contemplation of the universe which is at variance with the hitherto accepted theology. If that contemplation of the world is wholly in the right, the theology which has been prevalent hitherto will fall altogether. If it is altogether in the wrong, theology will overthrow it. If truth and right side only in part with it, it will conquer as far as that part is concerned, and theology will by the strife change much, but also become purified and sanctified, and after some time blossom more brightly than before. But whatever may be the result, that result will only be possible through the free development of science. If science has inflicted wounds

* Since these notes, gathered for the most part during a visit to Holland in the winter of 1862, were published by the author in *Fraser's Magazine* for March 1863, an extremely interesting paper upon the same subject, from the pen of M. Réville, appeared in the *Theological Review* of July 1864. To it we would refer, more especially for a clear outline of the system of M. Scholten.

upon the church, those wounds, if curable, can only be cured by science itself. Dogmatisms, condemnations, and suspicions are of no use here. On the contrary, they make the matter worse.

" In former centuries it was believed—though, as has been shown by experience, unjustly—that the Reformed Church had the power of preserving a certain strictly-defined and fenced-in doctrine through *church authority*. This belief cannot be maintained any longer. The liberty of science, the public discussion about all the questions concerning philosophy and theology, render that authority powerless in the present.

" If, consequently, anything is to be done for the preservation of the Reformed Church and its doctrine, that order may rise out of the confusion, it can, in our opinion, only be done through the above-mentioned means, and particularly through the last-mentioned—science. We do not say, through scholarship, but through science, through one's own independent, thorough, unprejudiced, and coherent insight, based upon inquiry and meditation, which insight is obtainable also by those who continue strangers to scholarship, though they may not be able to do without the guidance of the scholars."

Surely it is no small thing for the friends of well-ordered democracy to be able to point to these glorious words and to say—" This was the answer of the governing body of a small little-considered Presbyterian Church, delivered at a time when the bishops of the mighty Anglican establishment, ' rich,' when compared with their brethren in Holland, ' beyond the dreams of avarice,' surrounded by all worldly pomp, and possessed of all *prestige* except that which is given by transcendent personal merit, could do nothing better than ape, amidst the sneers of the laity, the worn-out methods of the Vatican."

The state of education in the Netherlands has, at various times and for various reasons, excited considerable interest in Great Britain. It was no very uncommon thing, during the last century, for English or Scotch families to send one of their number to study at Utrecht or at Leyden. The revolutionary war put an end to this practice, but when the cessation of that struggle at length left us time to improve our constitution, and to spy out the dark places of our social state, we soon listened to those who told us that the Dutch had been making great changes in primary education, and began to think that we might possibly do well to imitate them. The French of the Empire were the first to make known to Europe the success of their then fellow-citizens. In 1811 the great naturalist Cuvier was sent, surely not without a certain *malice*, to investigate the educational methods of the *Amphibia*, and he brought back a report in which he gave them the highest possible praise. We were then too busy to think much of education, but five-and-twenty years later, M. Victor Cousin was despatched on a similar errand, and to him we gave heed. His book was, in great part, translated by Mr. Leonard Horner, and presently afterwards Mr. William Chambers visited Holland, and published in a very cheap and popular form the results of his personal investigations. The educational commissioners of 1858, in their turn, sent an envoy to examine and report, so that we have reliable accounts of the working of the Dutch school law almost from the period of its first coming into operation. The educational commissioners were fortunate in their choice. They selected Mr. Matthew Arnold, a man who could not only see clearly, but could embody what he saw in a form so graceful as to have a permanent literary value. His report is not so long as that of M. Cousin, and he does not think it fitting to describe the galleries of pictures which he visited, nor to collect, *apropos des bottes*, hitherto inedited letters of Descartes ; but, *pace* the *salons*, there is nothing so good in M. Cousin's book as Mr. Arnold's concluding pages. The author of *Obermann* and of the *Grande Chartreuse* contrives to give to everything, even to the paragraphs of a blue-book, that elevation of tone which he insists upon in others.

The improved primary education of Holland dates from the year 1784—that is, from the foundation of the celebrated "Society for the Public Good." It was not, however, till 1806, till the administration of the Grand Pensionary Schimmelpenninck, that the law was passed which made the primary schools of Holland what Cuvier found them. How they prospered under the direction of M. Van den Ende, the author of that law, may be read at much length in M. Cousin's report. The state of things, which he describes, continued until 1857, when, as we have seen, a series of debates took place, which resulted in a modification of the school law of 1806. The origin of these debates was the dissatisfaction that was felt by the High Tory party with the strict enforcement of the law of 1806, which they had tolerated as long as the education given was practically though not theoretically more or less strongly tinged by their own religious views. After 1848, however, the Roman Catholics began to complain loudly, and to say that the word "Christian" in the school law of 1806 had been throughout interpreted to mean "Protestant." With them sided the advanced Liberals, who held that the state had no business to meddle with the religious instruction of the people. A long and careful analysis of these debates was published at Ghent, in 1858, in French, by

M. Émile de Laveleye. Mr. Arnold has recorded the strongly favourable impression made upon his mind by reading them, and we agree with every word of the following passage, which we quote from M. de Laveleye :—

" Quand on étudie ces débats des Chambres Hollandaises dont nous avons essayé de donner une idée, on ne peut se défendre d'un sentiment d'admiration pour ce bon sens pratique, pour cet instinct de liberté uni au sentiment du droit, qui ont fait la gloire de ce peuple dans le passé et qui le rendent de nos jours, si digne de l'attention et de la sympathie de l'étranger. Ce qui distingue la discussion, c'est d'abord une urbanité extrême, une déférence réciproque des orateurs les uns pour les autres, un ton de courtoisie qui vient, non de l'affectation d'une etiquette officielle, mais du respect que chacun ressent pour la dignité dont ses collégues sont revêtus. Au plus fort de la lutte, aucune parole acerbe n'est prononcée, nulle allusion méchante n'est hasardée. Chacun, en parlant, semble obéir à sa conscience et il admet volontiers que ses adversaires en exprimant des convictions opposés, cherchent également le bien de la patrie. Quant au fond même du débat, ce qui le caractérise c'est un sentiment religieux très sincère, très profond, mais très éclairé, une certaine nuance théologique, mais en general nulle bigoterie hypocrite ou persécutrice.

Tous les orateurs, sans exception, semblent pénétrés de l'importance des questions religieuses et de la nécessité de donner pour mobile au progrès de civilisation la morale et la religion. Mais sauf un très petit nombre de protestants et de catholiques exagérés, tous aussi manifestent une répugnance sans bornes pour les envahissements d'une dogmatique étroite et intolerante. Ce qu'ils appellent l'esprit de secte leur cause un effroi qu'ils ne cherche pas à cacher."

The party which was really triumphant was that of the advanced Liberals, but all the many sections of the Dutch Church, except that which is identified with M. Groen van Prinsterer, were consenting parties to the new order of things.

Since 1857 the Dutch primary schools are, in so far as they are supported by the government, entirely unsectarian, but the school buildings are put at the disposal of the pastors of the different denominations for the purpose of instructing those members of their flocks whose parents desire them to have this advantage.

The partisans of M. Groen have naturally done what they could to promote the establishment of primary schools, more in accordance with their own ideas of what is right. They have not succeeded generally, and they will not succeed, for their views are not those of the enlightened classes in Holland. That country has distinctly cast in its lot with the ideas of the new time. Others may go to it, but it will not return to them.

" La Hollande qui a devancé les autres peuples de l'Europe sous tant d'autres rapports, est aussi la première nation de l'ancien monde, qui applique jusque sur le terrain de l'enseignment primaire, la separation de l'eglise et de l'etat."

The principles of the governmental schools were formulised by the Home Minister of the day, in the debates of 1857 :—

1. The culture of the Social and Christian virtues.

2. No dogmatic teaching given by the master of the school.

3. Respect for all beliefs, and a spirit of tolerance and charity.

The excitement of the dispute of 1857 has not yet quite died away, and the Groenist party is apt to claim exclusively for its own schools the title of Christian ; but this is obviously one of the usual exaggerations which flow from the *odium theologicum*. It would be fairer to say, that while the Groenist schools are founded on those principles on which all the Protestant confessions are agreed, the governmental schools are founded upon that portion of Christianity which has interpenetrated and leavened our modern civilisation—that Christianity which, as M. Thorbecke observed in the debates

to which we have alluded, is above the different churches, as
humanity is above the different peoples which it comprehends
—that Christianity which is the sum itself of which the different Christian confessions are only the divergent rays. It
would be a mistake to suppose that absolute unanimity prevails amongst the supporters of the governmental schools as to
the interpretation to be put on the law of 1857. Some years
ago a rather serious difference of opinion manifested itself,
which has for its exponent no less a personage than Professor
Hofstede de Groot, who thinks that the exclusion of the religious element has been more absolute in practice than the law
intended. Into this question our space forbids us to enter, but
it is obvious that in the working of an education law much depends on the character of the master. A man who is at once
able and religious will give a religious tone to a school where
no dogma is ever alluded to, while a man of a different turn of
mind will fail to do so although he is allowed the fullest
liberty in expanding his doctrinal views.

The law of 1857 applied only to primary education, and
was, as we have seen, the development of an existing, not
the construction of a new system. It was otherwise with the
law which regulated secondary education. Cuvier and
Cousin both reported unfavourably of Dutch secondary education ; but in a country so enlightened as Holland now is,
it could not escape notice that in this latter half of the nineteenth century a knowledge of the facts of the universe is
becoming every day a more important element of national
strength. The lowest class is debarred by its poverty from
giving the time necessary to obtain any real scientific knowledge, and the highest class may, if it pleases, repose in bliss-
ful ignorance, or, as in England, learn cricket while pretending

to learn the art of writing Latin verses. But for the middle class this will not any longer answer. The Dutch government and the Dutch people came to a clear understanding on this head some time ago, and so in 1863 a law was passed creating an admirable system of secondary education throughout the country. We doubt not that full details, with regard to it, will appear in the forthcoming report of our own commissioners for middle-class education, who have, we know, applied for information to a person well capable of giving it. The best, however, to which we in England can look forward is some wretched compromise between mediæval and modern views.

In the Netherlands the state could not, unhappily, fall back upon endowments, like those which in England were the glory of the generation that founded them, and are now the shame of an age that seems unable to use them. It did, however, all that was wanted, and created four classes of schools.

The first, a school with a two years' course for those who were to live by some handicraft trade, or by agriculture, taking up their education at the point where the primary school stops.

The second, a school for boys who desire a good but not a learned education. In this class are two divisions :—

a. The school with a three years' course.

b. The school with a five years' course.

The third, or polytechnic school, which is intended for those who mean to devote themselves to the higher walks of manufactures—engineering, architecture, and the like.

The fourth, or agricultural school, intended for those who desire a thorough knowledge of that science, which, since the decline of Dutch commerce in the last century, has made immense progress in Holland, and is, now that Dutch commerce is reviving under the happy influence of free trade, advancing alongside of it to new victories in the wide heaths which occupy so much of the soil of the Netherlands, and contrast so painfully with the riches of those districts of the country with which travellers are most familiar.

All these various schools are strictly superintended by the government, and—enthusiastically supported by an intelligent people—are working admirably. We need hardly add that the whole system found bitter opponents in the same section which is opposed to religious and to political progress, nor need we mention that no attempt is made to discourage private efforts for the establishment of other secondary schools on other principles. As a matter of fact, many such exist, though few of them, we believe, have much merit. It is only just to say that the staunchest and most celebrated Conservatives in the Netherlands speak, as we know from personal experience, with good-natured pity of the antique and barbarous system which still disgraces our most famous schools.

The universities are now in a much more flourishing state than they were, either at the period of M. Cuvier's or M. Cousin's visits. Two old seats of learning—Franeker and Harderwyk—were abolished in consequence of M. Cuvier's report, and the higher education was concentrated in Leyden, Utrecht, and Groningen, aided by two establishments called Athenæums—and which are really universities on a small scale, without the power of conferring degrees—at Amsterdam and Deventer. Leyden, Groningen, and Utrecht each boasts a Protestant faculty of theology, and each, as we have seen, differs entirely in its theological colour from the two others. Peerlkamp, whose name is so well known in connection with Horace, has retired ; but Professor Cobet is still engaged in teaching, and worthily maintains the honour of that kind of scholarship for which England was famous in the days of Elmsley and Porson.   Professor Dozy * of Leyden is one of the best living Arabic scholars, and one of the persons best entitled to complain of the niggardliness with which the University of Oxford refuses to allow her manuscript treasures to be consulted anywhere, except within her own precincts.   Utrecht has two medical professors of considerable note.   The most learned historian in the Netherlands, who is lately dead—M. Bakhuyzen van den Brink—was keeper of the archives at the Hague, and never occupied a position at the universities ; but Professor Fruin of Leyden ranked next to him; and the chairs of law and political economy are in general respectably filled.   Professor Goudsmid of Leyden is one of the very first authorities of the day upon Roman law, and excites among his pupils enthusiasm for that study.†   The use of Latin has been of late years in great measure discontinued ; but the tourist may still be struck with the gracefully-turned phrases of the programmes of study which he will see fixed upon the gates of the university buildings, and may smile when he observes the notice " Cubicula Locanda " at intervals along

* His *Israelites at Mecca* has lately created a great sensation amongst Orientalists and biblical scholars.

† An English barrister, lately called to high judicial office in India, who, believing that the present system, or rather no-system, of the Inns of Court, with regard to legal education, is producing very disastrous effects, has given great attention to the courses of law study enforced by foreign governments, lately visited Holland ; and we extract the following facts from the notes which he has kindly placed at our disposal :—

" The course of instruction is fixed by law, so far as relates to the subjects of the lectures and examinations.   In other respects the professors are entirely uncontrolled.

the streets. Esquiros mentions that he somewhere saw a fencing-master described as "qui elegantem gladii artem docet." Most of the professors still write Latin with great facility, and there are few, perhaps, who have not composed something in that language. An eminent professor of jurisprudence, travelling some years ago in England, and wishing to hear the debates in the House of Commons, found it the most natural thing in the world to write a Latin letter to the Speaker, who immediately sent him, with his usual courtesy, some orders for his gallery.

The ridiculous brawls, dignified by the name of duels,

"No person can hold any judicial appointment, or practise as a barrister, unless he has obtained the degree of doctor of law at one of the universities.

"Any person who can pass the examinations, and perform the necessary exercises, can claim a degree from a university.

"Before commencing the law course the student must pass an examination in Latin, Greek, Roman Antiquities, and Dutch and Universal History.

"The course of law lectures occupies *four* years, but the whole course with the examinations generally covers five.

"These examinations are two in number—1. *Pro gradu candidati;* 2. *Pro gradu doctoris.* The subjects of examination for the second are—

I. Jus Civile Hodiernum.

II. Jus Criminale.

III. Explication of a text of the Pandects.

IV. Explication of a text of the *Jus Civile Hodiernum,* or the *Jus Criminale.*

"Before obtaining the degree of doctor, the student must also write and publish either a *Dissertatio Juridica Inauguralis* upon some thesis, *or* defend (privately) some thirty or forty *loci disputabiles.*

"If the student has not passed three years at a university when he applies for the degree of doctor, he must *both* write the dissertation, *and* defend the *loci disputabiles* in public."

It is strange that a course like this should be necessary on one side of the German Ocean, when we find that on the other a man is enabled to discharge precisely the same functions, by eating a certain number of dinners, and attending two courses of lectures, or paying £100 to a barrister, in whose chambers he is supposed to pass a year ; and this in spite of the protests of all our best jurists, of the report of a Select Committee of the House of Commons, and of a Royal Commission.

which are happily not so common now as they once were in
the German universities, are unknown among the Dutch
students; and the style of living, at least amongst the
wealthier of them, recalls Oxford rather than Heidelberg.

It would, indeed, be a dark day for Holland if the light of
these great institutions were ever to be put out; but the
whole tendency of the times is in an opposite direction.
The organisation of secondary education mainly on a scientific
basis, so far from being in any way hostile to them, will have
quite an opposite effect; for if that reorganisation is really to
prove a success, the universities will constantly be called upon
for a supply of men, thoroughly grounded in theory, to keep
the secondary education up to the requirements of the day,
while the highest walks of professional or public life will
always require university training.

To some Englishmen the colonial empire of Holland is
much more familiar than Holland itself, but to many others it
is so little known that perhaps not a few very intelligent
readers will need to be reminded that Holland is, next to
England, absolutely the greatest colonial power in the world,
and that, relatively to the size of the mother-country, her
colonies are as extensive as our own. So important are her
colonial relations, so much does the East Indian group of
her dependencies, and more particularly Java, influence the
whole of the politics and life of Holland, that at any time but
the present we should have attemped—looking alternately
through the English spectacles of Crawford or Raffles, and the
Dutch spectacles of Temminck and Money—to say something
of those wide dominions whose centre is Batavia. This would
however, be a peculiarly unfortunate moment for doing so,
because, under the auspices of M. Franssen van de Putte, the

present very able Colonial Minister, the whole question of the management of Java has been opened up, and is, while we write, under discussion. The proposal of the government is strongly opposed by the Conservative party, who are all for the maintenance of the old state of things, with its forced labour, exclusiveness, oppression of the natives, and large yearly surplus. On the other hand, the more advanced Liberals do not think that the government measure goes far enough in its concessions to modern views. Whatever may be the fate of the project now before the House—which to a great extent depends, not upon its own merits, but on the line which may be taken by the Roman Catholic deputies, who, as in Ireland, are dissatisfied with mixed education—it is quite certain that the tendency of opinion in Holland is towards a wiser and juster colonial policy. Much has been done, but much remains to do ; and we trust and believe that when all that is desired by the best colonial reformers has been carried out, it will have added to the material prosperity as well as to the fame of a country, upon whose scutcheon a certain narrowness in dealing with her possessions beyond the sea, is the one remaining blot, and which in so many other respects deserves to be revered and imitated by more powerful and fortunate lands.

CHAPTER VII.

EVENTS, in these our times, crowd so rapidly upon each other, that we are already far away from that week of the early winter, when nearly all the newspapers in England were discussing, with many prophecies of coming ill, the life and character of the aged monarch who had just breathed his last at Laeken. We trust, however, that it is not even yet too late to ask some few readers to accompany us, while we retrace the events of his reign, inquire in what state he left his adopted country, and estimate the chances of that country in the immediate future.

The diplomatists of Vienna showed, in the arrangements which they made for the advantage of Holland, the same want of foresight for which they have been justly reproached in so many other instances. That they should have failed to appreciate the importance of the desire for national life which was beginning to be felt in so many small European communities, was not, perhaps, extraordinary; but it was extraordinary that in dealing with a country which had, like the Netherlands, been the scene of such fierce religious struggles, they should have overlooked the strength of the religious antipathy of Catholic and Protestant. Overlook it, however, they did; and thinking only of the importance of erecting a barrier against French ambition, they gave the provinces, which we now know as Belgium, " comme un accroissement de territoire," to that very Holland which had but a few years before been annexed to France, on the plea that it had been formed by the "alluvium of French rivers." This ill-assorted marriage lasted little more than fifteen years. Great benefits were, during its continuance, conferred upon the lower classes in Belgium; for the wide colonial possessions of Holland offered to them a noble market for their industry. This was the reason why the lower classes were the last to join in the revolt; and if they had not been so much under aristocratical and priestly influence, it may well be doubted whether they would have joined in it at all. While, however, the Dutch merchants felt towards the Belgians, who had been admitted to share the advantages of their long-established commercial prosperity, pretty much as the English felt towards the Scotch in the days of Darien, the middle and higher ranks in Belgium were thoroughly hostile to Dutch ascendancy. First, there was a religious grievance; for the clergy distrusted a Protestant king, and abhorred a constitution which treated all religions alike. Then Belgium returned only one member to the States-General for every 61,000 of its inhabitants; while Holland returned one member for every 37,000. Not less irritating was the preponderance which was given to the Dutch language in the transaction of business, and the unlucky arrangements which had been adopted for raising and distributing the taxes. To these great causes were added many smaller ones; such as annoyance at the abolition of the jury, political prosecutions, the greater favour accorded in the army to Dutch officers, the transference of the supreme court to the Hague, and the suspicions which the king brought upon himself by his habit of stock-jobbing.

These and other grievances, which had been long fermenting in the public mind, led in 1828 to the formation of a party which took the name of " The Union," the character of which was at first rather reforming than revolutionary, but which paved the way for the overthrow of the Dutch government.

Reform would, perhaps, have been longer in passing into revolution if it had not been for the three days in Paris, and the fall of the elder Bourbons. These events excited the passions of the people of Brussels. In August 1830 disturbances began ; and in September they had their " four glorious days." The Dutch troops retreated after some hard fighting, and an extempore Provisional Government had to decide on the future of the land.

Then ensued a period of anxious negotiation, of intrigues and counter-intrigues ; but the upshot of all was, that on the 7th of February 1831, the Provisional Government retired from office, and M. Surlet de Chokier—a man of advanced years and high personal character—assumed the conduct of affairs as regent. M. Hymans truly says, speaking of the Provisional Government :—

"Lorsque, le 26 Septembre, ils ouvrirent leur première séance à l'hôtel de ville, au bruit du tocsin et de la fusillade, ils avaient pour tout mobilier une table de bois blanc, prise dans un corps de garde, et deux bouteilles vides, surmontées chacune d'une chandelle. Leurs seules ressources consistaient dans la somme de fr. 21·96, que renfermait la caisse communale. Lorsqu'ils se retirèrent, le 24 Fèvrier, la dissolution du royaume des Pays-Bas etait proclamée par la Conférence de Londres, et la Belgique, à la veille d'être reconnue par les monarques de la sainte-alliance, avait une armée, une adminstration, un trésor, un pouvoir régulier, une assemblée constituante, et la charte la plus libérale de l'Europe."

In doing this great work they were assisted by a congress consisting of 200 members, which, in little more than two months, elaborated a constitution containing, amongst other well-known and excellent provisions, one which had not hitherto made its way into legislation—the complete separation of the church and state. A hundred and eleven members, as against fifty-nine, voted for this—a fact which shows, if we remember the intolerant spirit which was manifested in the appeal of the Belgian bishops to the Congress of Vienna against a Protestant king, that the principles of Lamennais had made no inconsiderable progress among the Belgian Catholics.

To detail the events of the next few months would be unnecessarily to inflict upon our readers the history of one of the most complicated negotiations, and one of the least interesting wars, which have taken place in modern times. They shall hear nothing of the London Conference and its many protocols. Suffice it to say that on the 21st of July 1831, Leopold, sixth son of Francis of Saxe-Coburg, became first king of the Belgians ; that the king of Holland showed alike in diplomacy and in war all the characteristic obstinacy of his race, even threatening at one time to follow the example of Van Speyk, the young officer who blew up his gunboat rather than let it fall into the hands of the enemy ; that the arms of Leopold, at first unsuccessful, were strengthened by French, to say nothing of English aid ; and that the French evacuated the soil of Belgium in the month of January 1833, after having crushed Chassé at Antwerp just before the end of 1832.

Of all the changes and chances of the time none was more auspicious for Belgium than that which transferred the Seals of the Foreign Office from Lord Aberdeen to Lord Palmerston.

" Qu'il me soit permis " (says General Goblet, an active negotiator in those days, in his *Memoirs*, quoted by M. Hymans) " de rendre hommage à ce ministre illustre.   La Belgique a toujours trouvé en lui le défenseur le plus dévoué ; et si la reconnaissance doit égaler les services rendus, la nôtre doit être sans bornes envers l'homme qui, à juste titre, regarde le nouveau royaume comme l'une de ses créations."

Testimonies of this kind to the real worth of Lord Palmerston may be consolatory to some of those who followed him through the last two parliaments, and had often to ask themselves whether one, known personally to younger politicians, chiefly as a dexterous manager of the House of Commons, was indeed the great man they would fain have believed him to be.

Long before the conclusion of the war with Holland, the political life of the new nation was developing itself in a steady and regular manner.   The congress was dissolved in July 1831, immediately after the inauguration of the king, and in September a House of Representatives consisting of 102, and a Senate consisting of 51 members, were already assembled.

Questions relating to the army and to foreign affairs were those which excited most attention in the first two sessions, but as early as 1831 the adverse parties of Liberals and Clericals were in presence of each other, and the breach between them was widened by the Encyclical Letter of Gregory XVI. in August 1832, which was directed against the constitutional liberties of Belgium.

Useful measures were not, however, neglected amidst the strife of parties, and before the settlement with Holland in 1839 had definitively fixed the boundaries of the new kingdom, the army had been remodelled, the tribunals had been regulated, the great railway from Antwerp to the Prussian frontier had been decreed and partially completed, the provincial and communal institutions of the country had been settled. A Catholic university had been founded at Malines and transferred to Louvain. A Liberal university had been founded at Brussels, while the two state universities of Liége and Ghent, together with the system of examination for degrees, had been reorganised. Most of these matters gave occasion to sharp debates, more especially the law of the *communes*, which occupied more than 100 sittings of the Senate and House of Representatives.

The final arrangements with Holland, which put an end to all danger from without, at the expense of the sacrifice of a population of 380,000 in Luxemburg-Limburg, who passed once more under Dutch rule, had naturally the effect of turning the attention of Belgian politicians to those internal questions, upon which they were divided in opinion. The society called the "Union," which paved, as we have seen, the way for the revolution, was composed indifferently of Catholics and Liberals, who were welded as closely together by hatred of the House of Nassau, as our churchmen and dissenters were in 1688. The elections to the Congress were likewise made without any reference to the religious opinions of the deputies. The same may be said of the first cabinets of the king; but the cabinet of 1834, at the head of which was M. de Theux, was distinctly intended to be a mixed cabinet, representing, as equally as might be, both the parties which divided the state. When, however, all fear of aggression from abroad was for the present at an end, a very general impression grew up that it was time to allow free play to party views, and that Belgium would, like other constitutional states, find it most to her advantage to be ruled by each of her parties in turn, as each from time to time secured a majority in the electoral body. Effective expression was given to these views in an article by M. Devaux, which appeared about this time in the *Revue Nationale*, and is generally spoken of as marking a turning-point in Belgian politics. Strangely enough, it was this same M. Devaux who first submitted the name of Leopold to the Congress. The Liberals made the first move, and overthrew the government of M. de Theux in 1840, substituting for it a cabinet whose leader was M. Rogier. Their adversaries soon returned the blow by prevailing upon the Senate to adopt, in 1841, an address to the Crown of more than doubtful legality, deprecating the system of government by party, and asking for a mixed cabinet. The king hesitated for three weeks, then yielded, and dismissed M. Rogier and his colleagues.

The head of the new government was M. Nothomb, a man of liberal inclinations, but so much afraid of being considered to lean too much to either side, as to be quite unable to give to his policy any decided character. The one important measure which marked his four years' tenure of power was the law regulating primary education, a subject upon which compromise was natural. Few ministers have been more fiercely attacked from both sides of a legislative assembly, and on one occasion he was supported by no follower out of his own cabinet. His government, which had been completely remodelled since it came into power in 1841, fell immediately after the general elections of 1845, which had shown that if the Liberals were not in a majority amongst the electors, they at least had on their side the vast preponderance of ability and energy, and a powerful following amongst the masses of the towns. Two acts which passed under the *régime* of M. Nothomb were much criticised at the time, and being nicknamed the "reactionary laws," attached to it disagreeable recollections in the minds of the people. The one limited to some extent the rights of the *commune*, to the advantage of the central authority ; the other broke up the larger *communes* into electoral sections, with a view—which turned out to be anything but prophetic—of causing the elections to turn, not upon great party questions, but upon trifling local ones.

The resignation of the Nothomb ministry in 1845 put the king in a difficult position. He sent for M. Rogier, but M. Rogier could not undertake the government without having the right of dissolving, because his cabinet would otherwise have merely existed on sufferance. The king, always inclined to moderate counsels, shrank from dissolving the Chamber which had only just been called into life, and summoned to his aid M. Van de Weyer, whose long absence from Belgium, as minister in England, had given to him a position outside and above her parties. Of the liberalism of a man so wise and so cultivated as M. Van de Weyer there could, of course, be not a shadow of doubt, but it was not precisely of a colour to suit that of his co-religionists at home. Their liberalism was militant and aggressive, his philosophical and conciliatory.

The ministry of M. Van de Weyer lasted only eight months, and the king once more appealed to M. Rogier, who explained in a long letter the conditions upon which he was willing to take the helm of affairs. Two of these conditions— that, viz., M. Rogier should be at liberty to dismiss public functionaries who embarrassed his government, and should have the power of dissolving the Chambers if he could not govern with them—were objected to by the king, and M. de Theux was again sent for. He came in with a purely clerical cabinet, and maintained himself in place for sixteen months, passing, in the meantime, some useful measures. The Liberal minority in the Chambers was, however, enthusiastically supported out of doors, and the country grew ever more and more indisposed to the rule of the Clericals. At last, the partial elections of 1847 having turned out decidedly unfavourable, the ministry resigned, and power passed into the hands of their opponents.

In waging war against the ministry of M. de Theux, the Liberals had availed themselves of their undoubted constitutional rights, to hold a great political gathering in the Hotel de Ville at Brussels. After the fall of the July monarchy, a letter from Louis Philippe was found and published in the *Revue Retrospective*, in which he expatiated to his son-in-law on the danger of permitting so revolutionary a proceeding, and assured him that France would be ready to support him against popular agitation.

> Invida fatorum series, summisque negatum
> Stare diu !

M. Rogier came into power on the 12th of August 1847, and amongst his colleagues was a "*novus homo*." M. Frère-Orban, the new Minister of Public Works, then five-and-thirty, had only just been elected, for the first time, a representative of the people, but he had been known as a distinguished advocate in his native town of Liége, and as a member of the *Association Libérale*. Born in very humble circumstances, he had married the daughter of a rich man, M. Orban, and had taken her name, which he has now made distinguished. Since 1847 he has been one of the most conspicuous figures in Belgian politics. He is the ablest of her financiers, and the soul of the present cabinet. Clear, ardent, and incisive, his speaking is of a very high order, and the Clerical party fears no one so much, although some of the best of the younger Liberals sometimes find fault with him for not moving fast enough. The publication of his principal work, " La Main-morte," formed an important episode in the struggle which culminated in the year 1857, and of which we shall hereafter have to speak.

The new ministers immediately put forth a programme of policy. Their whole system rested upon two principles :—

1. The state is a lay institution, absolutely independent of clerical influence.

2. All religions should be respected, and their ministers protected, as long as they keep within the circle of their duties.

They announced further that they were all agreed on the expediency of—

1. Reforming the body by which university degrees were conferred.

2. Abolishing the law by which the *communes* were broken up for electoral purposes.

3. Restricting the appointment of burgomasters by the central authority, to those cases in which such a method of appointment was recommended by the permanent committee of the provincial councils.

4. Adding " *capacités*" to the electoral lists (a sort of fancy franchise).

The session was in full course. The new cabinet was busily engaged in working out its programme, when suddenly, while all the society of Brussels was gathered, as thirty-three years before, at a ball, news arrived of the outbreak of the February revolution in Paris.

The first emotion was one of fear, but it was a wise and salutary fear, which M. Rogier and his colleagues translated in a few weeks into a number of wise and popular measures, some of which they had not ventured to put into their programme, and some of which they had not even wished to put into it. In the first days of March the two "reactionary laws" of 1843 were swept away. On the 12th the franchise was lowered as far as the constitution permitted, and much further than the Liberal gathering in Brussels, which so much alarmed Louis Philippe, had proposed. On the 8th of May a national guard was created; on the 25th the newspaper stamp was abolished, and on the 26th officials, with the exception of ministers, were forbidden to sit in the Chambers.

On the 27th of May Parliament was dissolved, and the Liberals had in the elections for the House of Representatives a majority of 62, the numbers being 85 to 23. The new Parliament met on the 26th of June, the very day on which the archbishop of Paris was killed. The good sense of the king, the wise foresight of the Liberal ministers, and the prudent reserve of the Clerical party, had enabled Belgium to pass unscathed through a most dangerous crisis.

One deputy alone had raised his voice in favour of a republic:—"The principles of the French Revolution," said M. Castiau, "are destined to make the tour of the world."

M. Delfosse spoke the sentiments of the immense majority of his countrymen when he said in reply:—" In order to make the tour of the world the ideas of the French Revolution need not take us on their way. We have already in Belgium the great principles of liberty and equality. They are inscribed in our constitution, as they are engraved upon our hearts."

This was in the spring, but the festival of September, on occasion of the eighteenth anniversary of the Four Days of 1830, with its shouts of "*Vive le Roi,*" showed that after all that anxious summer, the masses were still monarchical, as indeed they had good reason to be. King and people had shown themselves worthy of each other, and we recommend the study of these six months of Belgian history to those journalists who are so very much afraid that Belgian parties will fight with such Corcyrean animosity as to require the intervention of France.

All through the session of 1848-49, the liberal reforms went on. The duty on foreign corn was reduced; the government was empowered to allow cattle to be introduced without any duty; postage was diminished, and other measures taken in the interest of the poorer classes. But the truce, which the alarms of 1848 had established between the two great parties, was, as might have been expected, not of long duration. Their dissensions broke out again during the consideration of the bill which modified the regulations which had existed since 1835, with regard to the bodies to which were entrusted the examinations for degrees, '*les Jurys Universitaires,*' in the composition of which there was always great difficulty in adjusting the rival claims of the state and of the clergy—substantially, we may observe, in passing, the question which is giving so much trouble to our government with regard to the Queen's University in Ireland. It was, however, upon the long-vexed subject of secondary education that the old passions were fully revived. The bishops protested against the ministerial measure, and the pope pronounced an allocution against it. Yet the proposals of the cabinet were perfectly moderate: ministers only asked the right to establish ten Royal Athenæums, certain *écoles moyennes* (institutions like the German "Real Schulen"), the right of refusing subsidies to the communal schools unless they would accept their programme of studies, and the right of forbidding the *communes* to support adventure-schools unless they permitted the visits of the government inspector. What more especially offended the Clericals was that the government only *invited* the clergy to give or superintend the religious instruction, without making its assistance absolutely necessary. In spite, however, of all opposition, the bill became law.

In the partial elections of 1850 the Clericals had some successes, and the Liberals were further weakened by dissensions amongst themselves, chiefly about financial questions. Defeated upon one of these, the ministry resigned, but as none of the persons to whom the king applied would undertake to make a government, they presently resumed their portfolios. M. Frère-Orban, the finance minister, then slightly modified his propositions, succeeded in the House of Representatives, but had the mortification of seeing his proposal for a new form of succession-duty rejected by the large proprietors of the Senate, led by the Prince de Ligne and other members of the Liberal party. The Senate was immediately dissolved, and a modified form of succession-duty was agreed to by the new House. This episode, however, sadly disorganised the Liberal party, and the spirits of their opponents were further raised by the *coup d'état* in Paris, and by the tone of the French press, which seemed to make the safety of Belgium depend upon the overthrow of the Rogier ministry. Weakened in the election of June 1852, and further weakened by the retirement of M. Frère-Orban, the cabinet received a severe check on the question of the election of the president of the

House of Representatives, and on the 31st of October 1852 M. Henri de Brouckere took the reins of power.

This was just the moment for a ministry of conciliation, and he was just the man to be at the head of one. The period of his power may be considered as a sort of armistice, although his own opinions were distinctly liberal. Before he retired he had succeeded in settling the long controversy with France about the piratical reprinting of French books in Brussels ; in passing an act more expedient than altogether defensible against attacks by Belgian subjects upon foreign sovereigns, which is known by the name of his colleague, M. Faider ; in getting Belgium officially recognised by Russia, and in making a sort of treaty with the archbishop of Malines, with regard to the interference of the clergy in secondary education, which is called by Belgian writers the "Convention of Antwerp."

Nevertheless, things did not go altogether well with him. Slight checks in the Chamber were frequent, the expulsion of Colonel Charras was unpopular ; the Russian war then raging made many fear, without perhaps much reason, that Belgium would be obliged to renounce the neutrality which is the foundation of her political existence. Above all, the great question of benevolent foundations, which in 1857 almost over-turned public order, began to excite the minds of men. Har-assed by many difficulties, and not least by those we have mentioned, M. de Brouckere and his moderate Liberals sur-rendered the government in 1855 into the hands of a moderate clerical government, presided over by M. Vilain xiiii. and M. de Decker. As the names of those politicians, eminent in their own country, are but little known in England, we may say a word or two about them.

Charles Vicomte Vilain xiiii.—by no means xiv. as it is

often written—is descended from a family of substantial
burghers, one of whom was ennobled in 1758 by Maria Theresa.
The xiiii. which so much puzzles people, is a mediæval rebus
which expresses the family motto 'veertien in hop'—'earn in
hope,' expressed by the device of xiiii. surrounded by a wreath
of the hop-plant. He was born in 1803, and was brought up
by the Jesuits, who, however, although they did not succeed,
as they have so often done, in making their pupil the bitter
enemy of Catholicism, failed also to injure his noble and
generous nature. He studied at the university of Liége,
married a woman of large property, took some part as a journalist in preparing the way for the revolution, and became an
active and distinguished member of the Congress. A decided
but by no means bigoted Catholic, he has always been the foe
of centralisation and the friend of an almost boundless liberty
for his opponents as well as for his friends ; nor would it be
difficult to gather from his speeches many passages which are
worthy to stand by the side of the noblest sentiments which
were expressed by M. de Montalembert at the Congress of
Malines in the autumn of 1863.

His colleague, M. Pierre de Decker, was born in East
Flanders in 1812, and was, before he entered into political
life, a well-known journalist and man of letters. His shade
of political opinion is much the same as that of Vilain xiiii.,
whom he resembles in high honour and unblemished integrity.
He, however, arrived at his political opinions by a different
road. Vilain xiiii. was a conciliatory minister, because he
recognised the right of his opponents to absolute freedom,
believing, as he did fully, that what he conceived to be truth
must conquer in the end. M. de Decker was, if we understand him right, a conciliatory minister, partly because his

temper was conciliatory, and partly because he was pro-
foundly impressed with the idea that behind and beneath
the parties which divide Belgium, there was another party
which was likely to be dangerous to both,—the party which
was crushed for a time at Paris in the days of June 1848.
It was this last prepossession that made him so ardént an
advocate of the law of charity by which his government was
wrecked in 1857 ; and it was his conciliatory, or, as it has
been called, synthetic turn of mind, which won for him the
bitter hatred of the real leaders of the Clerical party, who
stood in somewhat the same relation to him as Dr. Cullen and
his immediate allies do to such politicians as Mr. Monsell.
We need not then be surprised to learn that in a country
where the lines of political demarcation are drawn so distinctly
as in Belgium, his high personal character has not succeeded
in securing him any great amount of public confidence. He
is, it has been said, "a gun with two barrels, which goes off of
itself; the contents of the one barrel strike down his friends,
and those of the other his enemies." It was during this administration that Count Walewski brought the transgressions of
the Belgian press before the Congress of Paris, on which
occasion the plenipotentiaries, those of them even who reserved the principle of the liberty of the press, passed a
severe censure upon some newspapers which appeared in
Belgium. The censure was by no means undeserved, but the
incident was calculated to offend national susceptibilities, and
M. Orts put a question about it in the Chamber. We give the
account of what followed in the words of M. Hymans :—

L'honorable M. Orts (répondit M. Vilain xiiii.) désire savoir si l'un
des gouvernements représentés au Congrès a demandé au gouvernement
belge quelque modification à la constitution.—Aucune !—L'honorable
M. Orts me demande si le cabinet, dans le cas où une pareille de-

mande lui serait faite, serait disposé à proposer à la chambre quelque changement à la constitution.—Jamais !

The spirited reply of the Foreign Minister gained for the government no little credit, although it was afterwards explained by the official journal that ministers by no means pledged themselves, while upholding the *constitution*, not to introduce some changes in the *laws* relating to the press. A series of unfortunate incidents, soon, however, destroyed this popularity. One of these was the bringing in of a sort of conspiracy bill, to take away all political character from projects of assassinating a foreign sovereign, thereby reducing them to the level of ordinary crime, for which the constitution permitted extradition. The session of 1856 was not an eventful one, and the same might perhaps have been the case with its successor, if the ultramontane press and the Belgian episcopate had not been foolish enough to think that the time had arrived for commencing a new campaign against free inquiry.

The bishop of Ghent began the fray by publishing a violent invective against state education. His lead was followed presently by the bishop of Bruges, and the deliverances of those ecclesiastics gave the tone to the language of the whole of their party. The free university of Brussels and the state university of Ghent were the chief objects of attack, and the name which drew upon itself most abuse was that of Professor Laurent, the author of *Études sur l'Histoire de l'Humanité*, and numerous other works. M. de Decker bore himself in the *mêlée* with great dignity. He altogether disavowed the violent teachings of his party, spoke with contempt of the *Index*, declared with regard to a publication in the nature of the *Index*, which had appeared at Brussels, that those who followed such guidance would prepare for Belgium

a generation of *crétins,* and lamented in striking words the
gust of intolerance which was passing over the land. When
the Chambers met in the autumn there was a serious discussion with regard to the liberty to be allowed to professors in
explaining their opinions upon questions which might affect
religion. The amendment of the Liberals upon the clause of
the address, which related to this matter, was defeated; and
when men's minds were in the irritable state which such discussions tend to produce, the Minister of Justice, M. A.
Nothomb, had the unfortunate idea of introducing a bill with
regard to charitable foundations, which was highly favourable
to clerical pretensions. If this bill had passed into law, a
royal ordinance would have been enough to authorise the
establishment of private foundations, exempt from the control
of the state—its inspectors and superintendents. Founders
would have been able to reserve for themselves and for third
persons the administration of their foundations, and they
might even have created family trustees or have attached
the control of their foundations to the successive occupants
of civil or ecclesiastical offices. This would have been to
restore mortmain in a form suitable to modern exigencies,
and would enormously have increased the power of the 800
religious associations which exist in Belgium, and which
count already about 12,000 members. Hence the bill got the
name of the "Loi des Couvents," and very soon the cry was
raised for the " Abolition des Couvents." The Liberal party
asked for an inquiry into pauperism, which was refused, and
the debates went on getting fiercer and fiercer for twenty-seven
days. As the spring advanced the whole country became
extremely agitated, and on the 27th of May 1857 the multitude assembled in front of the House of Representatives ap-

plauded the Liberals and hissed the Clericals as they came
out, proceeding the next day to break windows, and to commit other insubordinate acts. Similar scenes were enacted in
most of the large towns, but the only really dangerous outbreak took place in the *commune* of Jemappes, where an
establishment belonging to the Frères de la Doctrine Chrê-
tienne was sacked by the mob. It had now, however, become
quite clear that it would be madness to go on, and the bil.
was withdrawn. The Chambers were then adjourned, and on
the 14th of June the official journal published a decree
closing the session, a letter from the ministers to the king,
and the answer addressed by him to M. de Decker.

A portion of the letter may be cited as illustrative of the
moderating influence which the king exercised over Belgian
party contentions :—

" Vous avez agi avec la plus grande loyauté et la plus entière bonne
foi. Vous êtes fermement persuadé que le projet de loi, mis à exécu-
tion, ne produirait pas les conséquences fâcheuses que l'on y a attri-
buées. Je ne porterai point de jugement sur le projet ; je n'aurais
jamais consenti à donner place dans notre législation à une loi qui
aurait pu avoir les funestes effets qu'on redoute, mais, sans me livrer à
l'examen de la loi en elle-même, je tiens compte, comme vous, d'une
impression qui s'est produite, à cette occasion, chez une partie con-
sidérable de la population. Il y a, dans les pays qui s'occupent eux-
mêmes de leurs affaires, de ces émotions rapides, contagieuses, se
propageant avec une intensité qui se constate plus facilement qu'elle ne
s'explique et avec lesquelles il est plus sage de transiger que de
raisonner.

" Les libres institutions de la Belgique ont été pratiquées, pendant vingt-six ans, avec une admirable régularité. Que faut-il pour
qu'elles continuent à fonctionner dans l'avenir avec le même ordre,
le même succès ? Je n'hésite pas à le dire, il faut chez les partis
de la modération et de la réserve ; je crois que nous devons nous
abstenir d'agiter toute question qui peut allumer la guerre dans les
esprits. Je suis convaincu que la Belgique peut vivre heureuse et
respectée, en suivant les voies de la modération ; mais je suis égale-

ment convaincu, et je le dis à tout le monde, que toute mesure qui peut être interprétée comme tendant à fixer la suprématie d'une opinion sur l'autre, qu'une telle mesure est un danger. La liberté ne nous manque pas, et notre constitution, sagement et modérément pratiquée, présente un heureux équilibre."

Thus ended a crisis which might have been a very serious one, in a country less influenced by the maxims of common sense. In the whole transaction the persons most to blame were the Belgian bishops, who, without rest, though not without haste, have ever since 1830 used their liberty as an instrument to obtain power. We fully acquit M. de Decker of any desire to play into their hands, but the measure introduced by his colleague would undoubtedly have been turned to evil uses ; and although we cannot approve of the violence which was exhibited by some of the Liberal party, tinged as it was by much of that narrowness and intolerance which they reproached in their adversaries, they were in the main right.

The agitations were followed by loud demands for the resignation of ministers, and a serious difference of opinion arose in the cabinet as to whether or not these demands should be complied with. M. de Decker and M. Vilain xiiii., who represented, as we have seen, the moderate section of Catholic opinion, were in favour of retiring, but M. A. Nothomb and others were opposed to it. The views of the violent section at first triumphed, but ere long the pressure from without became too strong ; the ministry resigned, and the king sent once more for M. Henri de Brouckere. A Brouckere cabinet, however, was no longer possible. The period of coalitions was, at least for a time, over, and the Belgian Liberals insisted upon having a government which should be distinctly of their own colour, whereas M. de Brouckere stood in the same re-

lations to them as M. de Decker did to the Clerical party.
M. Rogier accordingly took the reins of power, and the
ministry which then (9th October 1857) came in is substantially the same as that which governs Belgium at the present
hour. The new government dissolved the House of Representatives, and both parties exerted themselves to the utmost
at the elections, which took place early in December. The
result was a complete triumph for the Liberals, the numbers
being 70 to 38. The ministers, however, did not, in the session of 1858, give as much satisfaction to their more zealous
supporters as might have been expected. They were, perhaps
wisely, extremely cautious, and thought more of securing the
victory, which they had gained, than of pushing it further.
There is a strong resemblance between Lord Palmerston's last
government and that of M. Rogier. Perhaps the only just
reproach that can be addressed to either is, that they were
both led by chiefs who had done so much public service that
it was not in the nature of things that they could retain the
force and *verve* which would be expected in men who were
not worn out. In Belgium, accordingly, just as in England,
a party of "Young Liberals" has grown up, which will, no
doubt, when it in its turn attains to power, attempt to realise
in practice, somewhat more quickly than its predecessors, the
conclusions of our best theoretical guides.

The Clerical party, during the session of 1858, being well
aware of the tendency to disunion amongst their opponents,
tried to aggravate it, by a systematic silence during the debates. Their tactics were well defined by one of their number, who said, "Nous leur donnerons si peu de clérical à
manger qu'ils finiront par s'entre-dévorer." They did not,
however, obtain by this any real party advantage, and the

Liberals held their own at the beginning as at the end of the session. Its two principal events were—first, an alteration in the law of 1852 with respect to attacks made by the Belgian press upon foreign sovereigns, which grew out of the same circumstances that led to our "conspiracy bill," and was opposed for similar reasons by a small number of deputies ; and secondly, the failure of the ministerial proposal with respect to the fortification of Antwerp.

In the session of 1858 and 1859, the Clerical party refused to take part in the discussion of the address, in consequence of some words which the majority had inserted in it, and throughout its course they adhered for the most part to their policy of silence. They opposed, however, as might have been expected, the somewhat severe provisions which the Liberals, in revising the criminal code, wished to re-enact, or rather to maintain in a modified form, for the purpose of restraining those priests who turned their pulpits into tribunes from which to fulminate against the government.

The *Journal des Débats* did at this time good service to the Belgian Liberals, by calling their attention to a proposal which the government, acting doubtless under Imperialist influence, had made for increasing its control over the press. Thanks to a vigorous resistance, the attempt altogether failed.

New questions began now to be agitated by the "Young Liberals ;" amongst them compulsory education, the rights of the Flemish population to more consideration for their language, and the liberty of combination amongst workmen.

A proposal for altering the method in which the votes were taken at elections, which would have had the effect of mixing the voters from town and country together, and so withdrawing the latter at the decisive moment from the influence of the curé, was fiercely opposed by the Clericals, but accepted in principle by the majority of the House of Representatives; while an enactment, further restraining the rights of private foundations, became the law of the land.

The partial elections of June 1859 were favourable to the government. In 1860 it was able to commence a series of financial reforms by abolishing the Octroi,* and substituting for it taxes less oppressive to industry. The removal of the hateful *barrières*, which all travellers remember but too well, took place on the 21st of July, on the 29th anniversary of the king's accession.

The affair of Savoy and Nice naturally revived amongst large classes of Frenchmen a desire to annex Belgium, and that desire was more emphatically than courteously expressed in many French newspapers. The result was a great outburst of anti-Gallican feeling, and a reaction in favour of the Dutch, which, after increasing for many months, culminated on the occasion of the visit of the king of the Netherlands to Liége. In the great hall of the noble and ancient pile which once was the episcopal palace, William III. and Leopold showed themselves at the window to the assembled multitudes, who, poli-

---

* Mr. Barron, in his report, dated March 26, 1864, speaks as follows :— "Of all these taxes the most profitable, but also the most objectionable, were the octroi duties. Seventy-eight communes, containing a population of 1,223,000, were privileged to levy duties on the import of certain articles, mostly liquors, food, forage, and fuel. The tariffs included seventy-six taxable articles, but the list of rates varied in every town. These towns were fenced round with walls, palisades, ditches, etc., were entered by a limited number of gates, and were defended by seventy-eight armies. The brewers and distillers were watched by two sets of officials,—those of the state and those of the town. Then there was often a system of drawbacks on the export of goods made of taxed materials. All these tariffs were framed on good old protectionist principles, so as to favour local and personal interests. The towns even indulged in little tariff wars with each other. Such is still the condition of almost all the rest of the Continent."

tically disjoined from Holland, have now no feelings of animosity to that country, which regards them with equal goodwill.

The chief events of the year 1861 were the conclusion of a commercial treaty with France, the natural result of our treaty of the previous year with that country, and the recognition of Italy. By the latter measure, tone, so to speak, was restored to the Liberal party, in the ranks of which dissatisfaction had been steadily increasing. During a portion of the summer and autumn the ministry lacked the powerful aid of M. Frère, who retired as soon as the commercial treaty with France was concluded, early in the month of June, in consequence of a motion adverse to his financial policy, which had been carried against him in April by M. Dumortier, a member of the Clerical opposition, and a consistent advocate of traditional errors,—political, economical, and religious. Before the autumn was over, however, he returned to power.

The debate on the recognition of Italy was a very lively one, and the views of the majority were well summed up in the remark of M. Orts : " Belgium, which only exists by the will of the nation, should respect national will wherever it is displayed."

The union, which was to some extent re-established in the Liberal party by this wise step, was soon rudely broken by the question of the fortifications of Antwerp, which came to a head in 1862. For many years it had been evident that this great fortress required to be very much altered and improved, if it was to serve as the last refuge of Belgian independence in case of a French invasion. After long consideration, a plan was elaborated, of which the inhabitants of

Antwerp cordially approved. The area included in the fortifications was to be enlarged about sixfold; the wharf and dock accommodation was to be greatly increased and better protected, while every effort was to be made to conciliate, as far as was possible, the interests of commerce and defence. The Antwerpians had looked at first only on the bright side of the picture; but by degrees the notion of being bombarded at all, even at the most respectful distance, grew extremely horrible to them, and they began to object to every detail of the government plan, as well as to make demands for compensation, which could not be listened to. A deputation which they sent to the king was very coldly received; and his majesty read a paper which set forth extremely clearly the grounds upon which the government proceeded. Antwerp soon avenged itself by sending to the House of Representatives the bitterest possible opponents of the ministry. One of these was M. Hayez, who had had a personal quarrel with the Minister of War; and another was M. Delaet, whose duel with that functionary was the tragi-comedy of the session of 1865. Any one who happened to be at Antwerp towards the end of 1862, will remember how much of the conversation in public places was engrossed by the *servitudes militaires* and other features of the great fortification question. We need hardly say that the Clerical party used the Antwerp agitation as a weapon, because in Belgium, as elsewhere, it neglects no weapon which can in any way injure its opponents.

A commercial treaty with England was concluded in 1862, not, however, without some murmurs, on the part of our government, at what Lord Russell considered to be an unnecessary and unfriendly delay. Some concessions were made in the treaty to the earnest representations of Ghent, the last citadel of Belgian protectionism.* 1863 saw the abolition of the Scheldt dues, a great benefit to Belgian commerce, and an advantage to that of the whole world.

The partial elections of June 1863, which soon followed, and some by-elections which took place later, were not favourable to the Liberals ; and in the beginning of 1864 the ministers found their majority so reduced, as to make it seem desirable to resign. This they did, but their clerical adversaries wholly failed in making a government, and after one of the longest cabinet crises upon record, during which every imaginable combination had been essayed by the king—a Brouckere cabinet, a Dechamps and De Theux cabinet, a

---

* Mr. Barron tells us, in his report of February 26, 1865 :—" *The Superior Council of Industry and Commerce* was created by royal Arrêté of the 27th of March 1859. It is composed of two delegates from each of the Chambers of Commerce of Antwerp, Brussels, Charleroi, Ghent, Liége, and Mons ; of one from each of the other eighteen Chambers ; and of eight nominees of the Crown—in all thirty-eight members. Its attributions are to give advice on proposals emanating from the government, from Chambers of Commerce, or from individual members. Its opinions, therefore, may be quoted as the highest authority on all commercial questions.

" *With reference to the tariff*, their resolutions of 1864 are that it should cease forthwith to be anything but a means of collecting revenue ; that machines and raw materials must first be expunged from it, and then gradually all other articles which produce trifling sums ; that taxation should be concentrated on a small number of articles, the customs and excise duties being always kept in harmony ; that, as the absolute suppression of the custom-house would act more energetically on the development of public wealth than any mere reduction, it is expedient that the government should constantly tend to attain that end, and seek for a practical solution of the financial difficulties of the question ; that it would be unjust to augment the taxes on real property for the sole purpose of suppressing customs and excise duties ; that the conventional ' régime ' should be at once extended to the world at large ; that the government should negotiate for the purpose of suppressing the vexatious certificate of origin ; that the customs' officers shall abstain as often as they safely can from searching passengers' luggage."

Faider cabinet, a Nothomb cabinet, a cabinet with the Prince de Ligne for its head—every combination was found impossible, and the old ministers once more accepted the power and the responsibilities which circumstances had absolutely forced upon them. On the 31st of May M. Rogier explained the circumstances of the ministerial interregnum, and the policy which he meant to pursue. Much of the discussion which followed, and was continued for fifteen days, turned upon the merits of a programme which had been laid before the king by M. Dechamps.

M. Dechamps, who is the recognised leader of that section of Belgian Catholics which adopts the views of M. de Montalembert—a party which, be it remembered, is only strong enough to exist by the sufferance of the more violent Clericals, —was born in 1807, studied at Brussels, and adopted, like so many of his contemporaries, the views of Lamennais. When, however, it came to a parting between that remarkable man and his friends, his Belgian disciple followed Lacordaire and submitted to Rome. A distinguished journalist, M. Dechamps was elected in 1834, and made himself conspicuous, as well by his speeches upon education and communal organisation, as by taking an active part in promoting railways and other material improvements. He had a seat in the De Theux, Van de Weyer, and Nothomb cabinets, of which last he was an unruly member. After 1847 he naturally fell somewhat into the background, but rose again into great importance in the period preceding the ministerial crisis of 1864, during the course of which he submitted to the king the programme of policy to which we have alluded. It is too long to quote, and would require a commentary, but the ideas which presided over its composition were :—

1. To turn away the attention of the people from the distinction between Liberals and Clericals.

2. To lower the provincial and communal franchise, *with a view to increase the power of the clergy and the aristocracy.*

3. To decentralise, *partly, we presume, with the same view, but chiefly because the country wishes it.*

4. To propose some minor changes, which might either conciliate particular interests or give popularity to the party.

M. Nothomb, the last Clerical orator who spoke, proposed a vote of want of confidence. A division was taken, and the numbers were—for the government 57, against it 56. Three members—two Liberals and one Clerical—were absent. On the 30th of the same month, M. Orts, one of the representatives of Brussels, proposed, with a view to strengthen his party, that in consequence of the increase of population since 1859, when the number of representatives had been last increased, the numbers of the Lower House should be raised from 116 to 122, and those of the Upper from 58 to 61. Hereupon the Clerical party declared that if the government supported this proposition, they would retire from the Chamber, and thus make it impossible to vote the estimates for public works, which were then being discussed. In this unconstitutional proceeding they persisted, until the king, seeing no other way out of the difficulty, dissolved the House of Representatives on the 16th of July. The elections returned, as might have been expected, a Liberal majority, and M. Dechamps, the head of the party which had disgraced itself by a manœuvre so damaging to Liberal institutions, was himself defeated for Charleroi, and obliged to employ his mischievous activity in the production of a long article and a long pamphlet, the latter of which has seriously injured his country by misleading the English press as to its real position and tendencies. In the autumn session of 1864, the dangers which Belgium might possibly incur from her connection with Mexico were discussed in an unnecessarily alarmist tone, but no very important event occurred before the end of the year. The pope's Encyclical of the 8th December, with its exaggerated pretensions and old-world dreams, was a sad blow to the moderate Catholics, and the controversies which it raised were an important element in the political activity of 1865.

These discussions were more interesting and more important than the encounters of parties on corrupt practices or ministerial responsibility during a somewhat sterile session, but all other events of the year 1865 in Belgium were cast into the shade by the death of the good and wise king who had for so many years presided over her councils.

The secret of Leopold's success was, that he had early the sagacity to perceive that the age of kings, in the old sense of the term, was passing away for ever, and that such a country as Belgium could only be happy if it were treated as a republic under monarchical forms. When the secret history of the last generation is written, we shall know how much the king of the Belgians, not less than our own queen, owed to one whose name, when he passed away from the scene, was hardly mentioned by a single English paper—we mean the late Baron Stockmar, of whom Lord Palmerston said to the late Baron Bunsen :—" He is simply the greatest statesman I have ever known."

That Leopold I. was an intelligent man and a sensible man there can be no doubt, and he was, both before and after his marriage with the heiress of England, put in a position which in the mind of any one who had no illusions as to the direction in which the world was slowly moving, could not fail to develop good sense and intelligence into the highest of all political qualities—wisdom. That he was gifted with any brilliant or remarkable abilities we do not in the least believe, and in spite of the shrieks of alarm which we heard on all sides when it was clear that the sceptre was passing from his hands, we have never met with the slightest evidence that the present king is at all less likely than his father to play well the part which destiny has assigned to him. It has been constantly repeated in the English papers that he is in the hands of the ultramontane party. That notion is founded on the simple fact that he was brought up as a Roman Catholic, which of course it was inevitable that he should be. If the first ideas of his youth were not coloured to some extent by the religious views of his instructors, *they* must have been preternaturally inefficient, or *he* must have been singularly wanting in some of those qualities out of which grows the sort of character which is least susceptible of ultramontane influences. Since his early youth he has travelled very widely, and unless we are much misinformed, has travelled with an open mind. Nor in his alliance with an Austrian archduchess do we see anything to fear. Whatever may have been the case while the Archduchess Sophia was still a person of primary importance, it does not appear that the Austrian imperial family of to-day carries its private religious opinions into politics ; and on the only occasion on which the present queen of the Belgians has played any conspicuous part— namely, at the deathbed of her father-in-law—while we thoroughly appreciate the dignified and stoical behaviour of the old king, we think that her conduct, as related by those who had the best means of knowing exactly what passed, was as worthy of her position as Leopold's was of his. Founded it was, no doubt, upon a different theory of life, but one which is held by millions whom it would be absurd to accuse of being under priestly influence, and who have not even the faintest sympathy with that form of Christianity which is generally professed in Belgium.*

We have traced in rapid outline the leading events of the reign of Leopold I. We have now to ask—In what condition did he leave his adopted country? On the whole, we answer, in a very satisfactory one. True it is that her parties are closely balanced, and that the Liberals only hold their own by a moderate majority. But before he began to reign, it was quite doubtful whether the Liberals would be able to make head at all against their opponents. There were, we have seen, many causes at work in producing the breach with Holland, yet of all these causes the most potent was the hatred of the priests against the free-thinking Protestant house of Nassau. For some years after Belgium became independent, the Liberals, as we have seen, were satisfied to maintain the *status quo,* and made no important attempt to improve the institutions of the country. Since 1847 they have generally been in power, and their tone with each successive year becomes more confident.

If we turn from the moral to the material condition of the country, as it was when the old king died, and as it still continues, we see agriculture flourishing; manufactures recovering from the depression of the American war; education in an improved if not yet quite satisfactory state; the tariff, which

---

* The Belgian Protestants are unhappily not numerous. One of them, M. Bost, pastor at Verviers, but belonging, we believe, to a Swiss family, has lately obtained distinction by a work entitled *Le Protestantisme Liberal.*

was till recently extremely illiberal, now one of the best in Europe ; large foreign transactions, carried on indeed almost without a national marine ; Antwerp becoming a second Gibraltar ; an army, burdensome no doubt to the resources of the land, and likely, we hope, to be one day somewhat reduced, but maintained more inexpensively than almost any other ; cheap and easy communication everywhere established by rail and telegraph; deep peace with Holland, undisturbed relations with France, diminished jealousy of England, and general, if languid, goodwill from all the world.

We must supplement these general observations by a few particulars before we say a little about the last point on which we proposed to touch—the near future of Belgium. Not that we need go into any details as to the Belgian constitution, or the general statistics of the country. They may be found in well-known works of reference. The article on Belgium in Block's *Dictionnaire Général de la Politique*, which ought to be oftener found than it is in English libraries, is by M. Heuschling, an eminent statistical authority at Brussels, where statistics are attended to more carefully than in any other capital. Much information about the country is also agreeably summarised in a paper which appeared in the *Quarterly* in 1862 ; and Mr. Barron's reports, especially that of 1864, are most valuable. To these authorities we refer our readers, adding only a few facts taken from sources less easily accessible. The writer in the *Quarterly*, who devotes much space to agriculture, does not seem to have had under his eye the *Essai sur l'Économie rurale*, by M. Émile de Laveleye, which was perhaps not then published, but which is written with all the clearness and vivacity for which the readers of the *Revue des Deux Mondes* so often feel obliged to that clear and well-informed writer, who at present occupies the position of a professor in the university of Liége.

In a linguistic point of view, Belgium consists of two populations, one speaking French or Walloon, and the other speaking Flemish. French is, of course, understood and habitually used by all educated persons in the country, but of late years there has been a very serious Flemish literary revival, an interesting account of which will be found in the *Annuaire des Deux Mondes* for 1851-52. Quite recently attempts have been made to give to this movement a political character, in the interest sometimes of Germany and sometimes of Holland. The impulse in the former direction is purely artificial and without any real importance, but the impulse in the latter direction comes from within, and is the natural reaction against the essentially Walloon revolution of 1830. No political importance could attach to it, unless French schemes of annexation were revived, and Holland would receive most unwillingly any accession to the already troublesome masses of her Catholic subjects. The only Flemish *littérateur* whose name has become known to Europe is the novelist Henri Conscience, but their number would appear to be considerable. The resuscitation of the Walloon, as a literary language, is due to a society whose head-quarters are at Liége, and some poems of considerable merit have recently been published in it ; but, overshadowed by its stronger sister, the "French of Paris," it has no chance of rising out of a subordinate position. So far as French literature is concerned, it cannot be denied that Belgian literary efforts have never shaken off a certain provincial character, and they are most successful in local and provincial history—the very department in which alone there is some

literary activity in French provincial towns. In this department the name of J. B. Nothomb, the first of the two ministers of that name whom we have mentioned, occupies a distinguished place as the author of a valuable essay on the
Belgian revolution; M. Kervyn de Lettenhove, a respected
member of the Clerical party in the House of Representatives,
has written an elaborate history of Flanders; and M. Juste has
laboured upon kindred subjects. M. Gachard, whose name
stands so high for his original researches in the history of the
sixteenth century, was born in France, but has become a
naturalised Belgian, and is archivist of the realm. A writer
of a very different stamp and of a quite opposite order of
merit is M. Laurent, the professor at Ghent, to whom we have
already alluded, and who is so cordially detested by the
clergy; a detestation which it must be admitted he cordially
reciprocates. His *Études sur l'Histoire de l'Humanité* have
been compared to the work of Mr. Buckle, but the Belgian
far exceeds in learning his English rival, although he is perhaps inferior to him in affluence of ideas. The life, by M.
Brialmont, of the Duke of Wellington has made his name
better known in England than those of M. Thonissen and Van
den Peereboom, who have written important works on the
parliamentary history of their country from a Clerical and
Liberal point of view respectively; but the charming *Opuscules*
of M. Van de Weyer, and the useful *Literary History* of M.
Delepierre, have had many readers in this country.

Amongst Belgian economists, the name of M. de Molinari
deserves mention, as well for his importance in his own
land as for his connection with Mr. Cobden, and for his
attempts to extend a knowledge of free-trade principles in
Russia. M. Quetelet, who was at one time the instructor of

the late Prince Consort, and has long been at the head of the Observatory in Brussels, holds a distinguished place, alike as an astronomer and a statistician. Amongst painters, the names of Leys, Gallait, and Verboeckhoven are known to all; and amongst musicians, De Bériot and Vieuxtemps have also a respectable place.

These names, which we might supplement by those of geologists, botanists, and persons fairly distinguished in many other departments of intellectual labour, will show that the kingdom of 1830 has not been idle. Thirty-five years are a very short space in the history of a nation, and we have no doubt that the Belgians will yet do far more than they have done. The generation which made the revolution is only just passing away, and that which first inherited the full benefit of its labours is only coming upon the scene. Political life and the good ordering of social arrangements have occupied hitherto the chief energies of the people. Intelligence and information, rather than genius or learning, have hitherto been characteristic of Belgium. It is the chosen land of lectures and scientific congresses—of associations for the furtherance of all good things.

The paper of the extreme right is the *Bien Public* of Ghent, which upholds the views of the *Monde* and the *Cività Cattolica*, and is written with considerable vigour and ability. The less *acharné* section of the party is represented by the *Journal de Bruxelles* and its satellite the *Émancipation ;* to some extent also by *La Paix*, which is, however, the organ of M. Coomans, who is apt to fight for his own hand, and is more especially devoted to the interest of the Peace party. The governmental section of the Liberal party has for its principal exponent in the press the *Echo du Parlement*, which is understood to be inspired by M. Frère-Orban himself, and the *Journal de Liége*, one of the oldest papers in Belgium, which has been, ever since its foundation a hundred and one years ago, in the family of its present proprietor, M. Desoer. The influence of M. Frère-Orban, who is connected with Liége and with the Desoer family, is very perceptible in its pages also. Further to the left is the *Indépendance*, with which every one is familiar, and which is at present edited by a man of remarkable intelligence, M. Bérardi. The *Indépendance* is, however, more European than strictly Belgian. The most consequent section of the Liberals has an able organ in the *Revue Trimestrielle*; the Clericals a respectable one in the *Revue Générale*, to which Ducpétiaux and other well-known names contribute.

The name of that great statistician reminds us that we have omitted one subject on which a few words may be expected. We shall not be very far wrong in stating the present population, in round numbers, at about 5,000,000.

This is a very dense population for an area which is only equal in size to about one-third of Ireland. From 1840 to 1850 the alarm caused by the amount of pauperism was very great, and during the last three years of that period two out of five amongst the operative classes are said to have received relief, while the whole number of assisted paupers rose during the ten years from 401,000 to 901,000. It is not, then, to be wondered at that in 1848 the government voted a sum of about £20,000 for transporting a body of emigrants to the United States. In 1856, 13,861 emigrated, but in 1860—thanks, we may hope, to the improvement of the times—the number had fallen to 9339. It should not be forgotten that the years from 1847 to 1857 saw the death-struggles of agricultural protection, and that in Belgium, as amongst ourselves, the failure of the potato caused at first an extraordinary amount of distress. More recently the American war inflicted much misery upon the working class in Ghent and other manufacturing towns ; but some of the accounts which then reached England were greatly exaggerated. Pauperism, however, continues, and is likely, we fear, long to continue, a subject of serious anxiety as well to the Belgian as to the Dutch and the English legislature. Unlike this country and Holland, Belgium is, however, very lightly taxed ; the average amount payable by the Belgian citizen to the state being only twenty-six francs, to which three may be added for provincial and communal assessments. The corresponding amount payable by the English citizen is said to be about seventy francs, and that of the French citizen over sixty francs. In Belgium there is no floating debt at all, and the whole of the funded debt might be easily wiped off by the sale of the state railways and canals. These are facts upon which M. Frère-Orban has good reason to congratulate himself, and they are facts which ought not to be lightly disregarded by those who speculate upon Belgium being merged with her own goodwill in the French empire.

We have, it will be observed, spoken throughout of the parties which divide Belgium as Clericals and Liberals. This is the true distinction, and it is one which extends far back into history, and which made itself manifest to all Europe when, during the "Brabantian revolution" against Joseph II., the Clerical revolutionists under Van der Noot, and the Liberal revolutionists, or Vonckists, began to fight to the death long before they had secured their victory over Austria. M. Dechamps, in his careful and very interesting article, which appeared in January 1865 in the *Revue Générale*, expresses the utmost horror at the increasing tendency of Belgian politicians to divide themselves into two camps, according to their religious or philosophical opinions ; but M. Dechamps shows in this, as indeed he does in all his political conduct, that he does not comprehend the world in which he is living. In grouping themselves ever more and more into two great parties, according to their views as to the highest questions which can occupy mankind, Belgian politicians are only yielding to the resistless stream of tendency. M. Dechamps points to England and Holland, but in both these countries, if he will only look closely at them, he would see the stream of tendency flowing in the same direction. We should like to take the distinguished Belgian politician under the gallery of the House of Commons on a "Church Wednesday;" and as for Holland, we think that M. Groen van Prinsterer would enlighten, not to say alarm, him a good deal if he were to ask that stout defender of the faith, how far Holland is free from symptoms like those which he deplores in Belgium.

Those who read M. Dechamps' article—and every one who wants to understand Belgium ought to make a point of reading it—should study as a corrective the admirable paper on the same subject by M. Émile de Laveleye, in the *Revue des Deux Mondes* for 1864. In it we see the hand of a man who does know the world in which he is living, and who, without making to himself any illusions as to the formidable character of Belgian party-strife, has faith in liberty, and believes that the wisdom of the Congress will be justified of her children. Many of our readers will remember the four emblematical figures around the column which commemorates the Congress at Brussels, representing respectively :—

Liberty of Worship,

Liberty of the Press,

Liberty of Instruction,

Liberty of Association.

Belgium enjoys these liberties in more unstinted measure than any European country, our own not excepted; and that she should succeed is of the utmost possible importance to mankind, and above all to that portion of it which does not speak the Anglo-Saxon tongue.

Si vous réussissez (cried the Prince de Broglie to the Belgians), l'épreuve est faite, et tout le monde peut réussir après vous, et la société moderne est sauvée. Mais si vous ne réussissez pas ? Ah ! je ne veux pas prévoir cette hypothèse ! Quand on marche et quand on lutte, il ne faut pas regarder du côté de l'abîme, pour n'être pas pris par le vertige. Tout ce que je sais, c'est que si vous ne réussissez pas par le noble moyen que vous employez, personne ne réussira par aucun autre.

We have no difficulty in admitting that M. Dechamps is in the main correct, and that the active principle, so to speak, in Belgian Liberalism is the same which caused the great revolt of the human mind against the Latin Church, and which brought about the revolution of 1789. Call it the right of private judgment, the *libre-pensée*, or what you will, we will not quarrel about words. M. Dechamps is, however, very unfair in attributing to the present Liberal politicians of Belgium, as represented in actual affairs, the exaggerations or errors of M. Laurent and others whom he names. It would be just as unfair to attribute to M. Dechamps himself, the worst superstitions and the most dishonest aims of those who pull the strings of the Clerical party. We give M. Dechamps the fullest credit for sincerity when he tells us that, in his capacity of Belgian citizen, he accepts the constitution with the same submission with which, in his capacity of Catholic, he accepts the Encyclical of December 1864. It is an astounding feat of intellectual legerdemain. We cannot even conceive how it is done, but that it is done, in perfect good faith, we have not the smallest doubt. Nevertheless, we think that the ideas of M. Dechamps, and of the better class of Belgian Clerical politicians, are no more the active principle of Belgian clericalism than are those of M. de Montalembert the active principle of French clericalism. The active principle is to be found in the ideas of the Encyclical, in the ideas of the *Monde.* The Clerical party of Belgium is really not a conservative but a reactionary party, and only one of two things is possible—either that it should fairly succumb to the opposite opinion, and become a permanent minority, or that it should be strong enough fairly to put down its opponents, and once more to reintroduce the *régime* of the dark ages. M. Dechamps contemplates a third possibility. He points out to the ministry that it is only in the Walloon districts that they are becoming stronger, and that they cannot hope to overpower the Catholics in the Flemish districts. Such a division of parties points directly towards a division of the country, with, say, the Scheldt for a boundary. Cut off between Protestant Holland and an anti-Catholic Walloon country, one would think the faithful would have a bad time of it ; and for other reasons which we shall adduce in the sequel, we have no faith in this solution of the difficulty.

No, the two old enemies—priestcraft and free-thought— must remain in the " Cock-pit of Europe," and fight it fairly out. We trust that we may by this article call the attention of some who have hitherto only thought of Belgium as an uninteresting little secondary state, to the fact that this great battle is being there fought out with ever-deepening earnestness.

Any one who has followed our résumé of the reign of

Leopold will have perceived that the Liberals have since 1830 not only held their own, but considerably improved their position. If this were not so, M. Dechamps would not shriek and protest so loudly. He feels in his heart of hearts that the sceptre is passing away from the power which he reveres, and that his friends, in spite of all declamations, will become a permanent minority. The hour, however, of final triumph for the Liberals will not strike for some time yet; the adversary is still very strong, or M. Laurent would not call for his destruction *per fas et nefas*. The adversary is strong from the ignorance of the masses in the country districts, from the hold which the priests have still over the women in all ranks, from the prejudice which connects in the minds of large classes of the population the old usages of Catholicism with the first principles of morality. He is supported by a large and powerful section of the aristocracy, by great wealth, by the ever-increasing religious associations, by the family diplomacy in arranging marriages and the like, which has been reduced to a science by the Romish clergy in all lands, by an unrivalled organisation, and last, not least, by the many virtues which are bound up with the farrago of superstitions which forms the stock-in-trade of the party. The Liberals, inferior in many points to their opponents, have on their side that one great force which is stronger than all the others put together— the modern spirit, the example of all progressive countries, the nature of things. One weapon which the Clericals are largely using will have to be wrested from them by the strong hand of a parliamentary majority—that is, the power of creating, by evasions of the law, religious institutions which become possessed of vast amounts of property, and are corporations in all but name. At the foundation of such institutions, a strong state may wink, but they are altogether contrary to public policy; and sooner or later, as they become troublesome, experience has shown us that, even in the most Catholic countries, the rough hand of power falls upon them and proclaims that when religion, stepping out of its own sphere, becomes a rival of the powers of the earth, she must expect to meet from them the same treatment which they give to each other. The pamphlet published by M. Dechamps, entitled *La France et l' Allemagne,* which appeared some months after the article to which we have called attention, is a production of very inferior merit, although it excited much more attention beyond the limits of Belgium. The leading idea is the same—that, namely, the dissensions of Belgian parties are dangerous to the independence of the state ; but the sketch of the general politics of Europe, upon which it is founded, betrays a very imperfect knowledge and radically false ideas upon many important points.

A very different and infinitely more valuable *brochure* is that which was published by M. Van de Weyer, under the title of *Richard Cobden, Roi des Belges.* We may regret the altogether too depreciatory tone in which the eminent diplomatist speaks of a man who, if he held, as we think he did, erroneous views, not only with regard to Belgium, but with regard to several other matters of foreign politics, was very far indeed from being an authority *merely* upon free trade. When Mr. Cobden's writings are collected, as we trust they may ere very long be, by some competent hand, his general political reputation will, we suspect, rise considerably, and his body, so to speak, of doctrine, if not exempt from heresy, will be found far more wide-reaching and complete than it is usually thought to be. Putting aside, however, all his reflec-

tions upon Mr. Cobden, and making some allowance for the
irritated national feeling of one who saw what was to some
extent his own work threatened, we think that M. Van de
Weyer's answer is complete. The neutrality of Belgium, to be
good for anything, must be an armed and powerful neutrality,
sufficient to prevent the guaranteeing powers being tempted to
accept the subjugation of Belgium as an accomplished fact.
The personal individual interest of England in the independence of Belgium may easily be over-rated. We doubt whether
the interest of whatever is good in France in the independence
of Belgium can possibly be over-rated. Of course a time may
come when France is perfectly different from what it is now ;
when Chauvinism is as dead as Druidism ; when the revolutionary period has fairly come to an end, and Belgium and
France are separated not by a huge political chasm, but by a
mere imaginary line. The politician has, however, little to do
with such far-off speculations. For the present, and for any
time to which we can look forward, it is of essential importance
to the weal of France herself, that Belgium should go on working out her own problem in her own way.

M. Dechamps' pamphlet and the newspaper discussions to
which it gave rise, did no good. They roused the slumbering
spirit of the annexationist party in France; they excited uneasiness in the minds of many Belgians who, only desiring to
be let alone, would have nevertheless, if they saw annexation
coming, desired to set their house in order and make the best
of it; and they gave occasion to persons on both sides of the
channel to misrepresent the policy of England by declaring
that we should "abandon" Belgium as we "abandoned"
Denmark. Let our English critics and foreign detractors take
comfort. The very men in the House of Commons who would

have strained every nerve to throw out the government which they had supported for years, if it had dared to take one more step in favour of Denmark, and whose intended defection, intimated to Lord Palmerston at a critical moment, did much to prevent that crowning folly, would be the first to urge armed intervention in favour of Belgium, if she were at present threatened. The case of Denmark, in her relations to Schleswig-Holstein in 1864, is closely analogous to that of Holland in its relations to Belgium in 1830. In reading the history of that time, we sympathise nearly as much with Holland as with Belgium ; in living through the events of 1864, we sympathised nearly as much with Denmark as with Germany; but sympathy and antipathy have no right to govern political action. Taking a broad view of the question of 1830, it was right to throw the influence of England into the scale of Belgium ; taking a broad view of the question of 1864, it would have been right to throw the influence of England into the scale of the Diet, thus obtaining far better terms for Denmark, and taking away from the Prussian government the temptation to play before high Heaven those pranks in which it has lately been indulging itself.

Conscious of no jealousy towards France, but desirous on the other hand of seeing her increasingly prosperous, free, and powerful—nay even content to see her, if she once more returns to a parliamentary system of government, taking the *pas* of us in Europe, while we fall back upon our unquestioned cosmopolitan hegemony—we should nevertheless rather incur the great calamity of a war with her, than allow her to annex Belgium by force or fraud. If, on the other hand, it could be proved that Belgium ardently desired to be united to France, we should not think ourselves justified in attempting to forbid the banns. As we have already hinted, we think it not in the least improbable that our children's children may live to see that day arrive.

It is true, no doubt, that as long as France is under an absolute government, not Belgium only, but every state in this part of Europe is continually in danger, for a fit of ill-temper on the part of the occupant of the Tuilleries may at any moment put an end to the general peace. This state of things is, however, we all trust and believe, only temporary, and it is only simple justice to the emperor of the French to say that we do not believe that he has the remotest intention or desire to interfere with his northern neighbour. He might be driven to attempt to annex Belgium, as he might be driven to attack England or Germany, but it would only be, as long as he continued in his sane mind, if he saw that the popular desire in France for such an enterprise was so great as to make him tremble for his own position if he did not yield to it. Every year that has passed over us since 1858 has made his personal position stronger and has diminished the influence of the "old parties," although it has fortunately not diminished the desire on the part of the best minds in the nation for free institutions. That there is a large class in France which would hail with delight an attack upon Belgium we do not doubt. We know but too well by how many the most hazardous and unprovoked attack upon England would be hailed with satisfaction ; but for the opinions of the most intelligent French politicians, on this subject, we would refer the reader to the admirable remarks of M. Forcade, in the *Revue des Deux Mondes* of the 15th of December 1865. If a free government is once more re-established in France, these are the views which we should expect to prevail in a majority of the legislative body ;

and as long as the existing system lasts, we trust to the good sense of the Emperor, to his wide knowledge of European politics, as well as to his love of ease and his desire to keep his dynasty on the throne of France. If the malignant mischief-making of Count Bismark, the unwisdom of the Austrian government, or the madness of the Italian people, should plunge Europe into war, it is far from improbable that his "complete liberty of action" will be used ere that war ends for the aggrandisement of France, but nothing seems less probable than that he should meddle with Belgium.

INDEX.

ABERDEEN, Lord, 335
Administration of Spain, 30 *et seq.*
Adrianople, treaty of, 145
Africa, places on northern and western coasts of, belonging to Spain, 28
Agricultural serfs of Russia, division of, into two great classes, 80
Aksakoff, M., a Russian journalist, 110, 117
Albaida, Marquis of. *See* Orense
Alcalá, the famous university of, 51
Alcaldes (mayors), Spanish, 30, 32, 33
Alexander I. of Russia, 66, 79 ; unfortunate policy into which he was led, 67 ; the Holy Alliance, 67-69 ; the Poles, 88
Alexander II., his accession to the throne, 71 ; results since achieved, 131, 132. *See* Russia
Alicante, 35
Altenstein, a Prussian statesman, 203.
Amador de los Rios, a Spanish author, 49
Amat, Rico y, his work on Spain, 3
American war, effect of, in Belgium, 362, 368
Amsterdam, Athenæum at, 327
Andalusia, attempts at colonisation in, 38
Anglican and Eastern Churches, union of, 101
Angoulême, Duc d', 5
Anhalt-Bernburg, 266
Anhalt-Cöthen, 266
Anhalt-Dessau, dukedom of, 267, 274.
Annabon, an island in the Gulf of Guinea, subject to Spain, 28
Annexationist party in France, 354, 374
Annuaire des Deux Mondes, valuable articles on Spain in the, 4
Antwerp, 353 ; citadel of, surrendered by Chassé to the French, 335 ; "convention" of, 345
Araktcheïeff, a favourite of Alexander I., 67
Aranjuez, 19

Arguëlles, a Spanish statesman, 8
Aristocracy in Prussia, 244
Armero, General, 21
Arminius, 298
Army of Spain, 43 ; of Prussia, 227, 243 ; of the Germanic Confederation, 270
Arndt, Ernst Moritz, a German professor, 262
Arnold, Matthew, 321
Arragon, 9 ; Carlist rising in, 19
Art and music of the Russian Church, 97
Asia, Russian aggrandisement in, 102, 103
Assis, Don Francisco de, husband of Isabella II. of Spain, 16
Athenæums, Dutch, 327
Attaché at Madrid, a work on Spain, professedly from the diary of a German diplomatist, 3, 33
Attorney, the Spanish, 31, *et seq.*
Auersperg, Count (Anastasius Grün), 159
Auerswald, a Prussian statesman, 208 ; becomes a member of the Hohenzollern cabinet, 224
Austria, modern history of, 135 ; recent writers upon, 136 ; Joseph II., his plans of reform, and the forces opposed to them, 136-138 ; regard for traditional rights in Hungary, 138 ; Leopold II. and his policy, 139 ; the *inactionary* SYSTEM, 140 ; the two dominating men during this state of things : the Emperor Francis and Prince Metternich, 140-144 ; the Greek insurrection of 1821 and the policy of Metternich—its influence on Hungary, 144-149 ; the Polish struggle of 1831, 148, 149 ; the triumvirate under Ferdinand, 150-152 ; course of events in Hungary from 1836 to 1848, 153-158 ; Croatia, 155 ; the nobles and the SYSTEM, 159 ; seizure of Cracow, and the Galician massacres, 160,

161 ; effects of the February revolution in Paris, 162 ; flight of Metternich, 163 ; Kossuth, 158, 163 ; the revolutionary period of 1848-49, 164-166 ; the reaction,—Schwartzenberg, 166 ; Bach and his system, 167-170 ; unpopularity of Austria at this time in France and England, 170 ; influence of the Russian war on her internal politics ; fall of M. Bach, 172, 173 ; system inaugurated by the October Diploma (of 1860), 174, 175 ; session of the "strengthened Council of the Empire," 175, 176 ; Bach's successor, M. Schmerling, 177 ; his policy and administration, 178-182, 185 ; the manifesto of September 1865 announcing the overthrow of the Schmerling policy, and its results, 186-189 ; difficulties with which Austria has to contend, 189-193 ; the commercial treaty with England, 191-193 ; the question of Venetia, 194 ; relations to Germany, 195, 196 ; to Turkey, 197 ; the Polish question, 197, 198 ; Austria's future, 199, 200

Ayacuchos, an epithet given to Espartero's party, 12

Ayuntamientos, Spanish, 32

BACH, Alexander, an Austrian statesman, 167 ; the Bach system, 168-170 ; fall of, 172, 173

Baden, Grand-duchy of, 267, 273

Bader, a German philosopher, 67

Balearic Isles, 22, 28

Balmez, 52

Baltic provinces of Russia, serfs of the, 81, 83

Banking, Spanish, 37

Barca, Calderon de la, 17

Barcelona rises in rebellion, 10 ; democratic agitations at, 12 ; university of, 52

Barzanallana, M., a Spanish statesman, 27, 40

Batavian Republic, proclamation of, 292

Batthyani, Count Louis, president of the Hungarian ministry in 1848, 184

Bavaria, 253, 271 ; Louis of, 246, 271

Baur, Ferdinand Christian, founder of the new Tübingen school of theology, 271, 283

Beasain, 1.

Bekker, Balthasar, 299

Belcredi, Count, Austrian Minister of Interior, 185

Belgian press, transgressions of, brought before the Congress of Paris by Count Walewski, 347

Belgium: united with Holland by the Congress of Vienna (1815), 332 ; grievances of the Belgians arising from this union, 333 ; the "four glorious days" of September 1830, and formation of a provisional government, 334 ; the revolutionary war, 335 ; inauguration of the king, Leopold I., 336 ; settlement with Holland, 337 ; attention turned to internal questions, 337 ; ministry of De Theux overthrown, 338 ; ministry of Rogier, Nothomb, and Van de Weyer, 339 ; De Theux again in power, and again succeeded by Rogier, 340 ; M. Frère-Orban, 340, 341 ; ministerial programme, 341 ; effect of the news of the February revolution (1848) of Paris, 342 ; liberal reforms, 343 ; dissensions on educational questions, 343, 344 ; dissolution of the Senate ; Rogier succeeded by De Brouckere, 345, and he by a moderate clerical government—Charles Vicomte Vilain xiiii., 345, 346, and Pierre de Decker, 346, 347 ; the Belgian press censured by the plenipotentiaries in the Congress of Paris, 347, 348 ; the crisis of 1857, 348-350 ; letter of the king, 350, 351 ; the ministry resign, 351, and Rogier is recalled, 352 ; party struggles, 353 ; effect on the Belgians of the cession of Savoy and Nice to France, 354 ; commercial treaty with France ; debate on the recognition of Italy ; question of the fortifications of Antwerp, 355, 356 ; commercial treaty with England, 356 ; fiscal improvements, 357 ; ministerial interregnum, 357, 358 ; M. Dechamps, 358, and his programme, 359 ; dissolution of the House of Representatives, and the return of a Liberal majority, 359 ; the Encyclical of December 1864, and the controversies it raised, 360 ; death of Leopold, 360 ; his character, 361 ; condition in which he left his adopted country, 362 ; recent works on Belgium, 363 ; the French (Walloon) and Flemish dialects, 364 ; contemporary literature, 365 ; names distinguished in other departments of intellectual labour, 365, 366 ; journalism, 366, 367 ; population and pauperism, 367 ; parties in Belgium, Clericals and Liberals, 368-374 ; France and Belgium, 374-376 ; the future, 377

Belgium and Holland, attempts to weld into one state, 293

Benedek, Ludwig von, an Austrian general, 160

Benevolent foundations of Belgium, 345, 349

Bergasse, 67

Berlin, on the receipt of the news of the February revolution in Paris, 206; state of siege proclaimed, 210; municipality of, remonstrates against Bismark's proceedings with regard to the press, 237

Bermudez, Zea, 6

Bernard, Dr., 4

Bernstorff, M., a Prussian statesman, 231, 233; his proposals for the reform of the Germanic Confederation, 279

Bethmann-Hollweg, M., a Prussian professor, and member of the Hohenzollern cabinet, 223

Beust, M. von, Saxon minister in the Germanic Diet, 272, 279

Bibikoff, General, of Russia, 81

Bidassoa, the, 1, 5

Bilbao pronounces for Don Carlos as pretender in Spain, 5

Bilderdyk, a Dutch poet, 301

Bismark, Count, 167, 233-235, 377; his proceedings with regard to the press, 237; treatment of Liberal demands, 238; the Schleswig-Holstein question, 238, 239; his offensive attitude towards Parliament, 239; the Danish war, 240; the reaction brought about by him, 249; his proposals for the reform of the Germanic Confederation, 281

Blaser, Spanish General, 17

Bludoff, Count, 81

Bockum-Dolffs' party in Prussia, 232, 238

Bohemia, influence of the Polish struggle of 1831 on the public mind there, 148, 158

Bondholders, Spanish, 41

Boner's "Transylvania" referred to, 133, 135, 180, 190

Bonin, General von, 224

Books on Spain, 2; on Poland, 92, 93; on Russia, 115-117; on Holland, 291; on Belgium, 373

Borrow, Mr., author of Bible in Spain, 7, 33, 50; his expedition a perfect failure, 57

Bost, M., a Belgian preacher, 362

Brandenburg, Count, 209, 212

Bravo, Gonsalez, a Spanish statesman, 14, 25, 29

Brenier, Baron, 266

British interest in the regeneration of Spain, 64

Brouckere, Henri de, government of, in Belgium, 345, 351

Bruck, an Austrian cabinet minister, 171, 173, 217

Brunswick, 267, 272

Brussels, Belgian revolution of 1830 commenced at, 334; Liberal university of, 337, 348; Liberal gathering in, 340, 342

Bryce, James, B.A. of Oxford, on the Holy Roman Empire, 253

Buckle, Mr. Henry T., his opinion of Spain and the Spaniards, 1, 2, 28, 59

Buda and Pesth, proposal to unite by a chain-bridge, 153

Bull-fight, the, in Spain, 62

CABALLERO, Fernan, 50

Cadiz, Constitution of, 4, 5

Calderon, 59

Calvinism in Holland, 298

Camphausen, "transition" ministry of, 209

Canary Islands, 28

Carcel del Corte, the, in Madrid, 33

Carlists of Spain, 46, 47

Carlos (Don), his pretensions to the Spanish throne, 5; the interests he represented, 6

Carlowitz, M., a Prussian Liberal, 235

Carlsbad, Congress of, 259

Cartesian philosophy, influence of, on Dutch theology, 299

Castelar, Emilio, of the university of Madrid, 26, 47

Catherine II. and Russian serfdom, 80; commission called by her, 111

Chambers, William, 321

Chamiakoff, a Russian poet, 101, 106

Charles III. of Spain, 43, 49

Charles IV., 48

Charles, Archduke of Austria, and brother of Francis I., 140

Charras, Colonel, his expulsion from Belgium, 345

Chassé, General, surrendered the citadel of Antwerp to the French, 335

Cheremetieff, the Russian family of, 81

Chokier, M. Surlet de, regent in Belgium in 1831, 334

Christina of Spain: her proceedings as regent during the minority of her daughter Isabella II., 6; yields to the mutineers of La Granja, 8; at Barcelona, 10; resigns the regency, 11; military revolt in 1841 in her

interest, 12 ; her quarrel with Narvaez, 17
Church, the Russian, 95-102 ; its clergy of high rank and its ordinary priests to be distinguished, 98 ; the Dissidents, 99, 100 ; idea of union between the Eastern Church and the Anglican communion talked of by Russian priests, 101
Circassia, 109.
Civil wars of Spain, 42
Clarke's (Dr.) travels in Russia, 65, 73
Clergy of the Russian Church, 97, 98
Clerical and Liberal parties in Belgium, and their contests, 336 et seq., 368-374
Clerical interference with education in Belgium, 343, 345, 348
Club, Milani, the, 217
Cobden, Richard, 365, 373, 374
Coburg and Gotha, twin duchies of, 277
Cocceius, Johannes, theological professor at Leyden, 299
Collin, General, 160
Colonies of Spain, 28, 44-46, 62, 63
Cologne banquet, stopping of the, 241
Colonial empire of Holland, 330, 331
Comines, Philip de, 101
Commerce, Spanish, 38
Commercial treaty between England and Austria, 191-193 ; between Belgium and France (1861), 355 ; between Belgium and England (1862), 356
Communes in Belgium, law of the, 337, 339, 350
Commune in Russia, or "the Mir," 77 et seq.
Concordat with Spain of 1852, 17 ; of 1860, 24 ; with Austria in 1855, 168
Confederation of the Rhine, 253-255
Congresses, European, 68, 171, 258, 259
Conscience, Henri, a Flemish novelist, 364
Constantine, Grand-duke, of Russia, 81, 109
Constantinople, have we reason to fear Russian designs upon ? 104
Constituent Cortes of 1837 in Spain, 8 ; of 1840, 10 ; of 1854, 18, 19 ; of 1855 —debate on religious toleration, 56
Constitutionalists, Spanish, 46, 47
Constitutional question, the, in Prussia, 235-242
Constitution (Spanish) of Cadiz, 4 ; the Estatuto Real, 6 ; that of 1837, 8 ; of 1845, 15 ; the constitution now in force, 29

"Convention" of Vergara, 9 ; of Gastein, 214 ; of Antwerp, 345
Convention (secret) of Prussia with Russia, 236
Cortes of Cadiz, its constitution of 1812, 4 ; overthrown by Ferdinand VII. in 1814, 5
Cortes, Donoso,—De Mazade's article on, in the Revue des Deux Mondes, 4
Cossacks, the, of Russia, 72, 73, 83
Coup d'état of 2d December 1851 in Paris, 213
Courses in Dutch universities, 329
Cousin, Victor, 321, 327
Cracow, seizure of, by Austria, in 1846, 161
Crimean war, 70, 71 ; results of, in Russia, 107, 131 ; attitude of Austria during, 171-173 ; Prussia, during preceding negotiations, 214, 217
Criminal law in Spain, 31 et seq.
Croatia, 155
Cuba, 27 ; filibustering expeditions to, 44 ; slavery in, 45
Cumberland, Duke of, King of Hanover, 263, 272
Cuvier, 321, 327
Czartoryski, Prince Adam, 88
Czechs, the, of Prague, 155 ; recent agitation amongst them, 200

Da Costa, M., a Dutch theologian, 302
Dalberg, duke of, 254
Danish war, the, 238-240, 250, 286-288, 374, 375
Deak, Francis, an eminent Hungarian patriot, 181, 184
Death, punishment of, in Spain, 31
Dechamps, M., leader of a section of Belgian Catholics, 358 ; "programme" of his policy, 359 ; his political pamphlets after being defeated when candidate for Charleroi, 368 et seq.
De Decker, an eminent Belgian politician, 345-348, 351
Delfosse, M., a Belgian politician, 342
Democratic party in Spain, 47 ; democratic organisation in Russia, 113
Denmark, 238, 250
De Theux, ministry of, in Belgium, 337 et seq.
Devaux, M., important article by, in the Revue Nationale, 338
Deventer Athenæum, 327
De Wette, 318
Diet (Bundes-Versammlung) of Germany, why so called, 267 ; legislative and executive powers of the Confederation vested in, 267 ; constitu-

tion of, 268 ; summary of what is within the competence of, 268, 269

Diet of Frankfort, 258 ; its hostile sections, 261 ; resigns its powers to Archduke John of Austria as Vicar of the Empire, 261 ; transfers its sittings to Stuttgardt, 262

Disaffection in Belgium during the union with Holland, 333

Dissidents, the, in Russia, 99 ; their divisions and subdivisions, 100

Doblado's *Letters* on the religious state of Spain, 54

Dolgoroukoff, Prince, 81, 110.

Don, Cossacks of the, 73

Dort, Synod of, 298

Douro, river, 39

Dresden Conferences, 266

Drought, next to misgovernment, the great curse of Spain, 38

Dulce, Spanish general, 17

Dunes of Holland, 289

Düppel, 240

Dutch and English Society, few links of connection between, 291

Dutch Reformed Church, 306 *et seq. ;* reply of its General Synod to the request of some zealots, 319, 320

EAST PRUSSIA, states of, 203

Ebro, river, 39.

Ecclesiastical system in Holland, 298

Echo de la Presse Russe, 124, 125 ; passage quoted from, on the foreign politics of Russia, 108

Education in Spain, 48-54 ; in Russia, 118, 119 ; in Prussia, 221 ; in the Netherlands, 297, 321 :—schools, 322-327 ; universities, 327-330

Edwards, Mr. Sutherland, on the Polish insurrection, 92 ; music in the Russian Church, 97 ; his "Russians at home," 116, 117

Eichhorn, unpopularity of his appointment as Minister of Public Instruction in Prussia, 203, 204

Emancipation of serfs in Russia, 81 ; state of feeling prevalent between the announcement of the intention of Government and the production of its plan, 82 ; the extent of emancipation, and proclamation of enfranchisement, 83 ; actual and probable results, 86, 87

Ende, M. Van den, author of the law as to the primary schools of Holland, 322

English ideas about Russia, 65, 66 ; are our interests in Asia likely to clash? 102, 103 ; misapprehension

by English journalists of the situation in Prussia, 242, 286-288 ; the English press misled as to the real position and tendencies of Belgium in 1864 by the writings of M. Dechamps, 360

Enzinas family in Spain, 58

Eötvös, Baron Joseph, leader of a Hungarian party, 157 ; his "Village Notary," 180 ; his pamphlet *Die Nationalitäten-Frage*, 193

Erasmus, 298

Erfurt Parliament, 232, 235, 264

Ernest Augustus, Duke of Cumberland and King of Hanover, 263, 272

Ernest II., Duke of Coburg and Gotha, brother of Albert, Prince Consort of the Queen of Great Britain, 277-279

Escosura, a Spanish politician, 20

Escribano (notary), the Spanish, 31, 32

Espartero, Spanish commander-in-chief, 9 ; becomes regent, 11 ; his government attacked, 12 ; its fall, 13 ; sailed for England, 13 ; again in power, 18-20 ; his property near Logroño, 38

Esquiros, Alphonse, his work on Holland, 291, 329

Estatuto Real, the, a constitution promulgated by Christina of Spain, 6

Esterhazy, Count Maurice, an Austrian statesman, 185

Exports, Spanish, 38

FEBRUARY 1848, events of, 16, 162, 206, 260, 293, 297, 341

Federal Act, the, by which the Germanic Confederation is created, — stages through which it passed, 257, 258

Ferdinand VII. of Spain, 5, 63.

Feudal party, and its leaders, in Prussia, 214 *et seq.*, 243-245

"Filioque," feud of the, 95

Final Act of the Germanic Confederation, 259

Finance, Spanish, ministry of, 39-42 ; financial disorder in Russia, 109

Finland, 108

Fire insurance in Spain, 37

Fires in Russia, in 1864, and the causes to which they are attributable, 122, 123

Fiume, an Adriatic port, 155

Flaquer, Mañe y, a Spanish journalist, 47

Flottwell, a Prussian statesman, 224.

Fomento (Public Welfare), department of, in Spain, 34-39

Forcade, M., a French writer, on the Prussian situation, 245, 376

Ford's *Handbook for Spain*, 5, 29, 33, 38, 62

Foreign Affairs, Spanish Minister of— the policy he should follow, 46

Foreign politics of Russia, 107, 108

Fortresses, great, of Germany, 270

Fortschritts Partei of Prussia, its principal aims, 228, 229, 231 ; address embodying the demands of the Liberal party, 237, 238

France and Belgium, 374-376

Francis I. of Austria, as a man and a ruler, 141, 142

Francis Joseph, emperor of Austria, and his advisers, 166, 246

Frankfort Parliament of 1848, 212 ; the Diet, 258, 268 *et seq.*

Fraser, article in, on Spain, quoted, 28, 48 ; article on Circassia, 109

Free-trade party in Russia, 109

Frederick William III. of Prussia, 202

Frederick William IV. of Prussia, 201 ; popular acts at the opening of his reign, 202, 203 ; desirous of a change in the constitution of the Germanic Confederation, 260 ; offered the crown of the resuscitated German Empire, but declines, 262 ; humiliation, 207 ; goes to Warsaw to meet Nicholas, 213 ; his illness, 221 ; regency of his brother, the Prince of Prussia, and changes in policy, 221-225

Frederick William, Crown-Prince of Prussia, 247

Frederick VII. of Denmark, his death gives a formidable turn to the Schleswig-Holstein question, 238

Frederick the Great, 248

French books reprinted in Brussels, controversy between France and Belgium regarding, 345

French government, assistance of, to Christina of Spain, 12

Frère-Orban, an eminent Belgian statesman, 340, 341, 344, 368

Freytag, M., on the Thirty Years' War, 248

Future of Russia, 119-122 ; of Austria, 199, 200 ; of Prussia, 247-251 ; of Belgium, 377

GAGERN, Heinrich von, a German statesman, 261, 276 ; his father, 255

Gai, Louis, a journalist in Croatia, 155

Galiano, a Spanish statesman, 7

Galicia, massacres in, 160, 161

Gansfoort, Wessel, of Groningen, 298

Garcia, Sergeant, 8

Garibaldi at Marsala, 173

Garrido, Fernando, his work on Spain, 3, 4, 31, 38, 44, 45

Gastein, convention of, 241

George Victor, Prince of Waldeck, 274

Gerlach, the President von, a leader of the Feudalists in Prussia, 215 *et seq.*

" German party of Progress," the, 228

German question, the, in Austria, 170, 195, 197 ; in Prussia, 212, 249

German unity, problem of, 282-286

Germanic Diet, the ; desirability of its disruption, 248, 249 ; political organisation of, 252 ; Confederation of the Rhine, 253 ; disintegration of Germany consequent on the breaking-up of the Confederation, 254 ; negotiations of 1814, 255, 256 ; the Federal Act : various stages through which it passed, 257 ; its chief stipulations, 258 ; the Final Act, 259 ; ministerial conferences at Vienna in 1834 consequent on the revolutionary agitation which had been called forth by the fall of the elder branch of the Bourbons, 260 ; the Frankfort parliament of 1848, and its hostile sections, 261 ; Frederick William of Prussia is offered the crown of the resuscitated German Empire, but declines it, 262 ; the " Union," 263 ; the reaction, 263, 264 ; the crisis of 1850, 265 ; states included in the Confederation, 267 ; the Diet and its assemblies, 268 ; summary of what is within the competence of the Diet, 268, 269 ; its departmental committees, funds, army, etc., 270 ; extent and population of the various states, 270, 271 ; remarks on the political life of some of these, in their individual capacity :—Bavaria, Würtemberg, Saxony, 271 ; Hanover, Brunswick, Weimar, 272 ; Hesse-Darmstadt, Hesse-Cassel, Baden, the two Mecklenburgs, Oldenburg, 273 ; Anhalt-Dessau, Schwarzburg-Sondershausen and Schwarzburg - Rudolstadt, Lichtenstein and Waldeck, 274 ; Reuss-Greitz and Reuss-Schleitz, Lippe - Detmold, Schaumburg - Lippe, Schleswig - Holstein, Luxemburg and Limburg, 275 ; Robert von Mohl, 273-276 ; plans suggested for the reconstruction of the Confederation, 276-281 ; Count Bismark's proposals, 281 ; objections to the Grossdeutsche idea, 282 ; difference in various respects between Northern and Southern Germany, 282 ; problem of German unity, 283-286 ; the Schleswig-Holstein imbroglio, 286-288

Germany, difference between Northern and Southern, 282, 283
Ghent, state university of, 348
Gibraltar, British possession of, 63
Gneist, Dr., 241
Gobernacion (Minister of). *See* Interior
Goblet, General, cited, 335, 336
Godunoff, Boris, a Russian usurper, 80
Goluchowski, Count, of Austria, 172, 175
Gomarus, a Dutch theologian, 298
Gomez, the famous Carlist leader, 9, 25
Gotha despatch of Lord Russell, 234
Gotha, party of, supporters of the "Union," 263
Grabow, M., a Prussian Liberal, 230, 235, 238 ; his speech at the opening of the session of 1865, 246
Granja (La), mutiny of, 7, 9
Greek Church, the, 96
Greek insurrection in 1821, and Metternich's policy, 144, 145
Gregory XVI., Pope, encyclical letter of, and its effects on parties in Belgium, in 1832, 336
Groen (van Prinsterer), M., an eminent statesman and historian in Holland, 303 *et seq.*, 323 *et seq.*, 369
Groningen school of theology, 307-309
Groningen, university of, 327
Groot, Hofstede de, a Dutch professor, 307, 308, 325
Grotius, 299
Grün, Anastasius (Count Auersperg), 159
Guardia Civil, the, 33

HAGUE, the, 333
Hallischen Jahrbücher, the, 4
Hanover, 267, 272 ; king of, 263
Hansemann cabinet in Prussia, 209
Harbours, Spanish, 41
Hardenberg, Karl August, a Prussian statesman, 256 *et seq.*
Harkort, M., and the section of the party of progress known as the Fraction Harkort, 230
Havel, marshes of the, 201
Haxthausen, a writer on Russia, referred to, 65, 72, 78, 106
Haynau, General, 176
Hayward, Mr., 212
Heidelberg, the Vorparlaament of, 260, 261
Hengstenberg, E. W., a German theologian, 204, 224
"Herrenhaus," 218, 244
Herzen, M., a writer on Russia, quoted and referred to, 78, 79, 102

Hesse-Cassel, or Electoral Hesse, misgovernment of, 265, 267, 273
Hesse-Darmstadt, 267, 273
Hesse-Homburg, 267
Heydt, Von der, a Prussian statesman, 224, 231, 233, 238
Hinckeldey, director-general of police in Prussia, 219
"Historical" school of publicists and of jurists in Prussia, 204
Hohenlohe, Prince, 231
Hohenzollerns, the two, Hechingen and Sigmaringen, 267
Hohenzollern, Prince of, and his cabinet, 222-225
Holland as described by Pliny, 289 ; changes since his time, 290 ; books on, 291 ; earlier and more recent history, 292, 293 ; rapid political advance since 1848, 293-297 ; ecclesiastical system, 298-320 ; schools of theology, 306-315 ; education : schools, 321-327 ; universities, 327-330 ; her colonial empire, 330, 331
Hollweg, M., 223. *See* Bethmann-Hollweg
Holstein, people of, 287. *See* Schleswig-Holstein
Holy Alliance, the, 67 *et seq.*, 145, 259
Holy Roman Empire, 252, 254
Horner, Leonard, 321
House of Commons, British, debates on Poland, 95
Hübner, M. de, Austrian Minister of Police, 172
Huet, M. Busken, a Dutch theologian, 313, 314
Humboldt, Alexander von, 202, 247
Humboldt, William von, 255
Hungary, books on, 134-136 ; changes introduced by Joseph II. 137, 138 ; influence of the Greek revolution of 1820, 146-148 ; and of Polish insurrection of 1831, 148, 149 ; debates in the Diet 1832-1836, 152, 158 ; course of events down to 1848, 153-158 ; Hungarian parties, 157, 158 ; Kossuth, 158, 163, 172 ; the laws of 1848, 163, 164 ; Bach and the Hungarian magnates, 172 ; Vay, the leader of the Hungarian Protestants, summoned to Vienna, 176 ; policy of Schmerling, 177 *et seq. ;* Diet of 1861, 178 ; resistance to Austrian policy from the dissolution of the Diet till the Patent of September 1865, 180 ; the "Old Conservatives," 181 ; programme of the Liberals, 182 ; the letters from

Pesth, and the chief points laid down in them, 182-184

Hymans, M., cited on provisional government in Belgium in 1831, 334, 336

INDUSTRIES of Spain, 38

Interior (ministry of), in Spain, 32 *et seq.*

Isabella II. of Spain, her accession to the throne, 5 ; pretensions of Don Carlos, 5-9 ; her marriage, 16 ; discussion of the question in the Cortes as to whether she was to be kept on the throne, 19 ; makes over to the nation the patrimony of the Crown, 26 ; extent of her dominion, 28

Isturiz, a Spanish statesman, 7, 21

Italian war of 1859, the impulse given to national feeling in Prussia by, 228

Italy, kingdom of, recognised by Spain, 27 ; by Prussia, 232 ; debate on, in the Belgian Chambers, 355, 356

JACOBY, Dr., of Königsberg, prosecuted on account of a pamphlet, 204, 208

Jagow, M. von, a Prussian statesman, 231

Jemappes, outbreak in the commune of, 350

Jews in Germany, 258

John, Archduke, of Austria, elected Vicar of the empire, 261

Jonas, M., a Prussian Protestant preacher, 209

Joseph II. of Austria ; his plans of reform and the forces opposed to them, 136, 137; his policy in Hungary, 138

Journalism in Spain, 47, 48 ; in Russia, 115-117, 124, 125 ; in Prussia, 237 ; in Belgium, 366, 367

Junkers, or Feudal party, in Prussia, 226, 243 *et seq.*

KALTENBORN, an authority on the constitution and history of the Confederation of the Rhine, 253

Kant, Immanuel, 224

Karamsine, N. M., the Russian historian, 110

Katkoff, a Russian journalist, 116, 123, 125

Kisseleff, Count, 81

Klaczko, M., his article on Poland, 198

Klebelsberg, an Austrian statesman, 149

Kleist-Retzow, a Prussian Feudalist, 226

Koloomzine, M., on Russian universities, 117, 118

Kolowrat, Count, a member of the triumvirate in Austria under Ferdinand, 150, 151

Kossuth, 153 ; his memorable words in March 1848, and their results, 158, 163 ; in the Italian campaign of 1859, 172

Kremlin, the, at Moscow, 96

Kremsier, Austrian National Assembly removed to, during the revolutionary period of 1848-49, 165

Kreuz-Zeitung party in Prussia, 214 *et seq.*, 221, 238 ; its principles dominant in Mecklenburg, 244, 245

Krüdener, Madame de, 66 *et seq.*

Kutusoff, Russian field-marshal, 254

LAFUENTE's history of Spain, 49

Lamennais, 358

Lampe, Professor at Utrecht, 299, 300

Land-question in Poland, 126-130

Lands belonging to Spanish clergy, sale of—its effect on the material revival of Spain, 35 ; waste lands, 38

Larisch, Count, an Austrian statesmen, 185

Larra, inscription suggested by, to be over the gate of the Madrid Exchange, 39

Larra, De Mazade's article on, in the *Revue des Deux Mondes*, 4

Laurent, Professor, a Belgian writer, 348, 370

Laveleye, M. de, cited, 323

Law, Russian, 115

"League of the Three Kings," 262-264

Leiningen, Count, his mission to Constantinople, 170

Leitha, the, 158, 175

Leon, General, 12

Leopold I., chosen king of the Belgians, 335 ; letter of, illustrative of his moderating influence over party disputes, 350 ; his death, 360 ; his character, and secret of his success, 360, 361

Leopold II. of Belgium, 361

Leopold II. of Austria, 139

Lerida, 31

Lewis, Sir George, 295

Leyden school of theology, 310, 311

Leyden, university of, 327

Leyen, Prince von der, 253

Liberalism in Russia, 109-112; in Prussia, 228-230, 249

Lichtenstein, principality of, 267, 274

Liège, state university at, 337

Lighthouses, Spanish, 41

Ligne, Prince de, 344

Lippe-Detmold, principality of, 267, 275

Literature of Spain, 47-52; of Russia, 115-117 ; of Belgium, 364 et seq.
Llorente, M., a Spanish statesman, 26
"Loi des Couvents," a bill in the Belgian Chambers so called, 349
·Loja, socialist rising at, 23
Lopez, ministry of, 13
Louis, Archduke, of Austria, 150, 151
Louis Bonaparte, king of Holland, 301
Louis Napoleon, 170
Louis of Bavaria, 246, 271
Louis Philippe, 32 ; his fall and flight, 206 ; letter to Leopold on the political gathering at Brussels, 340, 342
Louvain, Catholic university at, 337
Lübeck, 267
Lucena, Count of. See O'Donnell
Luchana, Count of. See Espartero
Lunatic asylums of Spain, 33
Lutherans in Holland, 316, 317
Luxemburg and Limburg, 267, 275, 276 ; transferred from Belgium to Holland, 337

MAAGER, M., 174
Madoz, Don Pascual, a Spanish statesman and statistician, 23, 49
Madrid, university of, 51-53
Magdeburg, 201
Magyars, the, 154 et seq. See Hungary
Majláth, George von, chancellor of Hungary, 185.
Malaga, 23
Malines, Catholic university at, transferred to Louvain, 337
Mancha (La), 9
Mann, Horace, on education in Prussia, 220
Manteuffel, Freiherr Otto von, ministry of, 210 et seq., 221, 222.
Manufactures, Spanish, 38
Margall, Pi y, a Spanish journalist, 47
Maria Theresa, 165
Maroto, a lieutenant of Don Carlos, 9
Marsh's Man and Nature quoted, 93
Matamoros, and the religious movement in Spain to which his name is attached, 57
Material revival in Spain, progress of, and field for, 34-39.
Matthiæ, 223
Maurice of Nassau, 298
Maximilian, king of Bavaria, 232
Mazade, M. C. de, papers on Spain and Russia in the Revue des Deux Mondes, 4, 27, 125
Mecklenburg-Schwerin, the worst governed district in Germany, 244, 245, 273

Mecklenburg-Strelitz, 267, 273
Mendizabal, ministry of, in Spain, 7
Mennonites in Holland, 316, 317
Metternich, Prince, 67 et seq., 140 ; his baneful influence on the foreign policy of Austria, 143, 144 ; takes part in the negotiations of 1814 as to the Germanic Confederation, 257 ; misapprehended by the mob of Vienna in 1848, 150 ; his opposition to all reform, 151 ; flight of, 163
Military question, the, in Prussia, 226, 231
Mill, John Stuart, 295, 315
Milutine, M., his pamphlet on the emancipation of the Russian serfs, 83-85, 94, 127
Ministerio del relampago, the, 16
Ministry, the Spanish, departments of, 30
Mines, Spanish, 34
Minutoli's work on Spain referred to, 2, 33, 42, 51
Miraflores, Marquis of, succeeds O'Donnell as President in 1863, 24, and is succeeded by Narvaez, 25
Moderado party in Spain, 6, 10-12, seq.
"Modern theology," school of, in Holland, 311-315
Mohl, M. Jules, professor of Persian at the Collège de France, 273
Mohl, Robert von, representative of Baden in the Germanic Diet, 273-276
Molinari, M. de, a Belgian economist, 365
Molins, Marquis of. See Togores
Mommers, a Dutch clergyman, 300
Mon cabinet (Spain), 24
Montalembert, M. de, 90, 346, 358, 371
Montalvan, M., rector of the university of Madrid, 26
Montemolin, Conde de, 22
Montenegro, 170
Montesinos, Colonel, governor of the prison at Valencia, 33
Montesinos, a Spanish politician, 56
Morocco, war between Spain and, 22
Moscow, 117
Motley, J. L., author of the Rise of the Dutch Republic, 292
Mouravieff, a Russian general, 94, 132
Mühler, M. a Prussian minister, 231
Munich, 232
Münster, Count, 255
Murillo, Bravo, 17

NAPOLEON, 67, 68, 248 ; hereditary protector of the Confederation of the Rhine, 254 ; return from Elba, 256
Narvaez (Duke of Valencia), 13, 15, 16,

25 ; implicated in the conspiracy of June 1854, 18 ; succeeds to power for a short time, 21 ; is recalled in 1864, 25 ; superseded in June 1865 by O'Donnell, 27

National Assembly of Prussia in 1848, 207 *et seq.*

National Verein, the, 277

Navarino, battle of, 145

Navarre, war of, 9

Navy, Spanish, 43, 44

Negotiations of 1814 as to a Germanic Confederation, 255

Neo-Catholicism, Spanish, 46, 47

Netherlands. *See* Belgium, Holland

Neutrality in Belgium the foundation of her political existence, 345

Newspaper stamp abolished in Belgium, 342

Nicholas of Russia, 150, 265 ; characteristics of his reign, 69 ; his foreign policy, 70 ; change on Russian society consequent on his death, 71 ; intrusted to Speranski the codification of Russian law, 115 ; a return to his system would be political ruin, 119, 131

Nicholas (Czarewitch), hereditary Grandduke of Russia, his death, 123

Niebuhr, 287

Nitzsch, C. L., similarity of his views with those of the Groningen school, 308 ; he is the father of

Nitzsch, Karl I., a distinguished German theologian, 224

Nobility, Russian, 113, 114

Nocedal, a Spanish politician, 21

Norway and Sweden, a confederation with a common hereditary sovereign, 252

Nothomb, M., government of, in Belgium, 338, 339, 349, 351, 359

Novara, battle of, 170

Obermayer, 33

Oca, Montes de, 12

Ochoa's collection of extracts from Spanish writers, 49

Octroi, Spanish, 40

O'Donnell (Duke of Tetuan), his intrigues against Espartero, 12 ; heads a military revolt in 1854, 18, 20 ; division in the cabinet between him and Espartero in 1856, 20 ; again in power for three months, being succeeded by Narvaez, and was once more called by the queen, 21 ; hostilities with Morocco, 22 ; succeeded in the ministry by the Marquis of Miraflores, 24 ; supersedes the Narvaez government, 27

Œder, and the Œder class, 211, 223

Ofalia, a Spanish statesman, 9

Officers of Prussian army belong chiefly to the Junker or Feudal party, 227, 243

Ogareff, his *Lettres à un Anglais* worthy of study, 80

Olazagutia, 1

" Old Church," the, or Jansenist Church, in Holland, 316

Olden-Barneveld, judicial murder of, 299

Oldenburg, Grand-duchy of, 267, 273

Olmütz, 212, 213, 232, 266

Olozaga, a Spanish statesman, 4, 14, 15, 23 ; his flight to Lisbon, 15

Oosterzee, M., a Dutch professor, 306

Opzoomer, M., a Dutch theologian, 314, 315

Orange, Princes of, 292, 293

Orense, Marquis of Albaida, his work on Spain, 3, 37

Organ in worship, dislike of the Russian peasantry to, 97

Ortega, captain-general of the Balearic Isles, 22

Orts, M., a Belgian politician, 355, 359

O'Shea's *Guide to Spain*, 28, 29

Oviedo, 24

Paget, Mr., author of *Hungary and Transylvania*, 134

Palm, Van der, his translations of the Bible into Dutch, 301, 309

Palmer, Mr. William, 101

Palmerston, Lord, and Belgium, 335, 336; his last government, 352 ; his opinion of Baron Stockmar, 360

Pamplona, military revolt at, 12

Pansclavism, 105-107

Papal aggression in the Netherlands in 1853, 296, 297

Paris, congress of, 171 ; fall of, 254

Paris to Madrid by railway, 1

Parties in Spain at present, 46

" Patent," Prussian, of February 1847, 205

Paton's works referred to, 135, 190

Patow, M., a Prussian statesman, 219, 223

Patrocinio (Nun), 23

Peasantry, Russian, not all serfs, 72 ; natural characteristics of, 96 ; recent introduction of a territorial arrangement highly favourable to them, 94

Pedro V., Dom, late king of Portugal, 222

Peninsula, the, travellers to, 1 ; war in, 42

Personal serfs of Russia, 81

Peru, conflict with Spain, 24

Pesth, 153

Peter the Great, 78, 80, 111

Pfuel, General von, 209

Philip II. of Spain, 30

Philip III. 38

Pichegru, Charles, a French general, 292

Pidal, Marquis of, 50

Pius IX., Pope, his encyclical letter of December 1864, and its results in Belgium, 360, 370

Pliny's description of Holland, 289

Poland, insurrection of, in 1831, and its influence on Austria, 148, 149 ; disturbances in 1846, and the Galician massacres, 160, 161 ; Austria more favourably disposed to Poland than either of the two other partitioning powers, 198 ; insurrection of 1861, 87 ; the Poles in the reigns of Alexander I. and Nicholas, 88, 89 ; tendencies manifested in the early years of Alexander II.'s reign, 89 ; policy of the Zamoyski and the Wielopolski parties, 89-92 ; books on Poland, 92, 93 ; the future of, 93, 94 ; land-question in, 126-130

Police, Spanish, 33

Population and pauperism in Belgium, 367

Porte, the ; hostilities with Russia, 145

Portugal and Spain, 63

Posen, 160

Post-office management in Spain, 33, 34

Poverty, evidences of, in Spain, 34

Prague, recent Czechish agitation at, 208

Presburg, the Diet of, 155, 156 ; events of March 1848, 163

Press (Spanish), regulation of, in the hands of Minister of Interior, 34 ; prosecutions in Prussia, 203, 204 ; Bismark's high-handed proceedings with regard to, 237 ; resolutions against freedom of, at the Congress of Carlsbad, 259

Priestcraft and free thought, 371

Priests of the Russian Church, 97, 98

Prim, exiled by the Mon cabinet, 24

Prisons and prisoners in Spain, 31-33

Professors, Belgian, discussions in the Chambers as to the liberty to be allowed them in explaining their opinions on questions affecting religion, 349

Progressista party in Spain, 10, 47 ; in favour of a regency of three, 11

Prussia : four well-marked periods of its recent history, 201 ; Frederick William III., 202 ; Frederick William

IV., 203 ; early events of his reign ; unpopularity of the appointment of Eichhorn as Minister of Public Instruction, 203, 204 ; the "patent" of February 1847 : the "historical" school of publicists and jurists, 205 ; opening of the "Vereinigte Landtag," 205, 206 ; the revolution of 1848, 206, 207 ; the National Assembly and its cliques, 207-209 ; dissolution of the Assembly, and announcement of new constitution, 210 ; the first parliament, 211 ; the Manteuffel cabinet, 213 ; the Kreuz-Zeitung party, and its leaders, 214-216 ; the Freiherr von Vincke, 217 ; breach between the Prince of Prussia and the government in consequence of differences of opinion about the Russian war, 217-220 ; education, 220, 221 ; the Prince becomes regent : consequent changes, 221-225 ; political parties, 225 ; coronation of William I., 226 ; the military question, 227 ; programme of the Fortschritts Partei, or party of Progress, 228, 230 ; the new ministry (May 1862), 231 ; M. von Bismarck-Schönhausen becomes President of the Council, 233-225 ; the constitutional question, 235-241 ; the Danish war, 240 ; the British press on Prussian policy, 242 ; the Feudal party, 243-246 ; present difficulties, 246 ; the future of Prussia, 247-251 ; the disruption of the Confederation desirable, 248, 249.

Public Welfare, ministry of, in Spain, 34-39

Putiatine, Admiral, 118

QUETELET, M., a distinguished astronomer and statistician in Belgium, 365, 366

RADOWITZ, Joseph von, Prussian genera and statesman, 210, 212, 217, 266

Railways, development of, in Spain, 35, 36 ; in Holland, 297

Ranke, 232

Rationalism, German,—Dutch variety of, 300, 301

Rechberg, Count, Austrian Foreign Minister in 1859, 172

Reconstruction of the Germanic Confederation, plans suggested for, 276-281

Reformed tenets, opposition to, in Spain, a chief cause of its decline, 56

Reforms necessary in the Prussian Church, 97

Reichensperger, A., an eminent Catholic lawyer in Prussia, 209

Reichsrath, Austrian, 173 et seq., 180

Reimarus, H. S., author of the "Wolfenbüttel Fragments," 214

Religious struggles in the Netherlands, 332

Religious toleration in Spain, 8, 19, 38 ; state of religion, 54-59

Remonstrants, a religious section in Holland, 316

Renan, Ernest, on the authorship of the "Imitation of Christ," 294, 315

Representative government in Russia, 110, 111

Reprinting of French books in Brussels, controversy as to, 345

Reuss-Greiz and Reuss-Schleiz, principalities of, 267, 275

Revenue of Spain, 40

Réville, M. Albert, a Dutch theologian, 312, 313

Revue des Deux Mondes, Spanish papers in, 4, 44 ; article on Portugal, 63 ; articles on Russia, 80, 125 ; papers on Poland, 92, 198 ; on Prussia, 245, 246 ; on Belgium, by Émile de Laveleye, 369

Rhine, Confederation of the, 253-255

Rhineland, Kreuz-Zeitung rule in, 226, 245, 250. See Mecklenburg

Riego, revolt of, 5

Ritter, Karl, Professor Extraordinarius of Geography at Berlin University, 223, 236

Rivers, Spanish, 39

Roads in Spain, 33, 36

Rochow, M. von, a member of the Prussian Feudal party, 219

Rodbertus, 208

Roggenbach, M. de, a German statesman, 213

Rogier, M., a Belgian statesman, 338. See Belgium

Roman Catholic religion, and Spanish constitutions, 8

Romanism, form of, prevalent in Spain, 58

Roon, Von, a Prussian general and statesman, 231-236

Rosa, Martinez de la, called to the councils of Christina of Spain, 6

Rosas, Rios y, a Spanish statesman, 20, 23

Ross, Mr. Owen : his pamphlet on Spain and Morocco, 41

Royalists of Isabella II., 46, 47

Ruge, Arnold, 4

Russell, Earl, 356 ; his famous Gotha dispatch, 234

Russia : English ideas about, 65, 66 ; Alexander I., 66 ; the Holy Alliance, 67, 68 ; reign of Nicholas, 69, 70 ; the Crimean war, 70, 71 ; accession of Alexander II., 71 ; classes of peasantry not serfs, 72-75 ; the commune, and communal institutions, 77-80 ; serfdom, 80 ; working out of the idea of emancipation, 81, 82 ; the proclamation of enfranchisement, 83 ; its probable results, 84 ; the Polish insurrection of 1861, 87-95 ; the Russian Church, 95-102 ; question of the Dissidents, 99, 100 ; Russian aggrandisement in Asia, 102, 103 ; Panslavism, 105, 106 ; foreign politics of, 107, 108 ; financial disorder, 109 ; liberalism and its different sections, 109-112 ; the nobility, 113, 114 ; Russian law, 115, 116 ; journalism, 116, 117 ; education : universities, 117-119 ; future of Russia, 120-122 ; death of the heir to the crown, 123 ; results of the present reign, 131, 132

Russian war. See Crimean war

Russophobia, 102

Ruthenian peasantry of Galicia, 160-162

SALAMANCA, university of, 52

Sand-deserts in Poland, 93

San-Domingo, conflict with Spain, 24, 25

Santones, an epithet applied to Espartero's party, 12

Saragossa, university of, 52

Sartorius, Count of San Luis, 3, 16, 17

Saussaye, M. Chantepie de la, a popular preacher in Rotterdam, 306, 307

Saxe-Coburg-Gotha, Duke of, 277-279

Saxe-Meiningen, duke of, 279

Saxony, 267, 271 ; king of, 263

Schaumburg-Lippe, principality of, 267, 275

Schédo-Ferroti (nom de plume of a well-informed writer on Russia), 96, 97 ; quoted, 99 ; his journal, L'Echo de la Presse Russe, 124, 125

Scheldt dues, the, 357

Schimmelpenninck, 322

Schlegel, 301

Schleiermacher, 209

Schleinitz, the Freiherr Alexander von, member of the Hohenzollern cabinet, 222

Schleswig-Holstein question, 234, 249, 267, 275, 286-288 ; new phasis on the death of Frederick VII. of Denmark, 238

Schlosser, 223

Schmerling, M., an Austrian statesman,

176 ; succeeds Bach in the ministry, 177 ; his policy and administration, 178-182 ; his retirement and its results, 185-189, 261

Schnitzler's works on Russia, 115

Scholten, Professor, of Leyden, 310, 319

Schools in Spain, 50 ; in Russia, 118 ; in Prussia, 221 ; in Holland, 321 et seq. ; in Belgium, 343

Schön recalled to office by Frederick William IV., 202, 225

Schultens, Albert, 300

Schultze-Delitzsch, 208, 230

Schwab's (Dr. Erasmus), work on Hungary referred to, 135

Schwartz, Dr. Carl, Court preacher at Gotha, 283

Schwartzenberg, Prince of Austria, 166, 167, 177, 184, 266

Schwarzburg-Rudolstadt, principality of, 267, 274

Schwarzburg-Sondershausen, principality of, 267, 274

Schwerin, Count, 217, 225

Sclaves, or Sclavacks of north-western Hungary, 155

Sects, the, of Holland, 316 et seq.

Semler, 299

Serfs in Russia ; exceptional classes of the peasantry not coming under that denomination, 72, seq. ; writers giving a faithful picture of the working of serfdom, 76 ; origin of serfdom, 80 ; the communal institutions, 77-80 ; emancipation, 81-83

Siberia, serfs of, 83

Siéyès, Abbé, 208

Simson, M., a Prussian statesman, 230

Slave-trade, the, and the Spanish government, 45

Slavery in the West Indies, measure of emancipation adopted in Holland, 297

Small proprietors, or odnodvortzi, a class of Russian peasantry, 72

Sobieski, John, a Sclavonic hero, 147

Soldier, the Spanish, 42

Spain : prevalent erroneous notions about, 2 ; books on, 2 ; worthlessness of most of the modern English books of Spanish travel, 4 : ignorance of Englishmen of her recent history, 4 ; events in, during the minority of Isabella II., 5-16 ; crisis of June 1854, 18-20 ; reaction of 1857, 21 ; patrimony of the Crown made over to the nation by the queen, 26 ; the nine ministers of the government, 30 ; administration of justice in, 31 et seq. ; material revival, 34-38 ; finance department, 39-42 ; war department, 42-44 ; colonial department, 44-46 ; ministry of foreign affairs, 46 ; parties in Spain at present, 46-48 ; literature and education in, 49-54 ; religious state of, 54-59 ; question of the dynasty, and difficulties to be contended with, 59-62 ; true policy of, 62-64

Speranski an eminent Russian jurist, 115

Speyk, Van, a young Dutch officer, 335

Spinoza, 316

Springer, Professor, of Bonn, his work on Austria, 134, 163

St. Petersburg, disturbances at the university of, 118

Stahl, a leader of the Feudal faction in Prussia, 214, 215

Stanley, Dean, his lectures on Russia, 95, 98

States of the Germanic Confederation, 266-276

Stein, a Prussian statesman, 202, 255

Stockmar, Baron, 360

Stolberg, 301

Strauss, Dr., his observations on the late king of Prussia, 214, 215

Stuttgardt, the Frankfort Parliament transfers its sittings to, 262

Suvaroff, a Russian statesman, 117

Switzerland, a Federative State (Bundes-Staat) 252

Sybel, Professor von, 232, 250

Sydow, M., a Prussian Protestant preacher, 209

"System, the," in Austria, 140, 158, 159 ; received its last blow in consequence of the Galician massacres of 1846, 160

Széchenyi, Count Stephen, 153, 157 ; his proposal to unite the two halves of the Hungarian capital by a chain-bridge, 153

Tagus, the, 39

Tchinovniks, Russian, their venality and incapacity, 114

Tariff, Spanish, 40

Tetuan, Duke of. See O'Donnell

Theology, schools of, in Holland, 298, 299

Thirty Years' War, the, Prussia just recovering from, 248

Thomas-à-Kempis, 294

Thorbecke, M., an eminent Dutch statesman, 294-296, 324

Thun, Count Leo, as Austrian statesman, 168, 169

Ticknor, 48, 49

Togores, Roca di, Marquis of Molins, Spanish minister in London, 17, 44

Toledo, cathedral of, 59
Toreno, a Spanish statesman, 6
Tourguéneff, M. Ivan, a Russian novelist, 76
Tourguéneff, M. N., a writer on Russia, 72, 75 ; quotations from an unpublished work by, on the land-question in Poland, 127-130
Trafalgar, 43
Transylvania, Magyar population of, 154
Treaty of Vienna (1809), 140 ; of Paris (1814) as to the German States, 255 ; treaty between Austria and Prussia as to an interim management of the affairs of the Confederation, 263
Trieste, 22
Triumvirate in Austria under Ferdinand, 150, 151
Troitza, the, 96, 98
Trueba, Don Antonio de, a Spanish poet, 50
Tübingen University, 271
Turkey, policy of Austria with regard to, 197
Tyrol, clergy of the, 151

"Ungeist" in uniform, the, 247, 251
"Union, The," a society in Belgium, which paved the way for the revolution of 1830, 334 ; its composition, 337
"Union, The," 262 ; withdrawal of Hanover, 264
Union-Liberals of Spain, 47
Unruh, Von, 208, 238
Universities of Spain, 51-53 ; of Russia, 117, 118 ; of Holland, 327-330
Usedom, Baron von, 234
Utrecht university, 314, 315, 327

Valdez, General, and slavery in Cuba, 45
Valencia, 9, 33, 37 ; Duke of, see Narvaez
Valladolid, university of, 52
Vambéry, M., 102
Vay, Baron Nicholas, leader of the Hungarian Protestants, 176
Venema, 300
Venetia, the question of, a difficult one for Austria, 194, 195
Vergara, Convention of, 9
Vereinigte Landtag, the, of Prussia, 205 et seq.
Vessels, Spanish, coasting and for foreign trade, 37
Vicalvaro, 18

Vicalvarist, a name given to the followers of O'Donnell, 18, 48
Victory, Duke of, 12, 13
Vienna, disturbances in, consequent on the news of the February revolution in Paris, 163 ; taking of, by Prince Windischgrätz, 165 ; congress of, 258
Világos, surrender of the Hungarian army at, in 1849, 263
Vilain xiiii., Charles Vicomte, an eminent Belgian politician, 345, 346, 351. See Belgium
Vincke, the Freiherr von, a leader of the Prussian Liberals, 206, 217, 232
Virchow, Dr., medical professor at Berlin, 230, 235
Vinke of Utrecht, 315
Vitringa, 300
Vittoria, 12
Voet, of Utrecht, 299
Voltaire, 253 ; religious ideas of, in the Netherlands, 300
Vorparlaament, the, of Heidelberg, 260, 261

Waldeck, principality of, 267, 274
Waldeck, an eminent member of the Prussian National Assembly, 208, 229
Walewski, Count, and the Belgian press, 347
Wallis's work on Spain, 3, 30, 31, 44
Walloon churches, the, of Holland, 306, 311, 312
Walloon immigrations into Holland, 298
Walouieff, a Russian statesman, 117, 122
War Department, Spanish, 42-44
Warsaw, 90, 160
Water-supply of Spain, 38
Weimar, 267, 272
Wellington, Duke of, 254
Wesselemgi, leader of the patriotic movement in Transylvania, in 1834, 154
Wessenberg, an Austrian statesman, 257
Westminster Review, article in, on the "situation in Austria," quoted, 187, 188
Westphalen, M. von, 213, 222, 225
Westphalia, peasantry of, 229
Weyer, M. Van de, a Belgian statesman, 339
Widdrington, Captain, his works on Spain, 4, 57
Wielopolski, Marquis, his views as to Poland, 89 et seq.
Wild, Dr Albert, his work on Holland, 291
William, Prince of Prussia ; breach be-

tween him and the government on the question of the Russian war, 217-220 ; becomes regent : consequent changes, 221-225 ; coronation as William I. at Königsberg, 226 ; his abdication would be the most satisfactory but least probable solution of present difficulties, 246, 247

William I., king of the Netherlands, his system of stock-jobbing a source of annoyance to the Belgians, 333

William I., king of Würtemberg, 264

William III., king of the Netherlands, 293

William V., Prince of Orange, 292

Windischgrätz, Prince, of Austria, 165, 184

Wine, the most important of Spanish exports, 38

Witsius, 300

Wittenagemote at Kieff, A.D. 997, 110

" Wolfenbüttel Fragments," the, 215

Wolowski, M., a writer on the financial disorder of Russia, 109

Wouvermans, 201

Würtemberg, 267, 271 ; king of, 264

XIMENES, Cardinal, 51

YPSILANTI, 148

ZAMOYSKI, Count André, his views as to Poland, 89, 90

Zillerthal, Protestants of the, 152

THE END.